THE COURTLY CONSORT SUITE IN GERMAN-SPEAKING EUROPE, 1650–1706

To my wife, Barbara

The Courtly Consort Suite in German-Speaking Europe, 1650–1706

MICHAEL ROBERTSON
University of Leeds, UK

Routledge
Taylor & Francis Group
LONDON AND NEW YORK

First published 2009 by Ashgate Publishing

Published 2016 by Routledge
2 Park Square, Milton Park, Abingdon, Oxon OX14 4RN
711 Third Avenue, New York, NY 10017, USA

Routledge is an imprint of the Taylor & Francis Group, an informa business

Copyright © Michael Robertson 2009

All rights reserved. No part of this book may be reprinted or reproduced or utilised in any form or by any electronic, mechanical, or other means, now known or hereafter invented, including photocopying and recording, or in any information storage or retrieval system, without permission in writing from the publishers.

Notice:
Product or corporate names may be trademarks or registered trademarks, and are used only for identification and explanation without intent to infringe.

Michael Robertson has asserted his right under the Copyright, Designs and Patents Act, 1988, to be identified as the author of this work.

British Library Cataloguing in Publication Data
Robertson, Michael
 The Courtly Consort Suite in German-Speaking Europe, 1650–1706
 1. Lully, Jean Baptiste, 1632–1687 – Influence. 2. Chamber music – Germany –
17th century – History and criticism. 3. Instrumental ensembles – Germany – History
– 17th century. 4. Dance music – Germany – 17th century – History and criticism.
 . Title
 785'.00943'09032

Library of Congress Cataloging-in-Publication Data
Robertson, Michael, 1949–
 The Courtly Consort Suite in German-Speaking Europe, 1650–1706 / Michael Robertson.
    p. cm.
 1. Suite (Music) – 17th century. 2. Suite (Music) – 18th century. 3. Dance music – Europe, German-speaking – 17th century – History and criticism. 4. Dance music – Europe, German-speaking – 18th century – History and criticism. I. Title.
 ML3420.2.R63 2008
 784.18'83094309032–dc22   2008050806

ISBN 9780754664512 (hbk)

Contents

List of Figures	*vii*
List of Tables	*ix*
List of Music Examples	*xi*
Abbreviations	*xv*
Library Sigla	*xvii*
Acknowledgements	*xix*
Foreword	*xxi*

	Introduction	1
1	*Une splendeur et une magnificence incroyable* Music and Dance at the German Courts	3
2	*Nach der lustigen Frantzösischen Manier zu spielen* National Style and the Transmission of Dance Music	23
3	*Composées sur le même Mode ou Ton* Defining the Suite	45
4	*Frantzösische Branles, Courantes, Sarabandes, Ballettas* Manuscript Sources of the Courtly Suite before 1682	65
5	*Burgermeistern Syndicis* Printed Editions by Court Composers before 1682	93
6	*Ouverturen und Airs* The German Lullists – I	117
7	*Verschiedenen Ouverturen, Chaconnen, lustigen Suiten* The German Lullists – II	149
8	*'Cette nouvelle harmonie'* Unifying French and Italian styles	175
9	*Einer teutschen Führung* Vienna, the Imperial Court	201

10 *Eine frische Frantzösische Ouverture ihnen allen zu præferiren*
    Conclusion and Case Studies   227

Bibliography   *251*
Index   *265*

List of Figures

1.1.	S-E von Mecklenburg-Güstrow, 'Glückwünschende Freudensdarstellung dem hochgebornen Fürsten Herrn Augusten' (Wolfenbüttel, 1655)	14
3.1.	*D-Kl* 2° MS mus. 61g, outer wrapper	58
4.1.	*D-Kl* 2° MS mus. 61d², outer wrapper	77
4.2.	*D-Kl* 2° MS mus. 61b¹, violin part	78
7.1.	Manuscript M. 1092, 'dessus'; index.	168
10.1.	Manuscripts *GB-Lbl* Mus. 1585/90 and 91, outer wrappers	242

List of Tables

1.1.	Movements from the first part of the anonymous 'Ballet Royal du Dereglement des Passions' (*F-Pn* Rés. F. 499)	10
3.1.	Selected movements by Lully from manuscript *SV-X* Mus. MS 6	59
3.2.	Excerpts from R. Keiser, *Hercules und Hebe* in *S-VX* Mus. MS 6	60
3.3.	Movements, and their keys, in *Tous Les Airs de Violon de l'Opera D'Amadis Composez par Monsieur de Lullÿ, Escuier, Conseiller Secretaire, du Roÿ &. Imprimé a Amsterdam par Antoine Pointel* (Amsterdam, c.1687)	61
4.1.	Selected contents of manuscripts in *D-Kl* 2° MS mus. 61	68
4.2.	Concordances between *S-Uu* Instr. mus. hs 409 and *D-Kl* 2° MS mus. 61	85
4.3.	Dance movements grouped by key in the final section of manuscript *S-Uu* Ihre 281-3	90
5.1.	Printed suite collections by court composers, 1652-80	94
5.2.	Bransle sequences in N.B.N. (comp.), *Exercitium musicum* (Frankfurt am Main, 1660)	98
5.3.	Suites that start with an allemande in A. Drese, *Erster Theil Etlicher Allemanden, Couranten, Sarabanden, Balletten, Intraden und andern Arien* (Jena, 1672)	112
6.1.	Contents of: J.S. Cousser *Composition de musique* (Stuttgart, 1682)	125
6.2.	Contents of: P.H. Erlebach, *VI. Ouvertures, Begleitet mit ihren darzu schicklichen airs, nach Französischer Art und Manier* (Nuremberg, 1693)	139
6.3.	Contents of: 'L'Eraclio, Arie per i Sudetti Balli ... Da Melchiore D'Ardespin Consigliere e Maestro de Concerti Di S: A: E: 1690' (*A-Wn* Mus. Hs. 19 171)	147
7.1.	Contents of: J. Fischer, *Neuverfertigtes musicalisches Divertissement*, (Augsburg,1700)	151
7.2.	Contents of *à 4* suites in J. Fischer, *Tafel-Musik* (Hamburg, 1702) and *Musicalische Fürsten-Lust* (Lübeck, 1706)	157
7.3.	Contents of 'Sett IV' in manuscript *GB-Cmc* F-4-35, 1-5	165

8.1. Contents of: R. I. Mayr, *Pythagorische Schmids-Füncklein* (Augsburg, 1692) 176
8.2. Contents of: G. Muffat, *Suavioris harmoniæ instrumentalis hyporchematicæ florilegium primum* (Augsburg 1695) 184

9.1. Opening movements of the *balletti* by Johann Heinrich Schmelzer in *A-Wn* Mus. Hs. 16 583[I] 204
9.2. Suites by Poglietti in *CZ-KRa* that contain bransles or bransle-derived movements 214
9.3. J. Hoffer, 'Parti à.4. Sampt getantz worden von den kaÿs: Hofftanzern am Fest Leoboldi beÿ hoff 1694 Del Hoffer', (*A-Wn* S.m. 1809) 220
9.4. Keys and movements in J.H. Schmelzer, 'beder Kaÿl: Princessinen Ballet ist gehalten worden den 14 Februarÿ 1668' (*A-Wn* Mus. Hs. 16 583[II]) 221
9.5. Keys and sections in J.H. Schmelzer, *Sacro-profanus concentus musicus*, 'Sonata II a otto' (Nuremberg, 1662) 222

10.1. Contents of: J.C. Shieferdecker, *XII. musicalische Concerte, bestehend aus etlichen Ouverturen und Suiten* (Hamburg, 1713) 228
10.2. Contents of: J.J. Fux, *Concentus musico-instrumentalis* (Nuremberg, 1701), as given in the 'catalogo' of the first violin part-book' 237
10.3. Contents and groupings in Fux, *Concentus musico-instrumentalis*, 'N.I. Seranada à 8.' 239
10.4. Selected contents of: *GB-Lbl* MS Mus. 1585 243
10.5. Suites by Johann Fischer in the Liechtenstein collection in Kroměříž (*CZ-KRa*) 244

List of Music Examples

2.1. G. Bleyer, 'Partie â 4 â la Françoise' (*CZ-KRa* A 801), courante; M. Cazzati, *Correnti balletti galiarde a3 è 4* (Venice, 1659), 'Corente Seconda, La Guastallesa à 3' — 31

2.2. P. Erlebach, *VI. Sonate à violino e viola da gamba col suo basso continuo* (Nuremberg, 1694), 'Sonata seconda, Courante'; *VI. ouvertures* (Nuremberg, 1693), '2. Air Courante' — 33

2.3. G. Bononcini, *Arie, Correnti, Sarabande, Gighe, & Allemande ... Opera Quarta* (Bologna, 1671), '12 Sarabanda'; *D-Kl* 2° MS mus. 61b², 'La Sarabande' — 34

2.4. *S-Uu* Ihre 281–2, '38. Ballett', '39. Ballett' — 36

2.5. S. Valois, 'Ouverture de Mr Valoÿ' *D-B* Mus. MS 30274, 'gigue' — 38

2.6. J. Pachelbel, 'Partie a 4: 1 Violin, 2 Viole e Cembalo' (*D-B* Mus. MS 16481/2), 'gigue' — 39

2.7. Two versions of 'Libertas' in *S-Uu* IMhs 409 (ed. J.S. Mráček, Stockholm, 1976), and 'Recüeil de Plusieurs vieux Airs faits' (*F-Pn* Rés. F. 494) — 41

3.1. R. Ballard (ed.), *Pièces pour le violin a quatre parties* (Paris, 1665), — 50

3.2. J.H. Schein, *Banchetto musicale* (Leipzig, 1617), Suite IX, 'Padouana' and 'Courente' — 55

3.3. J.A. Reincken, *Hortus musicus* (Hamburg, n.d.), Suite III, openings of 'Sonata 11ma', 'Allemand 12ma' and 'Courant 13^{tia}' — 56

4.1. *D-Kl* 2° MS mus. 61e, 'Sarabande Italienne'; 'Recüeil de Plusieurs vieux Airs' (*F-Pn* Rés. F. 949), 'A l'imperio d'Amore' — 80

4.2. *D-Kl* 4° MS mus. 148a, 'Ouverture du Ballets' — 82

4.3. D. Pohle, 'Bransles à 4' (*D-Kl* 4° MS mus. 148e), 'simple' — 83

4.4. *S-Uu* Ihre 281-2, '8. Chaconne' — 91

5.1. W.C. Briegel, *Erster Theil. Darinnen begriffen X. Paduanen* (Erfurt, 1652), '11. Paduana', '12. Galliarda' — 100

5.2. Briegel, Erster Theil. Darinnen begriffen X. Paduanen, '24. Courante' — 101

5.3. J-J. Löwe von Eisenach, *Synfonien, Intraden, Gagliarden* (Bremen, 1657–58), 'VII. Intrada' — 102

5.4. Löwe von Eisenach, *Synfonien,* 'IV. Couranta' — 103

5.5. W.E. Rothe, *Erstmahlig musicalische Freuden – Gedichte* (Dresden, 1660), 'VII. Courant, à 5' — 104

5.6. J.W. Furchheim, *Musicalische Taffel-Bedienung* (Dresden, 1674), 'Sonata Sexta', 'Præludium' 106
5.7. E. Reusner, arr. J.G. Stanley, *Musicalische Taffel-erlustigung*, 'Saraband. 11' 107
5.8. Reusner, arr. Stanley, *Musicalische Taffel-erlustigung*, 'Ballo. 41', 'Ballo. 42' 108
5.9. G. Bleyer, *Lüst-Müsic Nach ietziger Frantzösicher Manier gesetzet* (Leipzig, 1670), 'XVI. Sarraband' 111
5.10. Bleyer, *Lüst-Müsic,* '1.Gavotte' 112

6.1. J-B. Lully, *Le Temple de la Paix*, editions by Pointel (Amsterdam, n.d.) and Ballard (Paris, 1685), 'Ouverture' 118
6.2. G. Bleyer, 'Partie â 4. â la Françoise' (*CZ-KRa* A 801), 'Ouverture' 120
6.3. J.S. Cousser, *Composition de musique* (Stuttgart, 1682), Suite III, 'Prelude. à 2. Dessus' 124
6.4. Cousser, *Composition de musique*, Suite III, 'Ouverture'; J.B. Lully, *Pysché* (Paris, 1720), 'Ouverture' 126
6.5. J.S. Cousser, *La cicala* (Stuttgart, 1700), Suite I, 'Chaconne' 131
6.6. J-B. Lully, *Proserpine* (Paris, 1680), 'Ritournelle pour Mercure'; J.S. Cousser, *Apollon enjoüé* (Stuttgart, 1700), Suite II, 'Ritournelle à 3' 134
6.7. J.S. Cousser, *Festin des muses* (Stuttgart, 1700), Suite IV, 'Vole de Demons' 135
6.8. Cousser, *La cicala*, Suite I, 'Les Porteurs de Flambeaux' 136
6.9. Ouverture openings in P. Erlebach, *VI. ouvertures* (Nuremberg, 1693), Suite I and Cousser, *Composition de musique*, Suite I 138
6.10. Erlebach, *VI. ouvertures*, Suite VI, 'Ouverture' 140
6.11. J.A.S., *Zodiaci musici* (Augsburg, 1698), Suite IV, 'Allemande' 144
6.12. J. Speth, *Ars magna consoni et dissoni* (Augsburg, 1693), 'Toccata secunda'; J.A.S., *Zodiaci musici*, Suite II, 'Ouverture' 146
6.13. M. D'Ardespin, 'L'Eraclio/Arie per i Sudetti Balli' (*A-Wn* Mus. Hs. 19171), 'Sinfonia' 148

7.1. J. Fischer, *Neuverfertigtes musicalisches Divertissement* (Augsburg, 1700), '41. Chaconne des Charpantiers' 153
7.2. Fischer, *Neuverfertigtes musicalisches Divertissement*, '45. Chique à 3. Pour Forgerons' 154
7.3. J. Fischer, *Tafel-Musik* (Hamburg, 1702), '12. Menuet en Rondeau' 156
7.4. Fischer, *Tafel-Musik*, '10. Ouverture' 158
7.5. *S-Uu* Instr. mus. i hs. 64:11, 'Ouverture a Hautbois 1$^{mo.}$ et 2$^{do.}$ Taille Basson', 'Ouverture' 163
7.6. *D-DS* Mus. MS 1221, Suite IV, '2. Menuet' 170
7.7. *D-DS* Mus. MS 1221, Suite I, 'Ouverture' 171

List of Music Examples xiii

8.1.	Sarabandes in R.I. Mayr, *Pythagorische Schmids-Füncklein* (Augsburg,1692), Suites III & IV	178
8.2.	Mayr, *Pythagorische Schmids-Füncklein*, Suite VI, 'Aria'	180
8.3.	G. Muffat, *Florilegium primum* (Augsburg, 1695), '3. Sarabande'	181
8.4.	G. Muffat, *Armonico Tributo* (Salzburg, 1682), Sonata V, 'Passacaglia'	183
8.5.	Muffat, *Florilegium primum* '17. Air'	187
8.6.	Muffat, *Florilegium primum* '39. Chaconne'	188
8.7.	G. Muffat, *Florilegium secundum* (Passau, 1698), '58. Les Bossus'; J.B. Lully, 'Entractes d'Oedipe'(LWV 23), 'Les Médecins'	190
8.8.	'Rondeau' in G. Muffat, Armonico Tributo, Sonata III; *Auserlesene Instrumentalmusik* (Passau, 1701), Concerto II	192
8.9.	J.C. Pez, 'Ouverture XI' (*B-Br* MS III 1077 Mus)	197
8.10.	J.C. Pez, 'Intrada. à 2 Violin. I Viol. è Cont:' (*D-B* Mus. MS 40 644), 'Intrada'	198
9.1.	*A-Wn* Mus. Hs. 19 265, 'Retirada'	206
9.2.	J.H. Schmelzer, '*Der Ninfen Ballet*' (16 583[I]), 'Allemande'	207
9.3.	*D-OB* MO 1037, 'Ballete De S. Mayeste Imperiale'; *A-Wn* Mus. Hs. 18 710, 'Allemande: 30ª'	208
9.4.	B.A. Aufschnaiter, *Concors discordia* (Nuremberg, 1695), Suite III, 'Fantasia'	216
9.5.	*S-Uu* IMhs 064:013, 'Final'	219
9.6.	A.A. Schmelzer, 'Balletto von gartnerinne' (16 588) 'Intrada N° 193'	225
10.1.	J.C. Schieferdecker, *XII. musicalische Concerte, bestehend aus etlichen Ouverturen und Suiten* (Hamburg,1713), Suite III, 'Concert'	232
10.2.	Schieferdecker, *XII. musicalische Concerte*, Suite VIII, 'Ouverture'	234
10.3.	Schieferdecker, *XII. musicalische Concerte*, Suite II, 'Menuet'	236
10.4.	J.J. Fux, *Concentus musico-instrumentalis* (Nuremberg, 1701), 'Aire francoise, Aire Italiana'	241
10.5.	Allemandes in J. Fischer, 'Balettæ a 4. Compositæ in Melancholia Authoris' (*CZ-KRa* A 780) and 'Partei a. 4' (*GB-Lbl* MS Mus. 1585)	246
10.6.	J. Fischer, 'Partei a. 4: ... La franceise'(*GB-Lbl* MS Mus. 1585), 'Rondeaux'	249

Abbreviations

The following abbreviations are used throughout this book:

AMA V/I   J. Sehnal and J. Pešková, *Caroli de Liechtenstein Castelcorno episcopi Olumucensis operum artis musicae collectio Cremsirii reservata, Artis Musicæ Antiquioris Catalogorum*, vol. 5/1

AMA V/2   J. Sehnal and J. Pešková, *Caroli de Liechtenstein Castelcorno episcopi Olumucensis operum artis musicae collectio Cremsirii reservata, Artis Musicæ Antiquioris Catalogorum*, vol. 5/2

EM   *Early Music*

Göhler   A. Göhler, (comp.), *Verzeichnis der in den Frankfurter und Leipziger Messkatalogen der Jahre 1564 bis 1759 angezeigten Musikalien*

IMhs   Instr. mus. hs (relating to MSS in the Universitetsbibilioteket Uppsala)

LWV   *Chronologisch-thematisches Verzeichnis sämtlicher Werke von Jean-Baptiste Lully*

New Grove 2   S. Sadie and J. Tyrrell, (eds.), *The New Grove Dictionary of Music and Musicians*

RISM   *Répertoire international des sources musicales*

RISM A/II   *International Inventory of Musical Sources after 1600*, online, http://biblioline.nisc.com

W&S   H. Watanabe-O'Kelly and A. Simon, *Festivals and ceremonies: a bibliography of works relating to court, civic and religious festivals in Europe, 1500–1800*

Library Sigla

A-Wn   Vienna, Österreichische Nationalbibliothek

B-Br   Brussels, Bibliothèque Royale Albert I$^{er.}$

CZ-KRa   Kroměříž, Archibiskupský zámek. hudeni sbirka

D-B   Berlin, Staatsbibliothek zu Berlin Preussischer Kulturbesitz

D-HN   Herborn, Bibliothek des Evangelischen Theologischen Seminars

D-HRD   Arnsberg-Herdringen, Schlossbibliothek

D-Dl   Dresden, Sächsische Landesbibliothek

D-DS   Darmstadt, Hessische Landes- und Hochschulbibliothek

D-JE   Jever, Marien-Gymnasium

D-Kl   Kassel, Landesbibliothek und Murhardsche Bibliothek der Stadt Kassel

D-LEm   Leipzig, Städtische Bibliotheken

D-OB   Ottobeuren, Benediktiner-Abtei, Bibliothek

D-ROu   Rostock, Universität Rostock, Universitätsbibliothek

D-SWs   Schwerin, Stadtbibliothek

D-SÜN   Sünching, Schloss

D-WD   Wiesentheid, Die Musikalien des Grafen von Schönborn-Wiesentheid

D-W   Wolfenbüttel, Herzog August Bibliothek

F-Pn   Paris, Bibliothèque nationale de France

GB-Cmc Cambridge, Magdalene College Library

GB-Lbl London, British Library

PL-Kj   Kraków, Biblioteka Jagiellonska

S-Uu   Uppsala, Universitetsbibilioteket

S-VX   Växjö, Lansbibilioteket i Växjö

Shelf marks for the Universitetsbibilioteket at Uppsala have been revised in order to match the six-digit format now used in the online Düben database, www.musik.uu.se/duben/Duben.php.

Acknowledgements

The author acknowledges the permission of the following to reproduce documents and musical examples.

Illustration 1.1 (Musica fol. 1.1.2 (3).)	Herzog August Bibliothek, Wolfenbüttel
Illustration 3.1 (2° MS mus. 61g)	Landesbibliothek und Murhardsche Bibliothek der Stadt Kassel
Illustration 4.1 (2° MS mus. 61d²)	Landesbibliothek und Murhardsche Bibliothek der Stadt Kassel
Illustration 4.2 (2° MS mus. 61b¹)	Landesbibliothek und Murhardsche Bibliothek der Stadt Kassel
Illustration 7.1 (M. 1092)	Christopher Hogwood, Cambridge
Illustration 10.1 (Mus. MS 1585)	The board of the British Library
Music examples 6.5, 6.7, 6.8, 6.9, 6.10, 7.1, 7.2, 10.1, 10.2, 10.3.	Der Musiksammlung des Grafen von Schönborn-Wiesentheid

Foreword

The origins of much of this work are in my 2004 PhD dissertation, *The consort suite in the German-speaking lands, 1660–1705*. My supervisor throughout the time of my research for this was Peter Holman and, in the years since, he has continued to give me help and encouragement. I am deeply grateful to him. I am grateful to David Marsh for his help with Latin translations, to Laura Perrin for her help with French translations and to Ursula Burchette for her help with German translations. I have also been helped in various ways by Simon McVeigh, Samantha Owens, John Butt, Stephen Rose, John and Rachel Cardell-Oliver, and Andrew Wooley. My visits and enquiries to various libraries and private collections have been met with unfailing help and courtesy, but I would particularly like to thank the following: The British Library (and in particular Nicholas Bell), Cambridge University Library, Universitetsbiblioteket Uppsala, Herzog August Bibliothek Wolfenbüttel, die Musikalien der Grafen von Schönborn-Wiesentheid (and in particular the curator, Frau Dr Dangel-Hofmann), Pepys Library, Magdalene College Cambridge, Christopher Hogwood, Niedersächsische Landesbibliothek Hanover, Österreichische Nationalbibliothek Vienna, Bayerische Staatsbibliothek Munich, Bibliothek des Evangelischen Theologischen Semiars Herborn, and Landesbibliothek und Murhardsche Bibliothek der Stadt Kassel.

    Finally, to my wife, Barbara, I owe the greatest debt of gratitude. She has been a constant source of help and support throughout the time that it has taken me to produce this work. Without her, it would not have been possible.

Michael Robertson, September, 2008.

Introduction

It is likely that most of the composers and courts considered in this book would have thought of themselves as being German, even if they were nominal citizens and members of the Holy Roman Empire. For the purposes of this study, we can describe the German lands in a geographical sense as stretching from the Baltic and North Sea coasts in the north to the Bavarian lands of the ruling Wittelsbach family in the south, and from the borders of the Spanish Netherlands in the west to Austria and the Kingdom of Bohemia in the east.[1]

Any comprehensive study of the court suite throughout this entire area would require greater length than this book permits, and, with two exceptions, I have regretfully excluded the suite in Austria and the surrounding areas. The first exception is a case study of a pair of suites that appear to have originated in the area of Vratislavia (now Wrocław in Poland). The second exception is the imperial court in Vienna. If a major part of this book will be spent in considering the influence of music from the court of Louis XIV, it is fitting that we should also consider the development of the suite at the court of Leopold I.

As Peter Holman has pointed out, 'orchestral' is hardly appropriate for ensembles of this period, and I use the term 'consort' to denote ensembles of two or more instruments in addition to the *continuo*.[2] Works for single instrument and *continuo* have been excluded, as have viol consorts. Likewise, little mention has been made of the lute suite in Germany, which surely demands a study of its own. Given that the intention of this book is to consider the suite in terms of a complete, self-contained entity, I shall not be examining individual movement types as a matter of course. But there are times when the characteristics of individual movement types have played a part in the development of the suite as a whole and, in such cases, these movement types receive examination in greater detail.

Seventeenth-century German music is beset with problems of movement nomenclature and inconsistency of spelling. I have not attempted to impose standardisation where none has previously existed, but to avoid confusion, the letter 'u', synonymous with 'v' in seventeenth-century German, is converted to a 'v' when required. In this respect, I have retained the standard spelling of 'paduan', but it is possible that we should be calling it the 'padvan'.

---

[1] W. R. Shepherd, *Shepherd's Historical Atlas* (ninth edition, New York, 1964), p. 123.

[2] P. Holman, 'From Violin Band to Orchestra' in J. Wainwright and P. Holman (eds.), *From Renaissance to Baroque; change in instruments and instrumental music in the seventeenth century* (Aldershot, 2005), pp. 241–257.

Confusion can also easily arise between 'ballet', 'ballett', 'ballo' and 'balletto'. These terms are used generically to describe complete suites, and also to describe individual movements, but without any sort of consistency. For clarity, I shall use 'ballet' to denote music that was danced on stage, the italicised *ballet*, *ballett* and *ballo* for individual dances or as generic terms for suites. Likewise, *balletto* and *balletti* are used to denote the singular and plural of the Viennese suite. Primary sources often fail to distinguish between 'courante' and 'corrente': I shall use 'courante' as a generic term for this dance, but 'corrente' where it is specifically Italian. The terms *à 4* and *à 5* are used to denote four- and five-part ensembles, and I use *ouverture* throughout. It is the one spelling that seems to bring any degree of consistency. Solely for identification, I have employed the terms of modern tonality in all discussions of key and relationships between keys.

Where quotations are taken from a previously existing translation, the original text is not given. The original language is only given when its translation is new. The musical examples within the text attempt to reproduce their sources as closely as possible, but they are not intended to be examples of modern critical editing. Obvious printing and scribal errors have been corrected without comment, but reconstructed material has been presented on small staves or with cue-sized notes. For clarity, I have used modern bar lines throughout, even when they do not appear in the sources. Accidentals, including natural signs, all follow modern usage. Where dots, rather than tied notes, have been used to extend the value of a note across the bar line, they have been reproduced in the examples. Clefs have been changed to reflect modern usage, but all clef changes are shown as incipits at the start of each movement. Beaming across quaver and semiquaver groupings, articulation and dynamic markings are shown as they appear in the sources, but bass line figures have been placed under the notes to which they refer. Time signatures have not been changed. I have followed seventeenth-century practice in using 't' rather than 'tr'.

Where it has been necessary in the text to differentiate between notes of different pitches, I have used the system where c' is the middle of the modern piano keyboard, c" is the octave above, and c the octave below.

For clear identification of manuscripts, I had originally intended to use RISM A/II numberings wherever possible. Unfortunately, the RISM A/II database has often proved to be unacceptably inaccurate. Therefore, I have only used RISM A/II references where they are required to illustrate a specific point.

New translations of primary source material have been accompanied by the original text, but the latter has not been given where previously existing translations have been used. Translations of secondary source material do not include the original text.

Chapter 1
Une splendeur et une magnificence incroyable
Music and Dance at the German Courts

On 5 November 1684 in Berlin, the wedding took place between Friedrich, Electoral Prince of Brandenburg and the music-loving Sophie Charlotte, Duchess of Braunschweig-Lüneburg. The celebrations included the ballet *La réjouissance des dieux, ballet Orné de Musique, de Machines & de Changemens de Theatre*.[1] The French-language preface to the printed libretto speaks of 'une splendeur et une magnificence incroyable' (incredible splendour and magnificence), the beauty of the music and 'la magnificence & la nouveauté des Machines & des Decorations' (the magnificence and novelty of the machines and decorations). Hardly less splendid were the costumes and the large number of performers. The ballet itself, with music by the Berlin court musician Johann Friedrich Bodecker, was in the manner of the French *Ballet de cour*. Vocal music formed an important part of each of the twenty *entrées*. Like the preface, the language of these was French.

The emphasis on the French language is hardly surprising, for it was France that provided the model for court culture in Germany for much of the seventeenth century. French was often used for conversation by the German nobility: a letter in French from the eleven-year-old Princess Emilie of Hesse to her brothers, Wilhelm and Philipp, shows how delighted she was to be able to communicate in the language, even if her command of it is less than secure.[2] Children also received tuition from dancing masters: in Kassel in 1656, payments were made to a 'Tantzmaister von Marpurgk' for his work on 'ceremonies' with the royal children.[3] As Wendy Hilton has asserted in connection with the French court, 'lessons in dancing, deportment and the complexities of social etiquette were begun in early childhood'.[4] It seems that the same was true in Germany.

---

[1] Only the printed libretto is preserved: *D-W* Textb. 4° 55. See: W&S 185.

[2] E. Bettenhäuser (ed.), *Familienbriefe der Landgräfin Amalie Elisabeth von Hessen-Kassel und ihrer Kinder*, Veröffentlichungen der Historischen Kommission für Hessen, 56, (Marburg, 1994), p. 12.

[3] *D-Kl* Ms. hass. 2° 350, *Rechnung aus dem Kammerverlag*. Entry for 5 October 1656.

[4] W. Hilton, *Dance and Music of Court and Theater: Selected Writings of Wendy Hilton*, Dance and Music, vol. 10 (Stuyvesant, New York, 1997), p. 3.

German court life could be regulated in 'sometimes pedantic detail'.[5] And the nobility often did its best to imitate everything that went on at the Paris court of Louis XIV. Even when Louis' territorial ambitions caused constant anxiety in many German states, sometimes resulting in open warfare, anything French still represented the height of fashion. But not just fashion: music became 'political propaganda, a display of power and wealth, a sphere for competition with rival courts'.[6] Louis XIV's personal appearance as a dancer in no less than forty ballets emphasized the link between dance and the representation of absolutist monarchy. As Geoffrey Burgess puts it, 'dance performs the central political message ... the representation and operation of the power of the sovereign'.[7]

Younger members of German ruling families often visited Paris as part of an education for the time when they assumed power. In 1647, the future Wilhelm VI of Hessen-Kassel visited Paris for what the *Theatri Europæi* termed 'unterschiedliche Præparatoria'[8]. These 'various preparations' were no doubt part of this education. For Wilhelm, apparently a lover of music and occasional composer, they included a performance of, amongst other items, 'un concert mélodieux' and 'un concert de clavesin avec deux lhutz, un theorbe, une viole et le Sr Constantin qui jouoit de son violin'.[9] Louis Constantin was one of the greatest violin virtuosi of his time. The prince also seems to have been present at a performance of Luigi Rossi's opera *L'Orfeo*, which was given in Paris during the carnival season of 1647.[10]

Such visits clearly made a deep and lasting impression, and it is hardly surprising that many German courts set out protocols in attempted imitation of Paris. But foreign visitors were apparently shocked by the lack of privacy in the daily life of Louis XIV: the so-called *Lever* and *Coucher* at the start and end of the day were witnessed by large numbers of people. With diplomatic and government business being held in the same surroundings as domestic events, his public and

---

[5] S. J. Klingensmith, *The utility of splendour: ceremony, social life, and architecture at the court of Bavaria, 1600–1800*, C. F. Otto and M. Ashton (eds.), (Chicago, 1993), p. 7.

[6] C. Hogwood, *Music at court* (London, 1977), p. 9.

[7] G. Burgess, 'The Chaconne and the Representation of Sovereign Power in Lully's *Amadis* (1684) and Charpentier's *Medée* (1693)' in S. McCleave (ed.), *Dance & music in French baroque theatre: sources & interpretations* (London, 1998), pp. 81–104 at p. 81.

[8] M. Merian, *Theatri Europæi Fuenffter Theil* (Frankfurt am Main, 1651), p. 293.

[9] C. Massip, *La vie des musiciens de Paris au temps de Mazarin (1643–1661)* (Paris, 1976), p. 7.

[10] It has been suggested that the music Wilhelm heard was connected at 'the marriage celebration offered by the Cardinal [Mazarin] and King [Louis XIV]' to Wilhelm. But as the prince did not get married until 1649, any celebration at this time seems rather premature. See: J. Le Cocq, 'The Early *Air de Cour*, the Theorbo, and the Continuo Principle in France' in J. Wainwright and P. Holman (eds.), *From Renaissance to Baroque; change in instruments and instrumental music in the seventeenth century* (Aldershot, 2005), pp. 191–210 at p. 205.

private lives often had little to separate them.[11] In this respect, German courts were perhaps less demanding of their rulers. The 1698 *Kammerordnung* regulations at the court of Prince-Bishop Joseph Clemens seem to have been fairly typical; they describe *Lever* and *Coucher* ceremonies, but with fewer people present than their French models.[12]

The *Lever* and *Coucher* were not the only type of French courtly institutions imitated by the Germans. In Munich during the late 1660s and early 1670s, Elector Ferdinand Maria and his pro-French wife, the Electoral Princess Henriette Adelaide of Savoy, were responsible for the 'loosening of the pious strictures that had hitherto determined the character of the court'.[13] The pre-Lent carnival 'now became the occasion for a cycle of festivities extending over several weeks'. So it was not surprising that their son, Maximilian II Emanuel, continued in the same fashion and introduced an entertainment modelled on the French *Appartement*. The Parisian model for this was:

> ... a reception for the entire Court in the great suite of rooms that runs from one end of the long gallery to the ante-chamber of the chapel. It lasted from seven until ten in the evening, when the king sat down to supper. At first there was music, and then tables were prepared for all kinds of games.[14]

In Munich, there were:

> ... five or six rooms ... all beautifully adorned and illuminated, with various tables for gaming, while at the same time there is dancing in another room. Besides the ladies of the court, those of the city are also present, and all the gentlemen. This conversazione is held three days a week – Sunday, Tuesday, and Thursday.[15]

There was further imitation of Paris in the precise regulation of behaviour 'according to rank and title', and visitors were not always generously received.[16] When De Blainville, a travelling diplomat from the Spanish court, attempted to gain an audience with the Bishop of Augsburg, the reply was hardly encouraging:

---

[11] See: Klingensmith, *Utility of splendour*, p. 11.
[12] Ibid., p. 157.
[13] For this and the following quotation, see: R. Babel, 'The Duchy of Bavaria: the courts of the Wittelsbachs c.1550–1750' in J. Adamson (ed.), *The Princely Courts of Europe 1500–1750* (London, 1999; repr. 2000), pp. 189–209.
[14] Klingensmith, *Utility of splendour*, p. 171.
[15] Ibid., p. 171.
[16] N. Henshall, *The myth of absolutism: change and continuity in Early Modern European monarchy* (London & New York, 1992), pp. 39–40.

> We sent to ask leave to pay our Respects to him. You won't easily guess what Answer was brought to us. His Grand Master of the Horse sent a Footman to acquaint us that if we were *Herrn Graaffen* i.e. Counts, or at least Barons, we might have that Honour. But if we were but Merchants, we could not be permitted to approach him.[17]

The court palaces themselves were often impressive. Chappuzeau's following description of the *Residenz* at Stuttgart may verge on hyperbole, but it is typical of the sentiments expressed by travellers when they arrived at German courts:

> Le château est des plus vastes & plus magnifiques d'Allemagne; il s'y void de grandes sales, & entre autres celle du Tournoy, qui a retenu ce nom, parce qu'on y a fait des Carozels, & l'escalier qui y conduit est si large, que deux hommes à cheual pourroient monter ensemble sans se heurter. ... [Les iardins] enferment une maison où les portraits, les statues, les Antiquitez arrestent long temps la veüe; & d'ailleurs les fontaines auec leurs tuyaux de bronze, des grenouilles, des lezards & serpens d'airain qui iettent l'eau par diuers endroits, des paysans & paysanes de fonte qui dansent à la rustique, ... un magnifique theatre, une grande cour couverte de sable pour les combats à cheval ... C'est dans ce grand palais que le Duc de Wirtemberg tient sa Cour, & qu'il entretient ordinairement plus de trois cens bouches.[18] (The Chateau is the largest and most magnificent in all of Germany; you will find large rooms and, amongst these, the *Tournoy* (tournament), which has this name because it is where the Carousels take place. This leads through to a staircase that is so big that two men on horses could go up it together without colliding. [The gardens] surround a house where the portraits, statues and antiquities have long since gained much attention; elsewhere [one finds] the fountains with their bronze pipes and bronze frogs, lizards and snakes which spurt water in all different directions, peasants of both sexes dancing a rustic dance ... a magnificent theatre and a large courtyard covered in sand for combat on horseback ...It is in this large palace that the Duke of Wirtemberg holds his court, and it is normally maintained by more than three hundred people.)

But we should not forget that French court culture had been fashionable in Germany well before the time of Louis XIV, and that French music had certainly been in circulation at the start of the century. However, the disruption to courtly life as a result of the Thirty Years War had been considerable and far-reaching. It is hardly surprising that 'the most spectacular court festival held in continental

---

[17] De Blainville, *Travels through Holland, Germany, Switzerland and Other Parts of Europe ... by the late Monsieur de Blainville,* trans. G. Turnbull and W. Guthrie (3 vols, London, 1757), vol. 1, p. 268, entry for 'July 12: Augsburg [1705]'.

[18] S. Chappuzeau, *L'Europe vivante, ou relation nouvelle, historique & politique de tous ses estats* (Paris, 1667), p. 60.

Europe during the Thirty Years War', the so-called 'Great Wedding' of 1634 between Christian, Prince Elect of Denmark and Norway, and Magdalena Sibylle, Duchess of Saxony, was Danish and not German.[19] Recovery from the war was patchy; it had not helped that the plague had returned to Germany in the 1630s with the resulting fall in population and decline in court income through taxation. Samantha Owens makes a telling comparison between the start of Lully's glittering career in late 1650s Paris and the Württemberg court at the same time where '*Kapellmeister* Samuel Capricornus (1628–65) was struggling with a reduced number of instrumentalists whose lack of skill clearly appalled him'.[20] But despite these difficulties, the libretto of *Die Triumphirende Liebe*, the ballet performed for the 1653 wedding of Christian Ludwig, Duke of Braunschweig-Lüneburg and Dorothea, Duchess of Schleswig-Holstein-Sonderburg, clearly demonstrates how the desire for spectacular entertainment was reaching the levels of former times.[21]

The carnival season, traditionally lasting from Twelfth Night to Ash Wednesday, was a time for entertainments of all kinds. In Germany, the immediate pre-lent carnival was known as the 'Wirtschaft', and we have already seen that, in Munich, it was extended to last not just a few days, but several weeks. There also seems to have been a degree of role reversal at this type of carnival. The *Histoire de la musique et des ses effets depuis son origine jusqu'a présent* describes the Munich 1670 *Wirtschaft* as follows:

> Je vais rapporter celle que fut faite en 1670, par son Altesse Electorale de Baviére, & Madame la Dauphine sa sœur. L'on prit le Palais de Munick pour servir d'Hôtellerie; ce sont ordinairement les plus grands Seigneurs & les plus grandes Dames de la Cour qui font la fonction de l'Hôtellier & de Hôtelliére, & d'autres personnes de Qualité qui font les fonctions des Domestiques, comme aux Fêtes Saturnales des Romains, où où les Maîtres servoient les Valets.[22] (I am talking of the [*Wirtschaft*] for 1670 given by His Highness the Elector of Bavaria and his sister, *Madame la Dauphine* [Charlotte Elisabeth of Bavaria, the princess Palatine]. The palace at Munich becomes a hotel; it is usual for the greatest lords and ladies of the court to take up the role of *Hôtellier* and *Hôtelliére*. Other people of quality function as domestics in the manner of the Roman feasts of Saturn where masters wait on servants.)

---

[19] M. R. Wade, *Triumphus nuptialis danicus: German court culture and Denmark* (Wiesbaden, 1996), p. 15.

[20] S. Owens, 'Upgrading from Consorts to Orchestra' in J. Wainwright & P. Holman (eds.), *From Renaissance to Baroque: change in instruments and instrumental music in the seventeenth century* (Aldershot, 2005), pp. 227–40 at p. 228.

[21] *GB-Lbl* 813.h.17; W&S 219.

[22] P. Bourdelot and P. Bonnet, *Histoire de la musique et des ses effets depuis son origine jusqu'a présent* (Paris, 1715; repr. 4 vols, Amsterdam, 1725), vol. 1, pp. 279–80.

But it was the court ballet, sometimes known by modern historians as the 'Singballet', that offered German ruling families one of the greatest opportunities to express their true cultural awareness.[23] And it has been estimated that, for every opera performed in the German-speaking lands between 1600 and 1700, around three ballets were presented.[24] Given this importance of court ballets in royal celebrations, we should now consider how they were put together, how they were performed and how they were perceived by musicians and dancers in seventeenth-century Germany.

The role of the dancing master was central. Many came from France and were specifically employed to educate the German aristocracy in dance, etiquette, fashion and behaviour. Dancing masters also took a large part in festive productions, having responsibility for providing the choreography and any required coaching of other dancers. They also took some of the solo parts themselves. At times, they were responsible for the composition of the music and, even when this was not the case, they were still able to exert influence over composers. Georg Muffat claims that he was 'sought out' by Christian Krünner, the dancing master at the Passau court, 'to compose totally new Arias utilizing certain useful ideas he had conceived, Arias which could be danced to in costume and which could utilize theatrical effects in order to be more impressive'.[25] Extra dancing masters were sometimes hired for large-scale events. The preface to the libretto of the 1684 *La rejouissance des dieux* notes that the Berlin court dancing master, Louis du Breüil, was assisted by 'Srs des Hayes, & de St. Romain Maistres de Danses', also from Berlin, along with 'Du Breüil de Lunebourg, de Mayeux Maistre de Danse de son Altesse Serenissime Monsigneur Le Prince d'Anhalt, & de Lehman Maistre de Danse a Hambourg.'[26] For the same occasion, 'Mr. Dufour de Paris' was in charge of 'des Decorations, des Machines' as well as the 'disposition' (arrangement) of the ballet as a whole. The preface wryly notes that Dufour could not speak German while the stagehands could not speak any French; the difficulty was only surmounted by the former's 'application' and 'industrie'.

All this implies a good deal of preparation, and it is surely an oversimplification to think that dancing masters plucked tunes from 'a head full of music, a veritable vademecum on which to draw whenever a new dance was required'.[27] Admittedly, much of the music provided by the dancing masters was probably simple and functional and, as we shall see in the following chapter, it often seems to have

---

[23] H-G. Hofmann, 'Singballett' in L. Finscher (ed.), *Die Musik in Geschichte und Gegenwart*, Sachteil 8 (Kassel, 1998), pp. 1409–11.

[24] S. Owens, 'Ducal musicians in the clouds: the role of seventeenth-century German Singballet' in *Context: Journal of music research*, vol. 24 (2002), pp. 63–7.

[25] D. Wilson (ed. & trans.), *Georg Muffat on Performance Practice* (Bloomington and Indianapolis, 2001), p. 28.

[26] *D-W* Gm 244 4°, W&S 185.

[27] J.M. Ward, 'Newly Devis'd Measures for Jacobean Masques' *Acta musicologica* LX/2 (May-August, 1988), pp. 111–142 at p.130.

been left to the professional musicians to provide the harmonies and instrumental parts. But even if Roger North in England equated dancing masters with 'common fiddlers or other ignoramuses',[28] it is surely too harsh to dismiss their music as 'common-denominator, sound-alike, nondescript, stop-and-go, add-a-strain style', especially when so little of it has survived.[29]

As Jill Bepler has pointed out, 'in so many court festivities of the day, the court provided both the actors and the primary audience for an entertainment which expressly excluded a broader public.'[30] Both male and female royalty danced alongside professional dancers and, in smaller-scale ballets that did not require so much professional help, they took most of the parts themselves. For the smaller courts with modest financial resources, this must have been a particularly attractive way of putting on an entertainment. Visiting royals were clearly expected to play a part in the entertainments put on for them, and it appears that dancers could be drawn from walks of courtly life other than royalty and dancing masters. *Die Triumphirende Liebe* included a part for the fencing master: 'M: Ville Longue Fechmeister' appears to have danced a solo where, not surprisingly, he took the part of a soldier.

Like other court entertainments, the model for these German court ballets, the French *Ballet de cour*, was 'rich in political allegory, galanterie, fantasy and sometimes satire'.[31] The subject matter was generally derived from classical myth, and a typical example in the first half of the seventeenth century would have included '*récits, vers, entrées*, and usually a concluding *grand ballet*'.[32] There would also have been mimed scenes and instrumental interludes.[33] By mid century, introductory *ouvertures* were an increasing part of this scheme. The *récits* were not recitatives in the conventional sense, but merely sung music for a single voice. Michel Depure's *Idées des spectacles anciens et nouveaux* (Paris, 1668) suggests that:

> Although [the récit] may be sung by a single voice, or accompanied by a very few others, without relation to a large choir, it has not taken its name from the

---

[28] M. Chan and J. C. Kassler (eds.), *Roger North's The Musical Grammarian 1728* (Cambridge, 1990), p. 173.

[29] Ward, 'Newly Devis'd Measures', p. 130.

[30] J. Bepler, 'Cultural life at the Wolfenbüttel court, 1635–1666' in H. Schmidt-Glintzer (ed.), *A Treasure House of Books: the library of Duke August of Brunswick-Wolfenbüttel* (Wolfenbüttel, 1998), pp. 131–146 at p. 135.

[31] L. Rosow, 'Power and display: music in court theatre' in T. Carter & J. Butt (eds.), *The Cambridge history of seventeenth-century music* (Cambridge, 2005), pp. 197–240 at p. 230.

[32] J.R. Anthony, *French baroque music from Beaujoyeulx to Rameau* (3rd edn., Oregon, 1997), p. 45.

[33] See: E.A. Bowles, *Musical Ensembles in Festival Books, 1500–1800* (Ann Arbor, 1989), p. 2.

resemblance but rather because of the action, of itself mute, and which has taken a vow to remain silent, borrows the voice of the Reciter, so that he may sing that which the dance would not dare to say, and to remove all the obstacles that the dance alone might cause in understanding the subject.[34]

It seems that, in Paris, the combination of dance and vocal music was not always happy; according to Depure, 'Dancers do not think that recitatives are in the least necessary to the ballet, and singers are persuaded that a ballet is imperfect if it lacks a symphony and some recitatives'.[35] We may imagine a similar situation in Germany.

Unfortunately, little of the vocal music appears to have been preserved in one of the most important sources of the *Ballet de cour*, the manuscripts retrospectively compiled in the 1690s by André Danican Philidor from material of at least forty or more years earlier. (Hereafter, the Philidor MSS.) Of course, he may not have had the vocal music available to him; or he may have extracted, and then grouped together, just the dances.[36] Table 1.1 details the movements from the first part of the 'Ballet Royal Du Dereglement des Passions De L'Interest De L'Amour et de la Gloire en 1652 Recueilly par philidor laisnée' (*F-Pn* Rés. F. 499).[37]

Table 1.1: Movements from the first part of the anonymous 'Ballet Royal du Dereglement des Passions' (*F-Pn* Rés. F. 499)

Movement title	Key	Time signature
Ouverture	G minor	C and ¢
1.ᵉ Entrée 6. titans	G minor	C
2.ᵉ Entrée	G minor	¢
3.ᵉ Entrée Sillene pere Nourissier de Bacchus	G major and G minor	¢ and 3
4.ᵉ Entrée Baccus	G minor	¢
5.ᵉ Entrée Darius	G major	¢

[34] C. MacClintock (ed.), *Readings in the history of music in performance* (Bloomington & Indianapolis, 1979, repr. 1982), p. 206.

[35] Ibid., p. 205.

[36] For a full discussion of the Philidor manuscripts, see: D. J. Buch, *Dance music from the Ballets de cour, 1575–1651: historical commentary, source study, and transcriptions from the Philidor manuscripts* (Stuyvesant, New York, c.1993).

[37] Buch suggests that Philidor's date of 1652 is incorrect, and that the ballet dates from 1648. His listing of the contents of this ballet does not agree with the titles given by Philidor. See Buch, *Dance Music from the Ballets de Cour*, pp. 90–91. An online facsimile of this manuscript is available at http://gallica.bnf.fr/ark:/12148/bpt6k1074201

Movement title	Key	Time signature
Les mesme	G minor	¢
6.ᵉ Entrée 5. Arimaspes	G minor	2
7.ᵉ Entrée 2. Marinieres suivent Thyphis	G minor	¢
8.ᵉ Entrée Jason Castor Pollox Zethes et Calais	G minor	¢
9.ᵉ Entrée 6. Compagnons D'Ulisse	G minor	¢
10.ᵉ Entrée les 4. Vents	G minor	¢

Even if the Philidor's source of the 'Ballet Royal du Dereglement des Passions' is not an accurate representation of a complete *Ballet de cour,* it does provide us with some indicators of how the mid-century French ballet was constructed. There is an *entrée* for each character or group of characters, and all the movements share a common key centre of G. This unity of key is typical of other ballets in the Philidor MSS: if there is a departure to another key, it is usually only for the duration of a single movement.[38] Acts are often concluded by a *Grand ballet* that serves to bring all the characters together. Bransles and courantes are noticeably lacking but, as we shall see below, these dances seem to have been particularly associated with the ballroom.

These same structural characteristics are apparent in *L'Art de bien danser* (Leipzig, 1713), a treatise by the Leipzig dancing master Samuel Behr that is clearly reliant on the French model. The section entitled 'Die Requisita aber eines Balets', sets out the prerequisites for a ballet. First there is the *ouverture* that Behr considers to be 'der haupt-Zweck der gantz Action' (the high [that is, starting] point of the entire proceedings). The subject matter is then established by 'die Invention derer Handlungen und Scenen' (the making of the plot and scenes) and the structure by 'die Entrées und Täntze' (the *entrées* and dance). Next is 'die Ordination des Balets' (the putting together of the ballet), 'die Decoration', 'der Machinett' and 'der Kleidungen' (costumes). Lastly, there is 'der Schluß' (the finale) and 'das Grand-Balet', which contains 'mehr Passagen and Figuren', more complicated movements and gestures. *Handlungen und Scenen* were obviously important, but we should not think of the plots in modern terms; as Samantha Owens has pointed out, there is a 'clear absence of an overall narrative sequence'. On the other hand, 'in almost every case the subjects of individual *Entréen* are related to the overall theme of the ballet, which thus acted as an important unifying thread.'[39] Unfortunately, Behr is silent about the vocal aspects of the German court ballet; clearly he was only interested in the dance.

---

[38] This conclusion is mostly based on the lists of movements and keys given in Buch, *Dance Music from the Ballets de Cour*, appendix B.

[39] Owens, 'Ducal musicians in the clouds', p. 65.

We can see many of Behr's *Requisita* in the 1678 *Ballet von Zusammenkunft u. Wirkung derer VII. Planeten* that was put on at the Dresden court to celebrate one of the occasional gatherings of the various arms of the ruling family. Elector Johann Georg II, in what has been described as 'one of the greatest festivities of his reign' personally took part as the allegorical figure of Nimrod.[40] Most unusually, the music has survived (manuscript *D-Dl* Mus. 2/F/31), although the identity of the composer is not known. A note at the beginning of the manuscript lists the seven characters and their voices, which include two 'Capell knabe' (chapel boys) singing the parts of 'Luna' and 'Cupido'. After the opening 'Prologus' for Cupid, the music for each of the seven 'planets' is contained within individual sections entitled 'Actus'. Each 'Actus' has the same basic structure and is brought to a close by three *entrées*, each comprising two dances, one a duple-time dance followed by one in triple time. Following the French custom, the entire work is brought to a close by a *Grand ballet*, here entitled 'Haubt-Ballet'. The *Ballet von Zusammenkunft* appears to have been exceptional in its grandeur and scope; even a second ballet given at the same Dresden celebrations, the *Frauen-Zimmer- und Mohren-Ballet*, seems to have been a much smaller-scale affair.

Many of the libretti suggest that the strophic song was a popular medium for the vocal elements of these ballets. This is borne out by the printed libretto of *Die Triumphirende Liebe* that, most unusually, includes the music of three of the ballet's songs. These songs are simple strophic settings for voice and 'Bassus'; there are no instrumental *ritournelli*. Does this mean that these strophic songs were usually performed in this way? The libretto of *Die Triumphirende Liebe* does note the presence of 'liebliche Instrumental-Music' (pleasant instrumental music), but it does not give any further details. Instrumental *ritournelli* are added to some of the arias in the *Ballet von Zusammenkunft* but, as I have already pointed out, this ballet may be exceptional. For a more representative example, we have to turn not to a ballet, but to the congratulatory music composed in 1655 by Sophie Elisabeth, Duchess of Mecklenburg-Güstrow, for the seventy-seventh birthday of her husband August, Duke of Braunschweig-Lüneburg.[41] Unusually, the music has been preserved.[42] Figure 1.1 shows the first of the strophic songs that make up the body of the work.

Despite the eccentric layout of the score, we can see that simple instrumental *ritournelli* were added at two points in each verse, and this may be more typical of how strophic songs were performed rather than the bare example in *Die Triumphirende Liebe*.

Music and dance were not just reserved for important occasions such as weddings. While the stage may have emphasized the absolutist aspects of

---

[40] See: H. Watanabe-O'Kelly, *Court Culture in Dresden from Renaissance to Baroque* (Basingstoke, 2002), pp. 184–5.

[41] The birthday celebrations also included a ballet with music again written by Sophie Elisabeth. See: W&S 214.

[42] *D-W* Musica fol. 1.1.2 (3).

monarchy, it was the music of the ballroom that perhaps played the greatest part in the regular day-to-day round of courtly entertainment. The Dresden *Hof-Journal* of 1665–6 describes a ball that concluded a wedding banquet:

> Most of the Dames and Cavaliers began to dance a bransle for which the royal prince's eight violins, sent by the king of France, were in attendance. After the bransle, courantes were danced, passing a couple of hours. ... After the meal, the dancing continued with courantes, bransles, and German dances, between which food and wine was carried around, and the ball ended with an English dance.[43]

There are interesting similarities between this and an account of a ball attended by Sir Bulstrode Whitelock, English ambassador to the Stockholm court of the Swedish Queen Christina. Referring to himself in the third person, Whitelock wrote the following in his diary for 5 January 1653:

> When he [Whitelocke] came into the roome, where the Queen was, she bid him wellcome, with more than ordinary respect, and ledd him into a large room where she usually hears sermons, and att other times it is for musick & dauncing. There was present a great number of Ladyes, & Gallants, her chayre of State was uppon a foot Carpett, a little distance from it, on the right hand, were 5 or 6 stooles, where wh. sate, next to the Queen, & after him Prince Adolphe and other Grandees, on the left hand sate about 20 ladyes, very gallant, after the French mode, the Queen's musick were in a place behind the Chayre of State, 7 or 8. violins, with base violes, Lutes and Citterns, perfecte masters. The Queen with her Ladyes, & Courtiers, first daunced the Brawles, [i.e. bransles] then French daunces.[44]

In both accounts, we again see the clear influence of French court culture, even to the extent of having the Dresden string players 'sent by the king of France'. Whitelock's observation that the musicians played 'behind the Chayre of State' is also interesting. It seems that it was common in the ballroom for the musicians to be placed at one end of the room, behind the dancers. We can see further evidence of this in various paintings; in the well-known 'Bal sur la terrasse d'un palais' (1658) by Hieronymous Janssens (sometimes known as 'le Danseur'), the musicians are clearly portrayed playing at the back of the room. And although the identity of the dancers has been questioned, the 1660 painting of 'Charles II dancing at the Hague' attributed to Gonzales Coques shows exactly the same placing of the musicians.[45] Both Whitelock and the Dresden *Hof-Journal* record the dancing of bransles and

---

[43] G. Spagnoli (ed.), *Letters and documents of Heinrich Schütz, 1656–1672; an annotated translation* (Ann Arbor, 1990), p. 68.

[44] *GB-Lbl* Add. MS 4902, 'A Journall of the Swedish Ambassy in the yeares 1653 & 1654 Impartially written by the Ambassadour', entry for 5 January, 1653.

[45] Reproduced on the front cover of *EM* 35/3 (2007).

14   The Courtly Consort Suite in German-Speaking Europe, 1650–1706

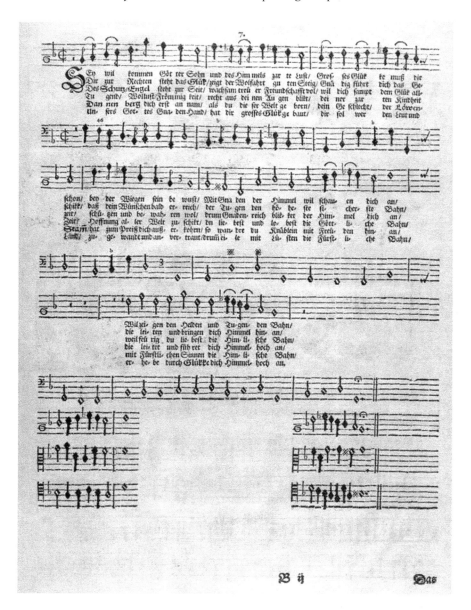

Fig. 1.1.   S-E von Mecklenburg-Güstrow, 'Glückwünschende Freudensdarstellung dem hochgebornen Fürsten Herrn Augusten' (Wolfenbüttel, 1655)

courantes and a bransle opening the proceedings.[46] Indeed, the tradition of opening a ball with a bransle seems to have been remarkably widespread; in France, according to Mersenne, it formed 'l'ouverture du Bal'[47], and in England, Pepys' diary entry for 31 December records:

> By and by comes the King and Queen, the Duke and Duchesse, and all the great ones; and after seating themselfs, the King takes out the Duchess of Yorke, and the Duke the Duchesse of Buckingham, the Duke of Monmouth my Lady Castlemayne, and so other lords other ladies; and they danced the Bransle.[48]

Pepys' account of the December ball also notes that, 'After that, the King led a lady a single Coranto, and then the rest of the lords, one after another, other ladies.'[49] The following of the bransle by a courante seems to have been an equally widespread tradition. As we shall see in Chapter 3, a considerable number of German musical sources of the bransle also include one or more courantes.

Did bransles have a similar function on stage? Even though it has been suggested that 'Bransles are an integral part of the earliest ballets', they are conspicuous by their absence in the ballets represented in the Philidor MSS.[50] Within the hundreds of individual movements in these manuscripts, there are only two movements that are specifically named as bransles: '6me Entrée La Mariée au montier' (Rés.F 496) and '18me Entrée Le Branle de Metz' (Rés.F 497).[51] Even allowing for the fact that some of the *entrées* in other parts of the manuscripts may be unnamed bransles, it is still hard to see how, on the available evidence, the bransle can be considered to be 'an integral part' of the *Ballet de cour*. Even though Mersenne suggests that the bransle could be used 'aux Balets, & aux Bals, qu'aux autres recreations', it seems that the principal use of the bransle and probably the courante was not on the stage, but in the ballroom.[52] If balls took place on a more regular basis than any other entertainment requiring dance music, it may help to explain why, in comparison with music for the dramatic stage, the music for so many bransles has survived.

The *Theatri Europæi* records 'allerley Instrumentè liblich musicirt' (all kinds of pleasant instrumental music) being given as part of wedding celebrations held

---

[46] The component parts of the bransle sequence will be discussed in detail in the following chapter.

[47] M. Mersenne, *Harmonie Universelle contenant la theorie et la pratique de la musique* (Paris, 1636), 'Traitez de la Voix, et des Chants', p. 167.

[48] R. C. Latham & W. Matthews (eds.), *The Diary of Samuel Pepys* (11 vols, London, 1970–83, repr. 1995), vol. 3, p. 300.

[49] Ibid., vol. 3, p. 300.

[50] D. Buch, The Influence of the *Ballet de cour* in the Genesis of the French Baroque Suite' *Acta Musicologica* vol. 57 (1985), pp. 94–109 at p. 98.

[51] This statistic is based on the information given in Buch, *Dance music from the Ballets de cour*, Appendix B.

[52] Mersenne, *Harmonie Universelle*, 'Traitez de la Voix, et des Chants', p. 167.

in Kassel in 1650, and there were surely occasions when dance music was played without being an accompaniment to actual dancing.[53] De Blainville's travels in 1705 took him to Düsseldorf, where he was 'present at a very fine Symphony in the Chapel of the Palace. For his Highness has a band of excellent Musicians.' And for a month, he 'shared regularly every Day ... Balls, Operas, Comedies' and 'Concerts of Music'.[54] Similar references to 'concerts' occur in the descriptions of other travellers. But we should not think of these 'concerts' as music being given as a self-sufficient entertainment. The birthday celebrations in Munich of Princess Henriette Adelaide were described by a French traveller, Charles Patin, as follows:

> Rien ne me parut plus beau que le Carousel. Il se fit dans un manége couvert qui n'est séparé de la Résidence que d'un petit canal. Madame l'Electrice fut conduite à son balcon par Monsieur l'Electeur. Deux galeries l'une sur l'autre qui occupent tout le circuit êtoient remplies de Spectateurs. On fut surpris d'abord par des Concerts de Musique, qui parurent dans des navires roulans, tirez par six chevaux chacun.[55] (Nothing appeared more beautiful to me than the Carousel. It was done in a covered riding school that is only separated from the *Residenz* by a small canal. *Madame l'Electrice* was escorted to her balcony by the Elector. Two galleries, one above the other [and] extending all along the circuit, were filled with spectators. One was initially surprised by concerts of music; these appeared in moving ships, each one drawn by six horses.)

We can only guess at the type of music being played here. But given Henriette Adelaide's exceedingly pro-French bias, it is reasonable to suppose that it was in the French manner. Certainly, carousels were another element of courtly entertainment imported from France. But such entertainments were clearly for the more wealthy establishments.

The music in German courts for all these entertainments was usually provided by the resident *Hofkapelle*, and it is to musicians and musical ensembles that I now turn. *Hofkapellen* were often limited in size but, according to John Spitzer and Neal Zaslaw, they were 'transformed in the last quarter of the seventeenth century into larger, violin-based ensembles, sometimes with two or more players on a part'.[56]

---

[53] M. Merian, *Theatri Europæi* vol. 6 (Frankfurt am Main, 1663), p. 1021; online facsimile at: www.bibliothek.uni-augsburg.de/dda/dr/hist/we_00001-00021. See also C. Engelbrecht, *Die Kasseler Hofkapelle im 17. Jahrhundert und ihre anonymen Musikhandschriften aus der Kasseler Landesbibliothek* (Kassel, 1958), p. 37.

[54] de Blainville, *Travels,* vol. 1, entry for 12 February–7 March, 1705.

[55] C. P[atin], *Relations historiques et curieuses de voyages en Allemagne, Angleterre, Hollande, Boheme, Suisse, & c. Par C.P.D.M. de la Faculté de Paris* (Rouen, 1676), pp. 80–81.

[56] J. Spitzer and N. Zaslaw, *The birth of the orchestra; history of an institution, 1650–1815* (Oxford, 2004), p. 217.

The same authors also suggest that 'performances of music by German Lullists must often have been one on a part because ... the *Kapelle* records document only four or five bowed-string players'.[57] Both these claims, particularly the latter, require some examination.

As a result of the financial impoverishment at the end of the Thirty Years War, many courts in the 1650s and 1660s could not maintain anything more than the smallest musical establishment. In 1651, even Dresden could only list, in addition to five singers, a Kapellmeister, Vicekapellmeister, two organists, six 'Instrumentisten' and an apprentice 'Instrumentistenknabe'.[58] The situation in Dresden did improve; by 1663, the number of instrumentalists had more than doubled.[59] In addition to financial considerations, the size and importance of each *Hofkapelle* was also heavily dependent on the whim of each individual ruler. Even during the Thirty Years War, Wilhelm V of Hessen-Kassel was looking for singers and instrumentalists for his *Hofkapelle*;[60] by 1651 the same court could manage to employ a *Kapellmeister*, an organist and seven 'Musikanten'.[61] On the other hand, in peace-time Wolfenbüttel, the musical establishment was drastically cut in 1666 on the accession of Rudolf August, a ruler who had little time for music or theatre.

But these figures do not give anything like a complete picture, and it is unwise to think of court music ensembles as having a permanent, fixed size. Extra players could be obtained by the ad hoc hiring of musicians from other courts, local towns and cities, and this seems to have been common practice throughout Germany. In Munich, no less than ten players – more than the basic size of some *Hofkapellen* elsewhere – were hired for the 1667–8 entertainment season.[62] In Vienna, Charles Patin reported on a ballet and *divertissement* given for the Empress that employed 'cent cinquante Violons'.[63] Patin's numbers may be an exaggeration, but it does indicate that, in Vienna, the hiring of extras seems to have taken place on an extraordinary scale. In complete contrast, local instrumentalists and singers were hired for a royal wedding in Gotha in 1666, but only on condition that they provided their own music![64] But extra players did not always need to be hired: the Arnstadt

---

[57] Ibid., 219.

[58] See: M. Fürstenau, *Zur Geschichte der Musik und des Theatres am Hofe zu Dresden* (2 vols, Dresden, 1861–2), vol. 1, p. 35.

[59] Ibid., p. 136.

[60] C. Engelbrect, W. Brennecke, F. Uhlendorff, H. J. Schaefer, *Theater in Kassel aus der Geschichte des Staatstheaters Kassel von den Anfängen bis zur Gegenwart* (Kassel, 1959), p. 16.

[61] Engelbrecht, *Die Kasseler Hofkapelle*, p. 38.

[62] C. Timms, *Polymath of the baroque: Agostino Steffani and his music* (Oxford, 2003), pp. 321–2.

[63] C. P[atin], *En Allemagne*, p. 23.

[64] E. Noack, *Wolfgang Carl Briegel. Ein Barockkomponist in seiner Zeit* (Berlin, 1963), p. 29.

Hofkapelle in early 1690s had, excluding the *Kapellmeister*, four violinists and an unspecified number of 'Gesellen und Lehrjungen' (apprentices and pupils) who played the *Alt-*, *Tenor-*, and *Bass-Viole*.[65] For larger-scale occasions, a further eight violinists and extra players of the lower parts were available. These additional players seem mostly to have come from the *Hofkapelle* singers and trumpeters.[66] Salary arrears were not uncommon, even for musicians in senior posts: in Dresden, Bontempi, the Kapellmeister 'appears to have acquired a property ... in exchange for a portion of his back salary, which clearly had gone unpaid for some time'.[67] For the ordinary *musicus*, the situation could be even worse. Georg Arnold, a 'former violinist' at the Hessen-Darmstadt court was owed no less than twelve years back pay at the time of his retirement, and he only received it on the condition that he continued to be available for occasions when more players were needed.[68]

As we have seen, eight violinists 'sent by the King of France' were in Dresden in 1665–6. But even if they were not usually sent by the King himself, French musicians were known at the German courts to a greater or lesser degree throughout most of the seventeenth century. For example, the French violinist Pierre Francisque Caroubel appears to have spent time at Wolfenbüttel around 1610 where he passed on dance music to Praetorius that came to be included in the latter's *Terpsichore* of 1612.[69] But it was the 1660s and 1670s in particular that saw the dramatic rise in popularity of violin bands in the French style, many with native French musicians. At Schwerin, Princess Isabella Angelika von Montmorency founded a French violin band in 1664; six Frenchmen were part of this band at its instigation and, seven years later, that number had risen to nine.[70] Six 'Frantzösische Musicanten' under the direction of Philipp la Vigne were employed at the Celle court from 1666. The payment record for them is marked 'halbjährig' (half-yearly), which may be an accounting *aide-memoire* or an indication that all or some of these French musicians stayed at the court for a no more than a brief period.[71] Certainly, some of the French violin bands did travel from place to place and the visit of one such band to Hesse-Darmstadt during 1683 resulted in the reorganization of the entire *Hofkapelle* along French lines. According to court records, the Hanover *Hofkapelle* in 1696 comprised an organist, a 'Hof-Musikant' (presumably the *Kapellmeister*), four 'Französische Musikanten' and two other 'Musikanten',

---

[65] P. Spitta, *Johann Sebastian Bach* (2 vols, Leipzig, 1873), vol. 1, p. 167.
[66] Ibid., p. 167.
[67] M. E. Frandsen, *Crossing confessional boundaries: the patronage of Italian sacred music in seventeenth-century Dresden* (Oxford, 2006), p. 40.
[68] E. Noack, *Musikgeschichte Darmstadts vom Mittelalter bis zur Goethezeit*, Beiträge zur Mittelrheinischen Musikgeschichte 8 (Mainz, 1967), p. 113.
[69] F. Dobbins, 'Caroubel, Pierre Francisque' in *New Grove 2*, vol. 5, p. 179.
[70] See: H. Erdmann, *Schwerin als Stadt der Musik* (Lübeck, 1967), pp. 25–6.
[71] F. Berend, *Nicolaus Adam Strungk (1640–1700), sein Leben und seine Werke* (Freiburg, c.1913), p. 219.

presumably German.[72] But these court records do not give anything like a complete picture of the music at Hanover. For this we have to turn to the writings of a French diplomat in Germany, Samuel Chappuzeau. His *Suite de L'Europe vivant* contains important evidence of how the musicians from various courts, including Hanover, combined at various times to form a large-scale ensemble:

> L'Evêque d'Osnabruc, & les Ducs de Cell & d'Hannover entretiennent depuis plusiers années une excellente Troupe de Comediens François riches en habits, & qui executent admirablement leurs rôles; & lors que leurs trois bandes de violons se trouvent ensemble, on les peut nommer la bande des vingt quatre, la plus part François & des meilleurs maîtres de cette profession.[73] (The bishop of Osnabruc, along with the Dukes of Celle and Hanover have, for a number of years, maintained an excellent troupe of French comedians; they have splendid costumes and carry out their roles admirably. Before [their performances] three bands of violins play together, and one might name them the band of the twenty four, for they are mostly French and the greatest masters of this profession.)

The comparison between these combined violin bands and the Parisian 'vingt quatre' is telling. And the significance of 'trouvent ensemble' was not lost on Chappuzeau. He goes on to give clear details of when and where these bands played together:

> Cette Troupe suit quatre mois l'Euêque, quatre mois le Duc de Cell, & quatre mois le Duc d'Hannouer. Mais comme ie l'ay dit, ces Princes se rencontrent quelquefois ensemble pour les affaires communes, ou pour se mieux divertir; & il y a trois ans qu'ils passerent l'hyver à Lunebourg l'une des grandes villes d'Allemagne au Duc de Cell, où le bal, le ballet, la Comedie, les courses de bague, les festins, & toutes les galenteries imaginables faisoient le divertissement ordinaire de ces belles Cours.[74] (This troupe follows the bishop for four months, the Duke of Cell for four months and the Duke of Hannover for four months. But, as I have said, the Princes meet together at times [to discuss] common affairs or, better, to entertain themselves. For the last three years, they have spent the winter at Lunebourg, one of the large towns in Germany of the Duke of Cell, where balls, ballet, comedy, running at the ring, feasts and all imaginable courtly activities become the standard entertainments of these fine courts.

Perhaps it was this combined ensemble that, according to Mattheson 'amazed everyone with their eupophonius sound'.[75]

---

[72] K. von Malortie, *Der Hannoversche Hof unter dem Kurfürsten Ernst August und der Kurfürstin Sophie* (Hanover, 1847), p. 38.
[73] Chappuzeau, *L'Europe vivante*, p. 348
[74] Ibid., pp. 348–9.
[75] Timms, Polymath of the Baroque, p. 47.

We can therefore say with some certainty that, even if the bringing together of different ensembles may have been exceptional, it is clear that extra players were routinely engaged for significant court entertainments. While there were bound to have been performances in which, as Spitzer and Zaslaw suggest, 'one on a part' was the norm, it seems that this was only acceptable when nothing else was available. But the influx of extra players did not mean that instrumental parts were doubled equally from top to bottom; I shall now go on to consider the type of sonority that seems to have been favoured for the performance of dance music.

Throughout the seventeenth century, *Hofkapelle* instrumental ensembles were mainly made up of string players. It was only in the final decade of the century that they were joined by the new French oboes and bassoons. And although it may be a 'myth ... that [in the sixteenth century] the two standard string scorings used by violin bands – violin, three violas and bass and violin, two violas and bass – were particularly associated with France', there can be little doubt that this association existed in many parts of Germany in the second half of the seventeenth.[76] But more important was the emphasis given to the *dessus* (treble) and bass parts in French music. Lüder Knöp described the third section of his 1660 *Ander Theil Newer Paduanen, Galliarden, Arien, Allemanden, Balletten, Couranten, und Sarabanden* as being 'nach der Frantzosischen Manier mit einem Bass und Discant gesetzet' (set in the French manner with a bass and treble). In addition, Knöp says that the 'Discant' part may be played 'mit unterschiedlichen Geigen in unisono' (with various [that is, many] violins in unison). While Knöp was a town musician, there is no doubt that he was reflecting a perception of French music that was also common amongst court musicians. For example, the court musician and later diplomat, Adam Drese suggests that 'Immassen denn die Ober-Stimme gar wohl mit zwey oder mehr gleichspielen Violinen ... zu bestellen' (when playing in large numbers, two or more violins playing in unison should take the top part).[77] Confusingly, Drese also goes on to say 'ob schon die untern Partheyen einfach verbleiben' (but, on the other hand, the lower parts [should be played] by single players) without fully explaining what he means by 'untern Partheyen'; are these just the middle viola parts, or the bass part as well? Certainly, the Kassel suite manuscripts, which include an allemande by Drese, provide a number of examples where bass and trebles parts are duplicated, but not the inner parts.[78]

We also find evidence of outer-part doublings in printed editions. In both surviving exemplars of Jean Sigismund Cousser's 1682 *Composition de musique*

---

[76] P. Holman, 'From Violin Band to Orchestra' in J. Wainwright, P. Holman (eds.), *From Renaissance to Baroque: change in instruments and instrumental music in the seventeenth century* (Aldershot, 2005), p. 243. See also: Spitzer and Zaslaw, *The birth of the orchestra*, p. 91.

[77] A. Drese, *Erster Theil Etlicher Allemanden, Couranten, Sarabanden, Balletten, Intraden und andern Arien* (Jena, 1672), preface.

[78] '2. Allemande Adam Dresen. à 4' (*D-Kl* 2° MS mus. 61d^4). The Kassel suite manuscripts are further discussed in Chapter 4.

(*F-Pn* Mus. Vm⁷1484 and *PL-Kj* Mus. ant. pract. C 1080), there are two copies of the 'Bassus' part. It is possible, though unlikely, that these extra bass parts were purchased separately, but their very existence is a further indication that bass-line doubling took place. There are also 'Premier dessus' and 'Second dessus' part books with the same music for many of the movements, which ensures treble-line doubling. Cousser's three later suite collections, all issued in 1700, have oboe and bassoon parts in addition to the *à 5* string ensemble. But the same concept of outer-part doubling is still evident. The second oboe does not double the string *haute-contre* part; instead, both first and second oboes double the *dessus* violin in unison. Naturally, the bassoon doubles the bass.[79] Similarly, late seventeenth- or early eighteenth-century wind parts added for Dresden performances of suites by Johann Christoph Pez have both oboes doubling the first violin part (*D-Dl* Mus. 2026 – N – 1–8). This is in addition to the multiple copies of the violin and bass parts for some of the suites. On the other hand, Georg Muffat, in the preface to his *Florilegium Secundum*, suggests that 'all the best players should not be assigned to the first violin (or upper) part, so that the middle voices seem robbed of the necessary players'.[80] Given the tradition of part doubling that I have just described, Muffat's comments suggest that he was somewhat at odds with his fellow Lullists in preferring a more balanced ensemble in which 'one can distinguish and perceive everything well and beautifully'.[81]

We should also not ignore the fact that five-, four-, and even three-part ensemble music may have been mixed together in the same performance, or even within the same suite. For example, the music written in 1655 by the Duchess Sophie Elizabeth for her husband's birthday contains pieces for *à 5*, *à 4* and *à 3* ensembles. (See page 12.) We have only the score of this music and no individual parts. So it is not possible to know if any instrumental doubling took place and if the players needed for the *à 5* and *à 4* ensemble also played in the *à 3* pieces. The situation is a little clearer in the first part of Georg Bleyer's *Lüst-Müsic* (Leipzig, 1670) that contains the following sequence of movements:

XXVII Air/XXIIX. Sarraband/XXIX. Courant/XXX. Gique.[82]

Given the careful ordering of *Lüst-Müsic's* contents, it is reasonable to suppose that Bleyer intended this sequence of movements as the last suite in this part of the collection and 'XXX. Gigue' as a finale.[83] The music for the first four dances is for four-part ensemble, the music for the gigue is expanded to five parts with an additional violin; the two violin parts in the gigue are printed on facing pages of

---

[79] Cousser's suite collections are further discussed in Chapter 6.
[80] Wilson, *Georg Muffat*, p. 45.
[81] Ibid., 45.
[82] This group of movements is followed by a sequence of seventeen dances that appear to have no association with each other.
[83] The collection will be further discussed in Chapter 5.

the same part book. The role of this additional violin in the preceding *à 4* dances is not specified. But, according to its title page, the collection is in the French manner, which indicates that outer-part doubling was intended as a matter of course. A number of violins would therefore be playing the treble part, and these would merely have divided for the *à 5* music. But division or combination of parts does not seem to have been confined to the treble lines. We can see this in two suites in the Kassel manuscript *D-Kl* 2° MS mus. 61d[7], which is a set of parts and not a score. In each individual part, the two suites are copied on opposite sides of the same sheet. The first suite requires *à 5* instrumentation with two viola parts; the second requires *à 4* instrumentation with one viola part. But both viola parts still contain music for the *à 4* suite: they simply double each other. This appears to indicate that the two suites were played together by the same ensemble, the violas combining for the four-part music. This would not have produced an unbalanced ensemble in the latter: the total number of players seems to have been comparatively large with three copies of the violin part, two of the second viola and two of the bass. Only the first viola has a single part. As we shall see in the next chapter, seventeenth-century suite construction appears to have been a fluid process; along with the frequent doubling bass and treble lines, this apparent practice of combining parts and including music for differently sized ensembles within the same piece is another facet of the same fluidity.

Chapter 2
Nach der lustigen Frantzösischen Manier zu spielen
National Style and the Transmission of Dance Music

The music of the seventeenth-century courtly suite had its origins in the type of courtly entertainment discussed in the previous chapter. But before examining the nature of the courtly suite itself, there are two important issues that need consideration. The first of these concerns the differences between the French and Italian styles of composition. The second concerns the transmission of the dance music itself.

Given that French court culture was so dominant in Germany, it is hardly surprising that a large proportion of seventeenth-century German courtly dance music was either imported from France or newly composed in imitation of the *frantzösischen Manier*. Court musicians were clearly aware of the existence of the French manner and were often keen to make the distinction between it and music in the Italian manner. The Rudolstadt court *Kapellmeister*, Philipp Heinrich Erlebach, complained in the preface to his *VI. Sonate à violino e viola da gamba col suo basso continuo* (Nuremberg, 1694) that he was unable to prevent the printer from using French dance titles rather than the Italian ones that he had requested. Even town musicians appeared to find the distinction important. In 1663, the Leipzig physician and musician, Johann Caspar Horn, published the first two volumes of his *Parergon musicum* (Erfurt, 1663). The first volume, made up entirely of suites, proclaimed its contents 'nach der ietzigen Italiänischen Manier zu spielen' (to be played in the current Italian manner), while the second volume, this time of ballet music, had 'nach der lustigen Frantzösischen Manier zu spielen' (to be played in the lively French manner).

How did seventeenth-century musicians perceive the French manner? Mersenne's *Harmonie universelle* suggests that the emotions of joy, love and hope are the principal ingredients of 'des airs François'.[1] But he has obvious difficulty in attempting to link emotions with music:

---

[1] M. Mersenne, *Harmonie Universelle contenant la theorie et la pratique de la musique* (Paris, 1636), 'Traitez des Consonances, des Dissonances', p. 371.

Cette proposition est tres-difficile à expliquer, tant parce qu'il semble que la Musique desire de certaines delicatesses, & des agreemens qui ne peuvent compatir avec la vehemence, & la rudesse des passions, & particulierement avec la cholere.[2] (This proposition is very difficult to explain, as much because it seems that music desires certain delicacies and diversions that cannot be in sympathy with vehemence, harsh passions, and particularly with anger.)

Over one hundred years later, writers were still experiencing difficulty and it seems that Quantz could do no more that suggest that the Italian manner of playing was 'arbitrary, extravagant, artificial, obscure, frequently bold and bizarre' while the French manner was 'slavish, yet modest, distinct, neat and true in execution'.[3]

Much of our information about stylistic issues in Germany comes from the prefaces to Georg Muffat's printed editions of music issued during the last two decades of the century.[4] But despite his assertion that his *Florilegium primum* (Augsburg, 1696) was written 'meistens auf Frantzösiche Ballet-Art' (mostly in the French ballet style), he seems unable to describe precisely what this means. The nearest we come to it is a defence of Lully and his followers who 'because of their flowing and natural motion, completely avoid irregular runs, frequent and ill-sounding leaps'.[5] Even this may not be as straightforward as it appears: Muffat served as a violinist at the Salzburg court of Archbishop Max Gandolph at the same time as Heinrich Biber. It seems that there was some rivalry between the two men and, as Eric Chafe has suggested, Muffat's criticisms could well have been a personally motivated reflection on Biber's playing rather than any direct reference to style.[6]

Muffat's 'Frantzösiche Ballet-Art' does at least demonstrate a link between the French manner and dance. But he was not the first to do this. *Musurgia universalis* (Rome, 1650), a widely circulated and influential treatise by the German priest, mathematician and scientist, Athanasius Kircher, has the following:

[The French have] been allotted a temperament that is cheerful, lively, and innocent of restraint. They love a style that is similar to this temperament: whence they give themselves for the most part to the hyporchematic style, that

---

[2] Ibid., p. 371.

[3] J.J. Quantz, *On Playing the Flute; the classic of Baroque music instruction*, E.R. Reilly (trans.), (Boston, 2001), p. 335.

[4] English translations of these prefaces are readily available. See: D. K. Wilson (ed. and trans.), *Georg Muffat on Performance Practice* (Bloomington and Indianapolis, 2001).

[5] Ibid., p. 113.

[6] E.T. Chafe, *The Church Music of Heinrich Biber*, Studies in Musicology 95 (Ann Arbor, 1987), p. 17.

is, to ensemble dancing, leaps, and similar very suitable dances (which they present to airs such as galliards, passamezzos, and courantes).[7]

The linking of French music to cheerfulness and liveliness seems to have been a familiar concept to German musicians throughout the second half of the seventeenth century. 'Lustigen Suiten' (lively suites) are mentioned on the title page of Johann Fischer's Lullian-inspired *Tafel-Musik* (Hamburg, 1702) and, as we have seen, Horn's *Parergon musicum* includes music in 'der lustigen Frantzösischen Manier' (the lively French manner). Muffat's 1701 *Auserlesene Instrumental-musik* speaks of 'the brisk liveliness of the ballet arias which spring from the Lullian fountain'.[8]

Many suite collection prefaces specifically ask for a lively pulse in the performance of their French-style dances. The preface to Hans Hake's *Ander Theil Newer Pavanen* (n.p., 1654) states that the bransle movements in the collection should be played 'mit einem geschwinden Tact' (with a swift pulse).[10] Virtually the same instruction, 'mit einem lustigem Tact' (with a lively pulse), is given for the French music in Lüder Knöp's collection of suites and dances, *Ander Theil Newer Paduanen, Galliarden, Arien, Allemanden, Balletten, Couranten, und Sarabanden* (Bremen, 1660). The preface to another printed collection from the same year, Wolf Ernst Rothe's *Erstmahlig Musicalische Freuden-Gedichte* (Dresden, 1660), is a little more specific:

> Hiernechst wolle ein Jeder die freundliche Erinnerung in besten vermercken/ daß die Balletten, Couranten, und Sarabanden nach Frantzösischer Art/mit einen frischen Strich und geschwinden Tact auff daß sie die Manier erlangen/gespielet werden müssen. (The following friendly reminder is intended for everyone as a most important observation: the balletts, courantes, and sarabandes in the French manner must be played with a lively bow-stroke and a rapid pulse in order to achieve the [correct] style.)

Although the equating of French music with nothing more than liveliness is obviously an oversimplification, it is clear that it was a clear and widely understood concept among German musicians. And if German seventeenth-century musicians seem to have seen the French style more in terms of performance practice than anything else, it partially explains why Georg Muffat gives such copious information on the matter in the preface to his *Florilegium secundum* (Passau, 1698).

One of the longest and most detailed sections in Muffat's preface is given over to 'The Use of the Bow'.[9] Here, there is genuine information concerning the

---

[7] O. Strunck (ed.), *Source Readings in Music History* (rev. edn., vol. 4), M. Murata (ed.), New York, 1998), p. 200.
[8] Wilson, *Muffat*, p. 71.
[9] Ibid., pp. 33–41.

difference, as perceived by Muffat, between Italian and French styles of playing and bowing:

> The first note of a measure which begins without a rest, whatever its value, should always be played down-bow. This is the most important and nearly indispensable general rule of the Lullists, upon which the entire style depends, as well as the main difference that distinguishes it from the other styles.[10]

There are also examples of how to bow common-time groups of quavers and semiquavers in accordance with this general rule, as well as various groupings in compound time. There are bowing exemplars for courantes, gigues, bourées, and the Lullian way of playing a menuet is compared with the 'German/Italian' way. Here, Muffat seems to be implying that the French bowing gives a rather more characterful performance of this dance than the German/Italian bowing, which is governed by convenience for the player. Uniformity of bowing is also emphasized, 'even if a thousand ... were to play together'.[11] But after all his considerations of performing style, Muffat could not end this section of the preface without returning to the concept of the lively French manner:

> The length of the lines is bound up with a marvellous liveliness, an astonishing uniformity of beat with the variety of movements, and a sensitive beauty with lively playing.[12]

Muffat was not the only one, nor the first, to concentrate on bowing as an essential ingredient of the French manner. In Ansbach, the young Jean Sigismund Cousser, freshly returned from a period of study in Paris, was employed at the court in 1683. His specific task was to instruct the *Hofkapelle* musicians in the correct way of playing French music through 'täglichen Exercitii' (daily exercises). (See page 122.) Presumably French uniform bowing was an element of these exercises. In Darmstadt, *Landgravine* Elisabeth Dorothea had heard French instrumentalists when they came to play at the court in 1683, and this made a deep impression on her.[13] She clearly felt that her own *Hofkapelle* was not capable of performing in this way; as a result, the musicians Cotta and Schober accompanying Princes Ernst Ludwig and Georg on the grand tour, were sent to Paris to study the Lullian style. Johann Cotta's principal task in Paris was to learn about French string techniques: the court accounts have the following entry: 'paid to the *musici* Cotta, 7fl.15 alb. for instruction on the violin in Paris'.

---

[10] Ibid., p. 34.
[11] Ibid., p. 33
[12] Ibid., p. 41.
[13] This and the following information regarding the Darmstadt court is all taken from: E. Noack, *Musikgeschichte Darmstadts vom Mittelalter bis zur Goethezeit*, Beiträge zur Mittelrheinischen Musikgeschichte 8 (Mainz, 1967), p. 130.

There were other performance practices that also defined national style. As Wiebke Thormahlen has pointed out, 'ornamentation [in the late seventeenth and early eighteenth centuries] had become a central category in the judgement of music, one that provided ammunition in the raging battle between French and Italian musical aesthetics.'[14] For the immediate pre-Lullian era, the preface given in each of the surviving part-books of *Erster Theil Etlicher Allemanden, Couranten, Sarabanden, Balletten, Intraden und andern Arien mit theils darbei befindlichen Doublen, oder Variationen* (Jena, 1672) by the Weimar and Jena court musician, Adam Drese, gives the following valuable advice on when to add ornamentation:

> wenn die Arien zuvor ein-oder zweymahl schlecht gemacht worden/in beyden Clausulen abgewechselt/und allezeit auff eine schlechte Clausul die variirte/von der einen Violine (in dem die anderen etwas schwächer und schlecht fortgehen) darzugespielet werden. (As long as the airs have been played in their simple form once or twice, both strains may be varied; and after every undecorated strain, one violin should play a decorated version while the others carry on more quietly and without decoration.)

Drese links this collection with the music of French dancing masters, and it is telling that he allows for each strain of a dance to be played three times: twice simply and once with decorations. It seems reasonable to think that dance music could have been played in this way at least until the end of the century. Unfortunately, no details are given of the type of ornamentation that Drese had in mind; for that, we need to examine French practices, and how German court composers perceived ornamentation in the French manner.

According to Jean Rousseau, 'les Ornements ne sont pas necessaires pour la subsistance du Bastiment, mais qu'ils servent seulement à le rendre plus agreable à la veuë' (ornaments are not essential for the substance of the argument; they only serve to make the outcome more agreeable).[15] He goes on to list seven varieties of ornament for the voice and a further three specifically for the viol. These include the 'Cadence ou Tremblement', the 'Port de Voix' and 'l'Aspiration' for the voice, and the 'Martellement' and 'Battement' for the viol.[16] But for complete tables of ornaments we have to turn to printed editions of keyboard by French composers. Perhaps the most influential of these in the late seventeenth century was the 'Marques des Agrements et leur signification' given in Jean-Henry d'Anglebert's *Pieces de Clavecin* (Paris, 1689). Here, there are twenty-nine examples with their explanations. But such tables seem to have been confined to keyboard and viol music: with one exception, there are seemingly no equivalent tables for consort music in either French or German sources. This exception is Muffat's preface

---

[14] W. Thormahlen, 'Georg Muffat – a document for the French manner?', *EM* 31/1 (2003), pp. 110–115 at p. 110.
[15] J. Rousseau, *Traité de la Viole* (Paris, 1687), p. 74.
[16] Ibid., p. 75.

in *Florilegium secundum*. Muffat claims that he 'will only describe the most important and essential' ornaments, but that does not stop his list running to nearly thirty examples.[17] In addition, Muffat embarks on lengthy verbal descriptions of each genre of ornament. Like Rousseau, Muffat considered ornamentation to have its origins in vocal technique, but a number of his ornaments seem to emanate from the keyboard. This is particularly apparent in the case of various types of trill, the mordant and the group of ornaments that D'Anglebert describes as a 'Coulé sur 2 notes de Suitte'. In all of these, Muffat's and D'Anglebert's examples are essentially the same.

If Muffat's writings represent his own practice, then the scope of his ornamentation seems to go well beyond that of Lully himself. Lully's own scores are mostly restricted to trill markings, and even these are not used with any great frequency. Anecdotal evidence seems to indicate that Lully disliked ad hoc ornamentation, and John Spitzer and Neal Zaslaw are surely correct in suggesting that, while Lully did not 'end ornamentation altogether', he 'reformed and restrained the performance practices of the *Vingt-quatre Violons* and other string players at the French court'.[18] Under Lully, players were strictly controlled; they became 'disciplined, hierarchical, polished ensembles'.[19]

At first, the German *Lullists* seem to have followed Lully's example to the letter, for it may not have been just bowing techniques that were passed on by German musicians who had worked in Paris. Concepts of ornamentation may have been part of the same education. Ornamentation in Cousser's *Composition de musique* is conspicuous by its absence. Perhaps this suggests that, if ornamentation was added at all, it was at rehearsal where it was also strictly controlled. *Composition de musique* is not alone in this; other printed collections by German *Lullists* from before 1700 follow a similar pattern and have little more the occasional trills. Even Muffat himself does not add anything more than trills, but the use of these trills is widespread; far more than in Lully's music, especially in the lower parts. It is possible that these trills are a generic sign for more complicated ornamentation, but, if so, it is strange that Muffat did not mention it in his preface. The trend for frequent trills is even more noticeable in the three collections of suites by Cousser issued in 1700 and, as with Muffat, their use is not confined to the upper part. Given the plethora of trills, Cousser's collections from 1700 appear to need little else, if anything, in the way of ornamentation.

Perhaps Muffat had Cousser in mind when he complained about 'those who unreasonably hold forth that Lullian violin ornaments ... are composed only of trills'.[20] But given the example of Muffat's own music, this seems perverse, and we

---

[17] G. Muffat, *Suavioris harmoniæ instrumentalis hyporchematicæ, Florilegium secundum* (Passau, 1698; H. Rietsch (ed.), DTÖ, vol. 4, Vienna, 1895, repr. 1959).

[18] J. Spitzer and N. Zaslaw, *The birth of the orchestra; history of an institution, 1650–1815* (Oxford, 2002), p. 98. See also pp. 96–7.

[19] Ibid., p. 99.

[20] Wilson, *Georg Muffat*, p. 46.

should also not forget that, by the end of the century, Muffat's personal experience of performances in Paris was nearly thirty years old. Thormahlen is surely right to question whether the preface to *Florilegium secundum* really does represent true French performing practice.[21] We are left with the suspicion that Muffat's later contact with French music may have come as much from keyboard collections as it did from consort pieces or the music of Lully. Muffat may have added this type of ornamentation to his own music, but it would be unwise for modern performers to add it to music by anyone else.

German court musicians did not just go to France; many were also given leave from their duties in order to spend time studying in Italy.[22] While they were there, 'they were often expected to engage the services of Italian musicians on behalf of their employer'.[23] Even in the strongly French-orientated court in Kassel, an Italian musician, Paolo Mazzuchelli, was admitted as a member of the *Hofkapelle* in 1659, thus demonstrating that an Italian could be employed in a musical ensemble that was run along French lines.[24] He was certainly not alone; as Geoffrey Webber has pointed out, 'numerous Italian musicians found work in the North German and Scandinavian courts during the seventeenth century'.[25]

If the greatest opportunity for German musicians to become familiar with the Italian style was through direct contact with Italian musicians and Italian sacred music, it was surely Italian opera that must have made the deepest impression. In the immediate aftermath of the Thirty Years War, it was only the larger courts with their substantial financial means that were able to contemplate performances of opera. In Munich, the Italian-trained Johann Caspar Kerll's opera *Oronte* was given at the opening of the new opera house. In Dresden *Il Paride im musica* by the Italian-born Giovanni Andrea Bontempi was given in 1662 to celebrate the marriage of Erdmuthe Sophia, Duchess of Saxony to Margrave Christian Ernst of Brandenburg-Bayreuth. Despite the Dresden court's precarious financial circumstances in the early 1660s, the lavish scale of the opera imitated 'the atmosphere of the festive early Italian court operas'.[26]

---

[21] Thormahlen, 'Georg Muffat – a document for the French manner?'

[22] G. Webber, *North German church music in the age of Buxtehude* (Oxford, 1996), pp. 44–47.

[23] Ibid., 47.

[24] C. Engelbrecht, *Die Kasseler Hofkapelle im 17. Jahrhundert und ihre anonymen Musikhand-schriften aus der Kasseler Landesbibliothek* (Kassel, 1958), p. 42.

[25] Webber, *North German church music*, pp. 48–49. See also M. E. Frandsen, *Crossing confessional boundaries: the patronage of Italian sacred music in seventeenth-century Dresden* (Oxford, 2006), pp. 50–51.

[26] B. Brumana and C. Timms, 'Bontempi, Giovanni Andrea' in *New Grove* 2, vol. 3, pp. 880–881. For a description of the Dresden finances, see Frandsen, *Crossing confessional boundaries*, pp. 37–39.

The combination of drama and singing was clearly linked to the expression of strong passions, and it was the expression of the passions that came to be considered essential elements of the Italian manner. As Mersenne put it, the Italians use:

> plus de vehemence que nous pour exprimer les plus fortes passions de la cholere par leurs accents, lors particulierement qu'ils chantent leurs vers fur le theatre pour imiter la Musique Scenique des anciens.[27] (more vehemence than us in order to express the strongest passions of anger by their inflection, especially when they sing their verses for the theatre imitating the scenic music of antiquity.)

Kircher does not specifically mention the voice, but he certainly agrees with Mersenne when he suggests that the Italians 'draw out both the torments and the passions of the soul, arousing them in every possible way with great power'.[28] Perhaps it was the expression of strong passions that also led Kircher – and other writers after him[29] – to suggest that 'upon first hearing, the music of the Italians, albeit charming, pleases the French and Germans very little'.[30]

Strong passions are not far removed from Muffat's suggestion that the Italian manner contains 'certain melancholy, exquisite affects', and we can see just what he meant by this in the first sonata of his 1682 *Armonico tributo*.[16] The 'Gravè' contains an extraordinary dynamic range, frequent dissonance and chromaticism: all musical devices that surely express emotions of exquisite melancholy. The first six bars alone contain a range of marked dynamics from 'forte' to 'pp', and the end of the movement is marked 'ppp'.

If seventeenth-century perceptions of stylistic elements seem to have focused on specific performing issues, or more generalised concepts such as the expression of the passions, there were some dances that had distinct musical characteristics. This was particularly the case with the courante and its Italian counterpart, the *corrente*. Example 2.1 compares the opening of a French courante from Georg Bleyer's 'Partie â 4 â la Françoise' (*CZ-KRa* A 801) with the first strain of 'La Guastallesa à 3' from Cazzati's *Correnti balletti galiarde a3 è 4* (Venice, 1659).

The Italian dance has vigour and deliberate simplicity and directness of rhythm, while in the French version, as Bruce Gustavson has put it, 'the hemiola qualities of the textures tend to undermine the sense of closure of melodic phrases'.[31] In Bleyer's courante, subtlety of phrasing and rhythmic ambiguity extend over several bars at a time. The only cross-rhythm in Cazzati's version is a *hemiola* at the end of the first strain. However, not all German musicians – especially those

---

[27] Mersenne, *Harmonie Universelle*, 'Traitez des Consonances, des Dissonances', p. 371.
[28] Strunck (ed.), *Source Readings*, rev. vol. 4, p. 203.
[29] For instance, see: Webber, *North German church music*, pp. 46–47.
[30] Strunck (ed.), *Source Readings*, rev. vol. 4, p. 202.
[31] B. Gustavson, 'France' in A. Silbiger (ed.), *Keyboard music before 1700* (New York, 1995, repr. 2004), pp. 90–146 at p. 130.

Nach der lustigen Frantzösischen Manier zu spielen

Ex. 2.1.   G. Bleyer, 'Partie â 4 â la Françoise' (*CZ-KRa* A 801), courante; M. Cazzati, *Correnti balletti galiarde a3 è 4* (Venice, 1659), 'Corente Seconda, La Guastallesa à 3'

from the towns – seem to have been aware of these differences. In the Italian and French volumes of Horn's *Parergon musicum*, it might be expected that he would have taken the opportunity to demonstrate his knowledge of national styles by composing an Italian *corrente* and a French courante. However, he does no such thing. There is little difference between the courantes of either volume; in both, frequent colourations indicating *hemiolas* provide the rhythmic ambiguity of the French model. Clearly, Horn did not understand the difference between the two dance types, or chose to ignore it. But as he uses 'Courante' as the dance title in the Italian volume, it is possible that it was the latter.

A comparison between Horn's courantes and those of a working court musician such as Philipp Heinrich Erlebach is telling. It is clear that the latter was fully aware of the differences between national styles of dance music, and we have already seen his annoyance at his publisher using French rather than Italian movement titles. Example 2.2 compares the opening of the Italian 'Courante' from Erlebach's 'Sonata seconda' of *VI. Sonate à violino e viola da gamba col suo basso continuo* (Nuremberg, 1694) with the first strain of his French '2. Air Courante' from the first of his *VI. ouvertures begleitet mit ihren darzu schicklichen Airs* (Nuremberg, 1693). '2. Air Courante' demonstrates all the rhythmic interest and subtlety expected in a French courante: it could easily have been written by a native French musician. But he was equally expert in the Italian style; comparison with Cazzati's 'La Guastallesa à 3' (given above) shows that the 'Courante' from *VI. Sonate* could also pass for one written by a native Italian musician.

There were some differences between the French and Italian versions of the sarabande, but these were far less marked than those between the courante and *corrente*. Richard Hudson has identified three types of sarabande: the sung Spanish, the fast French and, the last to emerge, the slow French.[32] The fast French version was imported into Italy and became the Italian *sarabanda*. Example 2.3 gives the first strain of a typical example, '12 Sarabanda' from Bononcini's *Arie, Correnti, Sarabande, Gighe, & Allemande ... Opera Quarta* (Bologna, 1671).

The slow version remained firmly associated with France. As Brossard put it, 'le mouvement est grave, lent, serieux &c.'[33] And while this slow sarabande may have been the last to emerge, it was certainly known in Germany by the 1660s and probably earlier. In order to compare French and Italian sarabandes, Example 2.3 also gives the first strain of 'La Sarabande' in *D-Kl* 2° MS mus. 61b². This movement clearly had its origins in France as it also appears Philidor's 'Recueil de Plusieurs belles pieces de Simphonie' (manuscript *F-Pn* Rés. F. 533). The

---

[32] R. Hudson, *The Folia, the Saraband, the Passacaglia, and the Chaconne: the historical evolution of four forms that originated in music for the five-course Spanish guitar* (4 vols, Neuhausen-Stuttgart, 1982), vol. 2, pp. xvi–xx.

[33] Brossard, S. de, *Dictionaire de Musique, contenant une explication des termes Grecs, Latins, Italiens, & François les plus usitez dans la Musique* (Paris, 1703; facsm.: F. Knuf (ed.), Hilversum, 1965), p. 312. But compare Rothe's comments on the nature of the French sarabande. (See page 25.)

Nach der lustigen Frantzösischen Manier zu spielen 33

Ex 2.2.   P. Erlebach, *VI. Sonate à violino e viola da gamba col suo basso continuo* (Nuremberg, 1694), 'Sonata seconda, Courante'; *VI. ouvertures* (Nuremberg, 1693), '2. Air Courante'

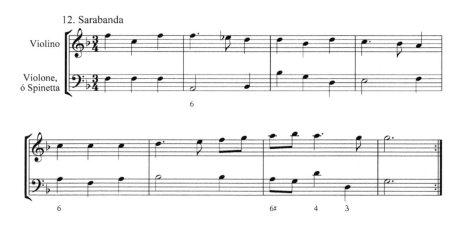

Ex 2.3. G. Bononcini, *Arie, Correnti, Sarabande, Gighe, & Allemande ... Opera Quarta* (Bologna, 1671), '12 Sarabanda'; *D-Kl* 2° MS mus. 61b², 'La Sarabande'

crotchet-dotted crotchet-quaver rhythm that permeates the piece is characteristic of the slow French sarabande, as are the three changes of chord that happen on the second beat of the bar.

We should also consider the *ballett* or *ballo*; these titles are frequently found in both Italian and French dance music. As we shall see in Chapter 3, *ballo*, *ballett* and *balletto* were all used as generic terms for complete suites. But *ballett* and *ballo*, and, to a lesser extent, *balletto*, were not just generic; they were also used as single-movement titles. As Brossard points out, the 'Balletto veut dire Ballet' is also 'une espece de dance dont l'air commence par une Croche en levant' (a type of dance starting with a quaver upbeat).[34] And while not mentioned by Brossard, *ballo* seems not only to be synonymous with *ballett*, but is also the most frequently used as a single-dance title. For example, in both Rothe's 1660 *Erstmahlig Musicalisches Freuden-Gedichte* and Reusner's 1668 *Musicalische Taffel-erlustigung*, 'balletten' is used on the title page list of dances, but, in every case, 'ballo' is used as the heading within the musical text.

If there was no apparent distinction in Germany between *ballo* and *ballett*, there was considerable diversity in the music used for the dance type itself. Brossard's quaver upbeat is certainly not a regular feature of the dance in either court or town repertoire. Rather more common is the use of constant, propulsive dotted quavers and semiquavers. There are also times, especially in the court repertoire, where two examples of quite different character are given in succession, presumably as a deliberate contrast. Example 2.4 gives the first strains of two consecutive *ballett* movements from the third section of the trio manuscript *S-Uu* Ihre 281–2; music that may well emanate from within the courtly repertoire.

The bass part has not survived, but I have provided a reconstruction. Both movements are in duple time, but, apart from this, there is little in common. '38. Ballett' has quaver upbeats in the manner suggested by Brossard, while '39. Ballett' starts on the downbeat, but with phrases ending on the last beat of the bar. Given the contrasts in phrase structure between these two examples, it seems unlikely that they were intended as a matched pair in the manner of the *en suite* courantes discussed in the next chapter; the same choreography would surely not have been transferable from one dance to the other. Richard Hudson has suggested that, before 1660, some *balletts* contained sections that were 'occasionally triple' in metre, and 'XXIV. Ballo â 5' in Rothe's *Erstmahlig musicalische Freuden – Gedichte* (Dresden, 1660), for example, is a bi-partite movement with a *presto* first section in common time and an *adagio* second section in 6/4.[35] But such instances are seemingly rare, and there can be little doubt that, for most German consort-suite composers in the second half of the century, the *ballo* or *ballett* was a lively, duple-time dance with a number of phrase and rhythmic options. Hudson has

---

[34] de Brossard, *Dictionaire*, entry for 'Balletto veut dire Ballet', p. 6.

[35] R. Hudson, *The Allemande, the Balletto and the Tanz* (2 vols, Cambridge, 1986), vol. 1, p. 179.

Ex 2.4. *S-Uu* Ihre 281–2, '38. Ballett', '39. Ballett'

lamented the 'lack of ... uniformity' in the dance.[36] Given the lack of uniformity throughout the court genre as a whole, this is hardly surprising and just one further example of the fluidity of courtly suite composition.

If the element of propulsion was an important part in some variants of the *ballo*, it was even more important in the gigue. As Bruce Gustafson has pointed out, the gigue had a 'propulsive duple-compound meter, an emphasis upon counterpoint, and the literal or approximate inversion of the first strain's theme in the second strain'.[37] This 'propulsive' quality no doubt assisted greatly in the adoption of the gigue as a finale to suites by German town musicians who tended to adopt this type of gigue or the simpler Italian *gigha*. Phrase lengths in the latter were often, but not always, confined to four- and eight-bar groupings.

But propulsive rhythms were not limited to Italian gigues and counterpoint was not limited to Germany. Lully employed energetic and contrapuntal gigues, often with lengthy, irregular phrases. Irregular phrase lengths were sometimes present in the Italian *gigha*, but they were far more common in the French gigue and were understood as a French characteristic by German musicians. Example 2.5 shows the gigue from the 'Ouverture de Mr Valoÿ' in manuscript *D-B* Mus. MS 30274. The French-born Stephan Valois was a musician in the Hanover *Hofkapelle*, and this *ouverture* with three dances are clearly in the French manner. While there is little use of counterpoint in the gigue, the *dessus* part starts by itself at the opening of each strain and the rest of the ensemble join in a bar later; the bass briefly imitates the *dessus* opening. There is a quasi-inversion at the start of the second strain. This type of opening to a gigue was very popular amongst the German Lullists and the movement type as a whole was often, but not consistently, known as the 'Gigue angloise'. Perhaps this was to separate it from its more contrapuntal cousin, or it may have been in recognition of the dance's possible English origins.

If the gigue became a popular way of ending a suite in the town repertoire, it was used rather more flexibly by court musicians, and could appear at any point in the dance sequence. In the first suite of Muffat's *Florilegium primum*, for example, we find the following sequence, which is by no means unusual:

1.Ouverture/2.Air/3. Sarabande/4.Gigue 1/5.Gavotte/6.Gigue 2/7.Menuet.[38]

Muffat's two gigues in this sequence are clearly intended to form a contrast, and this brings us to the first of two variants of the French gigue. This is the canarie, a dance that regularly appears in suites throughout the last three decades of the seventeenth century. Its simplicity strongly suggests the Italian *gigha*. Mattheson in 1713 described it as 'sehr geschwinde' (very rapid) and having a

---

[36] Ibid., pp. 178–86.

[37] B. Gustafson (ed.), *Lüneburg, Ratsbücherei, Mus. ant. pract. 1198*, 17th Century Keyboard Music 22) (New York and London, 1987), Introduction, vii.

[38] These titles are as given in the 1695 edition, but not as in *DTÖ*.

Ex 2.5.   S. Valois, 'Ouverture de Mr Valoÿ' *D-B* Mus. MS 30274, 'gigue'

3/8 time signature. He also points out that 'die ersten Noten in jedem Tact sind mehrentheils mit einem Punct versehen' (the first note in each bar is usually dotted).[39] Not all canaries have a 3/8 time signature, but the liveliness and frequent use of dotted rhythms are certainly common features of the dance, and there is a complete absence of counterpoint or imitation. Given the similarity between the canarie and the *gigha*, it is possible that they are parallel developments of the same dance. In Germany, there seems to have been some confusion or indifference over the titles of canarie and gigue. For instance, while not marked as such, Muffat's 'Gigue 2' from the sequence above is a canarie in all but name.

It appears that there may have been an association between the gigue and the allemande, especially in early seventeenth-century lute music, and this may explain the existence of the second French gigue variant, the version in common time. It is likely that the common-time rhythms were often performed as the more usual triple-time groups, but there are examples suggesting, particularly amongst the work of town musicians, that this may not have always been the case. Example 2.6 gives the opening of the gigue from Johann Pachelbel's manuscript 'Partie a 4: 1 Violin, 2 Viole e Cembalo' (*D-B* Mus. MS 16481/2).[40]

While it is possible to play this piece as a quasi-12/8, it would hardly be convincing, and it is difficult to understand why Pachelbel should have written a gigue in this way if he did not want it performed in common time. In the court repertoire, the common-time gigue does not figure strongly; Muffat included one in 'Fasciculus IV' of *Florilegium primum* where it follows '24. Canaries' where he clearly intended to produce a pair of gigues with as much contrast as possible. Here, the common-time '25. Gigue' is something of a hybrid; it contains dotted quaver and semiquaver groups in conjunction with sequences of triplet quavers.

---

[39]   J. Mattheson, *Das Neu-Eröffnete Orchestre* (Hamburg, 1713; facsm.: D. Bartel (ed.), Laaber, 2004), p. 192.

[40]   Modern edn.: J. Pachelbel, *Partie a 4 in F sharp minor*, R. Gwilt (ed.), (Hungerford, 1998).

Nach der lustigen Frantzösischen Manier zu spielen 39

Ex 2.6. J. Pachelbel, 'Partie a 4: 1 Violin, 2 Viole e Cembalo' (*D-B* Mus. MS 16481/2), 'gigue'

As with Pachelbel's example, it is difficult to see why Muffat should have written the movement in this way if he wanted all contrast to be ironed out by performing the whole movement as if notated in 12/8. On the other hand, the similarly notated common-time 'aria' in the fourth sonata of Muffat's 1682 *Armonico Tributo* was rewritten in 6/8 and renamed 'Giga' in the 1701 reworking of this collection.

We now need to examine the single-line transmission of dance music, a widespread tradition during much of the seventeenth century that lasted into the eighteenth. Within this tradition, dance music was transmitted merely in the form of a single-line melody; it was left to the recipients of the music to provide a bass line and inner parts. As early as 1612, the preface to Michael Praetorius' *Terpsichore* collection confirmed the existence of this practice.[41] 'Frantzösischer Branslen, Däntze und Melodyen' (French bransles, dances and melodies) were supplied as 'einige Discant Stimme' (a single treble line) by the French dance master Anthoine Emeraud. Praetorius himself added the bass line and inner parts. It is telling that specific mention is made here of Emeraud's role in providing the dance melodies.

---

[41] M. Praetorius, *Terpsichore* (Wolfenbüttel, 1612); G. Oberst (ed.), *Gesamtausgabe der musikalischen Werke von Michael Praetorius,* vol. 15, (Wolfenbüttel, 1929).

The role of dancing masters in providing single-line dance melodies is again highlighted, but in a different way, when Roger North in England complained that they 'make tunes, and then goe to their betters to put bases to them'.[42] At rehearsals of dance music the dancing master's violin was often the sole accompaniment and this may have been an important factor in establishing this tradition of single-line transmission. Of course, court musicians were perfectly capable of writing original dance music, and did so. But it seems that the provision of musically satisfactory accompaniments for existing dance melodies was considered to be an equally important duty.

Single-line transmission explains why the same dance melody might exist in a number of versions all with different basses and different harmonies. Example 2.7 shows the first strains of two versions of the widely circulated dance usually known simply as 'Libertas' or 'Libertace'.

The first version is taken from manuscript *S-Uu* IMhs 409, a collection of dance music notated in tablature and apparently derived from the music played by the French violin band at the Stockholm court of Queen Christina.[43] The second is taken from the Philidor manuscripts where it is part of the 'Recüeil de Plusieurs vieux Airs faits … sous les Regnes de François 1er, henry 3, henry 4 et Louis 13' (*F-Pn* Rés. F. 494). The different harmonies of each version clearly imply single-line transmission of at least one source, presumably IMhs 409. Bars 7–8 show how the arranger in IMhs 409 added a particularly attractive hemiola to enliven the cadence at this point. The same bars in the Philidor manuscripts, without the hemiola, seem rather staid in comparison. North's condemnation seems unjustified in such cases; the inherent flexibility in the process meant that a good musician could add something of his own to an existing piece of dance music. But not every musician worked with the same care as this or was prepared to follow Praetorius' example when he changed the instrumentation of an *à 5* dance in *Terpsichore* to *à 4* by providing completely new inner parts and bass line.[44] The practice of reducing *à 5* instrumentation to *à 4* by simply leaving out the lowest viola part was widespread. We see it in sources as diverse as the Amsterdam editions of music extracted from Lully's dramatic stage works and the Magdalen College part books (*GB-Cmc* F-4-35, 1–5). In the latter, Charles Babel copied the *à 5* 'Premier Air' from the sixth suite of Cousser's *Composition de musique* into 'Sett 26' where it lost the lowest viola part and became *à 4*.[45]

---

[42] M. Chan and J. C. Kassler (eds.), *Roger North's The Musical Grammarian 1728* (Cambridge, 1990), p. 173.

[43] Mráček, J. S. (ed.), *Seventeenth-Century Instrumental Dance Music in Uppsala University Library, Instr. mus. hs 409*, Musica Svecica Saeculi xvii: 5, Monumenta Musicae Svecicae, vol. 8 (Stockholm, 1976), preface 9*.

[44] M. Praetorius, *Terpsichore*, 'XXXIII. à 5. La Sarabande' & 'XXXIV. à 4. La Sarabande'. The four-part setting is a tone lower.

[45] Babel's work is discussed in more detail in Chapter 7.

Nach der lustigen Frantzösischen Manier zu spielen 41

Ex. 2.7.   Two versions of 'Libertas' in *S-Uu* IMhs 409 (ed. J.S. Mráček, Stockholm, 1976), and 'Recüeil de Plusieurs vieux Airs faits' (*F-Pn* Rés. F. 494)

The addition of lower parts to the single-line transmission of a treble part is apparent in manuscript *CZ-KRa* A 4826 from the Liechenstein collection in Kroměříž.[46] This manuscript source of music by Lully contains ten movements taken from *Le Temple de la paix* (LWV 69) and ten from *Achilles et Polixene* (LWV 74).[47] (LWV 74 is not entirely by Lully; he died before he could finish it, and it was completed by Pascal Collasse.) A 4826, a four-part score, is unfinished. Only the movements from *Le Temple de la Paix* and the *ouverture* from *Achilles et Polixene* have been completed, but neither the inner parts or bass lines match those given in Ballard's printed editions of LWV 69 and 74. Of the nine remaining movements extracted from *Achilles et Polixene*, six have a treble and bass line with staves left blank for the two inner parts; once again, the bass part does not match Ballard. In the remaining three movements, there is only a treble part with blank staves below it. It is, of course, possible that the scribe was merely copying from another manuscript, but the frequent crossings out and alterations make this unlikely. It appears that the inner parts and bass lines were all newly composed.

Five of the movements from *Le Temple de la paix* also exist in a second Lully source from the same collection, manuscript A 873.[48] This is not a score, but a set of parts containing exactly the arrangements of these movements found in A 4826, and from where they were probably copied. Vejvanovsky, the Kroměříž court trumpeter, composer and copyist, has been identified as the copyist of A 873, and he may also have been responsible for A 4826.[49] Not surprisingly the parts in A 873 were written with considerably more care than the score of A 4826, but the handwriting style of the two manuscripts is similar. Given the links between the two manuscripts, it seems highly likely that both are the work of the same person. The entire process may be summarised as follows: the single-line Lullian sources were copied into A 4826, and a bass part was added. This was followed by the inner parts. Selected movements from the completed sections of A 4826 were then copied into the individual parts of A 873.

Single-line melody was not the only form of reduced-format transmission. Two-stave transmission was also used, giving both treble and bass parts. Once again, there appears to be a link with the dancing masters: a notebook compiled by an 'unknown Frenchman active in Brussels at the beginning of the [seventeenth] century' includes a bass line for at least some of its treble parts.[50] But the format seems to have been most popular with publishers who wished to produce anthologies of dances. The Dutch anthology, *'T Uitnement Kabinet* – published

---

[46] *AMA* V/2, entry 880.

[47] Both this manuscript and *CZ-KRa* A 873 were unknown as sources of Lully's music until I drew attention to them in M.N. Robertson, 'The consort suite in the German-speaking lands, 1660–1705' Ph.D. diss. (University of Leeds, 2004).

[48] *AMA* V/2, entry 858.

[49] Ibid., entry 858.

[50] J.M. Ward, 'Newly Devis'd Measures for Jacobean Masques' *Acta musicologica* vol. 60/2 (May–August, 1988), pp. 111–142 at p. 128.

in Amsterdam between 1644 and 1649 – used the treble and bass format for much of its dance music[51] and, even in the early eighteenth century, Roger's publishing house issued a volume of treble and bass dance music as *Le Musicien Maistre de Dance contenant 118 Dances & Contredances tant angloises que Hollandoises & françoises à un Dessus & une Basse* (Amsterdam, n.d.). The two-stave format was also used in Vienna for the retrospectively copied manuscripts of ballet music by Johann Heinrich and Andreas Anton Schmelzer (*A-Wn* Mus. Hs. 16 583 and 16 588). There is an interesting parallel with some of the Philidor manuscripts that are written out in the same way.[52]

---

[51] Modern edition: R.A. Rasch (ed.), *'T Uitnement Kabinet* (10 vols, Amsterdam, 1973–78).

[52] Manuscripts *A-Wn* Mus. Hs. 165 83 and 165 88 will be discussed further in Chapter 9.

Chapter 3
Composées sur le même Mode ou Ton
Defining the Suite

During the course of this chapter, I will show that definitions of the suite by modern scholars sit uneasily with seventeenth-century court traditions. We therefore need to discuss these definitions and their origins. In modern times, it is no exaggeration to say that the suite has often been regarded by scholars as something of a poor relation to the sonata. Perhaps as a result, the so-called 'classical order' was imposed upon the suite, presumably in an attempt to give it a readily identifiable sonata-like hierarchy and structure. This structure was made up of specific dances placed in a specific order; every example of the suite could then be judged in terms of its relationship to this order. The main dances, labelled by Tobias Norlind as 'Haupttänze' were the allemande, courante and sarabande, with the gigue being added for suites written in the later part of the century.[1] Even in the later part of the twentieth century, scholars were still concerned with hierarchy. David J. Buch's definition of early French suites is as follows:

> A flexible hierarchy of types of movements, marked by a sense of proportion (and perhaps decorum) achieved by a somewhat loose ordering of dances of a specific meter, character and tempo.[2]

But while careful organization of a collection's contents seems to have appealed to a number of composers, hierarchy is not a concept that appears to have received much consideration in seventeenth-century dance music. Indeed, in many single-volume collections of dances from the mid-seventeenth century, it is sometimes difficult to distinguish between movements that were intended to be grouped together into suites, and movements that are lacking any apparent association. If we now consider the way in which seventeenth-century musicians and writers appear to have viewed the suite, we will see a different picture emerging.

Throughout the seventeenth century, the word 'suite' was used extensively in court and diplomatic circles to denote the entourage serving an important person. The word apparently had a similar connotation in music: groups of two,

---

[1] T. Norlind, 'Zur Geschichte der Suite' in *Sammelbände der Internationalen Musikgesellschaft*, vol. 7 (Leipzig, 1905–1906), pp. 172–203 at p. 187. See also: D. Fuller, 'Suite' in *New Grove* 2, vol. 18, p. 339.

[2] D. J. Buch, 'The Influence of the *Ballet de cour* in the Genesis of the French Baroque Suite' *Acta Musicologica* vol. 57 (1985), pp. 94–109 at pp. 96–7.

sometimes three, dances of the same type were sometimes marked by seventeenth century copyists as being 'en suite', 'de suite' or simply 'suite'. This occurs in both manuscript and printed sources and probably refers to the way in which such dances were often performed. We have seen in Chapter 1 how a dance might start with a pair of dancers, usually the most important couple present, followed in turn by everyone else according to their social rank. If a large number of couples were taking part in a dance in this way, a substantial amount of music would be required. Each strain of a dance would need to be repeated many times, and more than one piece of music would be required if endless repetition were to be avoided. It is also possible that the musicians did not know in advance how many people would be taking part, and that extra movements were grouped together to ensure that enough music was available, whatever the circumstances.[3] Therefore, it is reasonable to conclude that the term 'en suite' was often used to describe groups of like movements, gathered together for such purposes and presumably performed without a break. Given their popularity, it is hardly surprising that more courantes seem to have been brought together *en suite* than any other type of dance.

For much of the seventeenth century, the only other appearance of 'suite' in any sort of context of dance-movement association seems mostly to have been in connection with the bransle sequence. We can see an early example of this in the 1623 dance treatise *Apologie de la Danse* written by the French dancing master, F. de Lauze:

> Il est fort à propos maintenant qu'vn Escolier peut avoir acquis le port de la jambe, de luy monstrer la suitte des Bransles.[4] (It is important to propose now that a gentleman should acquire the *port de la jambe* in order to [correctly] demonstrate the bransle suite.)

But apart from this, the use of 'suite' as a generic label for a sequence of dances was limited. In many manuscript sources, it was the title of the first movement that often served to identify a suite, and, in most of the printed editions produced in seventeenth-century Germany, publishers of suite collections seem to have preferred title pages that merely listed movement types. Towards the end of the century, in collections written by the German *Lullists*, 'suite' was used to denote a sequence of dances following an initial abstract movement, usually the *ouverture*. In view of the association of 'suite' with a retinue of an important person, it may not be fanciful to see this as the central figure of the *ouverture* followed by its entourage of dances.

One early use of 'suite' in the modern sense that includes all movements of a sequence, both abstract and dance, appears to be in Drese's *Erster Theil Etlicher*

---

[3] I am grateful to Jennifer Thorp for this suggestion.

[4] F. de Lauze, *Apologie de la Danse et la Parfaicte Methode de L'enseigner tant aux Cavaliers quaux Dames* (n.p.,1623), p. 36.

Allemanden, Couranten, Sarabanden, Balletten, Intraden und andern Arien (Jena, 1672). Here, there are five sequences of movements with the following titles:

> Der Policriten Suite von Intraden, Balletten und Arien.
> Der Climenen erste Suite von Intraden, Balletten und Arien.
> Der Judithen Suite von Balletten, Intraden und Arien.
> Des Crœsus Suite von Balletten, Intraden und Arien.
> Der Climenen andere Suite von Intraden, Balletten und Arien.

Although the music has not survived complete, and the extant part books are riddled with errors, the titles themselves are unequivocal in their inclusion of *Intraden* as well as dance movements. Seventeen years later, we find 'Suitte' being used in two manuscript suite collections copied in at the Hanover court by the *Hofkapelle* musicians Barrey and Charles Babel (*D-DS* Mus. MSS 1221 & 1227).[5] As with Drese's 'suites', there can be no doubt that the term was used here to cover all the movements in the sequence. By the start of the eighteenth century, title pages such as that of Johann Fischer's *Tafel-Musik* (Hamburg, 1702) were starting to include the word 'suiten' in a generic sense, and 'suite' in its modern meaning was being used with far greater frequency.

But 'suite' was not the only generic term used at the turn of the century for sequences of dances. *Ballett, Balletto and Balletti* were all used at various times, and in various places. *Balletto* was particularly used in this way in Vienna. (See Chapter 9.) And while 'Ballo' was mostly used as a title for individual movements, it could also refer to entire suites. This was particularly the case in Italy. For example, the sequences of *Ballo/Corrente/Giga* and *Sarabanda* that appear in Salvatore Mazzella's *Balli, correnti, gighe, sarabande, gavotte, brande, e gagliarde* (Rome, 1689) are all given the generic title of 'Ballo' in the edition's *indice*.

In his 1703 *Dictionaire*, de Brossard equates 'suite' with 'sonata da camera':

> Le second genre comprend les *Sonates* qu'ils apellent *da Camera*, c'est à dire, propres pour la Chambre. Ce sont proprement des suites de plusieres petites pieces propres à faire danser.[6] (The second type concerns sonatas that are called 'da Camera', that is to say, suitable for the chamber. These are really suites of several short pieces suitable for dancing.)

This is borne out by the editions and catalogues issued by Roger, the Amsterdam publisher, where the same suite publication could be called a 'Suitte', a 'Sonata da camera', or sometimes both. His edition of J. C. Pez's op. 2 trio suites was

---

[5] Babel continued to use the term 'suitte' in the manuscripts that he copied after his move to England.

[6] S. de Brossard, Dictionaire de Musique, contenant une explication des termes Grecs, Latins, Italiens, & François les plus usitez dans la Musique (Paris, 1703; facsm.: F. Knuf (ed.), Hilversum, 1965), entry for 'Suonata', pp. 118-9.

published as *Sonate da camera a tre, Due flauti et basso del signore Christophoro Pez opera seconda*, but it was also listed in the same publisher's 1706 catalogue as 'Neuf suittes de Mr. Pez à 2 flûtes ou violons & Basse Continue qui sont son Opera seconda'.[7]

This dual nomenclature is probably Roger's attempt to give his editions a universal appeal, but in general, such use of 'sonata da camera' was extremely rare in seventeenth-century Germany. Indeed, its use in Johann Rosenmüller's 1667 *Sonata da Camera cioe Sinfonie* is entirely the result of the collection being published in Venice: had the collection been published in Germany, the title page would no doubt have been little more than a conventional list of movement types. However, 'suite' is well established in modern times as a standard nomenclature, and I shall use the term in the accepted way.

Were suites ever used as functional dance music? The town musician, Georg Wolfgang Druckenmüller clearly thought that suites could be danced. The preface of his *Musicalisches Tafel-Confect; Bestehend in Vll. Partyen/Balleten, Allemanden, Couranten, Sarabanden &c.* (Schwabisch Hall, 1668) states:

> 'Wo keine Violen di gam. vorhanden/oder nicht beliebig/oder zu Tantz/kan man die 11.Partie eine Octav höher/mit Violinen versuchen.' (Where no *viola da gambas* are available, or if you do not wish to use them, or for dance, you may play the second suite an octave higher with violins).

However, the music in Druckenmüller's collection shows that he was ill at ease in trying to write in the French manner, and his suggestions need to be treated with some suspicion. On the other hand, Georg Muffat certainly did understand the idiom, and his advertisement for his second *Florilegium* collection seems to confirm the notion that suites can be danced:

> These pieces were favourably performed with full harmony for the entertainment of distinguished guests at certain celebrations of the most esteemed Court of Passau, as well as for the dancing practice of the noble youth.[8]

But it is unlikely that Muffat meant that entire suites could be used in such a way. It was more likely to be individual movements. We come nearer to finding an answer to the question by considering not suites, but an individual movement, the allemande. It seems that this often-used movement was not danced in France in the second half of the seventeenth century.[9] According to Mersenne, allemandes are

---

[7] *GB-Lbl* Hirsch IV 1114.a.

[8] D. Wilson, (ed. & trans.), *Georg Muffat on Performance Practice* (Bloomington and Indianapolis, 2001), pp. 23-4.

[9] Richard Hudson calls this 'astonishing', but reluctantly comes to the same conclusion. See R. Hudson, *The Allemande, the Balletto and the Tanz*, (2 vols, Cambridge, 1986), vol. 1, p. 149.

'aujourd'huy de la jouër sur les instruments sans la dancer' (nowadays played on instruments, not danced).[10] The music in many allemandes seems to bear this out. Contrapuntal openings, such as the one in the 'allemande de Monsieur Mayeau' from Ballard's *Pièces pour le violin a quatre parties* (Paris, 1665) (see Example 3.1), were common in French ensemble allemandes; but they are at odds with the dance-music traditions that I have already described and would surely make dancing more difficult.

French allemandes seem to have been widely circulated in the German lands and imitated by German court musicians. Were such movements danced away from Paris? It has been suggested that they were danced in Kassel and Stockholm.[11] But this is not altogether satisfactory. As we have seen, French culture was a dominant feature at these two courts, especially when it came to dancing; and both courts appear to have employed French dancing masters. It would be strange if allemandes were being danced in Kassel and Stockholm when they were not being danced in France. Again, the argument is re-enforced by the music: the elaborate contrapuntal opening to the anonymous allemande in the first suite of *D-Kl* 2° MS mus. 61d^8 makes dancing highly unlikely. Gottfried Taubert's comprehensive dance treatise, *Rechtschaffener Tanzmeister oder gründlicher Erklärung der Frantzösischen Tantz-Kunst* (Leipzig, 1717), avoids all mention of the allemande. Taubert may have been reflecting practice in France, and not in Germany, but a local tradition of allemande dancing would surely have merited some sort of mention. Unfortunately, there is no surviving German dance treatise from the middle or later parts of the seventeenth century to add any further light on the subject.

Does the presence of an allemande indicate that all other movements in the same sequence are only intended for instrumental performance? It would be strange if some movements within a sequence were intended for dancing, and some not; but until further evidence is found, the question of whole suites acting as functional dance music must remain open. However, the evidence, such as it is, would seem to suggest that the presence of an allemande in a suite does indeed indicate that the entire sequence of movements was intended to be played instrumentally, but not danced. We should also note that in Vienna, as part of a quite separate tradition, the allemande appears to have been seen as a type of character dance with no set choreography (see Chapter 9).

If we now turn to suite construction, it is clear that suites of dances in the French manner by both court and town composers were rarely arranged in a specific order of movement types. We can see this in Lüder Knöp's *Ander Theil Newer Galliarden, Arien, Allemanden* (Bremen, 1660). Knöp was a town musician; he followed his father as a town organist in Bremen, and was clearly steeped in the municipal tradition. However, according to the preface, the third and final part of

---

[10] M. Mersenne, *Harmonie Universelle contenant la theorie et la pratique de la musique* (Paris, 1636), 'Traitez de la Voix, et des Chants', p. 165.

[11] Hudson, *Allemande*, vol. 1, p. 181.

Ex 3.1.   R. Ballard (ed.), *Pièces pour le violin a quatre parties* (Paris, 1665),

the collection is specifically set in the French manner, albeit with some curious use of language. There are six sequences of movements, each having a common key centre, and each is given the generic, though Italian, title of 'Ballo'. Each 'Ballo' ends with a 'Saraband', but there is no set number or sequence of dances and most of the movements are untitled. For example, 'Ballo Quarto' contains five movements untitled apart from a courante and sarabande; 'Ballo Quinto' contains nine movements, all untitled apart from a *bataglia*, courante and two sarabandes.

Although Knöp did not use any allemandes in the third part of his collection, it was not uncommon for court composers to include one, or even two, examples of the dance within a single suite. And, in many cases, the allemande was used to signify the start of a suite. But the movements that follow do not reflect anything like the 'classical' order discussed at the start of this chapter. This diversity of construction was to remain a characteristic of the courtly suite for the remainder of the century. Even in the German-Lullist tradition, where most suites started with an *ouverture*, the choice of dances thereafter did not usually follow any set pattern. *Le journal du printems* (Augsburg, 1695), a collection of *ouverture* suites by Johann Caspar Ferdinand Fischer is typical. The fourth suite of the collection has an *ouverture* followed by an entrée, rondeau, gavotte, menuet and passacaille; the fifth suite has an *ouverture* followed by an entrée, chaconne, traquenard and menuet.

The one exception to this diversity was the enduringly popular bransle suite: it remained remarkably constant as a structure throughout much of the seventeenth century, and we have seen how the word 'suite' was applied to the sequence from at least the second decade of the century. It had not started as a sequence, but as a single dance with many individual variants. Thoinot Arbeau's 1588 *Orchesography* dance treatise lists no few than twenty-five varieties although it is clear that, even in his time, different types were often put together and played in succession. As Arbeau describes it:

> Et affin de s'accorder par ensemble, ... comme les nostres de Lengres en iouent dix de suite, qu'ilz appellant branles de Champagne couppez. Ilz en iouent vn certain aultre nombre de suitte, qu'ilz appellant branles de Camp, vne aultre suitte ilz la nomment branles d'Auignon: Et aultant qu'il suruient de fresches compositions & nouueaultez, aultãt en font ilz de suites, & leur attribuent des noms à plaisir.[12] (When it is desired that collections should be put together, our [instrumentalists] from Langres play ten in succession; they call these mixed *branles de Champagne*. They play another sequence that is called *branles de Camp*, and yet another is named *branles d'Avignon*. And as fresh compositions and novelties appear, so they devise new sequences and bestow upon them what names they wish.)

If in Arbeau's time, the choice of bransle variants was up to individual musicians, it is apparent that a more clearly defined sequence was emerging at the start of the seventeenth century. In the fourth section of the preface to Praetorius' 1612 *Terpsichore*, there is advice on 'Interpretatio, oder Erklerung der Frantzösischen Wörter und Namen/in nachfolgenden Däntzen' (interpretation or explanation of the French words and names in the following dances). The *Interpretatio* lists a large number of bransle variants, but it is telling that the first five are:

> Bransle simple/Bransle gay/Bransle de Poictou/Montirande/Gavotte.

The *bransle de Poictou* is divided into two sections. The first of these has nine steps while the second, of twelve steps, is called 'Der dobbelte de Poictou' (the [bransle] double of Poictou).

A large number of bransle variants is also found in De Lauze's dance treatise, *Apologie de la danse*, which, as we have seen, uses the term 'suite' in relation to the bransle sequence. The description of the component parts of the 'suite des bransles' largely agrees with the order given by Praetorius, although the *bransle double* is now separated from the *bransle de Poictou* and given its own identity as the 'quatriesme bransle'. The 'Montirande' of Praetorius' sequence is not named by de Lauze but merely given as the 'cinquiesme bransle'.[13] By the time Mersenne published his *Harmonie universelle* in 1636, not only the sequence, but its nomenclature, seems to have been finally established. Mersenne describes it thus:

> Le premier s'appelle *Bransle simple* ... Le second Bransle s'appelle *Gay*, & se danse plus viste que le premier: ... Le troisiesme se nomme *Bransle à mener*,

---

[12] T. Arbeau, *Orchesographie en traicte en forme de dialogve* (Langres, 1589; facsm.: xxx (ed.), Bologna, 1981). Translation based on M.S. Evans (trans.), *Thoinot Arbeau: Orchesography* (New York, 1948, repr. 1967), p. 137.

[13] De Lauze, F., *Apologie de la danse et la parfaicte methode de l'enseigner tant aux Caualiers quáux dames* (n.p., 1623; trans. J. Wildeblood, London, 1952), p. 63.

ou *de Poitou,* ... Le quatriesme s'appelle *Bransle double de Poitou*: ... Le cinquiesme se nomme *Bransle de Montirandé*, sa mesure est binaire, mais elle est fort viste ... Le sixiesmes s'appelle *la Gavote*, c'est à dire la dance aux chansons: sa mesure est binaire assez grave.[14] (The first is called 'Bransle simple' ... The second bransle is called 'Gay' and this dance is faster than the first: ... The third has the name 'Bransle à mener' or 'of Poitou' ... The fourth is called 'Bransle double de Poitou': ... The fifth is named 'Bransle de Montirandé', its measure [that is, time signature] is binary [that is, duple], but it is strong and quick ... The sixth is called 'la Gavote', that is to say, the dance of songs: its measure is binary, but still slow.)

Perhaps one reason for the popularity amongst musicians of the bransle sequence was the combination of movements containing different characteristics. The *bransle simple* was a duple-time movement with a three-bar phrase structure. In contrast, the following *bransle gay* was in triple time with a characteristic quaver and crotchet upbeat to each of its four-bar phrases. Given that the bransle suite often appears to have functioned as a type of ballroom *ouverture*, it is possible that the juxtaposition of duple- and triple-time sections of the *bransle simple* and *bransle gay* had a greater influence on the Lullian *ouverture* than has hitherto been realized. The third dance of the sequence, the *amener* (or *bransle de Poictou*), was again in a triple metre with six-bar phrases split into two groups of three bars, or four and two. The *bransle double* was also in triple time, but with simple four-bar phrasing. Presumably to balance these sections in triple time, the concluding *montirande* and gavotte were both duple-time movements. The phrasing of both was mostly in groups of four bars, but the gavotte did not always have the double-crotchet upbeat of eighteenth-century versions. Until the end of the seventeenth century, it was more usual for this dance to start on the first beat of the bar.

There was also a shorter form of the bransle suite that existed outside France and had widespread use in Germany. Not surprisingly, Mersenne fails to mention this abbreviated sequence as it was rarely used in France. It had four movements, rather than six, the *bransle double* and *montirande* being omitted. Even six-movement bransles originating in France where often truncated in this way when copied by German scribes, but both long and short versions were often found with the addition of one or more courantes and a sarabande to the basic sequence. The bransle sequence was a popular addition to collections of suites by town musicians. They presumably used it to demonstrate that they too could write in what they considered to be the French style, even if their use of the four-movement version was a German phenomenon. Given that individual movements in many printed suite collections by town musicians were usually numbered, it is telling that the bransle sequences in these collections were nearly always combined under a single number.

---

[14] Mersenne, *Harmonie Universelle*, 'Traitez de la Voix, et des Chants', pp. 167–8.

In the following century, it seems that the courante's place in the sequence was supplanted by the menuet. John Essex's *The Dancing Master* (London, 1728), based on Pierre Rameau's *La Maître à danser* (Paris, 1725) has the following:

> But formerly the Courant used to be danced after the Brawls [Bransles]: And Lewis the Fourteenth danced one better than any Person of his Court ... but now the Menuet is danced after the Brawls.[15]

It is possible that the suite entitled 'Bransle à 4. le 20ma. 8bris 1668' in the Kassel manuscript *D-Kl* 2° MS mus. 61b[1a] may be any early indication of this trend. It has the following sequence of movements:

> Le grand Bransle à 4 /Gaÿ /À mener /Gavotte /Premiere courante ensuite / Deuxieme courante /3me courante /Sarabande /Menuet[16]

Likewise, there is a sequence of bransles followed by a courante and Menuet in the last suite of Cousser's 1682 *Composition de musique* (see page 125). But such instances are rare and it is surely significant that bransles with associated courantes were still being circulated in the early eighteenth century. Clearly, the combination of bransle and menuet was not common in the seventeenth century.

If German town and court composers viewed the bransle sequence in essentially the same way, there were fundamental differences in the way in which each approached all other genres of suite writing, and it is to these differences that I shall now turn. The town-music suite existed throughout much of the seventeenth century, only dying out in the 1690s. There were, particularly in the latter half of the century, some regional variations.[17] The style of the town-music suite was established in the early part of the century, especially in works such as Johann Hermann Schein's collection of twenty suites, *Banchetto musicale* (Leipzig, 1617). The preface to Schein's collection states that the suites 'correspond to one

---

[15] Quoted in W. Hilton, *Dance and Music of Court and Theater*, Dance and Music 10 (Stuyvesant, NY, 1997), p. 287.

[16] Nathalie Lecomte has suggested that Dumanior's Bransles and the manuscripts in *D-Kl* 2° MS mus. 61 represent the last stage of the 'Évolution de l'ordre des branles', although she fails to mention the Menuet in 2° MS mus. 61b[1a]. As we shall see in the following chapter, the Kassel manuscripts were largely imported from France and cannot be said to be evolutionary. See R. Harris-Warrick and N. Cecomte, 'Branle' in M. Benoit (ed.), *Dictionnaire de la musique en France aux XVIIe et XVIIIe siècles* (Paris, 1992), pp. 88–89.

[17] These regional variations are discussed in: M. Robertson, 'The consort suite in the German-speaking lands, 1660–1705' (Ph.D. diss., University of Leeds, 2004).

another in tone and invention'.[18] Accordingly, the movements of each suite remain in a single key and the same movement sequence is used throughout:

Padouana/Gagliarda/Courente/Allemande/Tripla.

Only six suites do not contain some form of melodic or harmonic link between one or more of their movements. This linking technique, associated with the so-called 'variation suite', involved the use of the same, or very similar, melodic or harmonic fragments at the start of the linked movements. In Example 3.2, we can see Schein's use of the technique in the 'Padouana' and 'Courente' of the ninth suite of *Banchetto musicale*.

But perhaps the most interesting use of movement linking in the collection is between the concluding allemande of each suite and its 'tripla' variation. In each case, the variation is a triple-time reworking of the associated allemande. This reworking from duple-time into a triple-time was a universally known technique dating from the previous century. In most seventeenth-century examples, it was usual for one bar of the duple-time movement to correspond to two bars of the triple-time movement. Such linking could be fairly strict, or it could be interpreted with a considerable amount of freedom as we see above in the two dances from *Banchetto musicale*. In dance suites, the technique was mostly applied to allemandes and courantes.

Given the interruptions of the Thirty Years War, it is no surprise to find that Schein's influence did not really start to exert itself until more than ten years after his death. But it is surely no coincidence that perhaps the earliest printed edition to demonstrate this influence was again from Leipzig: Rosenmüller's 1645 *Paduanen, Alemanden, Couranten, Balletten, Sarabanden, Mit drey Stimmen Und ihrem Basso pro Organo*. Here, the first twenty movements of this collection are divided into four suites with the same sequence of movements. In addition, all four suites are arranged in ascending order of key, and Rosenmüller makes frequent use of variation techniques. But Rosenmüller seems to be alone at this time in issuing carefully ordered suite collections. Most collections from town musicians in the 1650s are little more than sequences of like dances or pairs of dances. And, as we shall see in Chapter 5, it was two court musicians, Briegel and Löwe von Eisenach, who followed Schein's and Rosenmüller's examples more closely than anyone else in the middle decade of the century.

It is not until the 1663 issue of Horn's *Parergon musicum* that we see the concepts of ordering and careful arrangement that became common in collections of town-music suites issued during the remaining part of the century. Typically, these collections by town musicians were often arranged in ascending order of key and frequently used a common sequence of dances. We can see this in

---

[18] J. H. Schein, *Banchetto musicale Newer anmutiger Padouanen, Gagliarden, Courenten und Allemanden* (Leipzig, 1617; D. Krickeberg (ed.), Newe Ausgabe sämtlicher Werke, vol.9, Kassel, 1967).

Ex. 3.2.   J.H. Schein, *Banchetto musicale* (Leipzig, 1617), Suite IX, 'Padouana' and 'Courente'

Hortus musicus (Hamburg, n.d.), a collection of suites issued in the late 1680s by the Hamburg musician and 'Celebratissimi Directore' of the Cathedral music, Johann Adam Reincken. The six suites that go to make up Reincken's collection are not identified as such, but the contents are made clear. Each suite follows the same order of sonata/allemand/courant/saraband/gique, and five of the six suites are grouped in ascending order of key, starting in A major. Curiously, Reincken preferred not to write the final suite in F major or minor, but chose to return to A major. The collection is full of movement-linking techniques. Example 3.3 gives the openings of 'Sonata 11[ma]', 'Allemand 12[ma]' and 'Courant 13[tia]' from the third suite.

All three openings share the same rising bass line and the three repeated notes in the violin part. The start of the second violin part in 'Allemand 12[ma]' and 'Courant

Ex. 3.3. J.A. Reincken, *Hortus musicus* (Hamburg, n.d.), Suite III, openings of 'Sonata 11ma', 'Allemand 12ma' and 'Courant 13tia'

13^{tia}' is also linked. There are further links between other movements in the suite. It seems that the ability to make effective use of variation techniques was regarded as an important requirement for all German composers wishing to publish suite collections in the town tradition.

Court composers were clearly aware of variation techniques, but rarely seem to have used them in a court environment. There is no easily discernable reason for this; most court musicians were competent enough to use movement linking. Perhaps entertainments were put on with insufficient advance warning for court musicians to do anything other than gather together existing, and not necessarily connected, sequences of dances. There is a further comparison to be made between court and town suites: the importance of printing in the town repertoire. Suite collections by town musicians were usually issued in the form of printed part books. Leaving aside copies from existing printed editions, manuscript collections of dance music by town musicians are seemingly rare; presumably it was relatively easy and cheap for them to get music printed.

If printed suites by town musicians tended to be issued as single-composer collections, music in the court tradition, especially in the middle decades of the century, could be drawn from a wide variety of sources and from the work of a number of different composers. And given the way in which dance music was often transmitted as a single melody line, it is hardly surprising that its composers were not identified as a matter of course. The *Exercitium musicum* compilation of dance music published in Frankfurt am Main in 1660 was perhaps unusual in the way in which it drew on suites from both town and court traditions. But it is entirely typical of the latter in its seeming disinterest in the identity of its composers. Out of the one hundred and thirteen numbered movements that make up the collection, only four have indications of authorship. Perhaps it is significant that the only identified composers were the fashionable musicians at Louis XIV's court in Paris.

We can see evidence of the pastiche suite on the wrapper of a manuscript suite (*D-Kl* 2° MS mus. 61g) that clearly identifies the joint contribution of Jacques de Belleville and David Pohle (see Figure 3.1). There seems little obvious reason why music by these two composers should be combined together: they came from completely different backgrounds. Belleville seems to have worked in Paris during the 1620s and 1630s and Pohle briefly became of a member of the Hessen-Kassel *Hofkapelle* in around 1650. Thus, the combination of the two composers' work seems entirely to have been the personal choice of the copyist. Even the normally unified branle sequence could contain the work of more than one composer: the so-called 'Branles Nouvaux à 4' in *D-Kl* 2° MS mus. 61b[1] use music by both Dumanoir and Lully. We are fortunate that many of *D-Kl* 2° MS mus. 61 manuscripts identify their composers; there are many that do not. Given such evidence, it is unwise to assume that court suites always contain music by the

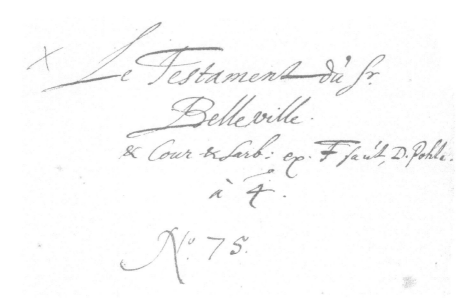

Fig. 3.1.   *D-Kl* 2° MS mus. 61g, outer wrapper

same composer.[19] Similarly, it is equally unwise to assume that 'in recording the dance suites, the scribe indicated the composer only in title of the first dance'.[20] Even in early eighteenth-century England, the copyist Charles Babel, who had spent his early career at the Hanover *Hofkapelle*, was still compiling suites with music taken from the widest variety of sources.[21]

But even in suites where the movements have been drawn from different sources, there is still one overriding consideration: the use of a common key centre. We have already seen Brossard's *Dictionaire* entry linking of the *sonata da camera* and suite; the most important part of his definition lies in what follows. He states that the movements of a suite are 'tout cela composé sur le même Ton ou Mode' (all composed in the same key or mode).[22] Brossard emphasizes 'le même Ton ou Mode' by using the phrase twice in the same definition. And with the exception of Austria, and particularly the imperial court of Vienna, the same is true for nearly every suite written in the German lands.[23] The importance of a

---

[19]   For instance, see: E. Albertyn, 'The Hanover orchestral repertory, 1672–1714: significant source discoveries', *EM*, 33/3 (2005), pp. 449–71.

[20]   J. S. Mráček (ed.), *Seventeenth-Century Instrumental Dance Music in Uppsala University Library, Instr. mus. hs 409*, Musica Svecica Saeculi XVII:5, Monumenta Musicae Svecicae, vol. 8 (Stockholm, 1976), preface, p. *11.

[21]   See Chapter 7.

[22]   Brossard, *Dictionaire*, entry for 'Suonata', pp. 118–19.

[23]   This aspect of the Viennese suite is discussed in Chapter 9.

common key centre is shown in a humorous way in 'Les Savants pretendus' (those who pretend knowledge), a movement in an anonymous manuscript suite in *S-Uu* IMhs 064:014. In this movement, ignorance is illustrated by an uncertain tonal centre: the music alternates between G minor and D minor. Tellingly, the rest of the suite is all in G major; the link between unity of key and ordered composition is clearly shown.

Grouping by key assumes paramount importance when we come to consider sequences of movements extracted from dramatic stage works. The last two decades of the seventeenth century saw the rapid expansion of this particular genre with excerpts from Lully's stage works starting to appear in print in the early 1680s. There was also a wide manuscript circulation of excerpts. But the idea of extracting music from dramatic stage works was not new. As early as the 1650s excerpts from Rossi's *L'Orfeo* appear to have been widely known, and we have seen earlier in the chapter that Adam Drese's *Erster Theil Etlicher Allemanden, Couranten, Sarabanden, Balletten, Intraden und andern Arien* (Jena, 1672) included various suites with the names 'Policriten', 'Climenen', 'Judithen' and 'Crœsus'. These titles make it reasonable to suppose that the suites are dramatic excerpts, and this supposition is largely confirmed by Drese's post as 'director of operatic and other theatre music' that he held in Jena from 1663.[24] However, most excerpts from stage works in the mid-seventeenth century appear to have been little more than one or two movements mixed together with music from other sources. As a result of the great popularity of Lully's music, this changed in the 1680s. Extended sequences of movements were now extracted from single works, presumably for audiences to get a faithful idea of Lully's original. Typically, the movements involved could be taken from widely separated points in the original opera or ballet, and the resulting sequences often employed a variety of keys. Table 3.1 details a sequence of movements by Lully in manuscript *SV-X* Mus. MS 6 taken from *Thésée* (LWV 51) and *Atys* (LWV 53). (The movement numbering is that of the manuscript.)

Table 3.1:   Selected movements by Lully from manuscript *SV-X* Mus. MS 6

Movement number	Title	Key	Source
46	prælude	A minor	*Thésée* (LWV 51)
47	La Sacrifice	A minor	*Thésée* (LWV 51)
48	Noll (*sic*)	A minor	*Thésée* (LWV 51)
49	Gique	A minor	*Thésée* (LWV 51)

---

[24]   G. Kraft and P. Downey, 'Drese, Adam' in *New Grove* 2, vol. 7, p 585.

60   *The Courtly Consort Suite in German-Speaking Europe, 1650–1706*

Movement number	Title	Key	Source
50	La de sinte de Mare	C major	*Thésée* (LWV 51)
51	Les Conbantons	C major	*Thésée* (LWV 51)
52	Noll (*sic*)	C major	*Thésée* (LWV 51)
53	Rondeau	C major	*Thésée* (LWV 51)
54	Les Songe Funeste	B flat major	*Atys* (LWV 53)
55	2me air de Songe	B flat major	*Atys* (LWV 53)
56	Allarm	B flat major	?

The first change of key is a simple one from C major to A minor; the second one is an awkward change from A minor to B flat major. While it would be possible to play these thirty-five movements as a single sequence, there is no real sense of Brossard's 'le même Ton ou Mode'. The same problems are not confined to music extracted from Lully's stage works. Keiser's opera *Hercules und Hebe* has not survived in complete form but the heading, 'Parties de Opera Hercules u. Hebe. Ao. 1699', leaves us in no doubt about the origins of this particular set of excerpts, also in *SV-X* Mus. MS 6. There are ten movements starting with a chaconne and these are listed, along with their keys, in Table 3.2.

Table 3.2:   Excerpts from R. Keiser, *Hercules und Hebe* in *S-VX* Mus. MS 6

Movement number	Movement title	Key
92	Chaconne	D minor
93	Menuet	F major
94	Saraband	B flat major
95	Menuet	D minor
96	Saraband	C major
97	Entreè	A minor
98	Trio	C major
99	Gig	C major

Movement number	Movement title	Key
100	Entreè	C major
101	Menuet	C major

The title 'Parties' is ambiguous, but, if these movements were played consecutively, a wide range of keys would be traversed, again with some awkward changes. To give a further example, 'Les Aires avec les flauts douces pour son Altesse Serenism Monseigneur le Prince Ludwig Rudolf, Duc de Bruns. e Luneburg fait par Nic. Ada. Strungk, Maistre de la Chapelle a Dresda' (manuscript *D-W* Cod. Guelf. 270 Mus. Hdschr.) is almost certainly a set of movements extracted from one of Strungk's dramatic stage works. There are ten movements with a range of keys similar to that of Keiser's music in Mus. MS 6: the last three are in G minor, B flat major and C minor.

Perhaps such shifts of key were acceptable if pieces were being played as background music. But there is some evidence to suggest that publishers and copyists were aware of this problem and took steps to alleviate it. Table 3.3 details the contents of *Tous Les Airs de Violon de l'Opera D'Amadis* (Amsterdam, c.1687).[25]

Table 3.3: Movements, and their keys, in *Tous Les Airs de Violon de l'Opera D'Amadis Composez par Monsieur de Lullÿ, Escuier, Conseiller Secretaire, du Roÿ &. Imprimé a Amsterdam par Antoine Pointel* (Amsterdam, c.1687)

Movement title	LWV number	Key
Ouverture	63/1	G minor
Air	63/4	G minor
Gigue	63/5	G minor
Trio	63/34	G minor
Marche	63/22	C major
Combat	63/23	C major
Rejouissance	63/24	C major

---

[25] The suggested date is taken from: C. Schmidt, 'The Amsterdam editions of Lully's music: a bibliographical scrutiny with commentary', in J. Heyer (ed.), *Lully studies* (Cambridge, 2000), pp. 100–165 at p. 137.

Movement title	LWV number	Key
Prelude	63/42	C major
Prelude	63/41	C major
Prelude	63/60	F major
Choeur	63/26	A minor
Centrez	63/49	A minor
Air	63/50	A minor
Air	63/55	A major
Menuet	63/57	A major
Rondeau	63/11	G major
Menuet	63/12	G major
Air	63/33	G major
Trio	63/35	G major
Menuet	63/36	G minor
Prelude	63/59	D major
Le Grande Chaconne de L'opera des Amadis des Gaules 1684	63/67	C major

Here, movements were selected out of order (see LWV numbers in the table), presumably to extend the key sequences. For example, the third and fourth movements in Pointel's edition are taken from much later in Lully's original, thus giving a longer sequence of movements in G minor. Pointel seems to have largely based his sequence of movements on an earlier Amsterdam edition of extracts from *Amadis* issued by Heus in 1684.[26] But Heus placed Lully's concluding 'Grande Chaconne' in an earlier group of movements in C major, thereby extending the key grouping but sacrificing all sense of an impressive finale. This was clearly not acceptable to Pointel who reinstated the chaconne to its original position at the end. Neither Heus' nor Pointel's ordering of these extracted movements completely solve the problem of awkward key changes. A simple transposition would surely have removed some of these, but Pointel, or his editor, was clearly unwilling to

---

[26] *Ouverture avec tous les airs de Violons de LOPERA (sic) d'AMADIS fait à paris par Mons. BAPTIST de LULLY. Imprimee à Amsterdam par Iean Philip Heus 1684.*

do this. This is not an isolated case: it seems that the option of transposition was rarely considered by either publishers or copyists.

A different approach to the problem, but one that looks back to the type of movement selection practised earlier in the century, is found in manuscript *A-Wn* Suppl. mus. 1813. This manuscript is a little-known source of Lully's music, although there are substantial errors in the transmission and the copyist has wrongly identified the excerpt from *Bellerophon*.[27] It contains seven 'partie', although it seems likely that the last seven movements in the manuscript have little to do with the final 'partie' and may well have been added later. Each 'partie' is clearly made up from the work of several different composers. However, the importance of this manuscript lies in the fact that, apart from the probable later additions, all the movements in each sequence are in a common key, and it is clear that they have been selected with this in mind. For example, the 'Cinquieme Partie' contains an extract from Lully's *Acis et Galathée*, a set of variations on the well-known 'La Folia' and dances by du Buisson and Jaques Gallot. Despite the disparate origins of the 'Cinquieme Partie', all its movements are written in the same key of D minor. This type of movement selection is not confined to manuscripts: there are printed editions where extracts appear to have been selected in the same way. In the two volumes of *Les trio des opera de Monsieur de Lully* published in Amsterdam in 1690 and 1691, both title pages state that the contents are 'Mis en ordre pour les concerts' and the arranger's preface to the first volume is equally clear: 'que j'ay mis dans un ordre tres commode pour les concerts'. It is apparent that, unlike other Amsterdam editions of dramatic excerpts, the contents of *Les trio des opera de Monsieur de Lully* were deliberately selected and grouped together in order to produce uninterrupted sequences of movements in the same key. The type of award transition that we have seen above is avoided. However, this type of care in movement selection is comparatively rare and, in the case of Lully, only possible towards the end of the century when large amounts of his music were readily available. Most dramatic excerpts use a variety of keys and, in the end, this is the fundamental difference them and genuine suites employing a single key centre.

In modern times, the failure to make this distinction between suites and series of dramatic excerpts has sometimes led to strange results. Manuscript *S-Uu* IMhs 064:007 comprises an *ouverture* and twenty-nine following movements organized into groups in the keys of A minor, G major and B flat major. The similarity between the contents of this manuscript and the types of sequence found in Heus' and Pointel's editions of *Tous Les Airs de Violon de l'Opera D'Amadis* is striking. But the RISM A/II database ignores the strong possibility that these are dramatic excerpts; the complete sequence is divided into five suites, each starting with a prelude or *entrée*, even though it is rare for a prelude or *entrée* to denote the start

---

[27] I first drew attention to this hitherto-unknown source in Robertson, 'Consort suite' pp. 137–40.

of a suite in the German-*Lullist* tradition.[28] For reasons that are not explained, the G major group is further split into two. Such arbitrary splitting up of these thirty movements is unconvincing: IMhs 064:007 is surely a set of movements extracted from a now-lost dramatic stage work.

If we now return to the definitions of the suite given at the start of this chapter, we can see how the traditions of suite writing by court composers have often been confused with those of town musicians. Despite definitions such as Brossard's that concentrate on 'le même Ton ou Mode', the importance of a common key centre in suites has often been ignored, just as the fluid, lively and rich tradition of the courtly suite is at odds with the concepts of a 'classical' ordering. Even if the latter was applied to the suites by town musicians, which is arguable, the idea of a well-defined and specific order of movements spread across the repertoire does not apply to suites by court musicians. Any concept of hierarchy imposes boundaries that clearly did not exist at the time. Seventeenth-century court suites were sequences of movements – mostly dances – which were united by a common key centre. With the exception of the bransle suite, the contents of these sequences varied widely and were subject to the whims of copyists or the performing musicians. It is unlikely that either scribes or members of German *Hofkapellen* ever gave a moment's thought to a 'classical' order.

---

[28] RISM A/II (generated online at http://biblioline.nisc.com), record 190.006.402. In addition, the movement numbering given in the manuscript is omitted and the opening of '1.Ouverture' is misquoted. The key of '9.Rondeau' is wrongly given as D major and the description of the instrumentation is incorrect.

Chapter 4
Frantzösische Branles, Courantes, Sarabandes, Ballettas Manuscript Sources of the Courtly Suite before 1682

German courtly dance music between the end of the Thirty Years War and the era of the German *Lullists* can be largely divided into two categories: manuscript sources containing suites or sequences of individual movements, and printed collections of suites, often written in the manner of town musicians. This chapter deals with manuscript sources; Chapter 5 deals with printed editions.

Research into the manuscripts of German courtly suites from this time is often hampered by lack of evidence. For example, the Weimar court music inventories for 1662 list 'Frantzösische Music' that includes a 'Bransle de monsier Constantin'.[1] The same inventory also lists 'Allemanden, Balletten, Cour: Sarab: à 4' by Adam Drese, the court *Kapellmeister* and a collection of 'Frantzösische, Arien, Allemanden, Balletten, Cour: Sarrab:'.[2] All these items are apparently now lost and our knowledge of manuscript suites from the German lands in this period comes mainly from one source: the Kassel manuscripts of dance music. But material does come from outside the German lands. The music and performing traditions at the court in Stockholm are valuable in what they tell us about dance music and its dissemination. And while the manuscripts in the Finspong collection now at Norrköping in Sweden may not be directly connected with any German court musical establishment, they do give us further evidence concerning dance music in Germany during the second half of the seventeenth century. Much of the music from Kassel and Stockholm has become known to modern scholars through modern editions, but the Finspong manuscripts are still little-known. As we shall see, all these sources have material in common: dance music emanating from mid-century Paris. But first, I shall deal with the most important German source of mid-century dance music: the manuscripts that are now preserved in the Landesbibliothek und Murhardsche Bibliothek der Stadt Kassel (hereafter *D-Kl*).

According to Chappuzeau, 'Les Hessiens passent pour les meilleurs Soldats & les plus infatigables d'Allemagne, qui font leur capital de la capital de la guerre,

---

[1] E. Möller, 'Die Weimarer Noteninventare von 1662 und ihre Bedeutung als Schütz-Quellen' in W. Breig (ed.), *Schütz-Jahrbuch 1988* (Kassel, 1988), pp. 62–85 at p. 78.

[2] Ibid., p. 75.

& qui n'ont presque point d'autre mestier' (People from Hesse, who make their capital the capital of the war, make for the best, most determined and single-minded soldiers of Germany)[3]. Perhaps as a result, Kassel was heavily involved in the latter stages of the Thirty Years War. But recovery seems to have started remarkably quickly and the 1650s marked a period of regeneration. Wilhelm VI and Wilhelm VII were the rulers at the court of Hessen-Kassel from 1650 to 1670, though the latter died in infancy and never fully acceded to the throne. Wilhelm VI's visit to Paris in 1647 (see Chapter 1) must surely have made a deep impression on him, and it is hardly surprising that some of the music he heard there found its way to Kassel – it is possible that Wilhelm personally took it back with him on his return to Germany. Wilhelm is sometimes given as the composer of the 'Sarabande de Son Alt[esse] de Hesse',[4] dated 1650 and included in manuscript *D-Kl* 2° MS mus. 61f. But 1650 was the year of his accession, and this title could equally well be a dedication rather than an indication of authorship.

Other music was brought back from Paris. Gerhard Diesener, the son of Christoph Diesener, one of the *Hofkapelle* violinists, spent time there, presumably in study, in 1660. He seems to have brought French dance music back with him when he returned to Kassel; the court *Rechnungen aus dem Kammerverlag* (business accounts) record a payment made in December of that year to Diesener for 'verschiedene Frantzösische Branles, courantes, sarabandes, ballettas' (assorted French bransles, courantes, sarabandes and ballets).[5] In addition, the *Rechnungen* record payments made in 1662 in connection with a performance of a ballet by 'G. du M.'. Presumably this was Constantin's successor in Paris, Guillaume du Manoir.[6]

The dance music of the Kassel manuscripts is now in two collections, 2° MS mus. 61 (hereafter Mus. 61) and 4° MS mus. 148 (hereafter Mus. 148). A number of the manuscripts carry initials, perhaps those of the copyist, which appear to be 'C. Th' or 'Ch. Th.'.[7] It is possible that this is Christoph Thomas who was employed in the *Hofkapelle* until at least 1660 and received unspecified payments in the *Rechnungen*. Perhaps these were for copying. However, this must remain highly speculative, especially for the later pieces. The players in the *Hofkapelle* appear to have been mostly German; if a violin band similar to those found at Celle and Schwerin existed at the Hessen-Kassel court, it does not appear to have included any Frenchmen. The only foreign musician appears to be the Italian

[3]   S. Chappuzeau, L'Europe vivante, ou relation nouvelle, historique & politique de tous ses estats (Paris, 1667), p. 352.
[4]   For instance, see: C. Gottwald (ed.) *Die Handschriften der Gesamthochschul-Bibliothek Kassel, Landesbibliothek und Murhardsche Bibliothek der Stadt Kassel* (Vol. 6, Wiesbaden, 1997), p. 188.
[5]   *D-Kl* MS hass. 2° 350, entry for 19 December.
[6]   Ibid., entry for 26 February 1662.
[7]   Israël suggests the latter: C. Israël, *Uebersichtlicher Katalog der Musikalien der Ständischen Landesbibliothek zu Cassel* (Kassel, 1881), p. 64.

Paolo Mazzuchelli who joined the *Hofkapelle* in 1659.[8] A selection of Mus. 61 was edited by Jules Écorcheville and published in 1906 as *Vingt suites d'orchestre du XVIIe siècle français.*[9] It was an impressive achievement for its time and included reproductions of some of the manuscripts along with an extended critical commentary. Perhaps for this reason, scholars have tended to accept this edition at face value, but as we shall see, Écorcheville's work should not be accepted uncritically, and this makes further examination of the original sources all the more important.

The suites in Mus. 61 and Mus. 148 are preserved as sets of parts; there are no scores. In Mus. 61, suites were sometimes copied together in pairs, although the wrappers and the layout on the paper make the composition of each pair perfectly clear.[10] Table 4.1 lists select suites from Mus. 61 along with the titles given on the wrappers or at the head of the parts and the numberings in *Vingt suites*.

These wrappers and movement titles are often rather vague when it comes to details of authorship, but it is clear that Mus. 61 contains dances drawn from a variety of sources, especially French. Indeed, some of this collection may well include the music that Diesener brought back with him from Paris in 1660. Of the composers listed in the table, Dumanoir, Bruslard, Mazuel and de la Croix were all 'Violons de la Chambre' in Paris,[11] Lazarin was an 'Ordinaire de la Musique du Cabinet du roi',[12] and Pinel was a 'joueur de luth'.[13] Dumanoir was also a dancing master and succeeded Constantin as 'Joüeur de Violon du Cabinet de Sa Majesté, l'un des Vingt-cinq de sa grand'Bande, et pourveu aussi de l'Office de Roy des Joüers d'instruments et des Maîtres à Dancer de France'.[14] Belleville was also a dancer and violinist and 'conducteur des ballets du roi' in the time of Louis XIII'.[15] The 'Sarabande Italienne' in Mus. 61e and the 'Fantasie Les pleurs d'Orpheé,

---

[8] C. Engelbrecht, *Die Kasseler Hofkapelle im 17. Jahrhundert* (Kassel, 1958), p. 42.

[9] J. Écorcheville, *Vingt suites d'orchestre du XVIIe siècle français, publiées d'après un manuscrit de la Bibliothèque de Cassel* (2 vols, Paris, 1906; repr., New York, 1970).

[10] Until quite recently, there was confusion over some of the individual shelf marks in Mus. 61, but this has been resolved in Gottwald, *Die Handschriften*.

[11] There were two Brullards listed as 'Violons de la Chambre': Louis Brullard and Jacques Brullard. It is not clear which of the two was responsible for the music in Mus. 61. See: M. Benoit (ed.), *Musiques de cour; chapelle, chambre, écurie, 1661–1733* (Paris, 1971), pp. 11 and 13.

[12] Gottwald incorrectly identifies Lazarin as the Italian-born Scipio Lazarini, an Augustine monk who never left Italy. See: Gottwald, *Die Handschriften*, p. 184.

[13] Benoit, *Musiques de cour*, p. 13.

[14] G. Dumanoir, *Le mariage de la musique avec la dance; contenant la reponce au livre des treize pretendus Academistes, touchant ces deux arts* (Paris, 1664; repr. Paris, 1870). Dumanoir's apparently self-styled title is given at the start of the final section, entitled 'Factum'.

[15] C. Massip, *La vie des musiciens de Paris au temps de Mazarin* (Paris, 1976), p. 110.

Table 4.1: Selected contents of manuscripts in *D-Kl* 2° MS mus. 61

Shelf-mark suffix	Composers (as identified in the MSS)	Movement titles	Wrapper titles	*Vingt suites*
61a[I]	Bruslard	[Bransle] /Gaÿ /àmener /double /Montirande /Gavotte /1.Courante en Suitte /2.Courante /3.Courante /Sarabande /Bourreè	Bransles de Mr. Brûlar à 4. 1664.	VI
61a[II]		[Branle] /Gaÿ /àmener /Gavotte /premiere Courante ensuitte /deuxieme Courante /3me Courante /Sarabande /Menuet	Bransle à 4. le 20ma. 8bris 1668.	VIII
61b[1]	Dumanoir	[Branle] [LWV 31/1] /Gaÿ [LWV 31/2] /àmener [LWV 31/3] Gavotte [LWV 31/4] /1.Courante ensuitte [LWV 31/8] /2. Courante [LWV 31/10] /Sarabande /Courante duManoir / Allemande/ Sarabande	Branles Nouvaux à 4.	X
61b[2]	Dumanoir	[Branle] /Gaÿ /àmener /Gavotte /1.Courante ensuitte /2.Courante /3.Courante /La Sarabande /Courante Madamoisella / Courante La Dauphine /Courante. La Preticuse /Sarabande	Bransles à 4. de Mr. du Manoir	IX
61c	D[iesineer]	Branle Nouvau de G.D. /Gaÿ /Amener/ Gavotte /1.Courante /2ma Courante/ La Sarabande	Branle Nouvau 1661	XI

Shelf-mark suffix	Composers (as identified in the MSS)	Movement titles	Wrapper titles	*Vingt suites*
61d¹	Lazarini, Mazüel	1.Allemand La Zarin /2.Allemand /Courants nouvelles de Mr. Mazüel 1 /[Courants] 2 /Gigue /Sarabande	Allemande Lazarini | à 4 …	XII
61d²[I]	Werdier	Alemande à 4 /1.Courante /2.Courante / 3.Courant Mon. Werdier /4.Sarabande	1.Allem. Cour: Sarb: à 4 …	XIII [ii]
61d² [II]		Alemande à 4 /1.Courante / 2.[Courante] / Sarabande	…2.Allem. Cour: Sarb. à 4	XIII [i]
61d³[I]	Mazüel	Alemande à 5 Mons Mazuel /1.Courante /2.Cour / 3.Cour/Sarab: /Boureé / Bourée [II]	1.Allemande. Mazuel. à 5 …	I
61d³ [II]	La Voÿs, La Haÿe.	Allemande. dela Voÿs /Gagliarde / Sarabande de La Haÿe	…2.Allem: de la Voÿs à 5	I
61d⁴[I]	La Croix	Allemande. du Sr. de la Croix. à 4 /1.Courante / 2.Courante /Sarabande	1.Allemande à 4. Cour: & Sarab: du Sr. de la Croix …	VII

Shelf-mark suffix	Composers (as identified in the MSS)	Movement titles	Wrapper titles	*Vingt suites*
61d⁴ [II]	Drese	Allemande à 4. Sigr Adam Dresen /1.Courante /La Duchesse, Courante figureè /Boureè	2.Allemande Adam Dresen à 4 & Courante la Duchesse	VII
61d⁵[I]	Nau	1.Ballet à 5. S. Nau /2.[Ballet] /3.[Ballet] / 4.[Ballet] /5.[Ballet] /6.[Ballet]	Ballet du Sr. Nau à 5 …	II
61d⁵ [II]		Alemande à 5 /Courante /[2.Courante] / [3.Courante] /4.[Courante] / Sarabande	… &. Allemande. Cour: & Sarab: à 5	II
61d⁶[I]	Artus, Herwig	1.Allemande /2.Allemande. Christian Herwig / Courante figureè /Gagliarde du Sr. Artus	Trois Allemandes avec Cour: Sarb: à 4	XIV
61d⁶[II]		Allemande /1.Courante /2.Courante /3.Courante /Bouree	Trois Allemandes avec Cour: Sarb: à 4	XIV
61d⁷[I]		1 Allemand /2 Courant /3 Courant /4 Saraband	Allemande Cour: Sarab: à 5 …	V [ii]
61d⁷[II]	Artus	Les passe pieds d'Artus /Sarabande /Boureè Geschwind / Courante /Boureè figureè La Christiana	… & les passe pieds à 4 & La Bouree Christiana	V [i]

Shelf-mark suffix	Composers (as identified in the MSS)	Movement titles	Wrapper titles	*Vingt suites*
61d⁸[I]		Allemande à5 /1 Courante Simple /2.Courante figureè /Sarabande	Allemande à 5. avec Cour, Sarb …	III [ii]
61d⁸ [II]		Bransles à 5 /Gaÿ /àmener /Double /Montirande /Gavotte	… & Bransles	III [i]
61e	Pinel	Libertas /Sarabande Italienne /1.Courante /2.[Courante] /3.Cour. du Sr. Pinelle /Sarabande	Libertas	IV
61f	Landgrave of Hesse	Sarabande de son Alt: de Hesse faitte l'an 1650 /Sarabande du Roy /Sarab /Courante /Sarabande /Sarabande /Frantzösich Liedt, wirdt etwas geschwindt gespielt /Fantasie Les pleurs d'Orpheé, aÿant perdu sa femme /Courante	Sarabande de son Alt: de Hesse faitte l'an 1650	XV
61g	Belleville, Pohle	Le Testament du Sr Belleville à 4 /1.Courante Simple /2.Courante /Sarabande /Sarabande /La Boureè	Le Testament du Sr. Belleville et Courante et Sarabande à 4 … Autore D. Pohle	XVI

Shelf-mark suffix	Composers (as identified in the MSS)	Movement titles	Wrapper titles	*Vingt suites*
61h	D[iesineer]	Ouverture de G.D. /1.Ballet les inconstans / 2 Ballet /3 [Ballet] /Allemande de G.D. / Allemande 2.	Ouvertures *(sic)*, Ballets et Allemandes	XVII
61k¹	Werdier	1.Courante nouvelle de l'annee 1658 /2.[Courante] / 3.[Courante] /Sarabande /2.Allemande verdier / 1.Allemande *(sic)*	Allemande & Courante nouvelle de l'an 1658 à 4	XVIII
61m [I]		Allemande à 4 /Courante 1 /Courante 2 /Sarab: /Gigue	Allemanden a 4	XX
61m [II]		Allemande à 4. /Courante /Sarabande /Bouree	Allemanden a 4	--

Notes:

Works by Lully are identified by their LWV numbers. Archive numberings, copyists' initials and key indications have been omitted from the wrapper details. Manuscript 61m [II] is incomplete, but was not included by Écorchville, even as part of the section entitled 'Suites incomplètes'.

ayant perdu sa femme' in Mus. 61f both come from Act 2 of Rossi's *L'Orfeo*. Although music by Constantin has not survived in the Kassel manuscripts, an allemande by him is mentioned as part of a note added to the title page of Mus. 61k[1]. Lully himself is represented in Mus. 61, but only anonymously. The first six movements of Mus. 61b[1] are only identified as 'Branles Nouvaux à 4', but they do appear in a number of French sources where Lully is given as the author.[16] It may seem strange that his authorship was not recorded in Mus. 61, but the spread of Lullism in Germany was still at least a decade away.[17]

Other names that appear in Mus. 61 are not so easily identifiable. 'Mr Seneca' was added in pencil to the wrapper of Mus. 61b[1a], and probably at a later date. Antoine Bauderon de Sénecé was in the service of Marie Thérèse, the wife of Louis XIV. He was highly critical of Lully, but presumably part of the court musical establishment. Gottwald gives Sénecé without question as the composer of all the movements in Mus. 61b[1a], and there is no reason why his music should not have come to Kassel.[18] But to do this on the basis of a subsequently added note is perhaps unwise, as it is to assume that one composer is responsible for all the movements in this suite. The identity of 'la Voÿs' (the allemande in the second suite of Mus. 61d[3]) is also problematical. Gottwald, presumably following Écorcheville, assumes that this is de la Voye-Mignot, the author of the theoretical treatise *Traité de musique* (Paris, 1656).[19] This may be correct, but there is no evidence that de la Voye-Mignot ever had direct links with the court musical circle in Paris, so we should be wary of this attribution. In fact, 'la Voÿs' could equally well be Nicolas Lavoizière, a dancing master in Paris during the 1660s.

Two further names have hitherto been problematic for modern scholars: 'la Haÿe' and 'Artus'. A 'Sarabande de la Haÿe' appears in the second suite of Mus. 61d[3], and other music was circulated in Germany under the same or a similar name. Mráček, with some reservations, suggests that 'Lahaeÿ', as he is called in *S-Uu* IMhs 409, is the French mathematician, Philippe de la Hire.[20] This is most unlikely. But while there does not seem to be any French or German composer of the period specifically called 'La Haye', Parisian court records clearly associate the name with musicians from the Crestot family working in Paris in the early- and middle-seventeenth century. For example, in a marriage contract of 1630, Jean Crestot is described as 'Jean Crestot, dit La Haye, maître joueur d'instruments, et violon ordinaire de la chambre du roi, demeurant rue de la Pelleterie, fils de défunt Claude Crestot, maître joueur d'instruments et violon de la chambre du

---

[16] See: LWV, pp. 123–7.

[17] Lully's authorship is also not given in Gottwald, *Die Handschriften*, p. 182.

[18] Gottwald, *Die Handschriften*, p. 183.

[19] Gottwald, *Die Handschriften*, p. 185; Écorcheville, *Vingt suites*, vol. 1, pp. 9–10.

[20] J. Mráček (ed.), *Seventeenth-Century Instrumental Dance Music in Uppsala University Library, Instr. mus. hs 409* (Musica Svecica Saeculi XVII: 5, Monumenta Musicae Svecicae, vol. 8 (Stockholm, 1976), pp. 14*–15*.

roi.'[21] Claude Crestot was working in Paris at the start of the seventeenth century, and it would unlikely for music from this time to be included in Mus. 61. But Jean Crestot was certainly active in Paris as a court violinist and dancing master during the 1640s, if not later. Given that much of the French music in Mus. 61 seems to come from around this time, it is reasonable to assume that 'La Haye' is Jean Crestot.

Dances by 'Artus' seem to have enjoyed wide circulation in the German lands. A number of his pieces also found their way to Sweden, and it is possible that pieces in IMhs 409 simply ascribed to 'A' are also by Artus.[22] A movement entitled 'La bouree dartus' appears in the *Exercitium musicum* collection of 1660. The name appears twice in the Kassel manuscripts: the first suite of Mus. 61d^6 has a 'Gagliarde. du Sr. Artus', and the second suite of Mus. 61d^7 contains 'Les passe pieds. d'Artus'. Écorcheville suggested three possible candidates for the name: Artus Leborgne, Louis d'Arthus and Artus Auxcousteaux (*sic*).[23] There is no dance music in any of the surviving printed editions containing music by Aux-Cousteaux; he was a church musician and there is no evidence that he ever had any association with the Parisian court. We may therefore delete his name from the list of candidates with some confidence. However, Artus Leborgne and Louis d'Arthus do require some further investigation.

Both were Parisian court violinists. D'Arthus is referred to as 'Louis Darthus dit Grandmaison, l'un des vingt-quatre violons ordinaires de la chambre du roi' in 1644,[24] and Artus Leborgne appears in the lists of 'Viollons de la Chambre' for 1664.[25] If Louis d'Arthus was known as 'Grandmaison' in court records, it seems reasonable to suppose that any music by him would have been identified with the latter pseudonym and not simply as 'Artus'. On the other hand, Artus Leborgne was not only a violinist; the *Papiers du Grand-Ecuyer* for 1661 list a payment to 'Jean Leborgne … maître baladin' (court dancing master), and it seems that he served in this post throughout the 1660s and 1670s.[26] In addition, Leborgne also held a more specific post. Court documents list the dancing master to the pages of 'la petite Escurie' simply as 'Artus'; but following his resignation from the post in 1684, the *Actes royaux* give the full name, 'Jean Artus le Borgne'.[27] Thus, it appears that Leborgne was known for much of his career simply as 'Artus' and, as a dancing master for 'la petite Escurie', he succeeded Dumanoir who had held the

---

[21] M. Jurgens (ed.), *Documents du Minutier central concernant l'histoire de la musique (1600–1650)* (Paris, 1974), p. 195.

[22] See Mráček, *Seventeenth-Century Instrumental Dance Music*, p. 11*

[23] Écorcheville, *vingt suites* vol. 1, p. 18.

[24] Jurgens, *Documents du Minutier central*, p. 196.

[25] Benoit, *Musiques de cour*, p. 11.

[26] Ibid., pp. 17, 21, 55.

[27] 'Retenue de maître a danser des pages de la petite Escurie, en faveur de François Ballon, sur la demission de Jean Artus le Borgne'. Ibid., p. 92. It seems that Le Borgne may have left this post four years earlier, perhaps informally. Ibid., p. 73.

same post between 1645 and 1656.[28] It is now with some degree of certainty that we can identify Leborgne as the 'Artus' of Kassel and elsewhere.

Despite the number of French composers represented in Mus. 61, comparatively little of the music in Mus. 61 has survived in French sources; Écorcheville recognized the existence of 'Libertas' and 'Sarabande Italienne' (Mus. 61e) in the 'Concert donné à Louis 13. par les 24 Viollons ... 1627' (*F-Pn* Rés. F. 494). To this, I have only been able to add the 'Sarabande' from the 'Recueil de Plusieurs belles pieces de Simphonie' (*F-Pn* Rés. F. 533, p. 216) that appears as both 'La Sarabande' in Mus. 61b[2] and '4. Saraband' in the first suite of Mus. 61d[7].

Little of music the in the Kassel manuscripts appears to originate from the musicians of the Kassel *Hofkapelle* itself. A number of manuscripts exist in *D-Kl*, and not just in Mus. 61, carrying the initials 'G.D'. The use of initials may be significant: with this single exception, where composers are identified, it is always by name. If we are looking for a person in the *Hofkapelle* who was too well known to require further identification, it is reasonable to assume that this is the court musician Gerhard Diesener whose role in the procurement of manuscripts was discussed earlier. Also represented in Mus. 61 are David Pohle who briefly joined the *Hofkapelle* in around 1650, and the lutenist Christian Herwig. The 'Allemande à 4. Sigr Adam Dresen' (Mus. 61d[4], second suite) also appears to have a connection with membership of the Kassel *Hofkapelle*. Following the disbanding of the Weimar *Hofkapelle* in 1662, Drese applied for a post at Kassel; he was unsuccessful, but it is not unreasonable to suppose that this allemande was part of his job application.

Perhaps the most curious manuscript in Mus. 61 is not included by Écorcheville in *Vingt suites*. It is the 'Balletti di Cavallo Composista di Georgio Christophoro Strattner' (Mus. 61i). Strattner was *Kapellmeister* at the court of Baden-Durlach from 1666 until 1682 when he moved to Frankfurt to take charge of the music at the *Barfüsserkirche*. From there, he moved to Weimar where he eventually became *Vice-Kapellmeister*. He died in 1704 or 1705.[29] The 'Balletti di Cavallo' is clearly modelled on Johann Heinrich Schmelzer's equestrian ballet of 1667; the latter being widely circulated throughout Europe and twice appearing in print. A partially complete set of manuscript parts of Schmelzer's ballet is mixed in with Strattner's music in Mus. 61i; clearly, Strattner had Schmelzer's music in front of him when he composed his own equestrian ballet.[30] How it all came to be part of Mus. 61 is unknown.

---

[28] Ibid., p. 3.

[29] R. Eitner, *Biographisch-Bibliographisches Quellen-Lexikon der Muskier und Musikgelehrten der Christlichen Zeitrechnung bis zur Mitte des neunzehnten Jahrhunderts* (11 vols, Leipzig, 1900–1904; repr. Graz, 1959), vol. 9, p. 308.

[30] Schmelzer's music in Mus. 61i has only been recently recognised. See M. Robertson, 'The Consort Suite in the German-speaking lands (1660–1705)' PhD diss. (University of Leeds, 2004), p. 200.

Turning now to the manuscripts themselves, the dating of some of the wrappers and water mark evidence suggest that most of their contents under discussion in this chapter were acquired and copied during a twenty year period from 1650 to 1670.[31] Perhaps their most important feature is the way in which suites are clearly defined. In many single-volume collections from the seventeenth century, it is sometimes difficult to distinguish between movements that were intended to be grouped together into suites, and movements that are lacking any apparent association. But Mus. 61 comprises physically separate sets of instrumental parts for each suite or pair of suites, and it is this that gives us the insight into the way that they were put together by the Kassel copyists. Unfortunately, and for reasons that are hard to understand, Écorcheville gives the impression that Mus. 61 is a single manuscript as he consistently uses the singular noun 'manuscrit' and, at one point, talks of 'cette volumineuse copie'.[32] Subsequent scholars have compounded the error by taking Écorcheville at face value and perpetuating the myth of a single manuscript.[33] It is worth emphasising that the manuscripts of Mus. 61 contain no evidence whatsoever to indicate that they were originally part of a single entity or ever bound together.

Even where suites have been copied in pairs, the wrappers make the division between each one completely clear. We can see this in Figure 4.1 that shows the wrapper of the two suites that make up Mus. 61d². And even where wrappers are missing, the layout of the music on opposite sides of each sheet of paper makes it clear where the first suite of the pair finishes and the second one starts. Écorcheville sometimes reverses the order of these pairings, and some suites are merged into a single entity that is at odds with the sources. This is particularly harmful in the case of his 'suite II' where he combines the two quite separate suites of Mus. 61d⁵ to produce a sequence starting in F major and finishing in G minor. As we have seen, key changes such as this during the course of a suite were exceedingly rare in seventeenth-century Germany and, in any case, both wrapper and parts make it quite clear that Mus. 61d⁵ comprises two suites. Likewise, Écorcheville's 'suite XX' is an unfortunate combination of a single movement from each of the two suites in Mus. 61m. Admittedly, the manuscript parts here have been damaged, but it is perverse of Écorcheville to include this truncated suite in the main section when he has an appendix dealing with incomplete material. To make matters worse, the allemande that Écorcheville includes in 'suite XX' was crossed out by the original copyist, and presumably not meant for inclusion.

With one exception, pairs of suites have the same instrumentation but, as I have pointed out in Chapter 1, Mus. 61d⁷ contains a pair of suites, the first à 5,

---

[31] For details of the watermarks, see Gottwald, *Die Handschriften*.

[32] Écorcheville, *Vingt suites*, vol. 1, p. 2.

[33] For example, J.R. Anthony: 'the so-called Manuscript of Kassel, ... [which] contains 200 pieces that are grouped into twenty "suites"'. See: J.R. Anthony, *French baroque music from Beaujoyeulx to Rameau* (3rd edn., Portland, Oregon), p. 355.

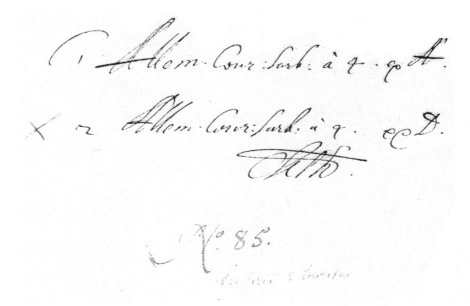

Fig. 4.1.   *D-Kl* 2° MS mus. 61d², outer wrapper

and the second *à 4*. The layout of parts seems to suggest that the two suites were performed together with the two viola players required for the *à 5* suite playing the same part in the *à 4* suite. This would not be the only instance of part doubling: throughout Mus. 61, the treble and bass parts are frequently duplicated in the manner discussed in Chapter 2. Écorcheville does not mention these duplicate parts, and they are not included in the so-called facsimiles.

Écorcheville also fails to take into account the various additions and changes that were made to some of the suites. Indeed, it is clear changes appear to have been made to some of the manuscripts even while copying was still in progress. Figure 4.2 reproduces a page from one of two duplicate violin parts in Mus. 61b[1].

Here, the sarabande that originally followed a pair of courantes was crossed out and a new sarabande, courante and allemande inserted in its place. The original sarabande was then recopied at the end. The duplicate part has been changed in exactly the same way. The remaining viola and bass parts were copied after this as they only have the revised sequence albeit with one further change: the new allemande was moved to the end. Of course, we cannot dismiss the possibility that these changes are a result of repeated error. But the changes seem to be more than that: they suggest that the copyist was making alterations as he worked. Mus. 61b[1] is not an isolated case: Mus. 61f, Mus. 61k[1], the second suite of Mus. 61d², the first suite of Mus. 61d³ and the first suite of Mus. 61m have all undergone changes in movement content or order.

Fig. 4.2.   *D-Kl* 2° MS mus. 61b[1], violin part

Given this variety of sources, it is hardly surprising many of the suites in Mus. 61 are pastiches and, as I have pointed out in the previous chapter, it seems that composers' names are often meant to refer to single movements rather than an entire sequence. For example, the second suite of Mus. 61d[4] starts with an 'Allemande. à 4. Sigr Adam Dresen'. But the third movement in this suite is the widely-circulated 'La Duchesse Courante figureè' and, almost certainly, the origins of this dance are French. It is therefore most unlikely that Drese's authorship extends to the entire suite.[34]

Some movements also have dramatic origins. The six-movement 'Ouverture de G. D.' in Mus. 61h may be extracted from a stage work, now lost. The *ouverture* itself closely resembles the pre-Lullian type found in *F-Pn* Rés. F. 498 and 499 of the 'Philidor MSS'; it is likely that the probable author, the Kassel musician Gerhard Diesener, wrote this and the three following 'ballet' movements in imitation of the stage works that he must have come across during his time in Paris. A pair of allemandes ends the suite; given that allemandes do not seem to have been danced in France at this time, they may have come from a quite different source of Diesener's music, if they are by him at all. It may be significant that the three ballet movements are numbered as a sequence, the allemandes are not.

The 'Sarabande Italienne' in Mus. 61e also has dramatic origins – along with the 'Fantasie Les pleurs d'Orpheé, aÿant perdu sa femme' (Mus. 61f), it comes from Rossi's *L'Orfeo* that Wilhelm VI heard in Paris in 1647. A source of Rossi's Sarabande, 'A l'imperio d'Amore' in Act 2 of the opera, also exists in the Philidor MSS (*F-Pn* Rés. F. 494, 'Recüeil de Plusieurs vieux Airs') and provides further insight into the transmission of dance music.[35] The harmonization is the same in both sources, except that there is no third viola part in the Philidor version. Did Philidor reduce the instrumentation and remove a viola part? The latter seems unlikely; while much of the music in the Philidor MSS is in treble and bass stave reductions, *à 5* movements do exist. So we must assume that either the Kassel copyist had access to an *à 5* source unknown to Philidor, or that he needed to add a third viola part for a specific performance.

There is one further, and more important, difference: in the Philidor source and in Rossi's original, the piece starts on the second beat of a triple-time bar.[36] But the Kassel copyist seems either to have misunderstood the rhythmic layout of his source, or chose to change it. In his version, which is clearly and unequivocally

---

[34] Both Gottwald and Meyer attribute the entire suite to Drese. See: E.H. Meyer, *Die mehrstimmige Spielmusik des 17. Jahrhunderts in Nord- und Mitteleuropa*, Heidelberger Studien zur Musikwissenschaft, vol. 2 (Kassel, 1934), p. 196; Gottwald, *Die Handschriften*, p. 185.

[35] A facsimile of *F-PN* Rés. F. 494 is available online at: http://gallica.bnf.fr

[36] See L. Rossi, *L'Orfeo*, C. Bartlett (ed.) (Huntingdon, c.1997), pp. 118–19.

marked, the piece starts on the first beat of the bar.[37] (The openings of both versions are given in Example 4.1.)

Ex. 4.1. *D-Kl* 2° MS mus. 61e, 'Sarabande Italienne'; 'Recüeil de Plusieurs vieux Airs' (*F-Pn* Rés. F. 494), 'A l'imperio d'Amore'

Despite this drastic change, the 'Sarabande Italienne' in its first-beat guise turns out to be an attractive dance with characterful shifts of rhythmic emphasis. The dissonance at the start of the second bar of the Kassel version goes for nothing in the Philidor version, while the two sets of near-repeated F major chords (marked

---

[37] Écorcheville confused the two sources: without comment, he used the five-part instrumentation of the Kassel version along with the rhythmic layout of the Philidor version. See: Écorcheville, *Vingt suites*, vol. 2, p. 54.

'x' in Example 4.1) make perfect sense when they are on the second and third beats of the bar. In the Philidor version, where they straddle the bar line, they are much weaker. There are similar instances in the second strain. All this may well be the fortuitous result of a copying error, but did the Kassel copyist see the inherent possibilities of the piece when it was made to start on the first beat? The answer is probably the former, but it is unlikely that we shall ever know for certain.

Music with dramatic origins also came from Sweden. The two duplicate bass parts of Mus. 61k^4 both carry the heading 'Ballet à 4. Zu Stockholm getantzt'. If this title is correct, and the ballet was danced in Stockholm, it is likely to be music for one of those put on at Queen Christina's court during the late 1640s and early 1650s. These Swedish ballets clearly followed the French model; *La Naissance de la paix*, put on in 1650, had a libretto by no lesser person than the French philosopher René Descartes who had arrived in Stockholm in 1649. Unfortunately, Mus. 61k^4 contains nothing more to aid identification of the work's origins. Peter Holman has suggested that the 'Ballet à 5. S. Nau' that forms the first part of Mus. 61d^5 possibly 'came from England via Sweden, and is the work of Stephen Nau'.[38] Like Mus. 61k^4, the music appears to be extracted from a stage work, and Holman has suggested that 'it was perhaps written for some English court masque or play of the 1630s'.[39]

The dramatic origins of Mus. 61d^5 and 61k^4 are further indicated by the use of more than one key centre in both sequences of movement. Elsewhere, it is clear that the movements of each suite were deliberately chosen to produce sequences of dances with the same key centre.[40] And even the seeming exceptions to this in Mus. 61f and g may not be what they seem. In Mus. 61f, the movements and keys are as follows:

> Sarabande de Son Alt. de Hesse: faite l'an 1650 [D major]/Sarabande du Roy [G major]/Sarab. [G major]/Courante [G minor]/Sarabande [G minor]/Sarabande [F major]/Frantzösisch Liedt [D minor]/Fantasie Les pleurs d'Orpheé [D minor]/ Courante [G minor]

But the last four movements have been added by another hand. Likewise, we cannot be certain that the 'Sarabande de Son Alt. de Hesse' was part of the original scheme. Given the strong unity of key elsewhere in Mus. 61, it is likely that this suite originally comprised a central courante flanked by sarabandes, all with a key centre of G. In Mus. 61g, there seems to be a combination of two sets of

---

[38] P. Holman, *Four and Twenty Fiddlers: the Violin at the English Court* (Oxford, 1993, repr. 1995), p. 249.

[39] Ibid.

[40] Écorcheville is particularly misleading in matters of key: his grouping together of originally separate suites produces key changes that were certainly not intended. Écorcheville, *Vingt suites*, vol. 2.

movements, one in F major and one in D minor: perhaps a similar process may have taken place.

Ex. 4.2.   *D-Kl* 4° MS Mus. 148a, 'Ouverture du Ballets'

The second collection of dance music at Kassel (Mus. 148) is on a much smaller scale than Mus. 61. In addition to a sonata by J. H. Schmelzer and a 'Pavan à 5' by Christian Herwig, there are five manuscripts of dance music. The largest of these, Mus. 148c[3], has over seventy movements, but only exists as a single, incomplete bass part. Écorcheville either ignored them or was unaware of their contents. Mus. 148a is clearly a set of movements extracted from a dramatic stage work. It has an 'Ouverture du Ballets' followed by a succession of *entrées*. Like Diesener's ballet music in Mus. 61h, the music appears to come from the 1650s or early 1660s. There are three instrumental parts but, as Example 4.2 shows, the frequently large gap between the top and middle parts suggests that at least one further viola part is missing.

If the contents of Mus. 148 c[1], c[2] and c[3] suggest little more than functional dance music, high quality work is to be found in the three extended bransle sequences (Mus. 148e) by David Pohle, a member of the Kassel *Hofkapelle* for a short time around 1650.[41] Unfortunately, two of the three sequences only exist as treble parts, but the complete suite is particularly fine. The start of the *bransle simple* is given in Example 4.3, and we can see how Pohle is prepared to use modulation and, especially in the bass line, a rhythmic subtlety that provides a vitality often missing from other examples of this dance type.

---

[41]   Engelbrecht, *Die Kasseler Hofkapelle*, pp. 36–7.

Frantzösische Branles, Courantes, Sarabandes, Ballettas 83

Ex. 4.3.   D. Pohle, 'Bransles à 4' (*D-Kl* 4° MS mus. 148e), 'Simple'

Had it been included in *Vingt suites*, this work would surely be better known.

Unlike the collection of separate manuscripts than make up Mus. 61, *S-Uu* IMhs 409 is a single manuscript containing over two hundred movements comprising complete suites, pairs of dances and sequences of seemingly unconnected dances.[42] Three dates in the manuscript indicate that the manuscript was probably put

---

[42] For a modern edition of the contents of this manuscript, see Mráček, *Seventeenth-Century Instrumental Dance Music*, See also: E. Kjellberg and K. Snyder (eds.) *The Düben collection database catalogue* (online, www.musik.uu.se/duben/Duben.php).

together over at least an eleven year period from 1651 until 1662.[43] It is part of the so-called 'Düben collection', apparently written 'for the most part in the hand of Gustav Düben', the court musician who succeeded his father Andreas in the post of *Kapellmeister* at Stockholm in 1663.[44]

The manuscript's contents are surely a reflection of the repertoire of the court of Queen Christina and her successor to the Swedish throne, Karl X Gustaf, and with a French violin band in residence, it is reasonable to assume that a good deal of the music at the Stockholm court was French.[45] Sir Bulstrode Whitelock's description, given in Chapter 1, of a ball and its music confirms this French influence and IMhs 409 contains many examples of French dance music. And as I have already pointed out, a good deal of this seems to have been transmitted as single-line melodies. The work of the Parisian musicians Belleville, Constantin, Dumanoir, de la Croix, la Haÿe (Crestot), Lazarin, la Voÿs, Mazuel and Verdier are all represented in the manuscript. It is also worth pointing out that de la Croix apparently served in Sweden as well as Paris.[46]

The manuscript also shows that both English and German music was known in Stockholm. The two 'Pavins' near the end of the collection are not by Verdier as Mráček suggests, but by the English composer Benjamin Rogers.[47] There is a further English connection with the music of the French-born Stephen Nau who is specifically identified in seven pieces. Nau was an important figure at the English court of Charles I, and his music may have been taken to Sweden by Nicholas Picart who served at the Stockholm court after a period in England.[48]

Stockholm had strong commercial relations with Lübeck and Gustav Düben 'studied in Germany from no later than 1645 until about 1648'.[49] There is also a link with the court at Kassel. Some of the music in IMhs 409 also appears in the Kassel dance-music manuscripts, Mus. 61, and these concordances are detailed in Table 4.2.

---

[43] Mráček, *Seventeenth-Century Instrumental Dance Music*, p. 22*.
[44] Ibid., p. 9*. See also, K. Snyder, *Dieterich Buxtehude: organist in Lübeck* (New York, 1987; revised edn.; Rochester, 2007), p. 121.
[45] Holman, *Four and Twenty Fiddlers*, p. 236.
[46] Écorcheville, *Vingt suites*, Vol. 1,
[47] See: Holman, *Four and Twenty Fiddlers*, pp. 247–9.
[48] Ibid., pp. 246–9.
[49] Snyder, Dieterich Buxtehude, pp. 120–21.

Table 4.2: Concordances between *S-Uu* Instr. mus. hs 409 and *D-Kl* 2° MS mus. 61

2° MS mus. suffix	Movements in Mus. 61	Movements in IMhs 409	Comments
61d²[II]	Alemande à 4 1.Courante 2.[Courante] Sarabande	Allamanda A: D: Cap[ellmeister]: 1.Courant A:D: Capp: 2.Courant A:D: Capp: Sarabande	Nos. 7-10 in Mráček, *Seventeenth-Century Instrumental Dance Music* (hereafter Mráček)
61d⁵[II]	Alemande à 5 Courante [2.Courante] [3.Courante] 4.[Courante] Sarabande	Allamanda G.D. 1.Courante G.D. 2.Courante Mons: A:D. 3.Courante Mons: A.D. 4.Courante Mons: A.D. Saraband G.D.	Nos. 150-155 in Mráček.
61d⁶[II]	Allemande	Allamand/La Croix	Mráček, p. 275. Incomplete in IMhs 409.
61d⁸[I]	1.Courante Simple 2.Courante figurée	Courante Mons: A.D. 2.Courante	Nos. 178-179 in Mráček.
61e	Libertas	Libertas a 4	Different inner and bass parts. No. 70 in Mráček.
61g	Le Testament du Sr Belleville à 4.	Serenade, Mons: de Belleville:	Different inner and bass parts; à 5 version in *S-Uu* IMhs 134:22 marked 'La Hays'. No. 139 in Mráček.

As we have seen, the music in Mus. 61k[4] was 'danced at Stockholm', and the 'Boureè figureè La Christiana' in second suite of Mus. 61d[7] may be a reference to the queen herself. The 'Courant du Landgraff de Hesse' in IMhs 409 may be the work of Wilhelm VI of Hessen-Kassel, or it may have just been written in his honour, just as '3. Courante La Reÿne de Suede' in the same manuscript was written by 'Mons: Lahaeÿ' (Jean Crestot). It seems that the Kassel court musician, David Pohle, visited Stockholm on a number of occasions between 1648 and 1660, just at the time that Düben was probably working on IMhs 409. Pohle may also have visited Weimar, and Peter Wollny has suggested that music originally from

Weimar may have made its way to Stockholm via Kassel.[50] This would include a number of anonymous dance movements in Mus. 61 that also appear in IMhs 409 where they are attributed to 'A: D: Cap:[ellmeister]' or simply 'A. D.'. (See Table 4.2 above.) Wollny has pointed to the fact that, in the inventory of the music of the Weimar *Hofkapelle*, 'A. D.' is the court *Kapellmeister* Adam Drese whose music was certainly known in Kassel. The widely held assumption that 'A. D.' is Andreas Düben, the father of IMhs 409's main copyist, has accordingly been challenged by Wollny who suggests that the initials are in fact those of Drese. He also suggests that 'G. D.' in IMhs 409 is not Gustav Düben, but the Kassel court musician, Gerhard Diesener.[51]

It is unfortunate for us that both Drese and Düben have the same initials and that both held the post of *Kapellmeister* at their respective courts; most of Drese's dance music is now lost, but it seems to have been widely known and circulated. Wollny's argument is persuasive, and he may well be correct. However we cannot completely ignore the possibility that 'A. D. Cap:' in Weimar may not be the same person as 'A. D. Cap:' in Stockholm. There is also no evidence to indicate that the music in question did not make its way from Stockholm to Kassel rather than the opposite route that Wollny suggests. If, after all, the Stockholm-Kassel route is correct, and 'D' stands for Düben rather than Drese or Diesener, then it might explain why 'A. D.' was added to music that was copied in Stockholm by Gustav Düben, but not in Kassel where it was recopied by someone else with no direct family connection to uphold. It is also strange that 'P.D.' seems to have been accepted in *The Düben collection database catalogue* as Gustav Düben's brother, Peter, while the participation of the rest of the family is questioned. Clearly, the identity of 'A. D' and 'G. D.' in IMhs 409 cannot be completely settled until further evidence comes to light, and it is perhaps unwise to attribute their music to Drese and Diesener without any caveats.

IMhs 409 was written in tablature and presumably copied from sets of parts. While the grouping of movements appears to been treated with considerable freedom in terms of dance type, much of the manuscript's contents seem to have been brought together in ascending order of key, starting with A and finishing with G. A number of pieces seem to have been added subsequently at the end of the manuscript without any thought of further ordering. Apart from this, there is no physical separation of the music into suites and few specific indications of movement association. However, Jaroslav Mráček, the editor of the modern edition of this manuscript goes to great lengths to place as many movements as possible into a quasi-suite format. According to his preface, selection of so-called suites is determined by 'the order of movements' and 'unity of key', and his

---

[50] P. Wollny, 'Zur Thüringer Rezeption des französischen Stils im späten 17. und frühen 18. Jahrhundert' in W. Seidel & P. Wollny (eds.), *Ständige Konferenz Mitteldeutsche Baroquemusic in Sachsen, Sachsen-Anhalt und Thüringen* (Jahrbuch 2001, Schneverdingen, 2002), pp. 140–52.

[51] Ibid., p. 142.

editorial suggestions of movement ordering appear to be heavily influenced by the twentieth-century concepts of 'classical' order discussed in Chapter 3.[52] This leads to some questionable results. For example, Mráček's editorial 'Suite V' contains the following movements:

> Allamanda/Brandle de Mons: Constantin/Gaÿ/Amenere/Dūble/Montirande/ Gavotte/1. Courant/2. Courant/Sarabande.

All these movements share the same key centre and, given the many similar examples throughout the courtly repertoire, Mráček is surely correct in linking the gavotte, courantes and sarabande to the bransles. But as bransles were frequently used to start off the dancing at a ball, Mráček's decision to precede the sequence with an allemande is open to question. Furthermore, it is telling that Constantin's authorship is noted at the start of the bransles and not at the head of the allemande. There are certainly a number of examples in IMhs 409 where the allemande is an indicator of the start of a suite; but to assume that it always has this function is to impose a degree of rigidity on the seventeenth century that is at odds with the fluidity of construction discussed earlier. How then should we approach the groupings of movements in IMhs 409? In some cases, the association between movements is clear. As I have already indicated, the bransle sequence tended to be transmitted as a six- or four-movement entity and IMhs 409 mostly follows the French six-movement tradition of *bransle simple, bransle gay, amener, double, montirande* and gavotte. Only in one case, the bransles by Pierre Verdier, is the four movement sequence used that omits the *double* and *montirande*.[53] The additional courantes and sarabandes that were frequently attached to the original bransle sequences are also present in IMhs 409, and it is telling that the copyist often drew attention to this association. For example, the bransle sequence by 'Lahaeÿ' is followed by a 'Courant Simpel Suittes des Bransles' (that is, following the bransles) and Constantin's bransle sequence is followed by '1. Courante Suitte des Bra[n]les Mons:. Constantin'.

In additional to the bransles, there are other groups of dances that may be intended as suites: The allemande and two courantes by 'A: D: Capp:' have linked harmonic and melodic material at the openings of each dance and are clearly intended as associated movements. On the other hand, the sequence of three courantes and a sarabande by Constantin may not have been associated with the preceding 'Allamanda Mons: Werdier' as Mráček suggests.[54] It is perhaps more likely that this group of movements was originally part of an extended bransle sequence. While the instrumentation of IMhs 409 is mainly *à 4*, there are also numbers of *à 5* dances and sometimes these are, as in the 'Courante la Reÿne de France', flanked by *à 4* movements. But this does not necessarily imply that they

---

[52] Mráček, *Seventeenth-Century Instrumental Dance Music*, p. 26*.
[53] Ibid., pp. 185–89.
[54] Ibid., 'Suite I', pp. 6–11.

are separate pieces. As we have seen, the Kassel manuscript Mus. 61d[7] contains an example of *à 4* and *à 5* music that is probably intended for the same ensemble and there is no reason why *à 5* and *à 4* dances should not have been performed together.

The so-called Finspong collection was apparently compiled during the early part of the eighteenth century, probably in the Low Countries, and was originally owned by the Swedish De Geer family. Manuscripts *S-N* 9096:5, 9096:10 and 9096:15 appear to have been assembled for teaching purposes and, in all three cases, their first entries are guides to staff notation. 9094 appears to be different: it has two volumes under the same shelf mark. The first is largely devoted to music extracted from Henry Purcell's *Fairy Queen* and is marked 'First Trebles'. The second volume, largely devoted to music by Lully, has no such marking and is largely a single-line treble clef source.

9098 is in two volumes; the first (hereafter 9098/1) is perhaps the most important of these manuscripts. The material, especially in the earlier part of the manuscript, is typical of the French dance music that was being circulated among the German courts during the 1650s and 1660s. It also contains two *intradas* by Johann Heinrich Schmelzer; the second of these is the widely-circulated 'Intrada der pulicinelli', a hitherto-unrecognized source of this dance. The manuscript may be the sole survivor of a set of parts but, even if it is no more than teaching material, it may be an example of single-line dance music transmission. And it would seem that, well into the Lullian era, French dance music from an earlier time was still being circulated in Northern Europe.

9098/1, in particular, sheds further light on the transmission of bransle sequences. It contains the bransle suite by Bruslard in *D-Kl* Mus. 61a that is also found in Ballard's 1665 *Pièces pour le Violon a Quatre Parties de Differents Autheurs*.[55] The lower parts of *Pièces pour le Violon* and Mus. 61a are quite different to each other, and this seems to indicate that the manuscript is an example of single-line transmission with the Kassel copyist providing his own harmonies. However, we should not ignore the possibility that Ballard in Paris may also have been working from a single-line melody; compared with the Kassel source, the harmonies of the printed edition often verge on the crude. In the melody line itself, there is remarkably little difference between all three sources. 9098/1 reduces the bransle sequence from six to four movements by omitting the *bransle double* and *montirande*. As we have seen, this was common in bransles outside France, but it is remarkable that, apart from the reduced bransle sequence, the remaining movements in all versions are the same. Even the final bourée, not usually part of the sequence, is present in all three. Albeit with the reduction in movements, these sources demonstrate the impressive power of the bransle sequence not only to remain unified through various stages of transmission, but to retain its ancillary movements.

---

[55] Modern edition: M. Roche (ed.), *Pièces pour le Violon a Quatre Parties de Differents Autheurs Ballard, 1665* (Paris, 1971).

Like IMhs 409, manuscript *S-Uu* Ihre 281–3 is now held in the University Library in Uppsala. It is bound together with the same library's exemplar of the *Exercitium musicum* printed collection of dance music and shares the same shelf mark.[56] The common shelf mark seems to have caused considerable misunderstanding. Paul Whitehead describes the entire manuscript as 'An allemand and a courand [that] have been added by hand to each of the part books [of *Exercitium musicum*]'[57] and, until recently, RISM A/II suggested that both manuscript and printed edition have material in common.[58] But none of this is accurate: although they contain similar types of music, there is no connection between manuscript and print other than a common shelf mark and binding. Ihre 281–3 is a collection of three manuscript part books for two upper parts, presumably violins, and bass; the latter part is incomplete. There are one hundred and twenty-nine numbered movements, mostly suites in the style of town musicians, none of which appears in *Exercitium musicum*.[59]

Ihre 281–3 contains a wide variation in musical quality. Some dances in the manuscript contain unpleasantly ungrammatical writing that suggests an extremely low level of musical competence, or a serious copying error. On the other hand, there is also high-quality music by Dieterich Becker and Gregor Zuber. But it is the last part of the manuscript that requires consideration here as it includes dance-types normally associated with the court suite. They are detailed in Table 4.3.

---

[56] Each subsection of the shelf mark refers to a different part book. Thus, Ihre 281 is the first treble part book, Ihre 282 the second treble part book, and Ihre 283 the bass part book.

[57] P. Whitehead, 'Austro-German Printed Sources of Instrumental Music, 1630 to 1700', (Ph.D. diss., University of Pennsylvania, 1996), p. 82.

[58] RISM A/II former number 000085888. Online records generated at http://biblioline.nisc.com have been renumbered and revised. In the revised records, Ihre 281–3 and *Exercitium musicum* are correctly described as being 'bound together'. See record 190.006.392.

[59] For a more detailed discussion of this manuscript, see: Robertson, 'The consort suite', pp. 240–44.

Table 4.3: Dance movements grouped by key in the final section of manuscript *S-Uu* Ihre 281-3

Movement titles	Key
1. Sonatina a 3/2.Allemande/3.Ballet/4.Gique/5.Bouree/6.Minuet/ 7.Gavotte	A major / A minor
8.Chaconne/9.Ballet/10.Gique/11.Bouree/12.Saraband/13.Aria	B flat major
14.Allemande/15.Ballet/16.Gique/17.Bouree/18.Gaillarde/19.Sarraband	C major
20.Ballet/21.Gique/22.Bouree/23.Canarie/24.Gavotte/25. Saraband	D major
26.Allemande/27.Gique/28.Ballet/29.Trezza/30.Bouree/31.Sarabande	E major
32.Allemande/33.Ballet/34.Gique/35.Aria/36.Sarrabande/37.Lamento	F minor
38.Ballet/39.Ballet[ll]/40.Gique/41.Minuett/42.Gavotte/43.Sarrabande	G major
44.Allemande/45.Ballet/46.Gigue/47.Sarrabande/48.Ballet/49.Trezza	D minor

Movements are grouped by key; arguably the most important is '8. Chaconne' that starts the second group in B flat major.

As the bass part of this movement has not been preserved, it is difficult to know if any sort of bass line repeated formula was used in '8 chaconne', but Example 4.4 shows the opening of this movement in a simple reconstruction that suggests that its use was at least possible.

And in the manner of many other chaconnes, there is a gradual intensification of the material towards the end of the movement that does suggest the use of a repeated bass. However, '8. Chaconne' does not have the characteristic rhythm of this dance that starts on the second beat of a triple-time bar; the opening and all subsequent subsections start on the first beat of the bar. Ihre 281–3 may well have been put together over a large period, and any precise dating is impossible. However, it would appear to come from a time before the advent of the Lullian era in Germany. From the start of the seventeenth century, the chaconne and passacaglia where well known in German keyboard music, but it is rare to find either in a consort suite before the 1680s. The importance of this part of Ihre 281–3 is not in the quality of its music, but the manuscript may provide evidence of how the repertoire of the German courtly suite was starting to expand before the era of the Lullists.

Frantzösische Branles, Courantes, Sarabandes, Ballettas 91

8. Chaconne

Ex. 4.4.   *S-Uu* Ihre 281-2, '8. Chaconne'

Chapter 5

Burgermeistern Syndicis
Printed Editions by Court Composers before 1682

In contrast to the increasingly lively town music tradition of the 1650s, 1660s and 1670s, where most suite collections were published, comparatively few collections of suites by court composers seem to have been printed during this time. Even allowing for losses, the 1650s and 1660s seem to have been particularly sparse in this respect, although there was an increase in the number of printed editions by court composers issued during the 1670s. Court composers' seeming reluctance to publish during the 1650s and 1660s may reflect the straightened financial circumstances of many German courts and their musicians after the Thirty Years War, although other documents including opera and ballet *libretti* frequently found their way to print. But given the apparently strong link between publishers and town musicians, it is also possible that publishers during this time were simply reluctant to put suites from the more varied court tradition into print. Table 5.1 provides a chronological list of select dance-music publications by court composers between 1650 and 1680 and I will consider how far these editions reflect court musical practice, and how far they reflect the increasingly well-ordered collections by town musicians.

But before this, it is important to examine two collections of dance music that were not just the work of single composers: Johann Ernest Rieck's *Neue Allemanden, Giques, Balletten, Couranten, Sarabanden, und Cavotten* (Strasbourg, 1658)[1] and *Exercitium musicum* issued in 1660 by the Frankfurt-am-Main publisher, Balthasar Christoph Wust.

Rieck was a town musician, organist at St Thomas' church in Strasbourg, but it seems that he also gave music lessons to Christian Ernst, Margrave of Brandenburg when the latter was a student at Strasbourg University. Rieck's collection is divided into eight suites that start either with an allemande or *ballet*. Six of these suites are in *à 3* instrumentation; the remainder are *à 4*. The first suite starts in the manner of those by town musicians; the openings of the allemande, courante and sarabande are all linked harmonically and melodically, but in other suites of the collection, Rieck includes arrangements of lute music by the French lutenist Jean Mercure and the German lutenists, Johann Gumprecht and Valentin Strobel. Both Gumprecht

---

[1] Modern edition: J-L. Gester (ed.), *Johann Ernst Rieck Neue Allemanden, Giques, Balletten*, Convivium Musicum 2 (Stuttgart, 1994).

Table 5.1: Printed suite collections by court composers, 1652-80

Composer	Employment at time of publication	Abbreviated collection title	Date	Comments
Briegel	Court musician (*Cantor*), Gotha	*Erster Theil. Darinnen begriffen X. Paduanen. X. Galliarden. X. Balleten, und X. Couranten.*	1652	Organised into pairs of movements.
Seyfrid	Court organist, Coburg	*Erster Theil neuer Balletten, Allemanten, Arien, Couranten und Sarabanden*	1656	Incomplete
Löwe von Eisenach	*Kapellmeister*, Wolfenbüttel	*Synfonien, Intraden, Gagliarden, Arien, Balletten, Couranten, Sarabanden. Mit 3. oder 5. Instrumenten*	1657-8	
Seyfrid	Court organist, Coburg	*Ander Theil neuer Paduanen, Baleten, Arien, Couranten und Sarabanden*	1659	Incomplete
Rothe	Court musician, Dresden	*Erstmahlig musicalische Freuden-Gedichte*	1660	Incomplete
Briegel	*Kapellmeister*, Darmstadt	*Allemanden, Couranten, Sarabanden, Balleten und Chiquen.*	1664	Incomplete
Reusner	Lutenist, Brieg	*Musicalische Taffel-erlustigung*	1668	Arrangements by Johann Georg Stanley of ten suites for lute
Reusner	Lutenist, Brieg	*Musicalische Gesellschaffts*	1670	

Composer	Employment at time of publication	Abbreviated collection title	Date	Comments
Bleyer	Courtier and musician, Rudolstadt	*Lüst-Müsic Nach ietziger Frantzösicher Manier gesetzet*	1670	Contains two volumes and an appendix.
Drese	Court musician, Jena	*Erster Theil, Etlicher Allemanden, Couranten, Sarabanden, Balletten, Intraden und andern Arien*	1672	Incomplete
Drese	Court musician, Jena	*Allem. Cour. Baett. (sic) Intr: u.[nd] andre Arien mit etzlichen Variationen*	?1672	Lost
Abel	Court musician, Hanover	*Erstlinge Musicalischer Blumen Bestehend in Sonatinen, Allemanden, Corranten, Sarabanden und Giqven... Pars Prima*	1674	
Furchheim	Court musician, Dresden	*Musicalische Taffel-Bedienung Mit 5. instrumenten, als 2. Violinen, 2. Violen, 1. Violon, Benebenst dem General-Bass*	1674	Title page and possible dedication missing from Violin 1 part-book.
Abel	Court musician, Hanover	*Erstlinge Musicalischer Blumen Bestehend in Sonatinen, Allemanden, Corranten, Sarabanden und Giqven... Pars Secunda*	1676	

and Strobel lived and worked in Strasbourg, so it is hardly surprising that Rieck should have used their music as a source of his arrangements. Rieck's techniques of arrangement are typical of seventeenth-century dance music: he added his own inner part to the little-changed existing treble and bass of the lute originals. While the new second-treble line is sometimes little more than sequences of notes a third below the existing treble part, Rieck can often be inventive. In 'XV. La Petite Altesse', apparently by the French lutenist, Germain Pinel, the new second treble part frequently rises above the original first treble part and has a strong character of its own.[2] *Neue Allemanden* is the opposite of many other collections discussed in this chapter; it is an example of a town musician using the type of material usually to be found in courtly suites.

Like most of Rieck's collection, Wust's 1660 *Exercitium musicum* compilation of dance music is in *à 3* instrumentation. There is much that is similar between the two collections, even if the latter is on a very much larger scale. The two upper parts of *Exercitium musicum* are labelled 'Cantus I' and 'Cantus II', though the inclusion of music using *scordatura* violin tuning makes it clear that violins are intended, at least for part of the collection. As I pointed out in Chapter 3, only four of the one hundred and thirteen numbered movements in the collection have indications of authorship. On the title page, Wust merely states that the collection contains music by 'den fürnehmsten Componisten dieser Zeit' (the foremost composers of our time). It is not clear if the publishing house received this music in an anonymous state, or if the publisher suppressed the names of composers. The title page also states that the music was 'zusammen getragen/Durch (put together and arranged by) N.B.N.' The identity of N.B.N. is not known, but we may assume that he was responsible for providing or removing middle parts where necessary. There appears to be some deliberate ordering of the contents into three main sections. Movements 'I-XIII' comprise twelve sonatas and one sonatina; this is followed by fifteen possible suites and a group of movements with no apparent association. Finally, 'LXXIIX-CXIII' form a group of five bransle suites. The preface shows that Wust, or his arranger, was concerned about the ordering of pieces being clearly set out:

> Diese Sonaten, Galliarden, Balletté, &c. ... zusammen getragen/und in eine solche Ordnung gerichtet/daß zweiffels ohne/einem jeden Music verständigen dieses alles/zumahlen die verstimte Stücke auff der Violino nicht unangenehm seyn. (These sonatas, galliards, ballets, etc. ... are put together and arranged in such an order that, without doubt, each musical [composition] is fully

---

[2] For Pinel's lute version, see: M. Rollin & J-M. Vaccaro (eds.), *Œuvres de Pinel* (Paris, 1982), p. 149. Hitherto unrecognised manuscript concordances of this dance are contained in *S-N* Finspong 9098 and 9096:10. It is clear that the Finspong source does not originate from Rieck's collection or from Pinel's lute version; there are substantial differences in detail.

understood and, in particular, that the *scordatura* pieces on the violin are not made unpleasant.)

However, the suites in the second section are not clearly identified, and Wust's preface can hardly said to be helpful in this respect. But we must not forget that seventeenth-century musicians would have seen the collection principally as an extraordinarily varied source of dance music for their various suites and courtly duties. And there are some clues for the players that help establish a relationship between groups of movements; what appears to be the opening suite of the collection (movements XIV–XIX) is for two violins in *scordatura* tuning and bass. It is headed '6. Drück/mit 2. verstimbten Violinen' (6 movements for two differently-tuned violins) at the opening, and 'Ende der verstimbten Balletten' (end of the differently-tuned ballets) at the close.

Given the size of the collection, it is hardly surprising that its contents are drawn from a wide variety of sources. There is music by the English composers Charles Coleman and William Lawes, although neither of them is named. Some of the music in the collection is also found in manuscript *GB-Lbl* Add. MS 31438 where it is ascribed to Locke. The attribution is doubtful, and it is possible that this part of Add. MS 31438 was in fact copied from *Exercitium musicum*.[3] 'LXXV Ballet' is also found as '15. Aria' in Add. MS 31438 in a section of the manuscript marked 'Gregorius Zubern 1.do 1649. a. 5 … u[nd] Franckfurt am Maÿn 1660'. This appears to be the otherwise-lost collection, *Paduanen, Galliarden, Arien, Balletten, Cour. Sarab. und einer Sonate* by the Lübeck town musician, Gregor Zuber, published in Lübeck in 1649, and re-issued in 1660.[4] 'LXXVl. Cour[ant]' in *Exercitium musicum* is also found in Add. MS 31438 as part of a section that is taken from Pleickard Carolus Beck's *1. Theil neuer Allemanden, Balletten, Arien* (Strasbourg, 1654).[5]

The standard court repertoire is represented in *Exercitium musicum* by five bransle sequences, and these are detailed in Table 5.2.

---

[3] See R. Harding, *A thematic catalogue of the works of Matthew Locke with a calendar of the main events of his life* (Oxford, 1971), p. 132. See also, M. N. Robertson, 'The consort suite in the German-speaking lands' (Ph.D diss. University of Leeds, 2004) p. 240.

[4] An incomplete further manuscript source of Zuber's collection apparently exists in *D-Uda*. See RISM A/II, record 230.008.881 (generated on-line at http://biblioline.nisc.com).

[5] Apart from the 1654 publication, it seems that nothing is known about Beck.

Table 5.2: Bransle sequences in N.B.N. (comp.), *Exercitium musicum* (Frankfurt am Main, 1660)

Movement titles	Keys
LXXIIX. Branle simple / XCVII.(*sic*) Gay / LXXX. Amener / LXXXI. Gavotte / LXXXII. Cour. de suitte / LXXXIII. Courante / LXXXIV. Sarabande	G major
LXXXV. Branle de Mons: du Manoir / LXXXVI. Gaij / LXXXVII. Branle Amener / LXXXIIX. Gavotte / LXXXIX. Courante de la suite / XC. Sarabande	A minor
XCI. Branle simple du manoir / XCII. Gay / XCIII. Amener / XCIV. Gavotte. / XCV. Courante de suitte / XCVI. Sarabande	D minor
XCVII. Branle simple du Manoir / XCIIX. Gay / XCIX: Amener / C. Double / CI. Montirante / CII. Gavotte / CIII. Courante / CIV. Courante / CV. Sarabanda	G major
CVII. Branle / CIIX. Gaij / CIX. Amener / CX. Gavotte / CXI. Courante / CXII. La bouree dartus (*sic*)/ CXIII. Sarabande	D major

Three of these bransle suites have their first movements ascribed to the French violinist and dancing master, Guillaume Dumanoir. As we have seen, Dumanoir's music appears to have been widely circulated in Germany in the 1650s: dance movements by him are included in the Kassel manuscripts of *D-Kl* 2° MS mus.61, and the manuscript collection *S-Uu* IMhs 409. These three bransle sequences by Dumanoir in *Exercitium musicum* again show how the six-movement sequence was often reduced to four in Germany: movements LXXIIX-LXXXIV form a typical six-movement bransle sequence, but 'LXXXV. Branle de Mons: du Manoir' and 'XCI. Branle simple du Manoir' are both followed by the shorter four-movement sequence. Given that the four-movement version was little used in France, these are unlikely to have originated from Dumanoir in this form. It is also possible that Dumanoir was only responsible for only parts of the three bransle sequences. The *en suitte* courantes could well be by someone else.

The earliest collection in Table 5.1 is Wolfgang Carl Briegel's *Erster Theil. Darinnen begriffen X. Paduanen. X. Galliarden. X. Balleten, und X. Couranten. Mit 3. oder 4. Stimmen* (Erfurt, 1652). Briegel was *Hof-cantor* at Gotha but, at the time of publication, it was still rare for a court musician to issue dance music in print. Perhaps as a result, the edition does not reflect any particular aspect of court practice. The optional tenor part is labelled 'Ad placitum'; this type of arrangement seems to have been a widely accepted way of producing trios throughout the seventeenth century. For example, the Leipzig composer Johann Rosenmüller added a note at the end of the index of his 1667 *Sonata da camera* suggesting that the contents of the collection could be performed as trios by leaving out the middle parts ('A presente Opera Composta à cinque Stromenti, si potrà ancora Sonare à doi Violini soli è Basso'). Briegel's collection is not just a series of dances; there is a good deal of careful organization. The ten *Paduanen* and *Galliarden* are grouped into pairs; each *Galliarda* is a triple-time recasting of the preceding *Paduana*. The pairs themselves are also mostly arranged in ascending order of key as follows:

C major /D minor /E minor /F major /G minor /A minor /B flat major /D major /G major /A major.

The ten pairs of *Balleten* and *Couranten* that follow are also arranged in an identical order of key. In addition to this organization of content, which is more carefully ordered than many collections from this time by town musicians, *X. Paduanen* is notable for the high quality of its music. Briegel allows himself some licence in the recasting of the *Paduanen* into *Galliarden*, and he often appears more concerned with maintaining the characteristics of each dance than with exact repetition. As we can see at the start of '11. Paduana' and '12. Galliarda' (Example 5.1), Briegel avoids imitation in the 'Cantus secundus' of the *Galliarda* and, at the end of bar 3, replaces a root position chord with a first inversion. In both cases, the momentum of the triple-metre dance rhythm is enhanced and we can see that the change is not simply gratuitous tinkering.

The courantes of this collection are mostly in the simple Italian manner with *hemiolas* at the end of strains or phrases. But in '24. Couranta' (given in Example 5.2), we find some of the cross rhythms of the French version. Does this mean that, like Horn in *Parergon musicum*, Briegel misunderstood or ignored the differences between the Italian and French versions? By the time he wrote this collection, Briegel had surely gained experience of both court and town traditions, and was fully aware of the differences between the two types of courante. And, unlike Horn, Briegel does not set out to deliberately contrast the Italian and French styles. Briegel's '24. Couranta' is a hybrid but, it appears, deliberately so.

Twelve years later, Briegel issued a further collection of suites: *Allemanden/ Couranten/Sarabanden/Balleten und Chiquen/Mit 2. oder 3. Stimmen sambt dem General-Bass* (Jena, 1664). Unfortunately, only the 'Vox III' bass part survives, so it is not possible to see exactly what is meant by the 'two or three voices' of the title page. There is some evidence of careful ordering, although not on the scale of Briegel's previous collection; the first twenty-six dances are grouped into suites and arranged in ascending order, starting in C major and ending in G minor. Most of these groups fall into the pattern of allemande/courante/sarabande/ gigue, but the first suite contains an extra *ballet* and courante, and the fifth starts with a *ballet* instead of the allemande. Four shorter suites finish the collection, but there is no grouping of these by key.

Johann Christoph Seyfrid issued two printed collections of dances: the 1656 *Erster Theil neuer Balletten, Allemanten, Arien, Couranten und Sarabanden*, and

Ex. 5.1. W.C. Briegel, *Erster Theil. Darinnen begriffen X. Paduanen* (Erfurt, 1652), '11. Paduana', '12. Galliarda'

the 1659 *Ander Theil neuer Paduanen, Baleten, Arien, Couranten und Sarabanden*. According to their title pages, Seyfrid was court organist at Rudolstadt. Both collections are trios for two violins and bass. Given the publication of Wust's *Exercitium musicum* trio collection in 1660 and Briegel's 'Tenor ad placitum', it is possible that the preponderance of trios at this time reflects the continuing straightened circumstances of a good deal of German music making in years following the Thirty Years War. Unfortunately, the first violin part does not survive, but like Briegel's 1652 collection, Seyfrid's movements appear to be mostly grouped in pairs, although there is none of the arranging by ascending order of key that is a feature of the former. Movements 23–25 (Allamant/Couranta/Sarabanda, all in D minor) and 48–50 (Ballet/Couranta/Sarabanda; all in G minor) may have been intended as suites. Curiously, none of the first three movements of the collection end in the key in which they started.

The 1659 collection is also incomplete, but the first violin part does survive. There are sixty movements in the collection but, after an opening group of five *Paduanen*, the dance type is limited to courantes, sarabandes, *ballets* and arias. Movements are mostly grouped by type and, like Bleyer's and Rothe's collections discussed below, they are clearly intended as a source from which musicians could

Ex. 5.2.   Briegel, *Erster Theil. Darinnen begriffen X. Paduanen*, '24. Courante'

choose in order to form sequences of dances. French influence on the collection is limited; most of the sarabandes and courantes are firmly in the Italian manner.

Perhaps the most remarkable collection considered in this chapter is Johann-Jacob Löwe von Eisenach's *Synfonien, Intraden, Gagliarden, Arien, Balletten, Couranten, Sarabanden. Mit 3. oder 5. Instrumenten* (Bremen, 1657–58). Löwe von Eisenach had studied in Vienna and Italy, and by the time of the collection's publication, he was *Kapellmeister* at the Wolfenbüttel court of Duke August the younger.[6] The 'Mit 3. oder 5' instrumentation of the collection is emphasized by the 'ad placitum' marking of the second viola part, and this presumably applies to the first viola part as well. The opening of 'VII. Intrada' (Example 5.3) shows how the musical argument is principally in the two violin and bass parts. As both violas do little more than fill in, it is possible that the collection may well have started life as trio music, and that these 'ad placitum' parts were subsequently added for publication.

The importance of the collection lies in the way that it is deliberately and carefully organized; the *Register* (index) at the back of each part book shows each sequence of movements grouped by key. Each sequence also starts with a 'Synfonia' and has a broadly similar construction. Only one movement, a final *Synfonia*, does not fall into this scheme. For a collection from the 1650s, and from a court musician, this is remarkable. It anticipates by six years the organizational concepts of J. C. Horn's 1663 *Parergon musicum*. Given Löwe von Eisenach's training, it is not surprising that the musical language of the collection is predominantly Italian. But the French manner is occasionally apparent as in the cross rhythms that open the otherwise Italianate 'IV. Couranta' (Example 5.4). The hybrid character of this dance is akin to Briegel's '24. Couranta' discussed earlier.

Both the quoted examples from Löwe von Eisenach's collection also demonstrate the vitality of the writing, especially the use of cross rhythms. The

---

[6]   H. Walter, 'Löwe von Eisenach, Johann Jakob' in *New Grove* 2, vol. 15, pp. 256–7.

102 The Courtly Consort Suite in German-Speaking Europe, 1650–1706

Ex. 5.3.   J-J. Löwe von Eisenach, *Synfonien, Intraden, Gagliarden* (Bremen, 1657–58), 'VII. Intrada'

latter is evident even in the 'ad placitum' viola parts. It is surprising that the collection is not better known.

Wolf Ernst Rothe's *Erstmahlig musicalische Freuden – Gedichte*, published in Dresden in 1660 by Wolffgang Seyfferts, has the following note at the head of 'XIIX. Alemanda â 5':

> NB. Folgende 8. Stück oder Tantze sind alle eines Clavis und weil man nicht so viel Semitoni hat/hat müssen abgebrochen werden/Dahero ein verständiger

Ex. 5.4.   Löwe von Eisenach, *Synfonien,* 'IV. Couranta'

Musicus in acht zu nehmen hat/wieder anfang dieser 8. Stücken alß die erste Zeile mit Semitonen verzeichnet/die andern auch so folgen müssen/oder tonnen darzu geschrieben werden. (NB. The following eight pieces or dances are all one key, and because there are not enough semitones, the [key signatures] must be spread out. Therefore, at the start of these eight pieces, a competent musician has to be especially careful to notice the order of semitones and tones, applying them to the staves that follow.)

At the start of each of these eight movements, all in D major, the anonymous printer has provided the requisite key signature; but on all subsequent staves, there is only an unfilled space between the clef and the start of the music. Clearly, the printer did not possess a sufficient number of type characters to manage a key signature of two sharps on every line when applied to a sequence of eight movements. In addition, there are many serious errors in the two 'Viola brazzo' parts; this raises the possibility that Rothe's collection was originally in *à 3* instrumentation and that the new inner parts where provided by someone possessing scant musical knowledge. At the time of publication, Rothe was a court musician at Dresden, though he later became *Kapellmeister* at Rudolstadt. Perhaps he did not have the financial means to obtain the services of an experienced publisher or printer of music. He also appears not to have had any royal patronage; there is no mention of nobility on the title page, and the collection's dedication is to civic dignitaries. Despite this, the collection reflects the traditions of the court suite and it is put together along the lines of manuscript collections such as S-Uu IMhs 409. There are forty-nine movements: some are grouped together by type, and some by key. Unfortunately, the 'Violon' and 'Basso continuo' part books are lost. There are some sequences of dances that appear to be grouped into suites, but there are also a number of movements without any apparent association. As we have seen in Chapter 2, Rothe described some of the *ballets*, courantes and sarabandes in his collection as being in the French manner. Rothe's dances, especially the courantes, are not as rhythmically detailed as Reusner's that are discussed below. And, like Briegel's, not all of them are in the French manner. But movements such as 'VII. Courant, à 5' are recognizable as French and could have graced any court ballroom. (See Example 5.5. Only the first violin line is shown; there are many mistakes in the remaining lower parts.)

It is clear that the main purpose of the collection is to provide a source of dance music from which various movements may be drawn. In this, it is entirely in line with what we have seen of German courtly suite construction in the 1650s and 1660s.

Ex. 5.5. W.E. Rothe, *Erstmahlig musicalische Freuden – Gedichte* (Dresden, 1660), 'VII. Courant, à 5'

Johann Wilhelm Furchheim was also a court musician at Dresden. It appears that he received his early training at the court, and joined the *Hofkapelle* around 1665.[7] The present-day existence of manuscript copies of his music in such

---

[7] K-E. Bergunder, 'Furchheim, Johann Wilhelm' in *New Grove* 2, vol 9, p. 350.

geographically diverse places as Kroměříž and Uppsala suggests that his music was widely disseminated. His *Musicalische Taffel-Bedienung Mit 5. instrumenten* was published in Dresden in 1674. The title page of the presumably 'Violino 1' part book is missing, and it is likely that a further page containing a dedication is also missing. The collection is carefully organized and is almost the exact opposite of Rothe's; it starts with three multi-sectioned sonatas that are followed by three suites. The three opening sonatas are quite separate from the suites, and each suite has, in addition to a prelude, its own opening sonata. The sonatas that start each suite are simpler in construction than the separate sonatas at the start of the collection: they are in an A-B-A format with the repeat of the first section simply being labelled 'Ut supra'. Only the fifth suite is any different: it has a brief *adagio* coda following the 'Ut supra' repeat. Throughout the collection, the sonatas are all in *à 5* instrumentation, but the preludes and dances that follow are all *à 4*. The reduction in ensemble size is achieved by uniting the two violin parts, a further example of the tradition of reinforcing the upper line of dance music. But in all the preludes, Furchheim uses *cantus firmus*-like outer parts while, in contrast to most dance or dance-related music, the violas provide the rhythmic impetus. (See Example 5.6.)

All three suites employ a similar sequence of movements. The first and second suites have the following:

Sonata/Præludium/Allemande/Couranta 1/Couranta 2/Sarabande/Gigue.

The third suite breaks the pattern by inserting a *ballo* between the two courantes. The use of two consecutive courantes seems to suggest the courtly *en suite* practice discussed earlier. There is movement linking only in the third suite, but Furchheim does not link the usual allemande and courante pair. Instead, he links the *ballo* and the second courante. A further volume of dance music by Furchheim is listed by Göhler, but is now lost.[8]

Esaias Reusner was a lutenist at the court of the Duke of Silesia in Brieg. A volume of his lute music, *Delitiae testudnis*, was published in 1667, and this was followed a year later by ten lute suites arranged for violin, two violas and bass by Johann Georg Stanley under the title *Musicalische Taffel-erlustigung*. It is clear that these arrangements were done with the full cooperation of the composer; indeed, Reusner himself was the publisher. The title page tells us that Stanley, the arranger also worked at the court of Brieg and that the pieces are 'nach französischer Art' (in the French manner). The dedication carries the names of both Stanley and Reusner. The *französischer Art* is confirmed by pieces such as 'Saraband. 11' (shown in Example 5.7): if we compare it with the sarabande from the 'Bransles à 4. de Mr. du Manoir' in *D-Kl* 2° MS mus. 61b² given earlier in

---

[8] Göhler, A., *Verzeichnis der in den Frankfurter und Leipziger Messkatalogen der Jahre 1564 bis 1759 angezeigten Musikalien* vol. 2, entry 576 (3 vols, Leipzig, 1902).

Ex. 5.6. J.W. Furchheim, *Musicalische Taffel-Bedienung* (Dresden, 1674), 'Sonata Sexta', 'Præludium'

Example 2.3 (page 34), we can see how closely Reusner follows the characteristic rhythms of the French model.

The same is true of the courantes in the collection. Although not marked as such, *Musicalische Taffel-erlustigung* falls clearly into two sections. The first section contains six suites using the basic order:

Paduan/Allemand/Courant/Saraband/Gavotte/Gigue.

Ex. 5.7. E. Reusner, arr. J.G. Stanley, *Musicalische Taffel-erlustigung*, 'Saraband. 11'

In four of these six suites, a second courante is added after the gigue. The second section of the collection has four suites, all using the same sequence of:

Ballo/Ballo [II]/Courant/Saraband/Gigue.

In each case, the constant dotted rhythms of the second *ballo* are clearly meant to form a contrast with the more even rhythms that have preceded it in the first *ballo*. (Example 5.8 shows the first strains of 'Ballo. 41' and 'Ballo. 42' from the seventh suite of the collection.)

The propulsive dotted rhythms of 'Ballo. 42' may also be a deliberate reference to the version of the dance often featured in the suites by town composers, but the sequence of *ballo*, *ballo*, courante, sarabande and gigue is seemingly unique to the Reusner-Stanley arrangements. It also seems that Reusner rarely used the *ballo* as movement in his other works.[9] But it must not be forgotten that these suites were originally written for the lute, and it is with Reusner's other collections of lute suites that we should make comparison. Unfortunately, the original lute pieces that make up *Musicalische Taffel-erlustigung* do not appear to have survived, but the sequence of *Paduan*, allemande, courante, sarabande, gavotte and gigue is found, with only minor differences, in *Delitiae testudnis*. The treble and bass lines of the suites in *Musicalische Taffel-erlustigung*, presumably close to Reusner's originals, are attractive and well-written music, but, as we have seen in the examples from the collection, Stanley does not appear to have been the most imaginative arranger. The viola parts are often awkward and unconvincing, and they detract from what otherwise might have been a most interesting collection of suites. And while there is some of the careful organization to be found in printed collections of

---

[9] See K. Koletschka, 'Esias Reußner der Jüngere und seine Bedeutung für die deutsche Lautenmusik des XVII. Jahrhunderts' in G. Adler (ed.), *Studien zur Musik*, Vol. 15 (Vienna, 1928), pp. 7–45.

Ex. 5.8.   Reusner, arr. Stanley, *Musicalische Taffel-erlustigung*, 'Ballo. 41', 'Ballo. 42'

suites by town musicians, *Musicalische Taffel-erlustigung* is closer to the varied court tradition of suite writing than any other collection considered so far in this chapter.

Reusner was still in the same post in Brieg when his *Musicalische Gesellschaffts ergetzung bestehend in Sonaten, Allemanden, Couranten, Sarabanden, Gavotten, und Giguen* was published in 1670. It is made up of ten suites, nine of which have the following sequence of movements:

Sonata/Allemanda/Courant/Sarab[ande]/Gavotte/Gigue.

The tenth suite omits the gavotte, and replaces the gigue with a second courante. The long list of errata at the start of the violin part book suggests that Reusner did not have much control over the early stages of the printing process. Like *Musicalische Taffel-erlustigung*, the instrumentation is for violin, two violas and bass, although there is no suggestion that the pieces in this later collection are arrangements of any sort. The lengthy sonatas are multi-sectioned; this type of sonata is more usually to be found in suites by town musicians, and the influence of the latter is clear from the careful movement ordering of each suite. However, many of the dances are French, especially the courantes, and it is the quality of the dance music that provides the real strength of the suites in this collection. This may be attributable to Reusner's work as a lutenist, and demonstrates how courtly composers often brought a quality of imagination to their dance movements that is sometimes lacking in the work of the town composers. A second edition of *Musicalische Gesellschaffts* was issued only two years after the first, but it is now lost.

After a musical training in Leipzig, Georg Bleyer served as a courtier and court musician at Rudolstadt. His *Lüst-Müsic Nach ietziger Frantzösicher Manier gesetzet* was issued in Leipzig in 1670. Unusually for an edition by a court musician, the publisher was also the dedicatee. The collection is described on its title page as being 'Nach ietziger Frantzösicher Manier gesetzet' (set in the current French manner). There are two volumes and an appendix to the second of these, entitled 'Zugabe', but all follow on from each other and were presumably printed and issued at the same time. Only the first volume has a full title page. There are one hundred and seventeen movements in the collection: fifty in each of the first and second volumes, and seventeen in the 'Zugabe'; despite the size of the collection, the range of movements is quite limited. The dance types that occur most frequently are the sarabandes and courantes and, curiously, there are no bransle sequences. The three movements entitled 'bransle' are all single examples of the *bransle simple*. Apart from this lack of bransle sequences, the similarity between Bleyer's *Lüst-Müsic* and manuscript compilations of suites such as *S-Uu* IMhs 409 is striking. There are many movements grouped by key but without any further apparent association with each other; these are clearly intended as material ready to be combined into suites or extended *en suite* sequences of like dances. There is a small amount of material in the 'Zugabe' that suggests dramatic origins, and there are also combinations of movements that appear to be ready-made suites. For example, in the second volume, we find the following sequence of movements, all in the same key of G minor:

IV.Allemand /V.Sarab. /VI.Cour. /VII.Bransle /VII.Sarrab. (sic) / IX.Cour. /X.Chique.

This type of sequence seems to be looking forward to the longer sequences of dance movements used by the German Lullists in the following two decades. And given the use of the allemande at the start of the sequence along with a single bransle, it may be an indication of how the courtly suite was starting to move away from its association with the stage and the ballroom in order to become more of an instrumental genre.

Bleyer's preface, like the title page, refers to the French manner; this time in connection with 'Bourreen Gagliarden, Gavotten, &c'. The Italian style is not mentioned, though rather whimsically in the case of the latter two, 'Allemanden, Aire, Chansoni' are given as examples of the German manner. But as the first strain of 'XVI. Sarraband' in Example 5.9 demonstrates, the use of the French manner is wholly idiomatic, as might be expected from a court composer.

The collection's part books are simply labelled as 'Violino', 'Altus', 'Tenor' and 'Bassus'. The highest note of the 'Altus' part is d", which is the same upper limit as many French-style first viola parts. We may assume from all this that the instrumentation here is, without doubt, the same as that used by Reusner, Stanley and most of the German four-part music written in the French manner: one violin, two violas and bass. The first strain of '1.Gavotte', the opening movement in the second part of the collection, is given as an illustration of this in Example 5.10. As we have seen, a single movement from the first part of the collection, 'XXX Gique', is written in five-part instrumentation with an additional 'violino' part.

The importance of *Lüst-Müsic* has sometimes been misunderstood by modern scholars. For example, the collection has been described merely as providing 'early evidence of the vogue in Germany for up-to-date French dances' while 'not fall[ing] into readily identifiable types or into stereotypical groupings'.[10] But this is to see the collection only in terms of the so-called 'classical' groupings. Like Rothe, Bleyer does not appear to be interested in issuing volumes of suites organized in the manner of town musicians. *Lüst-Müsic* is an important example of the provision of material for use by court musicians. It is a further example of the fluidity and ad hoc nature of the courtly suite at this time.

As we have seen, Adam Drese was 'director of operatic and other theatre music' in both Jena and Weimar, and he seems to have been a highly regarded figure in court music circles. On the title page of his 1672 *Erster Theil Etlicher Allemanden, Couranten, Sarabanden, Balletten, Intraden und andern Arien mit theils darbei befindlichen Doublen, oder Variationen*, he is also described as a 'Chamber Secretary' at the court in Jena and was clearly a court musician at the time of the collection's publication. Of this large collection of one hundred and fifty movements, only the 'Alt-Viola' and figured 'Basso' part books remain. The 1759 catalogue of music collected by Nicolas Selhof lists the collection as being scored 'a 4; Violino, Alto, Tenor & Basso'.[11] While the 'Alt-Viola' part has a high tessitura, it is reasonable to assume that the instrumentation is for violin, two violas and bass. Fortunately, the preface was printed in both surviving part books, and it gives us a most valuable insight into Drese's performing practice. We have already seen (page 20) the preface's comments on ornamentation and instrumentation. There is also advice concerning rhythmic adjustment:

> Diese Instrumental-Stükke und Arien, so gut als sie von der hand geflossen/ erfordern ins gemein einen feinen geshikten und gleich durchgegenden Takt/wie bey denen jezigen bekandten Frantzöischen Stükken von den Tanz-

---

[10] M. Spaeth, 'Bleyer, Georg' in *New Grove 2*, vol. 3, pp. 697–8.

[11] N. Selhof, *Catalogue d'une très belle bibliothèque de livres ... auquel suit le catalogue d'une partie tres considerable de livres de musique* (The Hague, 1759; facsm. A. Hyatt King (ed.), Amsterdam, 1973), p. 152.

Ex. 5.9. G. Bleyer, *Lüst-Müsic Nach ietziger Frantzösicher Manier gesetzet* (Leipzig, 1670), 'XVI. Sarraband'

Meistern beobachtet zu werden pfleget; Worbey/sonderlich die punctirten Noten jedesmahl ein wenig länger. (These instrumental pieces and airs have flowed easily from the hand. They generally require a degree of skill and the steady beat usually observed by the dancing masters in their fashionable French pieces. Consequently, the dotted notes, in particular, should be held a little longer each time: the following [notes] should be made that much shorter.

As the violin part is lost, Drese's comments on rhythm cannot be placed in their proper context, but some form of rhythmic enhancement seems to be implied where notes are already dotted. Perhaps Drese is referring to the type of rhythm used by Reusner in some of the *ballo* movements in his *Musicalische Taffel-erlustigung* (see Example 5.8 above). However, the most important part of Drese's preface lies in the opening comments. By suggesting that the 'Instrumental-Stükke und Arien' should be played in the style dictated by the French dancing masters, he seems to be implying that they were usually played in a different manner to music specifically intended for dancing.

Concepts of careful organization are rather more apparent than in Rothe's and Bleyer's collections. As we have seen (page 47), the central part of Drese's

112   *The Courtly Consort Suite in German-Speaking Europe, 1650–1706*

Ex. 5.10.   Bleyer, *Lüst-Müsic*, '1.Gavotte'

collection is devoted to five groups of movements, carrying the title 'suite', which appear to have their origins in the music of the stage. But the largest part of the collection is devoted to suites starting with an allemande and apparently possessing a common key centre for all their movements: there are twenty-one of these and they are detailed in Table 5.3.

Table 5.3:   Suites that start with an allemande in A. Drese, *Erster Theil Etlicher Allemanden, Couranten, Sarabanden, Balletten, Intraden und andern Arien* (Jena, 1672)

Movement numbers	Movement titles	Key
I-IV	Allemande/Courante 1/Courante 2/Sarabande	G minor
V-IIX	Allemande/Courante 1/Courante 2/Sarabande	E minor
XLV-XLIX	Allemande/Courante 1/Courante 2/Sarabande/ Sarabande	D major

Movement numbers	Movement titles	Key
L-LV	Allemande/Courante 1/Courante 2/ Sarabande/Aria/ Sarabande	E minor
LVI-LIX	Allemande/Allemande/Aria/ Sarabande	C minor
LXXIX-LXXXI	Allemande/Courante/Sarabande	A major
XCIV-XCVI	Allemande/Courante/Sarabande	B flat major
XCVII-XCIX	Allemande/ Courante/Sarabande	E minor
C-CII	Allemande/[untitled]/Giqvè.	C mjor
CIII-CV	Allemande/ Courante/ Sarabande.	B minor
CXV-CXVII	Allemande/ Courante/ Sarabande.	E minor
CXIIX-CXX	Allemande/ Courante/ Sarabande.	E minor
CXXI-CXXIII	Allemande/ Courante/ Sarabande.	B flat major
CXXIV-CXXVII	Allemande/ Courante 1/Courante 2/Sarabande.	D/G minor
CXXIIX-CXXXI	Allemande/ Courante/Sarabande/Rußen Aria.	B flat major
CXXXII[I]-CXXXIV	Allemande/ Courante/Sarabande.	C major
CXXXV-CXXXVII	Allemande/ Courante/Sarabande.	C major
CXXXIIX-CXL	Allemande/ Courante/Sarabande.	B flat major
CXLI-CXLIII	Allemande/ Courante/Sarabande.	C major
CXLIV-CXLVI	Allemande/ Courante/Sarabande.	C major
CXLVII-CI	Allemande/ Courante/ Aria/Sarabande.	E minor

Notes:

In *su*ite CXXIV-CXXVII, Courante II starts in G minor and ends in D minor. The other three movements are all in D minor. This courante is not the only movement in the collection to change key: 'XVII Lameto' starts in B minor and finishes in E minor, but its relationship to the surrounding movements is unclear.

There is also a six-movement extended bransle suite with two additional courantes and a sarabande. A now-lost further volume of apparently similar music by Drese, *Allem. Cour. Baett. (sic) Intr. u.[nd] andre Arien mit etzlichen Variationen*, is listed by Göhler.[12] It appears that this edition was also issued in 1672, presumably as the second part to *Erster Theil Etlicher Allemanden*. But as Göhler gives the wrong date for the latter, the publishing interval between the two volumes is unclear.

For much of his career, Clamor Heinrich Abel was employed at the courts of Celle and Hanover. During this time, he issued three volumes of *Erstlinge Musicalischer Blumen* (Frankfurt-am-Main, 1674, 1676, 1677). The first two volumes are described on their title pages as being set for 'Vier Instrumenten Sampt dem Basso Continuo', but the last is for violin, viola da gamba and continuo. The viola da gamba part has not survived.

In the first volume, all the suites have, with one exception, the same sequence of movements:

Præludium/Sonatina/Allemanda/Corrante/Sarabanda/Gique.

Even the exception, the second suite of the collection, only differs in having an extra sarabande and gigue at the end. In a similar manner to Furchheim's *Musicalische Taffel-Bedienung*, issued in the same year, the start of each suite is divided into a 'Præludium' and an *allegro* 'Sonatina'. These abstract movements are frequently substantial in length, and the same applies to the dances themselves, particularly the allemandes and gigues. Perhaps, like Reusner's sonatas, this was a deliberate attempt to impress the listener. But Abel does not always rise to the musical challenge that he sets himself by writing at length, and there is too much reliance on the repetition of phrases or note sequences.

Perhaps Abel realized this, for the 1676 second volume is simpler and musically more successful. There is also more variety. In all but two of the suites in the collection, he uses a single abstract movement, not divided into two sections as in the 1674 collection. The most unusual of these abstract movements is '51. Sonata Battaglia', which opens the final suite of the collection – the sounds of battle are clearly portrayed. The whole of this final suite is clearly meant to contrast with the others of the collection; the *allemanda/corrante/sarabanda/gique* sequence of dances that mostly predominates up to this point is, after the 'Sonata Battaglia' replaced by:

52. Allemanda/53. Ballo/54. Corrante/55. Gavott/56. Sarabanda/57. Ballet/
58. Sarabanda/59. Gique.

But Abel does not seem to have completely turned his back on issuing printed editions of dance music reflecting the traditions of court music. Göhler lists a

---

[12] Göhler, vol. 2, entry 390.

now-lost 1687 Braunschweig publication by him, *Drey Opera Musica, deren der Erste u[nd] Ander Th[eil] in sich enthält, Overturen nach französ[iche] Art*.[13] It appears that the instrumentation was for four-part string ensemble, but the title page's reference to 'Kriegsexerzitium der Infanterie' (fighting exercises for the infantry) may also suggest the presence of oboe-band music.[14]

From this discussion of printed editions of suites by court composers, it is clear that there are some collections, notably by Rothe and Bleyer, which reflect the fluid and varied tradition of the manuscript courtly suite. But a significant number do not. Why did court musicians make such a conscious decision to follow the suite-writing concepts of their town colleagues? Certainly, the printed suite collection after the mid 1660s was synonymous with careful organization of content, and it is possible that court composers were simply reluctant to depart from an increasingly well-established format. In some cases there may be a reason for this reluctance. While there is no specific evidence that any of the collections discussed in this chapter were linked with applications for posts in the towns, it seems that some of their composers were actively seeking municipal employment at the time of publication. Publication was clearly effective in helping to secure this type of employment. On the strength of his published collections, Johann Pezel was apparently offered the post of 'principal musician' in Bautzen in 1680 without the need for any audition.[15] So it is hardly surprising that collections by court composers were not always dedicated to princely employers, as might be expected, but to municipal dignitaries. For example, it seems that Abel was actively seeking employment as a town musician in Bremen; as a result, the second volume of his *Erstlinge Musicalischer Blumen* was dedicated to the 'Burgermeistern Syndicis' of the town. When the desired appointment did not materialise, Abel's third volume named each dedicatee burgher individually. Eventually, this brought success: Abel was given a post in Bremen in 1694. Likewise, Reusner moved to a university appointment in Leipzig only two years after the publication of *Musicalische Gesellschaffts ergetzung*; perhaps the publication was intended to provide an example of his work to the university authorities. And while Bleyer's *Lüst-Müsic* was issued in Leipzig where he had trained as a musician, it is perhaps significant that the collection has no dedication to the composer's princely employer at the Rudolstadt court. Instead, it is dedicated to 'herrn Christian Kirchnern/ Weitbekanten Bürger und Buchhändler in Leipzig'. There is also a dedicatory sonnet by the Leipzig musician, Johann Pezel. Bleyer had a chequered history of

---

[13] Göhler 2, entry 3.

[14] The link between oboe-band music and the military is discussed in Chapter 7.

[15] See H.W. Schwab, 'The Social Status of the Town Musician' in W. Salmen, (ed.), trans. H. Kaufman & B. Reisner, *The social status of the professional musician from the Middle Ages to the 19th. century* (Sociology of Music No. 1, New York, 1983), pp. 33–59 at p. 41.

employment at the courts.[16] It is not unreasonable to think that *Lüst-Müsic* was part of an unsuccessful attempt to gain a post as a town musician in Leipzig.

Of course, it would be unwise to assume that every printed edition of suites issued by a court composer was linked to an employment application in the towns. And, as I pointed out at the start of this chapter, it is likely that printed editions gradually assumed a well-defined format that many publishers were unwilling to change. But it is also clear that when court musicians wanted to impress possible municipal patrons, they composed and organized their suites in the manner of town musicians.

Did the suites in these quasi-municipal printed collections have a place in the regular run of court performance? The Rudolstadt court inventory drawn up by Philipp Heinrich Erlebach at the end of the seventeenth century lists, in addition to Erlebach's own works, only three printed editions of dance music: Wust's 1660 *Exercitium musicum*, *Hortulus musicus* (Bremen, 1662) by the otherwise-unknown Konrad Steneken and *Deliciae harmonicae oder Musicalische Ergötzung* (Leipzig, 1656) by the Leipzig town musician, Werner Fabricius.[17] It is telling that Erlebach does not list any of the printed-suite editions by Seyfrid, Rothe or Bleyer, all of whom had connections with the Rudolstadt court. On the other hand, it has recently been argued by Erik Albertyn that Abel's three *Erstlinge Musicalischer Blumen* editions are unequivocally linked to the repertoire of the 'Hanover court orchestra'.[18] Given the very strong French influence at Hanover and Abel's apparent desire to find employment elsewhere, it is perhaps unwise to make such a claim without any reservation. And, in the light of the practice by court musicians of drawing their materials from a wide variety of sources, it is rather more likely that individual movements or groups of movements from the printed editions described above were used by *Hofkapellen* on an ad hoc basis. As complete suites, the music in these printed collections may have seen little more than limited use at court.

Probably as a result of its fluid nature, the court suite between 1650 and 1680 seems to have made little progress as a genre, losing much of its variety and vitality during the 1670s. It is telling that court musicians wishing to appeal to a wider audience should have used forms of suite emanating from outside the court repertoire and, in these circumstances, it is hardly surprising that the influence of Lully's music swept all before it. The next three chapters deal with the phenomenon of the German *Lullists*, composers who worked within Lully's sphere of influence in Paris or used his music as an example for their own.

---

[16] Spaeth, 'Bleyer, Georg', p. 697.

[17] *Inventarium*, ThStA Rudolstadt, Geheimes Archiv B VII 4c Nr.2.

[18] E. Albertyn, 'The Hanover orchestral repertory, 1672–1714: significant source discoveries' in *Early Music*, vol. 33/3 (2005), pp. 449–71. See also my response to this article in *Early Music*, vol. 34/1 (2006), correspondence, pp. 179–80.

Chapter 6

Ouverturen und Airs
The German Lullists – I

It is difficult to date the arrival of Lully's influence in Germany with any precision. Although music from his dramatic works may well have been known during the later part of the 1670s, it was apparently not until the following decade that they were first performed in Germany. It may be significant that the Parisian publishing firm of Christophe Ballard did not start issuing printed scores of Lully's 'larger stage works' until 1679.[1] Carl Schmidt has drawn attention to performances in Regensburg, Wolfenbüttel, Ansbach, Darmstadt and Hamburg that all took place during this decade.[2] More followed in the 1690s, and it was claimed that Lully's works gave 'les plaisirs de touttes les Cours de l'Europe' (pleasure to all the courts of Europe).[3] This international aspect of Lullism is confirmed by Muffat when he speaks of 'those who play like the late Mr. Baptiste, that is, the French, the English, the Dutch and Flemish, and many others'.[4] We have already seen that German musicians such as Diesener visited Paris in the 1650s and, in the following decades, personal contact with Lully, or study of his methods, was clearly important. To quote Cousser, a German musician who studied in Paris, 'j'ay crû n'y pouvoir mieux parvenir, qu'en m'attachant a imiter ce fameux Baptiste' (I thought of nothing better than undertaking to imitate the famous Baptiste).[5] Manuscript extracts from Lully's stage works were disseminated throughout Germany. And, as we have seen, printed editions by Pointel and Heus started to appear in Amsterdam in the early 1680s, although they were not always faithful reproductions of Lully's music. Pointel's editions of *Le triomphe de l'amour* and

---

[1] C. Schmidt, 'The Amsterdam editions of Lully's music: a bibliographical scrutiny with commentary', in J. Heyer (ed.), *Lully studies* (Cambridge, 2000), p. 100–165 at p. 103.

[2] C. Schmidt, 'The geographical spread of Lully's operas during the late seventeenth and early eighteenth centuries: new evidence from the livrets' in J. Heyer (ed.), *Jean-Baptiste Lully and the music of the French baroque* (Cambridge, 1989), pp. 183–211 at pp. 184–5. See also J. Spitzer and N. Zaslaw, The birth of the orchestra: history of an institution, 1650–1815 (Oxford, 2004), p. 102.

[3] J.S. Cousser, *Composition de musique Suivant la Methode Francoise* (Stuttgart, 1682), preface.

[4] D. Wilson, (ed. and trans.) *Georg Muffat on Performance Practice* (Bloomington and Indianapolis, 2001), p. 13.

[5] Cousser, *Composition de musique*, preface.

Le temple de la paix are seemingly both trio arrangements. Unfortunately, the bass part book of the latter no longer survives, but Example 6.1 gives an excerpt from the opening of the *ouverture* in the Pointel edition supplemented by a bass part from the Ballard score issued in Paris in 1685; it also gives the same passage in the fully scored version from Ballard.

Ex. 6.1.   J-B. Lully, *Le Temple de la Paix*, editions by Pointel (Amsterdam, n.d.) and Ballard (Paris, 1685), 'Ouverture'

Together, they show how Pointel's arranger worked in the existing tradition of the free arrangement of dance and dance-related music: it is likely that he discarded all but Lully's treble and bass parts, and then added a completely new inner part. Carl Schmidt, in his discussion of the Amsterdam Lully editions, lists Pointel's *Le temple de la paix* as being for 'Four (?) parts'.[6] But as we can see from the example, the three parts appear to be complete and the existence of a fourth is unlikely. In the later Amsterdam printed editions of Lully's music, five-part texture was reduced to four by the simple process of omitting the *quinte* (third viola)

---

[6]   Schmidt, 'Amsterdam editions', p. 143.

part. Against this background, German court composers started to write suites in imitation of Lully. The first printed collection of suites in this style was Cousser's *Composition de musique*, and there can be little doubt that Cousser was highly influential in bringing the Lullian style to Germany. But it is also reasonable to assume that other composers may have been writing similar suites around the same time, if not earlier.

Two manuscripts suites by Georg Bleyer that exist in the Liechtenstein collection in Kroměříž may be an example of this; they are the 'Partie â 4. â la Françoise' (*CZ-KRa* A 801) and the 'Partie â 5. â la Françoise' (*CZ-KRa* A 847). The fact that these suites made their way to Kroměříž is significant. Bleyer had spent time in France, presumably Paris, 'probably before 1670', and he would surely have heard Lully's music while he was there.[7] Following this, in the mid-1670s, Bleyer also spent time in Vienna and, as we shall see in Chapter 9, there were close links between Kroměříž and the imperial capital. Given these circumstances, it is certainly possible that both A 801 and 847 pre-date Cousser's *Composition de musique*.[8] The instrumental norm for the German *Lullist* suite was one violin, two or three violas, and bass. A 801, with an *à 4* ensemble follows this, but the A 847 *à 5* ensemble includes a 'Second Dessus' part with a relatively high tessitura that seems to have been intended for a violin.

Both Bleyer's suites start with an *ouverture*, arguably the most important movement of any Lullian suite. Indeed, with the exception of parts of Austria, any *Kapellmeister* in the 1680s and 1690s who started an opera or ballet with anything other than an *ouverture* in the Lullian manner might well have run the risk of censure from his employer. This type of *ouverture* follows a bi- or tripartite pattern. The first section is always in duple-time; and harmonically, the opening bar is often no more than a simple tonic chord. This simplicity acts as a preparation for the following accented dissonance that is often such an important and striking feature of this part of the *ouverture*. Lully himself made frequent use of the 6/5 chord and often, even more dramatically, the accented 6/4/2 chord. The use of this latter chord had obvious appeal for many of the German *Lullists*; for them, it became something of a trademark. They used it even more than Lully did himself. Example 6.2 shows how Bleyer was clearly aware of this; the opening bar of the *ouverture* in A 801 is as simple as possible in preparation for the dissonance and chromaticism that follows.

In his 1732 lexicon, Walther describes the second section of the Lullian *ouverture* as 'eine reguliere oder irreguliere Fuge' (a regular or irregular fugue).[9]

---

[7] M. Spaeth, 'Bleyer, Georg' in *New Grove* 2, vol. 3, pp. 697–8.

[8] Presumably as a result of watermark studies, AMA vol. 5/1 gives the date of A 801 as the last quarter of the seventeenth century, and A 847 as 'c. 1680'. See entries 116 and 117.

[9] J. Walther, *Musicalisches Lexicon Oder Musicalische Bibliothec* (Leipzig, 1732; facsm. Kassel, 1953), p. 456.

Ex. 6.2.   G. Bleyer, 'Partie â 4. â la Françoise' (*CZ-KRa* A 801), 'Ouverture'

But even if it is qualified by being 'irregular', Walther's employment of the term 'fugue' is open to question. Certainly, the second sections of the *ouverture* tended to open with the voices entering one after another, from top to bottom, in imitation, and there was usually some overlapping of entries. But after this opening, there was usually little that was genuinely contrapuntal. Bleyer's *ouverture* in A 801 does not follow the Lullian norm here; it is in three sections, each of which starts with a fresh set of imitative entries, and this unusual feature adds further weight to the argument for it being a comparatively early example of the movement type in Germany. Both the *ouvertures* of A 801 and A 847 are bi-partite structures; every every German composer, following Lully himself, seems to have regarded the brief return to the rhythms and tempo of the opening as being optional.

The dances that follow Bleyer's *ouvertures* are not as individual as some of the examples in the same composer's *Lüst-Müsic*, though they are typical of the movement types used by the German Lullists. In A 801 they are:

Bransle/Sarabande/Gavotto/Courante/Bouree/Menuet

Here, the bransle is not a complete four- or five-movement sequence, but a single dance. As we have seen, Bleyer's *Lüst-Music* contains single bransle movements rather than the complete sequence and, if the bransle was going to be used in suites by the German Lullists at all, it was often in this single-movement form. Perhaps Bleyer was influential in establishing this single-movement use of the bransle. But this is unlikely; he was probably just reflecting the gradual shift away from the bransle sequence in suites written towards the end of the seventeenth century. Unusually for the court repertoire, there is clear movement linking between the gavotte and courante.

If the dating of Bleyer's suites is uncertain, we can be certain about the date of Cousser's *Composition de musique Suivant la Methode Francoise contenant Six Ouuertures de Theatre accompagnées de plusiers Airs*; it was published in Stuttgart in 1682. Cousser was certainly one of the most influential of the German followers of Lully. Born 'Kusser', he tended to use a French version of his name, and it is telling that his entry in Johann Gottfried Walther's *Musicalisches Lexicon* is under 'Cousser', not 'Kusser'.[10] But modern writers, particularly those in Germany, have tended to ignore this. The obvious alignment with Lullian culture may be pretentious, but it was Cousser's clear preference and should be respected. As a young man, he spent time in Paris, probably in the latter half of the 1670s. Cousser was strangely reticent over this stay in Paris and any contact with music at Louis XIV's court; in the preface to *Composition de musique*, he merely states that 'Je me suis reglé a suivre sa Methode, et a entrer dans ses manieres delicates, autand qu'il m'a esté possible' (I taught myself to follow [Lully's] methods and to follow his refined manners as far as possible). However it is clear that, at the very least, he had first-hand experience of the music of Lully during this time.

According to Walther's lexicon, 'Er [Cousser] hat gantz Teutschland durchreiset, und wird nicht leicht ein Ort seyn, da er nicht bekannt geworden' (He travelled through all of Germany; there was hardly a place where he was unknown).[11] This may be an exaggeration, but, especially in courtly circles, Cousser appears to have been well known, and it seems that he did more than any other to instruct court musicians in the French manner of playing. Indeed, his mature teaching was highly regarded: according to Mattheson, 'Er war unermüdet im Unterrichten' (he was tireless in instruction) and 'Er kan zum Muster dienen' (his work was a model of its kind).[12] But this was not always the case. In 1682, the same year as

---

[10] Three of Cousser's four suite collections use 'Jean Sigismond Cousser'. The exception is *La cicala della cetra d'Eunomio* where, despite the French musical content, the title page is in Italian. The composer is named as 'Giovanni Sigismondo Cusser'. See also p. 220.

[11] Walther, *Lexicon*, p. 189.

[12] J. Mattheson, *Der vollkommene Kapellmeister* (Hamburg, 1739; facsm. Kassel, 1954), p. 481.

the publication of *Composition de musique*, Cousser took up a position at the court in Ansbach, no doubt brimming over with the experiences and education that he had received in Paris. It seems that he was charged with the task of instilling French performance practices into the playing of the *Hofkapelle* and in order to do this, instituted a regime of 'täglichen Exercitij' (daily exercises).[13] The efforts of 'der junge Cusser von Stuttgart' do not seem to have been well received by the Ansbach musicians.[14] One of the violinists Johann Andreas Mayer, went as far as making an official complaint about the daily exercises:

> 'so ich diesen ganz kurzen Strich annehmen, ich nicht allein ein künstliches solo zu spielen, gänzlich unterlassen müste, sondern auch zu kirchen- und andern vocalsachen nichts sauberes mehr mitmachen könnte'.[15] (So if these constant short bow strokes are taken up [as the norm], I cannot play an artistic solo, and I cannot join in neatly with church and other vocal pieces; so I must refrain from playing them.)

Perhaps, at this early stage of his career, the qualities of teaching so praised by Mattheson were not yet evident, and we know that Cousser was often difficult and demanding on a personal level. Indeed, Mayer's complaint may have been more about his instructor's personality than performance practice. There may also have been some factional in-fighting taking place; it is telling that Mayer cites the newly-appointed *Kapellmeister* 'Cunradi' (Johann Georg Conradi) in support of his protest. Whatever the outcome, Cousser only stayed at Ansbach for a year.

Cousser's family connection with Stuttgart became rather more formal when, after a period of touring and working at the Hamburg opera house, he was appointed *Kapellmeister* there in 1699. Before that, *Composition de musique* had been dedicated to the court's then ruler, Friedrich Carl, Duke of Württemberg and Teck.[16] It is even possible that the Francophile Friedrich Carl had financed Cousser's study trip to Paris and given some encouragement or financial assistance over the publication of the collection.[17] The tone of the dedication in *Composition de musique* is suitably modest and seems to imply patronage:

> Si ces premiers Efforts ont le bonheur de luy plaire, je les redoubleray a l'advenir pour tesmoigner a V[otre] A[ltesse] S[erenissime] que l'honneur de

---

[13] H. Scholz, *Johann Sigismund Kusser (Cousser), sein Leben und seine Werke* (Leipzig, 1911), p. 13.

[14] C. Sachs, 'Die Ansbacher Hofkapelle unter Markgraf Johann Friedrich (1672–1686)' in M. Seiffert (ed.), *Sammelbände der Internationalen Musikgesellschaft*, vol. 9 (Leipzig, 1909–1910), pp. 105–137 at p. 131.

[15] Ibid., pp. 131–2.

[16] Friedrich Carl died in 1682.

[17] See: S.K. Owens, 'The Württemberg *Hofkapelle* c.1680–1721' (Ph.D. diss., Victoria University of Wellington, 1995), p. 19.

sa Protection inspire du Courage, comme l'augmentation du Zele et du profond respect, avec lesquels je seray toutte ma Vie. (If these first efforts give pleasure, I will redouble my efforts in future in order to prove to your Serene Highness that the honour of his protection inspires courage, and gives me great zeal and profound respect, which will remain with me all my life.)

The printer was Cousser's cousin, Paul Treu and, not surprisingly, the standard of printing is high. There are few errors, and we may assume that the composer exercised some authority over the finished publication. The collection was issued as six part books: *Premier Dessus, Second Dessus, Haute-contre, Taille, Quinte* and *Bassus*. As we have seen in Chapter 1, two copies of the *Bassus* part seem to have been provided for each set and, in addition to this, the two *dessus* parts double each other for most of the time.[18] Some of the suites must surely have been played by the Ansbach *Hofkapelle*, which comprised no more than a *Kapellmeister*, six *Hofmusices*, an unspecified number of *musices*, and two 'Stadtmusikanten' (town musicians). But even with these probably limited means, Cousser's intentions are still clear: the outer parts are re-enforced in line with the normal German practice of playing French music. In the trio sections of the large-scale dances, the *Second Dessus* breaks away from the *Premier Dessus* to provide the middle line of a three-part texture (see Example 6.3).

These 'à 2 Dessus' movements are used somewhat sparingly, and the trios themselves are not complete entities in the manner of Lully's writing or even Cousser's later collections. The three-part writing is often no more than an additional layer of instrumental colouring used to balance or reiterate a phrase. For example, in the two 'Rondeau à 2 Dessus' that make up the 'Premier Air' and the 'Dixiême Air' of the fourth suite, none of the *couplets* in these two movements are entirely given over to three-part texture. The trio texture is merely used to create echo effects that are further enhanced by 'doux' markings.

Despite its ground-breaking qualities, some aspects of *Composition de musique* still follow the example of suite collections published by town musicians. But as we have seen in the previous chapter, there was nothing unusual in court musicians following the traditions of their town colleagues when it came to publishing. The suites of *Composition de musique* are grouped in ascending order of key, and the minor mode alternates with the major. Movements are mostly numbered, albeit with one important departure from the normal pattern: the *ouvertures* themselves are designated 'I – VI', but the ensuing dances of each suite are identified as 'premier air', 'second air', and so on. (See Table 6.1.)

---

[18] Unfortunately, this doubling is not made clear in the modern edition of the collection. See: R. Bayreuther (ed.), *Johann Sigismund Kusser, Suiten für Orchester*, Musikalische Denkmäler vol. 11 (Mainz, 1994).

124   *The Courtly Consort Suite in German-Speaking Europe, 1650–1706*

Ex. 6.3.   J.S. Cousser, *Composition de musique* (Stuttgart, 1682), Suite III, 'Prelude. à 2. Dessus'

Table 6.1: Contents of: J.S. Cousser *Composition de musique* (Stuttgart, 1682)

Ouverture 1er:	Ouverture /Premier Air:Rondeau / Second Air / Troisiême Air: à 2. dessûs / Quatriême Air: Ballet / Cinquiême Air / Sixiême Air: Bourée / Septiême Air: Gigue à l'Angloise / Huictiême Air: Menuet / Neufiême Air: Menuet
Ouverture II:	Ouverture /Premier Air: Viste / Second Air: Eccho / Troisiême Air: Menuet / Quatriême Air: Gigue à l'Angloise / Cinquiême Air: Courante / Sixiême Air: Menuet / Septiême Air: Sarabande / Chaconne: à 2. Dessus
Ouverture III:	Ouverture /Premier Air / Second Air / Troisiême Air: Bourée / Quatriême Air: Menuet / Prelude: à 2. Dessus / Cinquiême Air: Rondeau / Sixiême Air: Courante / Septiême Air: Menuet / Huictiême Air: Passepied
Ouverture IV:	Ouverture /Premier Air: Rondeau à 2 Dessus / Second Air: Courante / Troisiême Air: Menuet Rondeau / Quatriême Air: Menuet / Cinquiême Air: Rondeau / Sixiême Air: Bourée / Septiême Air: Menuet / Huictiême Air: Gigue a l'Angloise: Rondeau / Neufiême Air: Menuet:Rondeau / Dixiême Air: Rondeau: à 2. Dessus
Ouverture V:	Ouverture /Premier Air / Second Air: Gauotte / Troisiême Air: Un autre Gauotte / Quatriême Air: Menuet / Cinquiême Air: Menuet / Sixiême Air: Courante / Septiême Air: Gigue à l'Angloise / Huictiême Air: Menuet / Neufiême Air: Ballet / Dixiême Air: Galliarde / Onziême Air: Bourée / Douziême Air: Canary
Ouverture VI:	Ouverture /Premier Air / Second Air: Menuet, Rondeau / Troisiême Air / Branle / Branle Guay / Branle Amener / Gauotte / Courante / Menuet / Bourée / Galliarde / Traquenar

Presumably this latter nomenclature was intended to be a further reminder of the French nature of the music. Cousser's last suite again follows the town tradition of ending a collection with a bransle sequence. And while the movement-linking techniques of town musicians were not usually employed in suites in the Lullian manner, the fourth suite of *Composition de musique* contains a number of thematic similarities between the *ouverture* and some of the following dance movements. It is possible that Cousser was again following the town tradition and intended some sort of movement linking at these points, but the material is mainly triadic and not

Ex. 6.4. Cousser, *Composition de musique*, Suite III, 'Ouverture'; J.B. Lully, *Psyché* (Paris, 1720), 'Ouverture'

distinctive enough to make this intention completely clear. We can only speculate that, if Cousser was experimenting with movement linking, he did not have the experience to use the technique properly.

Each of Cousser's opening *ouvertures* is closely based on the tri- or bi-partite Lullian model. Sometimes, it seems that Cousser had specific pieces in mind. *Pysché* (LWV 56), had first been performed in Paris in 1678, and it is reasonable to assume that Cousser heard it while he was there, perhaps even while he was working on the suites for *Composition de musique*. So it is not surprising that, in keeping with his desire 'a imiter ce fameux Baptiste', the opening of 'Ouverture III' of *Composition de musique* appears to have been closely modelled, especially in harmony, on the opening of the *ouverture* to *Pysché* (see Example 6.4). However, there are times when Cousser cannot bring himself to be as harmonically dramatic as his probable mentor. The opening of the sixth *ouverture* of *Composition de musique* appears to be based on Lully's *Monsieur de Pourceaugnac* (LWV 41). But where Lully springs straight to E flat major from an opening bar entirely in the tonic G minor, Cousser is less bold. He tempers the leap with an intervening bar in the dominant. In the second sections of these *ouvertures*, the young Cousser was again cautious, sticking rigidly to the triple-time model or to a similar compound-time 6/4. The optional third section is used for three of the six *ouvertures* of the collection.

If Cousser was cautious in his treatment of the *ouverture*, the same cannot be said of the 'plusier airs' of each suite. In complete contrast to the collections by town musicians, where the same sequence of movements is often repeated throughout the collection, Cousser's movement types are richly varied and change from suite to suite. Courantes, menuets and gigues all figure prominently, but it is the rondeau, seemingly hardly used in German consort suites before this time, which appears most often amongst the 'plusiers airs'. To the more knowledgeable members of the nobility, the rondeau would be instantly recognizable as French-inspired music, and its use seems to have been a prerequisite for any German composer wishing to demonstrate his familiarity with the Lullian manner. It is surely no coincidence that Cousser used this novel movement as the 'premier air' of the first suite. In the fourth suite, the rondeau occurs in six of the ten dances following the *ouverture*, and two of the nine rondeau movements in the collection use the 'à 2. Dessus' instrumentation that Cousser reserves for the larger-scale pieces. The structure of the movement usually comprised, in four- or eight-bar sequences, an opening *grand couplet* repeated in alternation with related secondary *petite couplets*. Cousser follows this with little variation and, in the 'Dixième Air' of the fourth suite, echo sections in the *petite couplets* are used to signal the return of the *grand couplet* in the most obvious way possible. Perhaps Cousser was making sure that even the less musically literate members of his presumably noble audience fully understood the structure of the music.

Cousser may well have had his noble audience again in mind when he included a chaconne in *Composition de musique*; although there is only a single example, it is the longest and most richly scored movement in the entire collection. Given the connection between this dance and the representation of sovereign power, it was arguably, in Cousser's mind, also the most important. With its emphasis on repetition, the chaconne was a near-relative of the rondeau; indeed, some so-called chaconnes by the German Lullists are rondeaux in all but name. At the start of the seventeenth century, most composers seem to have considered the chaconne to a major key piece, and the passacaglia a minor key piece. Indeed, the distinction was still being made in France at the end of the century: Brossard says 'les Passacailles sont presque toûjours travaillées sur des Modes mineurs',[19] and the second act *divertissement* in Charpentier's *Medée* contains a chaconne in the major key followed by a 'passecaille' in the minor key.[20] Brossard also suggests that the passacaglia is slower than the chaconne ('le mouvement en est ordinairement plus grave que celuy de la Chacone'). But for some, the two terms seem to have been synonymous; even Brossard contradicts himself by suggesting that the passacaglia is 'proprement une Chacone'. In France, the repetitive bass line formula often, but not always, used by Lully and his imitators was known as the 'basse contrainte'.

The chaconne in *Composition de musique* follows Brossard's definition by using the major mode; there is also a *basse contrainte* that appears throughout the movement. Perhaps most importantly of all, it is the only movement of the collection to fully exploit the differences between trio and *tutti* instrumentation. In fact, Cousser makes the difference in sonority as wide as possible: for the only time in the collection, 'Second Dessus' has an independent part throughout, and *à 3* texture is contrasted not with the usual *à 5* but with *à 6*. Such instrumental textures are rare in Lully's music, but not unknown; it is possible that Cousser may have known movements such as the *ritournelles* in the 1661 *Ballet des Saisons* (LWV 15/3a) or the 1669 *Ballet royal de Flore* (LWV 40/15). Both juxtapose *à 3* and *à 6*. In complete contrast, it is noticeable the last two suites in *Composition de musique* have no 'à 2 Dessus' writing at all; perhaps Cousser composed these suites for occasions where fewer players were available.

Each suite in the collection has at least two menuets, and the fourth has four. This reflects the increasing popularity of the dance during the last quarter of the seventeenth century, and the menuet features strongly in the music of the German *Lullists*. Wendy Hilton has argued that, between 1673 and 1687, the menuet was 'overwhelmingly predominant' in Lully's dance music.[21] She has also suggested

---

[19] S. de Brossard, *Dictionaire de Musique, contenant une explication des termes Grecs, Latins, Italiens, & François les plus usitez dans la Musique* (Paris, 1703; facsm. F. Knuf (ed.), Hilversum, 1965), entry for 'Passacaglio, Veut dire, Passacaille'.

[20] See: G. Burgess 'The chaconne and the representation of sovereign power in Lully's *Amadis* (1684) and Charpentier's *Medée* (1693)' in S. McCleave (ed.), *Dance & music in French baroque theatre: sources & interpretations* (London, 1996), pp. 81–104 at pp. 86–88.

[21] W. Hilton, *Dance and music of court and theater, selected writings of Wendy Hilton* (Stuyvesant, New York, 1997), p. 37.

that the courante 'lost its place of favor to the minuet during the 1660s'.[22] If the latter is correct, the transition in Germany seems to have been somewhat slower, and the menuet does not appear to have supplanted the courante as an appendix to the bransle sequence.

It is noticeable that *Composition de musique* does not contain any movements that suggest dramatic characterisation or narrative. These 'character' movements became very popular with the German Lullists and are a feature of Cousser's own collections from 1700. This may suggest that, despite the reference to 'Ouvertures de Theatre' on the collection's title page, that *Composition de musique* was written and conceived purely as a collection of instrumental music without any specific links to the dramatic stage. Paul Whitehead does not think so, and has suggested that the collection, along with others by Muffat and Aufschnaiter had its origins in specific, staged events.[23] But there is no evidence that Cousser composed any music for the stage during his time in Paris or immediately on his return to Germany, and Whitehead's suggestion does not take into account the sixth suite's bransle sequence with its ballroom associations. While it is not impossible that *Composition de musique* did have its origins in works for the stage, the absence of character movements and the apparent absence of dramatic music from this part of Cousser's career suggest that this is not the case. Finally, we should not forget that 'der junge Cusser von Stuttgart' was only twenty-two when *Composition de musique* was published. It makes the ground-breaking qualities of this collection seem all the more remarkable.

Eighteen years elapsed before Cousser put any more suite collections into print. During this time, after a prolonged period of travel and the post of opera director in Hamburg, he returned to Stuttgart in 1698 as *Kapellmeister*. This may not have been the happiest of situations; Cousser was obliged at one point to share the duties of the post with Theodor Schwartzkopff and Johann Störl.[24] However, it did not stop him from issuing no less than three large-scale suite collections in the same year of 1700: *Festin des muses*, *La cicala della cetra d'Eunomio* and *Apollon enjoüé*. The printer was again Cousser's Stuttgart cousin, Paul Treu.

All three collections are firmly in the German-Lullian style that he had done so much to establish and, like *Composition de musique*, are all described on their title pages as 'Ouvertures de Theatre accompagnées de plusiers Airs'. But there are a number of significant differences between the 1682 and 1700 collections. As well as containing far more ornamentation than *Composition de musique*, the three 1700 collections all have parts for a bassoon and two oboes. As James R. Anthony has pointed out, 'the ubiquitous *trio des hautbois* (two oboes and bassoon) was ideal for pastoral scenes and for achieving marked color contrast when used

---

[22] Ibid., p. 360.
[23] P. Whitehead, 'Austro-German Printed Sources of Instrumental Music, 1630 to 1700', (Ph.D. diss., University of Pennsylvania, 1996), p. 46.
[24] Owens 'Württemberg *Hofkapelle*', p. 67.

in alternation with the string orchestra'.[25] In Cousser's trios, the oboes play independently of each other, but, in all other places, the second oboe doubles the first oboe that in turn doubles the *dessus* violin part. In similar fashion, the bassoon doubles the string bass parts.[26] This use of the oboes and bassoon to reinforce the treble and bass parts once again shows the strength of the tradition of doubling the outer lines in French dance music. However, *Apollon enjoüé* contains numerous differences in the treatment of the bassoon. For example, in the first suite of the collection, the trio to the passepied is scored for two oboes and *Basse de violon*. But in the trio sections of the rondeau from the same suite, the string bass is silent and the bassoon provides the bass to the two oboes. In the second suite, the low C of the instrument is deliberately avoided in the eighth movement ('Air') but is used freely elsewhere. All this suggests that Cousser was compelled to use players of widely differing abilities and further illustrates how he seems to have drawn on music written at different times and for different situations.

The suites in the 1700 collections are noticeably longer than those from 1682: there are sequences of as many as seventeen movements. For example, the second suite from *Apollon enjoüé* has the following:

Ouverture/Les Chasseurs/Branle de Village qui se joüe alt./Trio/Rondeau/Trio/ Les Indiens/Air/ Bourée/Les Furies/Choeur/Gique/Gavotte/Ritournelle à 3/ Rejoüissance/Marche/Menuet Chaconne

Long sequences of movements were common in sequences of excerpts taken from Lully's dramatic music: the *Ouverture avec tous les airs de violons de L'opera de Persée* published in Amsterdam by Heus in 1682 has twenty-nine movements, and there are twenty-five movements in Pointel's *Tous les airs de violon de l'opera d'Amadis*, issued in 1684. But Cousser may also have been influenced by a similar trend in suite collections published in France. For example, the first suite of Marin Marais' 1692 *Pièces en trio pour les flutes, violon, & dessus de viola* has eleven movements and the second suite thirteen. In all three 1700 collections, Cousser makes frequent use of the *alternativement* A-B-A sequence of dances even though he did not do so in 1682. Occasionally, the number of *alternativement* movements is extended to three. The third suite of *Festin des muses* contains this typical sequence, which seems to have its origins in the sequences of 'en suite' dances discussed in earlier chapters:

Gavotte, qui se joüe alternativement avec les deux suivantes/2me Gavotte/3me Gavotte

---

[25] J.R. Anthony, *French Baroque Music from Beaujoyeulx to Rameau* (3rd edn., Portland, Oregon, 1997), p. 127.

[26] There is no extant 'basse de violon' part in *La cicala della cetra d'Eunomio*. However, restoring this lost part is a simple matter of doubling the bassoon in the appropriate places.

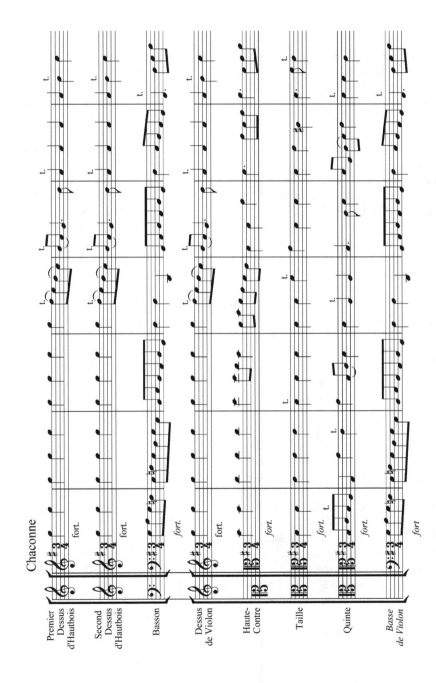

Ex. 6.5. J.S. Cousser, *La cicala* (Stuttgart, 1700), Suite I, 'Chaconne'

The rondeau format is used throughout the three collections, but there are times when Cousser seems to use it as a way of extending weak material. The rondeau in the second suite of *Apollon enjoüé* has little more than a rising sequence of repeated notes in the *grand couplet* and the two trio sections of the *petite couplet* offer little more. Cousser is less sparing in his use of the chaconne than he was in *Composition de musique*: there are three examples in *Apollon enjoüé*, four in *Festin des muses* and two in *La cicala*. The opening of the lengthy chaconne from the first suite of *La cicala* is given in Example 6.5. Most of the movement is made up of simple repetitions of unrelated four- or eight-bar phrases. Although it is hinted at in the bass line, there is no *basse contrainte* or use of rondeau-style *couplets*.

The fourth suite of *Apollon enjoüé* contains probably the most ambitious chaconne that Cousser ever wrote. It has some unusual features. Instead of the normal triple metre for this dance, it has a ₵ time signature, and prominent use is made of a solo oboe. A *basse contrainte*, often varied, is used throughout. The movement has two principal sections: the first in the major key, and the second in the minor; the first sixteen bars are repeated at the end of the movement. Cousser also makes considerable use of repetition, but not by simple repeating four- or eight-bar phrases. In each of the three sixteen-bar phrases that make up the first section of this chaconne, an eight-bar phrase for solo oboe and the *basse de violon* is repeated as a fully harmonized version by the whole ensemble. The second section, in the minor key, mostly follows a similar pattern. But instead of a solo oboe and bass, there are trios for a combination of two oboes with the two unison violas providing the bass line. These trios are, as in the major-key section, given fully harmonized *tutti* repeats.

In other trios in the collections, Cousser is more content to imitate Lully. Example 6.6 compares the trio 'Ritournelle pour Mercure' from the first act of Lully's 1680 *Proserpine* (LWV 58) with the 'Ritournelle à 3' from the second suite of *Apollon enjoüé*. It is not only the movement titles that are similar: rhythms and points of imitation all suggest that Cousser had trios such as the one from *Proserpine* clearly in mind when it came to writing his own.

All three 1700 collections contain 'character' movements with quasi-programmatic titles that are clearly meant to suggest a dramatic origin. Example 6.7 shows the opening of 'Vole de Demons' (Demon tricks) from the fourth suite of *Festin des muses* and, given the link with the theatre often proclaimed on the title pages of German *Lullist* suite collections, the inclusion of these quasi-dramatic movements is hardly surprising.

Some movements may have been given titles merely to give the impression of dramatic origin, but some of them do indeed come from Cousser's operas written during the 1690s. *Julia* (1690) is now lost, but five movements survive in manuscript Cod. Guelf. 295 Mus. Hdschr. in the Herzog August Bibliothek in Wolfenbüttel where they are entitled 'De l'Opera de Julie'. Three of these excerpts from *Julia* also appear in *La cicala*. In addition to this, two movements in *Apollon Enjoüé* ('Les Chasseurs' in the second suite, and 'Gique' in the fifth) have their origins in *Adonis*, probably written around 1699 and recently rediscovered by Samantha Owens.[27]

Given the absence of character movements from *Composition de musique*, what prompted Cousser to use this type of material in these later collections? There appears to have been a trend at the end of the seventeenth century to include quasi-dramatic movements in suites on a more regular basis; they feature prominently in the second volume of Muffat's *Florilegium*, published in 1698, and this may have influenced Cousser. But there may have been another, more pressing, reason for Cousser to reuse older material: even with constant use of the musicians of the Würtemberg *Hofkapelle* as copyists during the year leading up to their publication, the effort required to produce enough material for no less than three collections of suites must have been considerable, especially as he was also engaged in writing new operas.[28] We may suspect that the inclusion of movements extracted from his stage works may have been nothing more than a labour-saving device.

Cousser's quasi-dramatic movements enjoy varying degrees of success. 'Les Chasseurs' from *Apollon Enjoüé* is suitably bucolic, and the uneven strains and phrase lengths in 'Les Jardiniers' (first suite, *La cicala*) appear to be a wry portrait of ill-educated court labourers. 'Les Porteurs de Flambeaux' (also in the first suite of *La cicala*) is clearly meant to portray the touch bearers who were an essential of many royal processions, and the music is accordingly similar in style to an *ouverture* with a dotted-rhythm opening section and a triple-time second section. The rushing ascending scales at the opening are surely meant to represent tongues of flame (see Example 6.8), and this is one of Cousser's best essays in the genre.

On the other hand, there are movements such as 'Les Indiens' (second suite, *Apollon Enjoüé*) where any degree of exotic characterisation seems to be entirely absent. The bransle sequence is noticeably absent in the later collections. Like Bleyer, Cousser uses a single 'branle de village' in two of the suites in *Apollon enjoüé*, but even this single movement is absent from *La cicala* and *Festin des muses*.

The musical quality of these 1700 collections is uneven, and there are times when the music in them appears rather mundane and poverty of invention is only too obvious. Given the apparent haste in which the collections were put together, this is hardly surprising. On the other hand, we have seen that the chaconne from the fourth suite of the same collection shows Cousser to be capable of reaching the highest levels of accomplishment.

In 1681, a year before Cousser's Ansbach appointment, Philipp Heinrich Erlebach was appointed *Kapellmeister* at the Rudolstadt court. But unlike Cousser, Muffat, Mayr and Johann Fischer, he does not seem to have spent any time in Paris, and all his musical education appears to have been in Germany. His *VI. Ouvertures, Begleitet mit ihren darzu schicklichen airs, nach Französischer*

---

[27] S. Owens, 'The Stuttgart *Adonis*: a recently discovered opera by Johann Sigismund Cousser', *The Musical Times*, vol. 147 (2006), pp. 67–80.

[28] Owens 'Württemberg *Hofkapelle*', p. 61.

Ex. 6.6. J-B. Lully, *Proserpine* (Paris, 1680), 'Ritournelle pour Mercure'; J.S. Cousser, *Apollon enjoüé* (Stuttgart, 1700), Suite II, 'Ritournelle à 3'

Ex. 6.7. J.S. Cousser, *Festin des muses* (Stuttgart, 1700), Suite IV, 'Vole de Demons'

Ex. 6.8.   Cousser, *La cicala*, Suite I, 'Les Porteurs de Flambeaux'

Art und Manier were issued in Nuremberg in 1693 and *VI. Sonate à Violino e Viola da Gamba col suo Basso Continuo* followed a year later. It is unlikely that Horn's 1663 *Parergon musicum* was known at the Rudolstadt court, but, rather in the manner of these two volumes (see page 23), Erlebach's two collections are clearly meant to be seen as a contrasting pair.[29] The French *ouvertures* and airs for

---

[29]   Horn's volumes are not listed in the inventory of Rudolstadt court music drawn up by Erlebach himself. (ThStA Rudolstadt, Geheimes Archiv B VII 4c Nr.2.)

five-part consort are contrasted with trios in the Italian manner, and the preface to *VI. Sonate* draws attention to this. Erlebach also complains about a lack of 'Musicalischen Conventen'. Presumably, these 'conventions' were bowings and performance matters relating to the French style.

Cousser's *Composition de musique* seems to have provided the initial model for *VI. Ouvertures*. The latter's preface talks of 'Ouverturen nebst deren Suiten' (*ouvertures* next to their suites), just as Cousser labels his collection as 'Six Ouvertures de Theatre accompagnées de plusiers Airs'; in addition, the suites of *VI. Ouvertures* are grouped in ascending order of key, an order that is identical to that of *Composition de musique*:

A minor/B flat major/C major/D minor/F major/G minor

Both collections use movement numbering and layouts that are broadly similar. The title 'Air' is used as a generic term for dances, and there are clear similarities of instrumentation. *VI. Ouvertures* was issued as six part books; apart from trio sections, 'Premier Dessus' and 'Second Dessus' double each other giving the expected five-part texture with a reinforced top part.[30] Given that such instrumentation was part of an established German-Lullist tradition by the 1690s, Erlebach may have been following this rather than specifically imitating *Composition de musique*. But the opening of Erlebach's first *ouverture* movement is, without question, based on the opening of Cousser's first *ouverture* in *Composition de musique*. Perhaps Erlebach was paying deliberate homage (The two movement openings are given in Example 6.9). There is frequent use of trio textures throughout *VI Ouvertures* and this brings considerable variety. But in the second section of the *ouverture* to the first suite, Erlebach introduces a curious variant to the traditional concept of trio. The music at this point is marked 'trio', but it is not in three parts. Instead, there are four. 'Trio' is clearly meant in this instance to represent nothing more than a solo passage for a number of instruments; it obviously did not always have numerical significance for Erlebach.

As in most German-Lullian collections, the suites in *VI. Ouvertures* are clearly ordered and defined, even if they use quite differing sequences of dances each time. The contents of each suite are detailed in Table 6.2.

Apart from the progression in the third suite of 'Air la Plainte'/'Air de Sommiel'/'Air La Rejouissance', Erlebach uses similar dance types to Cousser. There is no apparent movement linking of the type found in suite collections by town musicians, but Bernd Baselt has suggested three kinds of 'thematic organisation' that link

---

[30] In the two surviving exemplars (in *D-WD* and *PL-Kj*), there is no evidence that the collection was ever issued with an extra copy of the bass part in the manner of *Composition de musique*.

Ex. 6.9. Ouverture openings in P. Erlebach, *VI. ouvertures* (Nuremberg, 1693), Suite I and Cousser, *Composition de musique*, Suite I

Table 6.2: Contents of: P.H. Erlebach, *VI Ouvertures, Begleitet mit ihren darzu schicklichen airs, nach Französischer Art und Manier* (Nuremberg, 1693)

Ouverture /1.Air Entrèe / 2.Air Menuet.I / 3.Air Menuet II / 4.Air Bourèe / 5.Air Courante / 6.Air / 7. Air Menuet qui se jouë alternativement avec le Trio / 8. Air Trio / 9. Air Gique / 10. Air Sarabande
Ouverture /1.Air Entrèe / 2.Air Courante / 3.Air Ballet / 4.Air Menuet qui se jouë alternativement avec le suivant / 5.Air Trio / 6.Air / 7.Air Sarabande / 8.Air Trio / 9. Chaconne
Ouverture /1.Air / 2.Air Bourèe / 3.Air / 4.Air Menuet qui se jouë alternativement avec le suivant / 5.Air Menuet Trio / 6.Air Courante / 7.Air Trio / 8.Air Ballet / 9.Air Gavotte / 10.Air la Plainte / 11.Air de Sommiel / 12.Air La Rejouissance.
Ouverture /1.Air Gavotte / 2.Air Menuet I / 3.Air Menuet II / 4. Air Bourèe / 5.Air Courante / 6.Air Entrèe / 7.Air Gavotte / 8.Air Traquenar / 9.Air
Ouverture /1.Air Entreè / 2.Air qui se jouë alternativement avec le Trio / 3.Air Trio / 4.Air Courante / 5.Air Bourèe / 6.Air Marche / 7.Air Rondeau. / 8.Chaconne
Ouverture /1.Air Entrèe / 2.Air Gavotte / 3.Air Menuet qui se jouë alternativement avec le Trio / 4. Air Trio / 5.Air la Plainte / 6.Air Entrèe / 7.Air Gique / 8.Chaconne

the openings of the *ouvertures* that start each suite.[31] He identifies these thematic characteristics as 'the falling interval of a fourth (*ouvertures* I and VI)', 'the rising interval of a fifth (*ouvertures* II and IV)' and 'a diatonic upward progression of notes comprising sequential dotted quavers (*ouvertures* III and IV)'.[32] He goes on to suggest that Erlebach may have intended a 'possible performance in pairs' for the two *ouvertures* in each of his categories.[33] There are reasons to doubt these suggestions. Thematic linking of movements was comparatively rare in suites by the German *Lullists*, and the linking of movements across suites would seem to be otherwise unknown in this repertoire. Example 6.10 shows the opening of

---

[31] B. Baselt, 'Philipp Heinrich Erlebach und seine VI Ouvertures, begleitet mit ihren darzu schicklichen Airs, nach französischer Art und Manier (Nürnberg, 1693)' in G. Fleischhauer, W. Ruf, B. Siegmund, F. Zschoch (eds.), *Michaelsteiner Konferenzberichte*, vol. 49, (Michaelstein 1996), pp. 9–30 at p. 23.

[32] Ibid., 23.

[33] Ibid., 24.

the sixth *ouverture* of the set; one that Baselt categorises as using a descending interval of a fourth.

Ex. 6.10.   Erlebach, *VI. ouvertures*, Suite VI, 'Ouverture'

It is true that the first two notes of the first violin part are a perfect fourth apart, but this interval is surely dictated by Erlebach's obvious desire to remain on the tonic chord in preparation for the characteristically dissonant 6/4/2 chord that follows. As I have already pointed out, the German Lullists frequently used this particular harmonic device at this point in their *ouvertures*. In all six of Erlebach's opening movements, the melodic line of the opening section appears to be subservient to the harmony, and this can be seen at the very start of the collection (see Example 6.9 above) where the melody is governed by the harmonic progression of the first three chords. If there is any similarity between the opening movements in Erlebach's collection, it appears to be a result of the type of harmonic progressions frequently used in the *ouvertures* of the German Lullists. It is not likely to have been a deliberate attempt at thematic unity. Apart from his trio suites issued in 1694, *VI Ouvertures* was the only collection of suites that Erlebach published. I have not been able to find any further examples of his suites in manuscript sources, but the '47 Partien' mentioned in Erlebach's Rudolstadt court inventory suggest that there may well have been more.

Johann Caspar Fischer's *Le journal du printems* was published in 1695 in Augsburg. Like Erlebach, Fischer was a court musician; he seems to have received all his musical education in Germany although, as we shall see, this view has recently been challenged. In the late 1680s, he was appointed *Kapellmeister* at Schlackenwerth. The collection's preface, entitled 'Admonito ad Philomusum' is brief, mostly limiting itself to basic information on tempi, repeats and time signatures. For example, the advice on playing the *ouvertures* is as follows: 'Tertiò attende in Ouverturis, ut secundam partem velociori motu aut mensurâ quàm primam inchoës' (thirdly: in the *ouvertures*, ensure that you begin the second section with a faster movement or measure than the first). Fischer's collection is hardly less in the German-Lullian tradition than Muffat's, and the brevity of his observations appears to suggest that, unlike Muffat, he expected his pieces to be played in the correct manner without much in the way of further comment.

The major difference between *Le journal du printems* and other collections in the German-Lullian tradition is the inclusion of trumpet parts in the opening and closing suites. The trumpets do not play in every movement, and, even when they do, there is no independent writing for them. The first trumpet doubles the upper string part and the second trumpet doubles, as far as it is able to, the *haute contre* part. This leads, in the latter, to frequent use of the B natural below the eighth partial, which players could produce by the technique known as 'lipping'. Fischer refers to them on the title page as 'Trompettes à plaisir': perhaps they were added as an afterthought.

Inka Stampfl has unfavourably compared *Le journal du printems* with suites by Muffat.[34] For example, in the first section of the *ouverture* to Fischer's final suite, she considers the succession of eight-bar phrases using the same or similar material to be a weakness. Certainly, Muffat would not have repeated material in this way when writing for strings, but we have no examples of *ouvertures* by Muffat that include trumpet parts. Trumpet music in its lower register was, of necessity, mostly triadic, and Fischer's harmonic language at this point is certainly simple. The first and second eight bar phrases at the start of the final *ouverture* are for strings alone, and they are then repeated with the addition of trumpets.

---

[34] I. Stampfl, *Georg Muffat Orchesterkompositionen. Ein musikhistorischer Vergleich der Orchestermusik 1670–1710* (Passau, 1984), p. 118.

A similar phrase structure is found at the start of the *ouverture* to the first suite, which again employs trumpets. It was presumably Fischer's deliberate intention at both these points not only to accommodate the trumpets, but to produce a grand effect by the simplest of means. It is telling that, where trumpets are not involved, he can be far more imaginative in rhythm and phrase structure. For example, the opening of the second *ouverture* has all the subtlety of rhythm and phrase structure that Stampfl admires in the *ouvertures* of Muffat. It also shows that Fischer, like Cousser and Muffat, had recognised and mastered Lully's use of dissonance in the opening sections of the *ouvertures* in *Le journal du printems*. Elsewhere, it is the influence of Cousser rather than Lully that seems to be evident in the collection. For example, the sixth suite of Fischer's collection mirrors the sixth suite of Cousser's *Composition de musique* in its combination of *ouverture* suite and bransle suite.

A manuscript source of *Le journal du printems* exists in the Philidor collection (*F-Pn* Rés. F. 529).[35] The manuscript does not carry any reference to composer or collection title, but all eight suites of the collection are included. There are few differences between the manuscript source and printed parts and this has prompted Herbert Schneider to suggest that 'both sources are fundamentally based on the same primary source or alternatively that the score copy was a later copy of the printed parts'.[36] It seems rather unlikely that a 'primary source' for a printed edition in Germany was also in circulation as a source in Paris, but it does seem clear that Rés. F. 529 was copied from a set of individual parts. The manuscript copyist was perhaps rather inexperienced; there are many slips that a more watchful eye might have corrected. For example, the first suite of the collection, bar 23 of 'Air des Combattans' contains an erroneous c sharp in the *haute-contre* against a c natural in the bass part. But the same error is also in the separate printed parts, where its presence would be far harder to spot; indeed, the error may even have come from the printed edition. The twelfth bar of the *ouverture* to the first suite shows that copyist did not anticipate the bass having more notes than the other parts at this point. As a result, he did not allow enough space when he ruled the bar line, and the bass part has had to be squashed in as best it can.[37] This is a typical error by a copyist, especially an inexperienced one, working from a set of parts; it seems unlikely that any 'primary source' is involved here, it is far more likely that Rés. F. 529 is nothing more than a copy of the printed edition.

If this is the case, how did this set of printed parts presumably get to Paris? Of course, it is possible that a musician or member of the German nobility may have taken the music on a visit to France. But Schneider has also pointed to the rarity of non-French music in the Philidor collection, and he goes on to suggest that the

---

[35] H. Schneider, 'J. C. F. Fischers Orchestersuiten, ihre Quellen und stilistische Einordnung' in L. Fischer (ed.), *J. C. F. Fischer in seiner Zeit: Tagungsbericht Rastatt 1988* (Frankfurt am Main, 1994), pp. 83–4.

[36] Ibid., p.84.

[37] This page can be seen online at BnF Gallica: http://gallica.bnf.fr/ark:/12148/bpt6k103679p/f2.cheminderfer

presence of *Le journal du printems* implies that Fischer was 'known personally in Paris'. Accordingly, the collection is 'an apprentice work' composed 'under [the instruction of] the master Lully', which then 'must have taken on a highly-important role at court'.[38] Of course, Schneider may be correct, but he does not attempt to explain why Fischer had his music included in the Philidor manuscripts whereas other Germans who studied in Paris did not. While it is still difficult to explain the existence of this French source, it is rather more likely that Fischer's printed collection found its way to Paris; he himself remained in Germany.

Zodiaci musici in XII partitas balleticas was published in Augsburg in 1698. The composer of *Zodiaci musici* is partially anonymous, only being identified as 'J.A.S.'. Publishers' compilations such as those issued by Wust in Frankfurt am Main or Roger in Amsterdam often withheld the identity of composers, but it was rare for printed collections devoted to the work of one composer to be issued anonymously. Even where work was issued under a pseudonym, clues to the identity of the composer were often provided at some point during the collection.

Despite his anonymity, J.A.S clearly intended his collection to be seen as an example of the Lullian manner, and the suites are also described on the title as 'Balletischen Parthyen' (balletic suites). The preface to refers the reader for information concerning performance practice to three printed editions by 'berühmten Auctoribus' (well-known authors): Fischer's *Le Journal de printems*, 'Balletischen Bleum-Bunds' (presumably J.C.F. Fischer's Augsburg 1696 keyboard collection, *Musicalisches Blumen-Büschlien*), and Rupert Mayr's *Pythagorische Schmids-Fincklein* (Augsburg, 1692).[39] But J.A.S. seems to stand outside the mainstream German-Lullian tradition. Unlike other printed suite collections by German *Lullists*, the contents of *Zodiaci musici* are carefully organized. The preface makes this organization quite clear: 'so in 6. Parthyen jede zu 8. Stuck eingerichtet/bestehet' (there are six suites, each made up of eight pieces). Each suite starts with an *ouverture*, and the following dance sequences all begin with an *entrée* or an allemande. Although collections such as *Composition de musique* show a degree of careful organization, this amount is rare in the German-Lullist suite.

Clearly, J.A.S. was an extremely competent composer. Example 6.11 gives the first strain of the allemande from the fourth suite, and it shows the care taken to vary the texture of the music.

We should also notice that imitation – a typical feature of the allemande – is not used at the start of the strain in the normal way, but halfway through. This interest in instrumental texture is apparent throughout the collection, and further highlighted by the frequent use of solo instruments. Most unusually, the opening of the *ouverture* of the third suite is given over to solo violin, *violetta* and viola. There are no movements that, by their titles suggest a dramatic origin; after the allemande or *entrée*, J.A.S. is mostly content to employ the same type of dances

---

[38] Schneider, 'J. C. F. Fischers Orchestersuiten', p. 84.
[39] Mayr's collection is considered in detail in the following chapter.

as the other German-Lullists. There is one exception: the final suite includes a movement entitled 'melodie'. This makes use of repetition in the way of a rondeau or chaconne, but with a much freer structure.

Ex. 6.11.   J.A.S., *Zodiaci musici* (Augsburg, 1698), Suite IV, 'Allemande'

Likes Bleyer's suite in manuscript *CZ-KRa* A 847, the very high range of the *violetta* part throughout the collection would seem to indicate the use of a violin rather than the customary viola, and the preface suggests that outer parts can be duplicated in the usual French manner:

> Worbey sonderbahr zu merken/daß die Violin und Violon vor denen andern 2. Mittel-Geigen/benanntlich der Violett und Alt Viola mercklich zubestetzen/und zu duplieren: (whereby, you are especially to note that the Violin and *Violon* should be brought out and duplicated in preference to the two middle parts, namely the *violett* and alto Viola).

But, there is a slight departure from the norm of re-enforcing both treble and bass when the preface also warns that 'die Violin allezeit umb eines mehr/dann der Violon verstärcket werde' (at all times, the violin should be re-enforced more than the *violon*). However, the opening of the *ouverture* to the fourth suite could come from any collection by a German *Lullist*: the first bar, entirely in the tonic, leads straight to an accented 6/4/2 dissonance on the first beat of the second bar. Clearly, J.A.S. was familiar with the idiom, even if he did not choose slavishly to follow it.

The issue of the composer's identity seemed to have been solved by Ernst von Werra in 1902 when he identified J.A.S. as being J.A. Schmierer on the basis of an attribution in the third volume of Göhler's Frankfurt and Leipzig trade-fair catalogues.[40] Apart from contact with Augsburg, little is known about Schmierer, but the case for von Werra's identification is obviously a strong one, and it is now generally assumed that Schmierer is the composer of *Zodiaci musici*. However, there are mistakes in the Leipzig and Frankfurt catalogues, and we have no way of knowing if their attribution was based on genuine knowledge or hearsay. We should not ignore other possibilities for the identification of J.A.S.

One possible candidate is Johann Speth, the cathedral organist in Augsburg. It appears that he was interested in German-Lullian music and he championed J.C.F. Fischer's music in Augsburg. Prior to publication, Speth introduced *Le journal du printems* to the Augsburg Cathedral authorities and apparently introduced Fischer to the Augsburg publishers, Lorenz Kroninger and Gottlieb Göbel.[41] Speth's only known instrumental publication is the collection of keyboard music, *Ars magna consoni et dissoni* (Augsburg, 1693), and an extract from its 'Toccata secunda' is given in Example 6.12 along with the opening of the second section of the *ouverture* to the second suite of *Zodiaci musici*. For ease of comparison, the latter has been set out in keyboard score.

The similarities between the two are intriguing, but probably not significant; there are many *ouvertures* by the German *Lullists* with this type of writing. However, the example does show that Speth was certainly competent enough as a composer to be responsible for *Zodiaci musici*. Given Speth's lack of first-hand experience of court music making, the departures in the collection from the

---

[40] E. Von Werra (ed.), *Orchestermusik*, DDT vol. 10 (Leipzig, 1902, repr. Graz, 1958), preface, vi–vii. Göhler, vol. 3, entry 405: 'J.A. Schmicerer (*sic*), Schmierers (*sic*) Zodiaci musici in XII Partitas Ballericas (*sic*), pars prima'. The publication date is wrongly given as 1699.

[41] J. Speth, *Ars magna consoni et dissoni*, T. Fedtke (ed.) (Kassel, 1973), preface.

normal Lullist manner may be another pointer to his authorship. In his search for the identity of J. A. S., von Werra had considered Speth, but rejected him on the grounds of name. Speth is only given the one forename of 'Johanne' in *Ars magna consoni et dissoni*, and there is no mention of a middle name. However, our knowledge of Speth is scant and we cannot be completely sure that he had no other forename apart from 'Johanne'. Given the attribution in the trade catalogues, Schmierer is still the most likely candidate for the authorship of *Zodiaci musici*, but it is unwise to put him forward without reservation as the composer of the collection. The first volume of *Zodiaci musici* appears to have been reissued in 1705 and reprinted 1710, and a second volume, now lost, followed in 1710.[42]

Ex. 6.12.   J. Speth, *Ars magna consoni et dissoni* (Augsburg, 1693), 'Toccata secunda'; J.A.S., *Zodiaci musici*, Suite II, 'Ouverture'

The description of the suites in *Zodiaci musici* as 'partitas balleticas' was probably little more than a means of heralding the Lullian influence over the collection. We have no way of knowing if any of the pieces in the collection were

---

[42]   Göhler, vol. 3, entries 406–407, p. 409.

ever danced. But in contrast, all the music in manuscript *A-Wn* Mus. Hs. 19 171, 'L'Eraclio/Arie per i Sudetti Balli ... Da Melchiore D'Ardespin Consigliere e Maestro de Concerti Di S: A: E: 1690', came from the stage. *L'Eraclio* was one of a series of operas written for the Munich court by the *Kapellmeister*, Giuseppe Antonio Bernabei, and D'Ardespin provided the music for the ballets at the end of each act. We shall see in Chapter 9 that it was common practice in Vienna for ballet music to be written by a different composer from the opera itself. Clearly, the same thing happened in Munich. The elegant manuscript, only in score, is dedicated to Leopold I in Vienna. The music in Mus. Hs. 19 171 comprises a sinfonia followed by ballet music, which itself is clearly divided up into 'Ballo Dopp'il Atto Primo', 'Ballo Dopp'il Atto Secondo' and 'Ballo Dopp'il Atto Terzo'. There are four dance movements in each ballet, and each ballet has a single key centre. The contents are listed in Table 6.3.

Table 6.3: Contents of: 'L'Eraclio, Arie per i Sudetti Balli ... Da Melchiore D'Ardespin Consigliere e Maestro de Concerti Di S: A: E: 1690' (*A-Wn* Mus. Hs. 19 171)

Act	Movement titles	Key
Ballo Dopp'il Atto Primo	Sinfonia/entree/gigue/menuet/rondeau	D major
Ballo Dopp'il Atto Secondo	Menuet/gigue/entrée/aria	F major
Ballo Dopp'il Atto Terzo	Aria/bouree/entree/chaccone	B flat major

Despite its title, the sinfonia is clearly a Lullian *ouverture* with its dotted rhythms and sharp accented dissonance in the second bar (see Example 6.13). Perhaps it was the *ouverture* to the entire opera. The dances themselves are equally in the French manner. The rondeau of the first act ballet has a *grand couplet* and two secondary *couplets*; the gigue in the same sequence is the canarie variety, and two of the three ballets include a menuet. The lengthy and magnificent concluding chaconne, complete with *basse contrainte*, could well have been the concluding movement of the entire opera.

The dances listed in Table 6.3 are no different from the dances that are found in many of the German-Lullian suites that I have discussed in this and the previous chapter. Our knowledge of the conditions surrounding the performances of these suites is still far from complete, and we can only assume that D'Ardespin's music was meant for purely instrumental performance once it reached Vienna. But if the dances in *L'Eraclio* are typical of the ballets frequent added to operas given at the German courts, then they show how the close link between the music of the suite and the music of the dramatic stage was maintained right up to the end of the seventeenth century.

Ex. 6.13.　　M. D'Ardespin, 'L'Eraclio/Arie per i Sudetti Balli' (*A-Wn* Mus. Hs. 19 171), 'Sinfonia'

Chapter 7
Verschiedenen Ouverturen, Chaconnen, lustigen Suiten
The German Lullists – II

If 1700 was the final year of Cousser's suite publications, it was the first year of Johann Fischer's. It seems that the name 'Johann Fischer' was common in the German lands at the end of the seventeenth century. At least three composers with the name Fischer were working in the area during the 1690s: a Johann Fischer of Vratislavia, Johann Caspar Ferdinand Fischer and the Augsburg-born Johann Fischer. It was Augsburg-born Fischer who spent time in Paris in the 1660s before the arrival of Cousser and, according to Eitner, worked as one of Lully's copyists.[1] It is his suites that I shall now discuss; they include the last published collections of suites by a German musician that worked in Paris during Lully's time. They also, as a body of material, contain arguably some of the best music by any of the German Lullists.

After periods of employment in Stuttgart and Augsburg, Fischer arrived at the court in Ansbach were he must have worked briefly with Cousser before the latter departed in 1683. From 1690 to 1697, he worked at the court of Duke Friedrich Casimir of Kurland in Mitau. It has been suggested that this was as a violinist, but there is evidence indicating that he was more than this.[2] In a manuscript of dance movements for recorder and bass, he is described as being 'Jean Fischer sy Devant Maitre de Chapelle de S. A. S. Monseigneur le Duc de Courlande',[3] and the title page of Fischer's *Musicalisch Divertissement* (Dresden, 1699–1700) similarly describes the composer as being 'gewesener Fürstl. Churländischer Capellmeister' (the former *Kapellmeister* of the Churland court). Fischer held the position of *Kapellmeister* at the Schwerin court of Duke Friedrich Wilhelm of Mecklenburg between 1701 and 1704, and he later held the same post at the court of Philipp Wilhelm of Brandenburg-Schwedt.

---

[1] Eitner lists the latter as 'Johann Fischer III': R. Eitner, *Biographisch-Bibliographisches Quellen-Lexikon der Muskier und Musikgelehrten der Christlichen Zeitrechnung bis zur Mitte des neunzehnten Jahrhunderts* (11 vols, Leipzig, 1900–1904; repr. Graz, 1959), vol. 3, pp. 464–5.

[2] G. Beechey, 'Fischer, Johann' in *New Grove* 2, vol. 8, p. 893.

[3] Manuscript *D-SWl* Mus. 1873.

It has also been suggested that Fischer was 'an important pioneer in requiring *scordatura* tunings'.[4] The evidence does not appear to support this. There are only two works by Fischer that require such tuning: the sacred collection *Himmlischen Seelenlust* (Nuremberg, 1686) and manuscript suite *S-Uu* IMhs 015:012 that has the somewhat whimsical title 'Das Eins-Drey und Drey Eins oder habile Violiste' (The one-in-three and three-in-one, or the skilful *violiste*).[5] The suite can only be described as something of a circus piece, designed to do nothing more than show off the virtuosity of the player who is expected to play, in turn, two violins and a viola. Each violin is in a different *scordatura* tuning, and the viola part, also in *scordatura* tuning, is written out as a transposing instrument in the treble clef. There are suitable, albeit brief, breaks in the music for the player to change instruments. 'Das Eins-Drey' may be a highly individual and even amusing work, but it hardly demonstrates pioneering attributes in *scordatura* string playing.

Apart from 'Das Eins-Drey', the rest of Fischer's extant suite output is clearly in the Lullian manner. This is hardly surprising; French influence at Ansbach and Schwerin, was particularly strong. At the latter, no fewer than eight Frenchmen were listed as members of the *Hofkapelle* in 1671, and it appears that this influence lasted until well into the next century.[6] Following *Musicalisch Divertissement*, a collection of suites for one instrument and bass, Fischer issued *Neuverfertigtes musicalisches Divertissement* in 1700, *Tafel-Musik Bestehend In Verschiedenen Ouverturen, Chaconnen, lustigen Suiten* in 1702 and *Musicalische Fürsten-Lust* in 1706. However, he was not as prolific as this list suggests: *Musicalische Fürsten-Lust* is no more than a re-issue of the 1702 *Tafel-Musik*. Apart from changes to the title page and removal of the latter's dedication, the two editions are identical. The exemplar of *Musicalische Fürsten-Lust* in *F-Pn* (Mus.Vm[7] 1497) has extra printed music added on supplementary sheets. But the authorship of this music is unclear, and it appears that some parts are missing.

All Fischer's consort suite collections have one problem in common: a very high proportion of errors, many of them major. Even the *authoris*-issued *Tafel-musik* did not escape this; and no attempt was made at correction when it was reissued, although it is possible that the reissue was carried out without Fischer's permission or knowledge. Any attempted explanation of this can be no more than conjecture, but it is telling that every one of Fischer's printed editions was issued by a different publisher or printer. Perhaps Fischer was not able to work amicably with any of them.

Neuverfertigtes musicalisches Divertissement is devoted to consort suites. In the one surviving exemplar, there are four part books: 'Dessus', 'Haut Contre',

---

[4] Beechey, 'Fischer', p. 893.

[5] A partial facsimile reproduction is given in D. Glüxam, *Die Violonskordatur und ihre Rolle in der Geschischte des Violinspieles* (Wiener Veröffentlichungen zur Musikwissenschaft 37, Tutzing, 1999), p. 161. See also G. Beckmann, *Das Violinspiel in Deutschland vor 1700* (Leipzig, 1920).

[6] H. Erdmann, *Schwerin als Stadt der Musik* (Lübeck, 1967), pp. 26–7.

'Taille' and 'Bassus'.[7] The 'Dessus' part book has 'Hautb.' added to trio passages in suites one and three, and participation of woodwind instruments was surely expected elsewhere. The second 'Hautb.' is written into the *haute-contre* part, and this seems to represent a break from traditional practice. As we have seen, both oboes play the same music as the violin in all three of Cousser's collections from 1700, which very much in line with the tradition of doubling the outer parts in French dance music. To have an oboe doubling an inner part is clearly not part of with this tradition. There are no corresponding 'basson' indications in the 'Bassus' part; in the trio sections, there are just rests. Therefore a second bass or, more likely, a bassoon part must either have been lost or omitted in error from the publication. Given the '4. Stimmen' of the title page, the latter is the most likely.

Neuverfertigtes musicalisches Divertissement is laid out in the same way as other German-Lullist suite collections. Each suite is clearly defined and starts with an *ouverture* in the Lullian manner. (Table 7.1 details the contents of the collection.)

Table 7.1: Contents of: J. Fischer, *Neuverfertigtes musicalisches Divertissement*, (Augsburg, 1700)

Suite	Movements	Key
Ouverture I	1.Ouverture/2.Entrée /3.Chique/4.Air/5.Chaconne en menuet/ 6.Menuet/7.Gavotte/8.Sarabande	G minor
Ouverture II	9.Ouverture/10.Rondeaux/11.Rondeaux trio/ 12.Meneut qui se joue alternativement avec le suivant/13.Menuet trio/14.Bourre/15.Chique/ 16.LesTonnelirs/17.Chaconne	G major
Ouverture III	18.Ouverture/19.Air/20.Menuet qui se joue alternativement avec le suivant/21.Menuet trio/ 22.Air/23.Bourrée/24.Chique/25.Chaconne	D major
Ouverture IV	26.Ouverture/27.Entrée/28.Menuet qui se joue alternativement avec le suivant/29.Menuet trio/ 30.Chique/31.Gavotte/32.Chaconne	A minor

---

[7] In the private library of Schloß Wiesentheid, Bavaria. See: F. Zobeley (comp.), *Die Musikalien der Graffen von Schönborn-Wiesenthied* (Tutzing, 1967), pp. 44–5.

Suite	Movements	Key
Ouverture V	33.Ouverture/34.Entrée/35.Entrée/ 36.Entrée/ 37.Menuet qui se joue alternativement avec le suivant/38.Menuet trio/39.Chique/40.Chique / 41.Chaconne des Charpantiers	B flat major
Ouverture VI	42.Ouverture de Vulcain/43.Entrée/44.Air. Auß meines Hertzens Grunde/45.Chique à 3. Pour Forgerons/46.Air à 4. chique/47.Menuet qui se joue alternativement avec le suivant/48.Menuet/ 49.Chaconne/ 50.Menuet/51.Chique/52.Chique/ 53.Menuet qui se joue alternativement avec le suivant/54.Air.	F major

The collection as a whole falls into two unequal parts. The first part comprises the first four suites. While certainly not identical, these suites are laid out on broadly similar lines with an opening *ouverture* being balanced by a closing chaconne or sarabande. The comparatively limited choice of dance-types seems to look back to *Composition de musique*. The second part of the collection, comprising the fifth and sixth suites is something of a contrast and seems to have dramatic origins. The fifth suite has a sequence of three *entrées* and a 'character' chaconne; the final suite has an 'Ouverture de Vulcain', an *entrée* and a 'Chique à 3. Pour Forgerons'.

The musical language of these suites is often distinctive; for example, it is unlikely that many other court musicians would, on the first downbeat chord of a dance, plunge into another key through an inversion of the dominant seventh. Fischer does just this in '22. Air' from the third suite. In '25. Chaconne', Fischer enlivens the simple four-bar *basse contrainte* formula with the use of repeated notes and strong rhythmic character that sustains interest in the piece through to the end. The relentless hammering of coopers is portrayed in '16. Les Tonnelirs', and hammers, this time belonging to carpenters, are again featured in the last movement of the fifth suite, '41. Chaconne des Charpantiers' (see Example 7.1).

In the latter, the element of satire is unmistakable: the elevated dance of royalty is turned into a mechanical dance of tradesmen accompanied by the constant noise of the hammers. The melodic line is passed between the violin and the two violas and it is not fanciful to see this as conversations taking place while the work is in progress. This movement shows wit and imagination; it can claim to be one of the most successful examples of characterization in any part of the German seventeenth-century suite repertoire.

At least part of the final suite of the collection seems to be connected with the character of Vulcan, the blacksmith to the gods of classical mythology. The suite is opened by an 'Ouverture de Vulcain' and the fourth movement of the suite is entitled '45. Chique à 3. Pour Forgerons' (for blacksmiths). There is some

Verschiedenen Ouverturen, Chaconnen, lustigen Suiten 153

41. Chaconne des Charpantiers

Ex. 7.1. J. Fischer, *Neuverfertigtes musicalisches Divertissement* (Augsburg, 1700), '41. Chaconne des Charpantiers'

disagreement among the part books about this title of the latter movement; it is given as either 'Chique' or 'Air'. The high tessitura of the *haute-contre* part in this movement, along with a change of clef from soprano 'C' to French violin, indicates that it is a *dessus* part intended for the violin. The bass, marked 'tacet', is silent through most of the movement, but it enters, as a solo, for the last eight bars. The characteristic sounds of the forge are apparent in the upper parts and, coupled with absence of bass until the end, may be a way of illustrating the strong upper torso but weak legs of the mythological character. Certainly, a classically educated noble audience would have been aware of the myth and would have understood such an allusion. The opening of this movement is given in Example 7.2.

Ex. 7.2.   Fischer, *Neuverfertigtes musicalisches Divertissement*, '45. Chique à 3. Pour Forgerons'

'44. Air' is the most unusual movement of the collection and has little, if any, parallel across the entire German-*Lullist* genre. The *haute-contre* part has 'Auß meines Hertzens Grunde' at the head of the movement, and this is the title of a widely used Lutheran chorale on which '44. Air' is based. This chorale, here played by the *haute-contre*, appears to have been frequently notated in triple time, as it is here. Perhaps this made it more suitable for use in secular dance-based music. There may also have been a now-lost tradition of using this chorale in a secular context, or the entire movement may have been included in this collection as a result of error. Given these possibilities, it is still difficult to know how or why a chorale-based movement came to be included in a suite that has at least some of its origins in classical myth.

Fischer's next collection of suites, the *Tafel-Musik* of 1702, has a wider range of music than *Neuverfertigtes musicalisches Divertissement*. There are four *à 4* suites, two trio suites and a number of apparently individual pieces. The collection is contained in five part books:

> Dessus [hereafter DI] – Dessus [hereafter DII] – Haute Contre & 2. Dessus – Taille – 1.Bass.

There are a number of problems of instrumentation posed by these part books. It is possible that '1.Bass' implies the existence of a second bass part, now missing. But the 1706 reissue is identical, and it may be that this labelling is the result of a printer's error. It would be one of many. A problem also exists with the two 'Dessus' parts. Here, despite a common title, the two part books are clearly separate entities; each one contains a different part for the two trio suites. But in the *à 4* suites themselves, the second treble part for the trio sections is contained in the 'Haute Contre & 2. Dessus' part book. This is confirmed by a change of clef and 'trio' markings. However, in the same trio sections, DII continues to double DI in the way that it does for the *tuttis*. Does this mean that the first treble lines in the trio sections were played by both *dessus* parts? This seems unlikely. It was probably yet another printer's error, adding to the lamentable quality of the collection in this respect.

Comparison with *Neuverfertigtes musicalisches Divertissement* does shed some light on how we might perform this music. As with *Neuverfertigtes musicalisches Divertissement*, oboes and bassoons are not mentioned on the title page *Tafel-Musik* and, in the latter, no mention is made of them in the music itself. But it is likely that Fischer expected wind instruments to be present and to fulfil the same role in both collections. As we have seen, the second oboe part of the earlier collection's trio sections are included in the *haute-contre* part book, and it is possible that the same is true of *Tafel-Musik*. Example 7.3 shows an edited excerpt from *Tafel-Musik* where the second oboe doubles the *haute-contre* part and then plays the solo music at the change of clef, exactly as it does in the 1700 collection. (The example retains the original clefs to show where this change takes place.) Perhaps a bassoon took the bass line at this point. The two 'dessus' parts are given to the first oboe and the violin, but the presumably erroneous duplication of solo material in the trio section is omitted.

Even if wind instruments were not intended for this collection, this arrangement of solo and *tutti* instrumentation is still presumably what Fischer intended.

Bruce Haynes places *Tafel-Musik* in the category of music that 'may also have been played by a double reed band', although he does not specify the parts of the collection to which this should be applied.[19] There is no indication that any of the *à 3* or *à 4* suites were specifically intended as wind music, but the sequence of marches and a concluding menuet that make up movements 33–9 are close to the type of oboe-band music discussed below. Marches also feature in two of the four *à 4* suites that open the collection. Perhaps this widespread use of marches was a factor in the triumphalist reissue of *Tafel-Musik* as *Musicalische Fürsten-Lust*. According to its title page, the latter collection was dedicated to the 'War hero' Prince Eugene and celebrated both the defeat of the French at the battle of Blenheim in 1704 and the capture of Tallard, the French general.

Ex. 7.3. J. Fischer, *Tafel-Musik* (Hamburg, 1702), '12. Menuet en Rondeau'

The contents of the *à 4* suites in *Tafel-Musik* and its reissue are given in Table 7.2.

Table 7.2: Contents of *à 4* suites in J. Fischer, *Tafel-Musik* (Hamburg, 1702) and *Musicalische Fürsten-Lust* (Lübeck, 1706)

Suite	Movements	Key
Ouverture I	1.Ouverture/2.Entree/3.Chaconne/4.La Marche/ 5.Menuet, qui se joue alternativement avec le suivant/ 6.Trio/7.Bourèe/8.Menuet, qui se joue alternativement avec le suivant/9.Trio	B flat major
Ouverture II	10.Ouverture/11.Entrée/12.Menuet en Rondeau/ 13.Chaconne/14.La Marche/15. La Marche/16.Air/ 17.Gique	C major
Ouverture III	18.Ouverture/19.Ballet/20.Menuet/21.Trio, Menuet/ 22.Air/ 23.Chaconne/24.Passepies/[24a Passepies II]	F major
Ouverture IV	26.Ouverture/27.Entree/28.Menuet, qui se joue alternativement avec le suivant/29.Trio/30. Air/ 31.Chaconne/32.Gavotte/25.Menuet [see notes].	A minor, A major

In both editions, the following note appears after the last movement of the third suite ('25. Menuet'): 'Diese Menuet kan zu Ende folgender Partie gemacht werden' (this menuet may be played at the end of the following *partie*). The key of '25. Menuet' is A minor, and it is unlikely that it was every intended to part of a sequence of movements in F major, the key of the third suite. But the fourth suite is in A minor and it is likely that '25. Menuet' was simply misplaced. The note is an attempt by the printer to cover yet another error. All four suites follow similar patterns: the *ouvertures* are followed by sequences of dances, but character movements are entirely absent. The writing may not be quite the standard of *Neuverfertigtes musicalisches Divertissement*, but it is still interesting; the inventiveness of the bass parts is a feature of many of the movements. Example 7.4 shows the opening of the *ouverture* to the second of the *à 4* suites.

Here, the principal material resides in the bass. By comparison, the upper lines verge on the prosaic. But Fischer does not limit this type of writing to the *ouvertures* in the collection. The same interest in the bass line is apparent in a number of the dances.

Ex. 7.4. Fischer, *Tafel-Musik*, '10. Ouverture'

The inclusion of two entire trio suites in a German-Lullist collection mainly devoted to *à 4* music is unusual. On the other hand, trios within movements, or as separate dances, were an indispensable part of music in the Lullian manner. Both trio suites in *Tafel-Musik* are similar to the preceding suites in *à 4* instrumentation, although the second suite uses an individual and often-dissonant allemande in place of the *ouverture*. Curiously, the rondeau of the first suite, apart from a repeat of the opening strain, has no further repetition of its opening *couplet*.

Two further suites by Johann Fischer are in manuscripts now in *S-Uu*. The first, 'Ouverture à 4 ... Composes par Mons: Jean Fischer Maistre De Capelle' (IMhs 015:010), is for a four-part ensemble of violin, two violas and bass. The reference to 'Maistre De Capelle' in the title suggests that the suite was copied during Fischer's time at Schwerin, and it is similar to the suites in his printed collections. The bass line writing is again noticeable for its exuberance: the bass line of the 'Gique Anglozice' is an almost exact repetition of the bass line in '19. Ballet' from the *Tafel-Musik*.

The second of these manuscript suites in *S-Uu* is entitled 'Ouverture. à 5. de divers pieces de Musique composcis par Jean Fischer' (IMhs 015:011). There are part books for:

Violino 1/Hautbois/Haute Contre/Tallie (*sic*)/Bassus

It is likely that these parts are incomplete: there is clearly a missing entry between the *haute contre* and *taille* parts in the imitative *allabreve* section of the *ouverture*. Later in the suite, the second menuet is only included in the parts for oboe and bass; at the same point, the first violin, *haute contre* and *taille* parts are all marked 'Menuet paus'. This makes it highly likely that a second treble part has been lost. Despite the labelling of the violin part as 'Violino 1', it is unlikely that the missing part is one for a second violin. A combination of oboe, second violin and bass in the second menuet is unlikely: the missing part must surely be a second oboe. This would give a suite for violin, two violas and bass with two important oboe parts and perhaps a bassoon. Reconstruction of the missing part is quite possible, and the suite is a most attractive composition that deserves to be added to the repertoire of modern performers.[8]

Despite his short stay at the Schwerin court, Fischer has been described as the best musician to work there during this period.[9] There is no reason to dispute this: Fischer's music may be slightly eccentric at times, but there is no doubt that his suites are well written, and often strikingly individual. It is unfortunate that his

---

[8] A modern edition of this work has been published with the parts as they stand; see: H. Bergmann (ed.), *Johann Fischer (1646 – nach 1716), Ouverture (Suite) á 5 F-Dur* (Magdeburg, 2006). Bergmann has either ignored or misunderstood the missing entry in the *ouverture*, and his version of the final *menuet* for solo oboe and bass has no parallel in the German-Lullist consort-suite repertoire.

[9] H. Erdmann, *Schwerin als Stadt der Musik* (Lübeck, 1967), p. 28.

music has suffered such neglect in modern times. The problems of establishing an authoritative text in the printed editions may help to explain why, despite their uniformly high quality, Fischer's suites have never received the recognition they deserve. Apart from the difficulty of establishing an accurate text, there is no reason why Fischer's suites should not be as well known as those of Muffat or any other of the German Lullists.

Meyer lists two further suites by Fischer in the Liechtenstein collection in Kroměříž (*CZ-KRa*).[10] In fact, there are six suites by this author in the collection, shelfmarks A 776–8 and A 780–2. The musical language and style of these suites are quite different from any of the music by the Schwerin Fischer that we have seen so far. It seems far more likely that Meyer confused the work of two different people: the 'Joanne Fischer' of *CZ-KRa* had connections with Vratislavia, and his work will be discussed in Chapter 9. He is not the same composer as the Fischer of the printed editions and *S-Uu* manuscripts that we have discussed above.

There is one aspect of French-inspired German suite writing that I have not yet considered: music for oboe bands. The new style of French oboe was first introduced into Germany in the 1680s. Bruce Haynes documents its early use, during this decade, at Celle, Stuttgart, Hanover, Berlin, Munich, Hamburg, Darmstadt and Nassau-Weilburg.[11] By 1700, 'almost every court of consequence' used oboes and oboe bands, and some of these bands went on tour.[12] A number of French oboists also came to work at German courts. At around the same time as the introduction of the oboe into Germany, the Nuremberg instrument maker J.C. Denner started to make bassoons in the French pattern. These instruments represented a considerable advance on the old German *fagott*, but their introduction into court ensembles seems to have taken some time.

It appears that there was a link between oboe bands and soldiering; bands of shawms were first used in Germany towards the end of the Thirty Years War and, in France, oboe bands became an integral part of Louis XIV's army.[13] Military oboe bands were still in vogue at the end of the seventeenth century, and it has been suggested that, even in the early eighteenth century, the oboist was 'not a member of the elite court chamber music, but was often regarded primarily as a soldier who happened also to be a musician'.[14] But it is unlikely that this applied to the French oboists working at German courts, and it certainly did not apply to the

---

[10] E. H. Meyer, *Die mehrstimmige Spielmusik des 17. Jahrhunderts in Nord-und Mitteleuropa*, Heidelberger Studien zur Musikwissenschaft, vol. 2 (Kassel, 1934), pp. 203–204.

[11] B. Haynes, *The Eloquent Oboe* (Oxford, 2001), pp. 136–7.

[12] W. Braun, 'The "Hautboist;" an Outline of Evolving Careers and Functions' in W. Salmen (ed.), *The Social Status of the Professional Musician from the Middle Ages to the 19th Century* (New York, 1983), pp. 125–58 at p. 130.

[13] J. K. Page, 'Band, II, 2 (i)' in S. Sadie & J. Tyrrell (eds.), *New Grove 2*, vol. 2, pp. 623–8 at p. 623.

[14] Haynes, *Eloquent Oboe*, p. 163.

French oboists in residence at the court of the Elector of Brandenburg. They were given equal status and salaries to the other court musicians from 1681.[15]

Manuscript *A-Wn* Suppl.mus.23982 may provide some indication of the type of music played by the oboe bands in outdoor activities. Unfortunately, only one instrumental part has survived, and this is probably incomplete. The label on the front of this part that gives the date as 1700 and the instrument as 'Hautbois' is almost certainly a later addition. However, the two-octave range of d-d" does make the oboe a likely candidate and the simple character of the music along with the sequences of like movements certainly suggest processional music. The movements, and their keys, are as follows:

> Sarabande (F)/Gavotte (F)/Passepied (F)/Menuet 1 (F)/Men. 2 (F)/La March 1 (F)/La March 2 (F)/La March 3 (F)/Sarabande (d)/Menuet (d)/Menuet (d)/ Menuet 1*(sic)* (d)/Menuet 2 (d)/Men: 3 (F)/Menuet 4 (F)/Menuet 5 (F)/Air (g)/ [untitled] (G).

It is possible that a first page is missing, and this may have contained an *ouverture*. It is noticeable that all but two of the movements centre on F major and D minor; traditionally good keys for the oboe of the time. There is also a parallel between this collection of dances and the processional music used by the French oboe bands in Paris. Of the 'ninety one short marches and airs for *hautbois* and snare drums' in the 'Partition de Plusiers Marches et batteries', (*F-V* MS mus. 1163) 'about two fifths ... are characteristic of such dances as bourées, gavottes, menuets, passepieds, loures, gigues and canaries'.[16]

Johann Philipp Krieger's *Die Lustige Feldmusik* (Nuremberg, 1704) further indicates the link between oboe bands and soldiering. The collection is for 'Four wind or other instruments, to be played while marching at the front of companies of soldiers or else while serving their officers'.[17] It is divided into six 'Partien' that are *ouverture* suites in all but name. At the time of its publication, Krieger was *Kapellmeister* at Weißenfels. Unfortunately, the only surviving copy was destroyed during World War II.[18] But three of the suites were published in modern editions before the destruction of the source.[19] It appears that multiple copies were provided with the original edition: three of the *premier dessus*, two of the *second*

---

[15] Braun, 'The Hautboist', p. 129.

[16] S.G. Sandman, 'The wind band at Louis XIV's court' in *EM* 5 (1977/1), pp. 27–37.

[17] German text and translation from Haynes, *The Eloquent Oboe*, p. 163.

[18] Bruce Haynes lists a further copy in *D-Hs*, but I have been unable to find any evidence for this. See: *Music for Oboe, 1650–1800* (2nd. edn., Berkeley, 1992), p. 211.

[19] Krieger, J.P., *Die Lustige Feldmusik* (Nuremberg, 1704; mod. editions: suites 1 & 2, R. Eitner (ed.), *Monatshefte für Musik-Geschichte*, 29/10, Leipzig, 1895; suite 3, M. Seiffert (ed.), *Organum*, vol. 3/9 (Leipzig, 1925). The latter has substantial editorial intervention.

dessus, one of the *taille* and three of the bassoon. In typical French manner, we see the reinforcement of the outer voices, but not the *taille* part. The music itself is also in the French manner: all three start suites with an *ouverture* that is followed by a sequence of dances. The movements of the third suite, all in F major, are typical of the set:

Ouverture/Entrée/Menuet/Passacaglia/Fantasia/Menuet/Gavotte/Air Menuet/ Gigue/Menuet.

However, in one important respect, the first two suites depart from this norm: both have movements in more than one key. Of the seven movements of the first suite, the first four and last two are in F major, but the fifth movement 'Marche' is in B flat major. The second suite has ten movements; the first three and last five are in C major, but the fourth and fifth are in G major. Why Krieger should have departed from the standard practice of having all movements of a suite in the same key is difficult to know; perhaps he felt that the oboe band offered little in the way of different sonorities, and that a change of key was the only way in which to obtain some variety.

The title page of *Die Lustige Feldmusik* refers to 'vier blasende oder andere Instrumenta' (four wind or other instruments); presumably this was strings. The *Ouverture à4 in G* (*D-Kl* 2° MS mus. 60b³) by the Gotha *Kapellmeister*, Christian Friederich Witt, is specific in its use of alternatives: the parts are marked 'Violino ò Hautbois', 'Viola 1 ò Haute Contre', 'Viola 2 ò Tailler', 'Violon ò Basson', 'Cembalo'. The latter is only sparsely figured. Like Krieger's suites, 2° MS mus. 60b³ is an *ouverture* suite, but it does not change key, and there is little difference between it and similar works for the standard string ensemble. Perhaps string ensemble and double-reed ensemble were interchangeable. If this is the case, manuscript *S-Uu* IMhs 064:011, 'Ouverture a Hautbois 1mo. et 2do. Taille Basson', is unusual in only mentioning wind instruments. But in all other respects, it conforms to the pattern that we have already seen. There are two copies of the 'Premier Hautbois' part, one each of the 'Secunde Hautbois' and 'Talie' parts, and two of the 'Basson'. Again, the music is in the form of an *ouverture* suite. It has the following movements:

Ouverture/Boure/Menuet/Lamento/Passpied/Gigue.

One bassoon part is figured throughout. Although continuo instruments could have been used outdoors, this is more likely to be an indication of an indoor performance, perhaps with string instruments playing in the usual way. It is noticeable that, despite the associations with marching, all these pieces for oboe band include an *ouverture*. The opening of the *ouverture* in IMhs 064:011 is given in Example 7.5.

Verschiedenen Ouverturen, Chaconnen, lustigen Suiten 163

Ex. 7.5.   S-Uu IMhs 064:011, 'Ouverture a Hautbois 1$^{mo.}$ et 2$^{do.}$ Taille Basson', 'Ouverture'

It is a particularly fine example of a German-Lullian *ouverture*, and the anonymous writer clearly had full command of the style. Care has obviously been taken to limit the upper range of the first oboe part, but that is the only allowance that appears to have been made for the instruments: the music is as complex as many of the *ouvertures* written specifically for strings. J. V. Burckart is unknown except for two manuscripts, S-Uu IMhs 013:020–21. Meyer suggests a date for Burckart of 'before 1700', but the two suites in these manuscripts could easily come from the eighteenth century.[20] Certainly, the suite in IMhs 013:021 was probably copied in the eighteenth century: naturals are used instead of flats to cancel sharps, and the paper has printed stave lines. IMhs 013:020 is a trio suite for two *flauti* and bass: the quality of the trio music is poor. Meyer lists the instrumentation of IMhs 013:021 as including flutes, but the parts are headed:

> Violino Primo. Seu Hautbios 1mo/Violino Secundo. Seu Hautbios 2do/Viola. Seu Talia./Basso Continuo. Seu Fagotto.

The similarities between this type of instrumentation and Krieger's and Witt's are clear, and we may assume that this was originally intended as oboe-band music. The parts themselves seem to confirm this, never going beyond the ranges of the wind instruments. The movements are similar to those that we have seen in other oboe-band music:

> Ouverture/Bouree/Gavotta/Aria/Menuet/Gigue.

But the music has little of the high quality found in Krieger's work, or in work, or in IMhs 064:011. Perhaps Burckart was not inspired by the task of writing music for this type of instrumental combination.

Finally, I come to a case study of the dance music written at the court of Hanover at the end of the seventeenth century and the start of the eighteenth. It appears that French influence was evident in the Hanover *Hofkapelle* as early as the mid-seventeenth century, and this influence seems to have carried on until the following century.[21] Indeed, at the time of the arrival from Munich of Agostino Steffani in 1688, the ensemble of five string and three wind players was 'almost entirely French'.[22] The *Kapellmeister* or 'Maître de concerts' was Jean-Baptiste Farinel. A decade later, there were 'at least seventeen instrumentalists on the payroll'.[23] Lully's works were known at the court by 1681, if not earlier.[24]

We have seen in Chapter 1 how the court music ensembles from Hanover, Osnabruck and Celle combined at various times to form a large-scale ensemble along the lines of the Parisian 'vingt quatre'. Unfortunately, there is no surviving music that specifically relates to the work of this ensemble, and we can only guess at its repertoire. And the music surviving from the repertoire of the Hanover *Hofkapelle* itself is disappointingly small. However, there are three manuscripts collections that do give us some idea of the Hanover court repertoire and may, in some cases, be related to the combined ensemble. These are *D-DS* Mus. MS 1221

---

[20] Meyer, *Die mehrstimmige Spielmusik*, p. 192.
[21] H. Sievers, 'Hanover' in *New Grove* 2, vol. 10, pp. 823–6.
[22] C. Timms, *Polymath of the baroque: Agostino Steffani and his music* (Oxford, 2003), p. 46.
[23] Ibid., p. 46.
[24] Ibid., p. 47.

and Mus. MS 1227, and the 'Livre Pour la flute Seule de Toutes Sortes de Pieces' *D-HVl* MS IV 417.

Both Mus. MS 1221 and 1227 were copied in 1689. According to the index of Mus. MS 1227, it was 'mise: en partition: à hanover 1689 ... par Mr Babel'. Charles Babel was a French-born bassoonist, one of the three wind players employed at the Hanover court at the time of Steffani's arrival. He left Hanover in 1690 and, after a time in The Hague, arrived in London in 1700.[25] In England, Babel was a prolific copier of music, and he must have carried a great deal with him, or had regular supplies of fresh music sent from Germany. Among the manuscripts copied and compiled by Babel during his time in England are the so-called 'Magdalen College part books' (*GB-Cmc* F-4-35, 1–5, hereafter, 'MCPB') and two manuscript part books in the private collection of Christopher Hogwood (M. 1092).[26] Between them, they give a valuable insight into Babel's working methods. It is clear that, in putting together the suites in these manuscripts, Babel drew on a wide range of sources. For example, Table 7.3 details the first twelve movements of the '4th Sett' in MCPB.

Table 7.3: Contents of 'Sett IV' in manuscript *GB-Cmc* F-4-35, 1-5

Movement title	Concordant sources	Key
Ouverture	Steffani, *La Superbia d'Alessandro*	G major
2. very slow	*D-DS* Mus. MS 1227 9th suite	G major
3.	Steffani, *La Lotta d'Hercole*	G major
4.	Steffani, *La Superbia d'Alessandro*	G major
5. slow	*D-DS* Mus. MS 1227 9th suite	G major
6.	*D-DS* Mus. MS 1227 9th suite	G major

---

[25] B. Gustafson, 'Babel, Charles' in L. Finscher, (ed.), *Die Musik in Geschichte und Gegenwart* 21 vols. (Kassel & Stuttgart, 1999–2008), Personenteil 1, p. 1250.

[26] I am very grateful to Christopher Hogwood for allowing me to inspect M. 1092 and to Andrew Woolley for drawing my attention to these and a number of other Babel sources in England. For the background to the MCPB, see: R. Herissone, 'The Magdalen College Part Books, origins and contents' in *Chronicle* 29 (1996), pp. 47–95.

Movement title	Concordant sources	Key
7. Flutes	D-DS Mus. MS 1221 4th suite	G major
8.	D-HVl MS IV 417, 4me. Concert de Farinelli pour le Nouvel an 1703	G major
9.	D-HVl MS IV 417, 6me. Concert de Farinelli pour le Nouvel an. 1701	G major
10. Trio h.	D-HVl MS IV 417, 6me. Concert de Farinelli pour le Nouvel an. 1701	G major
11. Very slow		E minor
12.	D-DS Mus. MS 1221 9th suite	E minor
13. Slow	Lenton, *The Ambitious Stepmother*	G major
14.		G major
15. Trio H		G major

Notes:

The concordances for the Ouverture and movements 2, 3, 4, 6 and 13 are taken from Herissone, 'Magdalen College Part Books'. Herissone incorrectly gives the key of the complete suite as being G major.

Not only are there different composers, but there is also a wide range of works. If most of the music in this '4th Sett' appears to originate in Hanover, other suites in MCPB include music from Cousser's *Composition de musique* (see Chapter 2), Aufschnaiter's *Concors discordia* and a wide range of English pieces.[27] Unfortunately, Babel was not particularly fastidious in recording details of authorship. While M. 1092 does contain an index with composers' names, there are some blank spaces suggesting that Babel could not remember or did not know all of them. (See Figure 7.1.)

---

[27] For a discussion of the English sources, see Herissone, 'Magdalen College Part Books'. The concordances with Ms IV 417, Mus. Ms. 1221, *Composition de musique* and *Concors discordia* are hitherto unknown.

This is not surprising when we consider just how much music Babel must have had in his collection. Rebecca Herissone has suggested that, in England, he 'established a copying 'factory''.[28] And we can see evidence of this in Mus. MS 1221 and 1227: the indices and general layout of each one are remarkably similar. Babel may have been following a 'house style' of copying established at the Hanover court, but he may also have established a 'factory' in Hanover with Barrey, the copyist of Mus. MS 1221, working under his personal supervision. Barrey was apparently one of the oboists in the Hanover *Hofkapelle*;[29] Mus. MS 1221 has the title 'Suittes mise en partition par Mr Barre à Hanover. 1689'. Babel's working methods clearly suggest that, like the English manuscripts, MS 1227 was drawn from the widest variety of sources. If Barrey was working under his supervision, the same is probably true of MS 1221. However, it has been tentatively suggested that Farinel, the Hanover 'Maître de concerts' is 'the most probable composer' of Mus. MS 1221 and that Valois, one of the French violinists in the Hanover *Hofkapelle* was the composer of the music in Mus. MS 1227.[30] As we shall see, a number of movements in the latter do appear to have been written by Valois but, in the light of Babel's activities in England, this assumption seems unwise.

Numerous crossings out in Mus. MS 1221 suggest that the material was used several times in performance: on at least one occasion, it appears that some of the opening movements were considerably shortened. Several of the movements in Mus. MS 1227 are marked 'aprendre'. This suggests that these movements were being selected for a particular performance or for fresh copying elsewhere. Other movements in both manuscripts are marked with a cross, perhaps for similar reasons. Again, we can see the ad hoc process of courtly suite writing at all stages of these manuscripts.

There are twelve anonymous suites in Mus. MS 1221, and they are all written out in score. It is incomplete, lacking several pages, and no sets of individual parts exist. There is a wealth of interesting and varied instrumentation in these twelve 'suittes'. The four-part string instrumentation of 'Violon'; 'Haut[contre]'; 'Taille' and 'Basse' is typically French. Specific recorder parts ('p^{re} flutte', '2^e Flutte') are added for the first and last movements of the eighth suite, but it is likely that, elsewhere in the suite, they simply doubled the violin line. The same suite has 'haub[ois]' markings in a different hand, and it appears that, at least on one occasion, oboes doubled the recorders. Oboes are not marked anywhere else in the manuscript, but it is reasonable to assume that they doubled the violin part for some performances. After all, the manuscript's copyist was an oboist. Perhaps the most striking feature of the instrumentation is the frequent use of 'triot' and 'tous' markings giving trios for two upper parts and bass. Example 7.6 shows

---

[28] Ibid., 48.
[29] Ibid., p. 467.
[30] E. Albertyn, 'The Hanover orchestral repertory, 1672–1714: significant source discoveries', *Early Music,* 33/3 (2005), pp. 449–71 at pp. 463 and 467.

the second menuet of the fourth suite with its 'triot' indications, 'viol' cues and original clefs; as the change of clef and 'viol' cue show, the second treble part in the trio sections is not taken by the *haut-contre* viola, but by a violin.

This is typical of the trio writing that we have seen elsewhere. If this example is comparatively simple, the use of different instrumental combinations elsewhere

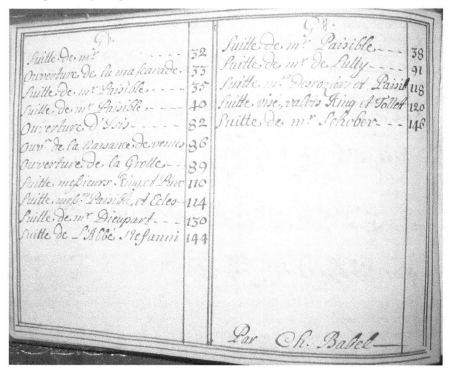

Fig. 7.1.   Manuscript M. 1092, 'dessus'; index.

often shows great variety: the first strain of the gigue of the second suite has three solo passages alternating with 'tous' sections for the complete ensemble. The first of these solos is for *haute contre* and *basse*, the second for *taille* and *basse*, and the third for *haute contre*, *taille* and *basse*. The instruments in the solos are all marked 'seul'.

A similar use of instrumental sonority occurs in the third suite. Here, only the violin plays at the start of the *ouverture*; the remaining instruments enter in turn. To highlight this opening even further, a 'tous' marking in bar 8 seems to suggest that the previous seven bars are intended for one player to a part. There are also frequent 'doux' markings throughout the manuscript. Example 7.7 shows the opening of the *ouverture* to the first suite; the quiet opening is most unusual.

The example also shows how 'doux' is cancelled by 'tous', implying a reduction of players for the soft passages. All this suggests that the ensembles playing the music in this manuscript, whether the Hanover *Hofkapelle* by itself or the combined ensembles mentioned earlier, made a special feature of frequent changes of dynamic and sonority.[31] Given the greater effectiveness of such changes within a larger body of players, these suites may well have been intended for the combined ensemble from Hanover, Osnabruck and Celle.

The manuscript's table of contents shows that the suites have been deliberately grouped in pairs according to key.[32] A number of movements also appear in various 'setts' in the MCPB, but there are no indications of authorship. The gigue and bourée of the tenth suite also appear in '47me. Suitte Mr. du visé' in M. 1092, the two part books copied by Babel. The index for this suite refers to it as 'Suitte visé, valois, King et Tollet' (see Illustration 7.1 above); perhaps the gigue and bourée are by Valois. But as I have already argued, Mus. MS 1221 is most likely to be a collection of the work of a large number of composers. Indeed, dances such as allemande of the seventh suite appear to come from the middle of the seventeenth century and certainly before 1689. But despite its disparate origins, the quality of the music in Mus. MS 1221 is often very high, and it is surprising that it is still barely known.

Mus. MS 1227 shares the date of 1689 with Mus. MS 1221, and also comprises twelve suites. I have already drawn attention to the similarities between the two manuscripts. With one exception, the instrumentation is unspecified; only the second suite, comprising nothing but an extended rondeau, has the following:

Dessus de violon/Haute contre/Taille/Basse Concertante/Basse Continuë

This suite is also the only one in either Mus. MS 1227 or 1221 to have a separate *continuo* part, which is a simplified version of the important 'Basse Concertante'. The '8me Couplet' of this rondeau is marked 'A demy Jeu' in every part. If this is a reference to only using half the players in the ensemble, it may be highly significant in the light of the combined ensembles from Hanover, Osnabruck and Celle. Perhaps the music in this suite was also intended for the large-scale ensemble. Elsewhere, the four parts appear to be the same as those in Mus. MS 1221: violin, two violas and bass. In contrast to the second suite, some of the suites seem to be intended for a small ensemble. For example, the violin part of the 'prelude' to the first suite is surely meant to be played by a single player, and it is reasonable to think that the whole suite was intended to be played by single players to a part. 'Flutte' markings are found in 'Chœur Honorons' in the tenth suite, but these are clearly a later addition, possibly replacing the oboes of an

---

[31] Colin Timms has drawn attention to similar 'tous' and 'violons seuls' markings in Steffani's Hanover works. See: Timms, *Agostino Steffani*, p. 206.

[32] Reproduced in Albertyn, 'Hanover orchestral repertoire', p.466.

Ex. 7.6.   *D-DS* Mus. MS 1221, Suite IV, '2. Menuet'

earlier performance. Once again, there are a significant number of trio sections and dynamic markings, the latter made with considerable care.

Not surprisingly, movements from Mus. MS 1227 also appear in Babel's English manuscripts. Eleven are to be found in the MCPB,[33] the prelude of the sixth suite is included in the '40me Suitte Messrs. Valois et Paisible' of M. 1092, where it is named 'ouverture', and the courante of the fourth suite is found in the sixteenth suite of the 'Recueil de pieces choisies pour le clavessin, 1702' copied by Babel for his son William. (*GB-Lbl* Add. MS 39569.) Like Mus. MS 1221, the twelve suites of Mus. MS 1227 are anonymous but, this time, we have some clues over the question of authorship. As well as the possible connection with Valois in M. 1092, a marking in pencil 'de Valloy', presumably Valois, has been added to the shortened version of the second suite found in the 'Livre Pour la flute Seule' *D-HVl* MS IV 417. The *ouverture* and gigue from the seventh suite of Mus. MS 1227 are also attributed to Valois in manuscript *D-B* MS Mus. 30274. (The gigue was quoted earlier in Example 2.5; see page 38) Valois may well have been a prolific composer of dance music at the Hanover court, and it may well be the case that a number of movements in Mus. MS 1227 are indeed by him.

---

[33]   Herissone, 'Magdalen College Part Books' pp. 59–82.

Ex. 7.7.   *D-DS* Mus. MS 1221, Suite I, 'Ouverture'

But, as I argued earlier, Babel's copying methods make it far more likely that the manuscript contains movements drawn from the widest variety of sources. The titles of many of the movements in Mus. MS 1227 strongly suggest that they were extracted from dramatic stage works, and 'Mise en partition' may not just have involved Babel in copying. As we have seen, Babel was adept at rewriting inner parts when the occasion demanded, and there is every reason to suspect that some of the material in Mus. MS 1227 may have undergone such treatment.

In Chapter 3, I argued that, during the second half of the seventeenth century, the allemande was not danced but performed as instrumental music. Given that much of Mus. MS 1227 appears to have its origins in music for the dramatic stage, it is not surprising the allemande only makes one appearance in the entire collection of twelve suites.

The 'Livre Pour la flute Seule de Toutes Sortes de Pieces' (*D-HVl* Ms IV 417) is large-scale collection of pieces from a variety of sources. It is probable that 'la flute' is the recorder. The binding, which does not appear to be original, has the date '1709' on its spine, presumably on the basis of the latest dated piece, the 'Pr[emier] Concert de Venturini pour le Nouvel an 1709'.[34] Given that the

---

[34]   Albertyn states that the manuscript is 'dated 1709', but this is misleading. Apart from the spine, there is no written indication of when it was compiled. See: Albertyn,

'livre pour la flute Seul' is the work of more than one hand, it is more likely that the manuscript was compiled over a period of time. Besides New Year pieces by Farinel and Venturini, it contains a collection of 'Des Pieces Angloise', and a large number of miscellaneous pieces. These include the rondeau by Valois discussed earlier, pieces by Corelli, and hitherto-unrecognized movements from recorder trios by Johann Christoph Pez.

The handwriting for much of the manuscript is large and clear, possibly the work of an amateur musician. There seems little likelihood of these pieces being intended for actual performance; there are numerous bars' rests (particularly in Farinel's *ouvertures*) and many awkward page turns. Many seem to have been copied directly from a *premier dessus* recorder or violin part. The New Year pieces by Farinel are labelled as ten 'Concert[s] de Farinelli pour le Nouvel an' and movements from the 'concerts' for 1701 and 1703 appear in the MCPB. Given that Babel left Hanover in 1690, Farinel's pieces must have drawn from earlier works or sent to Babel after his arrival in England. The MCPB also suggest that some, though not all, parts of the 'concerts' were transposed upwards, usually by a fourth, when copied into the 'livre pour la flute Seul'. Presumably this was to make them playable on the recorder.

The 'livre pour la flute Seul' does provide us with clues to the Hanover repertoire at the turn of the seventeenth century. Farinel's ten New Year 'concerts' are arranged and dated in sequence from 1706 back to 1697. The contents of the earliest 'concert' (from 1697) are as follows:

Ouverture /Gavotte /Air /Air /Bourée /Rondeau /Menuet /[untitled] /
Prelude /Air /Sarabande /Boureé /Menuet /Rigaudon Altern: /
Trio /Menuet /Air /Passepied /Sarabande /Gavotte /Menuett

There are eight movements in D minor, five in F major, five in G minor; the last three revert to D minor. As some pieces were probably transposed to fit the recorder, this may well not reflect the original key scheme. The substantial number of movements suggests that these pieces are dramatic excerpts and that the New Year 'concerts' may well have been staged as ballets. The sequences from the later years are somewhat shorter, but still in a variety of keys. We have no way of knowing, without further evidence, if fewer pieces were selected from the original scores by the copyist of the 'livre pour la flute Seul', or if the 'concerts' for these years were shorter.

If much of this music from Hanover appears to have links with the dramatic stage, there is example of a Hanover court suite that may well have been intended solely as instrumental music. It comes in the so-called Möller manuscript (*D-B* Mus. MS 40 644). This manuscript is far better known than any of the others discussed in this chapter: it is an important source of keyboard music known to the Bach family in the early years of the eighteenth century. The manuscript includes

---

'Hanover orchestral repertoire', p. 458.

early keyboard works by J.S. Bach, and has therefore received considerable attention from modern scholars. It has been suggested that the compilation of Mus. MS 40 644 'took place very probably between the end of 1703 and circa 1707'.[35] Concentration on the keyboard works in the manuscript has tended to obscure the fact that the first four pieces to be copied were not for keyboard, but for instrumental consort. Perhaps there was a fundamental change from consort to keyboard repertoire during the course of the manuscript's compilation. Within this group of consort pieces are two suites, one by Pez (discussed in the following chapter) and one by Johann Coberg, a Hanover court musician and a teacher of Princess Sophie Charlotte. Like all the consort pieces in Mus. MS 40 644, Coberg's is copied in score, and not as parts; it is the first piece in the manuscript and carries the title 'Ouverture à4 Composées par Ms. J.A. Couberg'. It has the following movements:

Ouverture/Sÿnfonia/Air/Ballo/Trio/Gavotte/Menuet/Gig

The *ouverture* itself follows the German-Lullian variety, but with a noticeably brief second section. No instrumentation is specified, but the clefs and the range suggest one violin, two violas and bass. While we have seen that Abel, Couberg's fellow Hanover musician, used two introductory movements for his quasi-town suites, it is unusual to have an *ouverture* followed by a sinfonia in a suite in the Lullian manner. Perhaps Coberg was following Abel's example, but he may also have been influenced by the use of an *entrée* to follow the *ouverture*, a pairing often used by the German Lullists. However, *entrées* tended to be shorter than their preceding *ouvertures*: Coberg's sinfonia is considerably longer.

In the music by the German *Lullists* that I have discussed so far, it is surprising that so few attempts were made to modify the basic Lullian pattern of suite writing. Even Coberg's suite in the Möller manuscript is still constructed on basically Lullian lines. In most cases, this was probably a reflection of the tastes of late seventeenth-century German nobility who, above all, wanted music that was easily recognizable as being in the French manner. But the next chapter deals with an important trend at the very end of the century, albeit apparently limited to only a few composers: an attempt at unification of styles and the consequent bringing together of French and Italian elements.

---

[35] R. Hill (ed.), *Keyboard music from the Andreas Bach Book and the Möller Manuscript,* Harvard Publications in Music, vol.16 (Harvard, 1991), introduction, xxiii.

Chapter 8
'Cette nouvelle harmonie'
Unifying French and Italian styles

This chapter deals with the music of Georg Muffat, Johann Christoph Pez and Rupert Ignaz Mayr. Much of their work appears to stem from a common desire to bring together elements of French and Italian styles even though French culture was still strong at the German courts in the years approaching the War of the Spanish Succession at the start of the eighteenth century. And, in many courts, it is likely that any attempt at experimentation was frowned on and actively discouraged. But as we saw in Chapter 1, court entertainments were often a mixture of French and Italian traditions, and a similar coexistence existed in other disciplines. Earlier in the century, the court of Queen Christina in Stockholm had a French violin band in residence, and its repertoire was clearly French inspired. But at the same time, books for the Queen's library were being collected in Italy. All over Europe, buildings were being erected in the Italian style, and Italy, perhaps even more than Paris, was an essential part of the itinerary of any travelling nobility. As a result of the prefaces to his two *Florilegium* collections, Muffat's enthusiasm for a combining music in the French and Italian manners is well known, but I shall argue that both Mayr and Pez appear to have been just as fervent in their quest for a mixed style. Mayr's collection is probably the earliest music here, and I shall deal with it first.

Throughout his career, Rupert Ignaz Mayr was a court musician and, for most of it, he was at the Munich court of the music-loving Elector Maximilian (II) Emanuel. During his time there, Mayr must have come into contact with Steffani and, latterly, with Pez. Early in his career, he was sent to study in Paris. He returned in 1685, and his only surviving complete collection of dance music, *Pythagorische Schmids-Füncklein*, was published in Augsburg in 1692. All that survives of an earlier volume of suites, *Arion Sacer, à 4. Strom[enti] e Basso Continuo* (Regensburg, 1678) is the bass part. In 1706, at the end of the War of Spanish Succession, Maximilian Emanuel's court was broken up. Mayr moved to the court of the Prince-Bishop of Freising as *Kapellmeister* until his death in 1712.

Despite the loss of most of *Arion Sacer*, we can at least see that the collection was divided up into six suites.[1] In the manner of Drese's 1672 *Erster Theil Etlicher*

---
[1] See: B. Ulrich, 'Die Pythagorischen Schmids-Fücnklein', *Sammelbände der Internationalen Musikgesellschaft*, vol. 9/1 (1907), pp. 75–82 at pp. 76–77.

Allemanden, Couranten, Sarabanden, Balletten, Intraden und andern Arien, these suites are given titles:

> Jepthias lugens (Jeptha lamenting); Joseph amissus (Joseph lost); Plausus Judithæ (Judith applauded); David saliens (David leaping); Samson ludens (Samson playing); Benjamin.

These appear to indicate music of a dramatic stage origin, but the contents of the suites themselves do not seem to bear this out. Each suite starts with a sinfonia that is followed by sequences of dances mostly starting with an allemande and ending with a gigue. Unless the missing part books come to light, it is difficult to say how the titles, presumably Biblical, relate to such music. Perhaps, as Muffat was to do later, Mayr used his titles to describe 'a state of mind'. (See page 185.) Johann Kuhnau used scriptural themes in a similar way in his *Biblischer Historien* (Leipzig, 1700) for keyboard.

Mayr's second collection, *Pythagorische Schmids-Füncklein*, dedicated to Maximilian II Emanuel, contains seven clearly defined suites for four-part string band and *continuo*. (Table 8.1 lists the contents.)

Table 8.1: Contents of: R. I. Mayr, *Pythagorische Schmids-Füncklein* (Augsburg, 1692)

Suite	Movements	Key
I	Ouverture/Allemande alla breve/Courante/Gavotte alla breve/Menuet allegro/Air allegro	F major
II	Sonata adagio/Spagniolet gravè/Courante/Menuet allegro/ Bourée alla breve/ Ritirata/Gique allegro	D major
III	Sinfonia/Ballo/Courante allegro/Menuet allegro/Gavotte alla breve/ Sarabande allegro/Menuet allegro	G major
IV	Ouverture/Allemande adagio/Courante gravè/Gavott alla breve/Sarabande adagio/Gique allegro	D minor
V	Prelude/Gavotte alla breve/Air allegro/Menuet allegro/ Bourée alla breve/Menuet allegro/Gique allegro	F major
VI	Aria adagio/Allemande allegro/Courante allegro/Aria allegro/Sarabande allegro/Fuga allegro	D major
VII	Passagaglia gravè/Gavotte alla breve/Menuet allegro/Rondeau allegro	B flat major

The upper range of the 'Violino Secundo' part, extending to a", makes it genuine violin music but, for most of the time, Mayr's use of the top string usually extends to no more than e". The comparatively low tessitura of much of the part gives it something of the characteristic of French *haute-contre* music. The figured 'Basso Continuo' is often a simplification of the corresponding 'Basso di Viola' part; trills in the latter are not included in the former. Muffat follows the same practice of omitting trills in the *continuo* parts of his *Florilegium* volumes. It is difficult to know if Muffat was copying Mayr in this, or if it was a widespread performance convention.

The collection draws on a mixture of both French and Italian styles. Perhaps it was the eclectic nature of Maximilian's court, where Italian opera rubbed shoulders with French comedy, which suggested this mix of styles to Mayr.[2] A 'Canon perpet[uo]: in unissono à 4 Violini ... Aut: R[upert] I[naz] M[ayr], 1692' is inserted before the title page of the 'violino primo' part book and a further 'Canon à 4. Voc.' comes in the middle of the collection's preface. Mayr had not, at this time, attained the rank of *Kapellmeister*; the title page of the collection describes him as a 'Violinisten und Hof-Musico'. So his apparent anxiety to demonstrate his ability as a learned musician is understandable. Given that the contents of *Pythagorische Schmids-Füncklein* are drawn from a variety of styles, it is possible that Mayr wanted to make completely sure that his use of such a stylistic mixture was correctly understood. He did not want to be seen as an incompetent with little understanding of the differences between the French or Italian manner. But surprisingly, and unlike Muffat, Mayr makes no specific mention of national style in his preface. He refers to the 'Französisch Reprise genant' (so-called French reprise) and discusses the use of the French four-string bass, but there is nothing else in the preface to indicate Mayr's approach to the music in his collection.

If the preface is largely silent on the various dance characteristics, Mayr takes particular care to use tempo markings for nearly every dance in order to indicate whether it is in the French or Italian manner. This is particularly important in the sarabandes where Mayr often uses an idiosyncratic one- or two-note upbeat. Example 8.1 shows the openings of the sarabandes from the third and fourth suites.

In the first of these, the phrasing and rhythm strongly suggest the Italian manner but, if the performer is still in any doubt as a result of the upbeat, Mayr adds 'allegro'. There can be little doubt that the sarabande from the fourth suite is in the slower, French manner and, presumably for the same reason, Mayr confirms its French status with an 'adagio' marking. The same is true for the courantes.

---

[2] A description of entertainments at Maximilian's court is given in R. Babel, 'The Duchy of Bavaria. The courts of the Wittelsbachs, c. 1500–1750' in J. Adamson (ed.), *The Princely Courts of Europe, 1500–1750* (London, 1999), pp. 189–209. See also S. J. Klingensmith, ,*The utility of splendour: ceremony, social life, and architecture at the court of Bavaria, 1600–1800*, C. F. Otto and M. Ashton (eds.) (Chicago, 1993).

178   The Courtly Consort Suite in German-Speaking Europe, 1650–1706

Ex. 8.1.   Sarabandes in R.I. Mayr, *Pythagorische Schmids-Füncklein* (Augsburg, 1692), Suites III & IV

Mayr apparently did not care about movement names in the same way as Erlebach; the so-called 'courante' of the sixth suite is Italian and carries the marking 'allegro'. The 'courante' in the fourth suite has the marking 'gravè', and is clearly French. But both have the same name.

The dances of the collection are restricted to a comparatively narrow range; in addition to the courantes and sarabandes, only allemandes, bourées, gavottes, menuets and gigues are used with any frequency. And unlike Cousser, for example, Mayr restricts the number of dances in each suite: none has any more than seven movements including the introduction. In the fifth suite, the bourée has the character of a gavotte, and the gavotte that of a bourée. The character of the latter certainly matches the other gavottes in the collection. We shall see later in the chapter that there was a good deal of confusion over these dances in Pez's music, but it is more likely that the printer of *Pythagorische Schmids-Füncklein* simply transposed the two titles by accident.

The final suite of the set does not start with an abstract movement; instead, it opens with a large-scale passacaglia. There is a bass line formula, but a truncated one of four notes and it is not used with great frequency. Instead, the movement mostly relies on repetition; every couplet is played once *forte* and then repeated *piano*. Mayr avoids the tedium inherent in such a formulaic approach by subtly varying the repeats especially at cadences, and the musical material itself is strong and inventive. The imitative opening is most unusual and, as in many movements of this type, the last section is typified by diminution of note values and an intensification of rhythm. It also follows the German-Lullist example by being the longest and most complex movement of the collection.

Only the first and fourth suites have the familiar opening of the 'Ouverture de Theatre'. Not surprisingly, the contents of these two suites are the most French of the entire collection. The opening of Mayr's first *ouverture* is idiomatic; even if the often-used dissonance is replaced by gentler harmonies, there is the characteristic emphasis on the bass and treble lines. But in the second section Mayr clearly departs from the norm with music that is much nearer to Walther's 'reguliere oder irreguliere Fuge' than most examples by German Lullists. The entries of the parts do not overlap, the subject is longer than usual, and Mayr gives us a genuine fugal exposition. This emphasis on stricter counterpoint is clearly linked to the canons given at the opening of the edition and the fugue that ends the sixth suite. Again we see Mayr's apparent anxiety to demonstrate his ability as a learned musician.

In the 'Sinfonia' of the third suite, Mayr does combine national styles in a way that may well, as we shall see, have influenced Pez. The structure of the movement is similar to a French *ouverture*: an *adagio* opening section followed by a 6/8 *allegro*. But the music of the opening is certainly not French and the *allegro* has some of the rhythmic character of an Italian gigue. And in typical German keyboard style, it has two strains with the opening of the second strain being an approximate inversion of the first.

The 'Aria' at the start of the sixth suite provides a complete contrast to the opening movements of the other suites; (Example 8.2 gives the first strain) and we can see that the phrase structure is built around the frequent re-iteration of a simple quaver and semiquaver rhythm. Perhaps in contrast to the musical sophistication of the opening movements in the remainder of the collection, this movement is clearly intended to be as simple as possible in its musical language. As we shall see, Muffat also used a simple opening movement as a contrast to the complexity of the usual *ouverture*. This prompts us to suspect that Muffat knew of Mayr's music. The similarity of '3. Sarabande' in *Florilegium primum* (shown in Example 8.3) to the *sarabande* of the fourth suite in *Pythagorische Schmids-Füncklein* (see Example 8.1 above) further suggests that he did.

180   The Courtly Consort Suite in German-Speaking Europe, 1650–1706

Ex. 8.2.   Mayr, *Pythagorische Schmids-Füncklein*, Suite VI, 'Aria'

There can be no doubt that Muffat had first-hand knowledge of both French and Italian styles, although his time in Paris started at the age of ten, and it is doubtful that he ever had direct instruction from Lully himself. But as a mature organist and chamber musician to Archbishop Maximilian Gandolf in Salzburg, he was also given leave to study in Italy with Pasquini. It was in Rome around 1680 that he also came into contact with the music of Corelli. And it was also in Rome, according to the preface of his *Auserlesene Instrumental-musik* (Passau 1701), where Muffat tried out some experimental compositions 'in the home of ... Archangelo Corelli'.[3] When Maximilian Gandolf died in 1687, he was succeeded by the anti-French Johann Ernst von Thun. It was probably this that made

---

[3]   D. Wilson (ed. and trans.), *Georg Muffat on Performance Practice* (Bloomington and Indianapolis, 2001), p. 71.

Muffat move to Passau in 1690, and this move may have delayed publication of *Florilegium primum*.[4]

Ex. 8.3.   G. Muffat, *Florilegium primum* (Augsburg, 1695), '3. Sarabande'

Muffat's first publication, *Armonico Tributo Cioé Sonate di camera commodissime a pocchi, ò a molti stromenti* was issued in Salzburg in 1682, the year of his return from Rome. Not surprisingly, it is dedicated to Maximilian Gandolf and presumably contains some the pieces tried out at Corelli's home. None of the five sonatas in *Armonico tributo* is a suite as such; they are a mixture of multi-sectioned sonatas, French and Italian dances. The opening of the fourth sonata has the following sequence:

Sonata/Balletto/adagio-presto

The multi-sectioned *adagio-presto* is clearly meant to be a resumption of the sonata, and Muffat is creating here a large-scale structure of combined dance and sonata. Such a combination was not completely new; many multi-sectioned sonatas end with a gigue. But as we shall see, this insertion of a dance into the middle of a sonata, not the end, was a device frequently used by Pez; perhaps he took his inspiration from Muffat. And it is possible that *Armonico tributo's* influence did not end here. It contains a number of important movements that may well have influenced German-*Lullist* collections by other composers. The most

---

[4]   Ibid., p. 5.

impressive of these movements is the passacaglia that closes the collection. It can claim to be the finest of its kind in the seventeenth century. The basic structure is that of a rondeau, but extended to the enormous length of three hundred and six bars. It also includes elements of a repeated bass line formula and phrase repetition that is often varied in the most imaginative way. The *grand couplet* at the heart of this movement is only used four times, although elements of it are used to create the basis of a whole series of variations. But Muffat made this *grand couplet* so melodically, rhythmically and harmonically distinctive that it easily supports the movement's enormous structure. It is shown in Example 8.4; for clarity, the solo, tutti and repeat markings have been omitted.

It is possible that this remarkable passacaglia was responsible for the trend of ever-increasing length of this type of movement, though few composers were able to equal the splendour of Muffat's writing.

It was thirteen years before Muffat issued his next printed edition of consort music; the first of the *Florilegium* volumes. The second volume followed in 1698. I have already quoted from the prefaces to these volumes, and there is no doubt that they are a rich, if flawed, source of information for modern scholars. However, we must question why Muffat still felt it so necessary to describe the French manner of performing in the 1690s when the Lullian style had been introduced into Germany in the early 1680s, if not earlier. There is no obvious answer to this question. But there can be little doubt that Muffat saw himself as the principal unifier of French and Italian style, as well as the leading German exponent of the Lullian manner. The prefaces are consequently written from this viewpoint, and the clear implication is that the French manner of performance had not been fully understood in Germany. But it would be strange if, thirteen years after the publication of Cousser's *Composition de musique*, there was still widespread ignorance of the correct way of playing such music. I have already argued that, especially in the towns, there was confusion in the minds of some German composers over the differences between the French and Italian styles. But there cannot have been many courts in the German lands where the Lullian manner was unknown in the 1690s. Perhaps Muffat was addressing himself to town musicians.

As David Wilson has pointed out, there is a philosophical element present in these prefaces, and Muffat frequently calls for a peaceful existence between nations.[5] These calls for peace were no doubt sincere as Muffat had experienced the French incursions into southern Germany early in his career. He also saw a fusion of musical styles as being genuinely desirable on both philosophical and artistic levels. Perhaps this explains the numerous comments on national musical styles in the prefaces to *Auserlesene Instrumental-musik* and both parts of *Florilegium*. But in the end, we cannot escape a suspicion of arrogance and presumption on Muffat's part. Indeed, the preface to *Auserlesene Instrumental-musik* seems to hint

---

[5] Ibid., p. 87.

at a degree of personal unpopularity when it speaks of 'critics', 'jealous people' and 'wicked efforts'.[6]

Ex. 8.4. G. Muffat, *Armonico Tributo* (Salzburg, 1682), Sonata V, 'Passacaglia'

The title pages of both *Florilegium* collections have a good deal in common; both use the phrase 'modelled on the current ballet style',[7] and both volumes are set for 'quatuor, vel quinque fidibus, una cum basso continuo'. In the light of the instrumentation of Violin, three violas and bass that is used throughout each volumes, this reference to 'four or five parts' may appear rather strange. But Muffat is merely reflection the dance-music tradition of variable instrumentation. If not

---

[6] Ibid., p. 72.
[7] Ibid., pp. 11 & 23.

enough violas were available, the third could presumably be omitted. On the other hand, Muffat was clearly unhappy with the practice of emphasizing the treble and bass at the expense of the inner parts. In the preface to *Florilegium secundum*, he says that 'all the best players should not be assigned to the first violin (or upper) part, so that the middle voices seem robbed of the necessary players.'[8] While this comment is a little ambiguous, and it is not clear whether Muffat is talking about the number or quality of players, the sense of disapproval is obvious. Despite this, Muffat's inner parts, particularly the viola and 'quinta parte', still follow the Lullian model and remain comparatively simple; in fact, there are many dance movements in both parts of *Florilegium* that would function perfectly well as trios using the existing violin, first viola and bass parts as they stand.

Unlike Cousser's three collections issued in 1700, there are no trio sections and no specific parts for oboes and bassoon, although it is possible that wind parts were added if players were available. Muffat allowed the option of replacing the string instruments in the trio sections of his *Auserlesener Instrumental-musik* with the 'French oboe or shawm' and a bassoon; but he also added a warning to 'select only concertos in keys convenient for those instruments'.[9]

There are seven suites in *Florilegium primum* and eight in *Florilegium secundum*; 'Fasciculus' is used as the generic term for suite throughout each volume. In the second volume, the movement titles are also given in the same variety of languages as the preface. Table 8.2 lists the contents of *Florilegium primum*, and it is to this volume that I now turn.

Table 8.2: Contents of: G. Muffat, *Suavioris harmoniæ instrumentalis hyporchematicæ florilegium primum* (Augsburg 1695)

Suite title	Movements	Key
Eusebia	1.Ouverture /2.Air /3.Sarabande/ 4.Gigue 1 / 5.Gavotte /6.Gigue 2 /7.Menuet	D major
Sperantis gaudia	8.Ouverture /9.Balet /10.Bourée /11.Rondeau / 12.Gavotte /13.Menuet 1 /14.Menuet 2	G minor
Gratitudo	15.Ouverture /16.Balet /17.Air /18.Bourreé / 19.Gigue /20.Gavotte /21.Menuet	D minor

---

[8] Ibid., p. 45.
[9] Ibid., p. 75.

Suite title	Movements	Key
Impatientia	22.Symphonie /23.Balet /24.Canaries / 25.Gigue /26.Sarabande /27.Boureé / 28.Chaconne	B flat major
Sollicitudo	29.Ouverture /30.Allemande /31.Air / 32.Gavotte /33.Menuet 1 / 34.Menuet 2 /35.Bourreé	A minor
Blanditiæ	36.Ouverture /37.Sarabande /38.Boureé / 39.Chaconne /40.Gigue / 41.Menuet /42.Eccho	E minor
Constantia	43.Air /44.Entreé des Fraudes /45.Entreé des Insultes /46.Gavotte /47.Bourreé / 48.Menuet 1 /49.Menuet 2 /50.Gigue. .	G major

In organization and arrangement, the collection follows in the footsteps of Cousser and Erlebach. Muffat suggests that the title given to each suite is 'according to a state of mind', although it is not always completely clear how the music relates to this.[10] It is possible that he may have been thinking of Mayr's *Arion Sacer*. But there can be no confusion over Muffat's claim that the music is 'mostly set in the French ballet manner'.[11] Each suite is clearly defined, and five of the seven start with an *ouverture*. The sixth suite starts with a *symphonie*. The openings of these *ouvertures* are often highly dissonant and, in most cases, the trademark 6/4/2 chord is never far away.

The second sections mostly follow the Lullian model, but '36. Ouverture' is rather more adventurous at this point. Its second section is set in common time with mostly quaver movement and, like Bleyer's *ouverture* in *CZ-KRa* A 801 (see page 119) falls into three distinct parts, all of which start with imitation. The first set of imitative entries is led by the violin, the second part by the first and second violas and the last by the violin, second viola and bass. This gives an increasing intensification to the musical language, rather in the manner of a chaconne, and Muffat imaginatively brings it to a close with a five-bar coda over a bass line of constant quavers.

If '36. ouverture' is one of the most inventive movements of the collection, then '22. Symphonie' of the fourth suite is the most complex and perhaps shows Muffat attempting to make obvious links with the chosen 'state of mind'. There

---

[10] Ibid., p. 16.
[11] Ibid., p. 15.

are three sections: the first, itself with three strains, is dominated by the rhythm of the first two bars. The central section, 'Grave' is, with its dotted rhythms and dissonance, identical to the opening of an *ouverture*. The third section is again based entirely on its two opening bars. It has a quick tempo and an impatient character. The structure of '22. Symphonie', fast-slow-fast, is the opposite of the standard *ouverture* structure, and impatience is the opposite of courtly etiquette. As well as the character of the third section, perhaps this is Muffat's way of illustrating the suite's title, 'Impatientia'.

In the final suite where there is no *ouverture* or *simphonie*, the opening movement is the 'gravè' and simple '43. Air'. As I pointed out earlier, Muffat's example appears to have a similar purpose to that of the 'Aria' that opens the sixth suite of Mayr's *Pythagorische Schmids-Füncklein* (shown above in Example 8.2). It provides a contrast to the sophistication of the normal *ouverture* and is clearly intended to be as simple as possible in construction. There are regular phrase lengths and every phrase starts in the same way on the second beat of the bar. Perhaps we may see Muffat again making an attempt to portray 'a state of mind' with the simple repetition of the opening linked to the title of the suite, 'Constantia'.

The range of dance-movement types in the collection is fairly narrow. Apart from the last suite, there are no character movements reflecting the music of the stage, although the 'Air' of the first suite does have many of the rhythmic characteristics of the Lullian *entrée*. Movements entitled 'air' appear in four suites of the collection, and they are all quite different in character. Perhaps Muffat was following Cousser's example in *Composition de musique* by apparently using the term generically. '31. Air' in the fifth suite is similar to a gigue. '17. Air' of the third suite is a triple-time movement and perhaps the most original movement of the third suite if not of the collection. There are two strains. The ten-bar strain that opens the movement is simple enough; there is no imitative writing and there is an emphasis on the second beat of the bar that is reminiscent of the French sarabande. The imitative start of the second strain is based on material derived from the first strain but to finish the movement, the musical interest moves to a bass line that mostly contains sequences of quavers under a simple chordal accompaniment. (See Example 8.5.) This is again reminiscent of the closing stages of a chaconne, although there is no suggestion of any type of bass line formula. Throughout '43. Air', there is an increasing intensification of musical argument progressing from the simple opening to the sophistication of the close.

If '43. Air' makes a passing reference to the chaconne, there are two genuine examples in *Florilegium primum*. The first is in the fourth suite, the second is in the sixth. Both follow a similar pattern: the chromatic descending bass suggests a repeated bass line formula, but it never reappears after the first strain. (The first strain of the chaconne from the sixth suite is shown in Example 8.6.)

'Cette nouvelle harmonie'

Ex. 8.5.   Muffat, *Florilegium primum* '17. Air'

While there are some parallels between these two movements and the French tradition, we should not forget that Muffat worked in Austria for a time. He may have been influenced by the *ciaconna* of the Viennese tradition, which was a triple-time movement with probable origins in early seventeenth-century Italy. Here, there were usually two or more repeated strains and the repeated bass line formula does not seem to have been used. Given Muffat's time in Salzburg, it is highly likely that he knew of this type of *ciaconna*; and allowing for the greater harmonic richness of Muffat's writing, there are clear similarities between the two chaconnes from *Florilegium primum* and those by the Schmelzers.

Ex. 8.6.   Muffat, *Florilegium primum* '39. Chaconne'

Unlike the first volume of *Florilegium*, which was published by Jacob Koppmayr, the second volume was published 'Apud Authorem' by Muffat himself. Perhaps this was a measure of economy brought on by the lengthy prefaces in each part book. The index to this volume makes it clear that two of the suites in the collection have their origins in music written for specific performances of dance. And this specific connection with dance is confirmed by Muffat's advertisement:

In this *Florilegio Secundo* you can hope to find my newly composed pieces, which have eminently entertained distinguished guests in Passau, and are nonetheless also suited to the ballet practice of the children of the highest nobility.[12]

The first suite of the collection has a series of dances and *entrées* associated with various nationalities ('des Hollandois', 'des Anglois', 'des Italiens' and 'des Francois') seemingly with origins in a 'Ballet des nations' type of stage work. The index appears to confirm this. It was 'composed and danced in 1691' and, along with the fourth suite, is the earliest in the collection. Likewise, the final suite has, according to the index, its origins as 1695 'Theatralischen Stücke' (theatre pieces) drawn from the mythological story of Damon and Pythias. The third suite stands apart from the others in the collection having no character movements, and its sequence of *ouverture* and dances is typical of the standard German-Lullian suite of Cousser, Erlebach and J.C.F. Fischer:

Ouverture/Gaillarde/Courante/Sarabande/Gavotte/Passacaille/Bourée/Menuet/Gigue

The index merely refers to it as 'containing the type of airs most suitable for the dance'. It is unlikely that such a sequence ever had its origins on the stage, although some of the music may possibly have had its origins in the ballroom. It is also possible that Muffat was following a tradition of town musicians by bringing these movements together for the sole purpose of creating a suite in a contrasting style to the rest of the collection.

Apart from dates of composition or compilation, no clue is given by the index to the origins of the other suites. But the titles of individual movements further suggest stage origins. For example, the second suite is as follows:

Ouverture/Les Poëtes/Jeunes Espagnols/Autre pour les mêmes/Les Cuisiniers/Le Hachis/Les Marmitons

However, as with Cousser's collections, we should not ignore the possibility that these titles were created merely to give the impression of dramatic origin. The pieces themselves may be nothing more than movements from newly composed or existing instrumental suites brought together to form this collection. Whatever their origins, it is the character movements that set the second *Florilegium* volume apart from the first. From Table 8.2 (given above), we can see that there are only two such movements in the whole of *Florilegium primum*, but they form the largest single movement type in *Florilegium secundum*. As a result, the collection has a quite different character to *Florilegium primum*.

Despite the dates of between 1691 and 1695 that Muffat gives to the music in this collection, some of the movements seem to look back to his time in Paris

---

[12] Ibid., p. 22.

190 The Courtly Consort Suite in German-Speaking Europe, 1650–1706

and the music by Lully that he must have encountered while he was there. Muffat could certainly have heard Lully's 1664 'Entractes d'Oedipe' (LWV 23), and '58. Les Bossus' from the final suite of *Florilegium secundum* seems to be modelled closely on 'les Médecins' (LWV 23/4) from the 'Entractes'.[13] (Example 8.7 gives the opening of LWV 23/4 along with the opening of '58. Les Bossus'.)

Ex. 8.7.   G. Muffat, *Florilegium secundum* (Passau, 1698), '58. Les Bossus'; J.B. Lully, 'Entractes d'Oedipe' (LWV 23), 'Les Médecins'

The similarities between the Lully's and Muffat's dances are telling, and '58. Les Bossus' may be taken from a very early work. This suggestion is supported by

---

[13]   LWV 23/4 also appears in the *Ballet Royal de la Naissance de Venus* (LWV 27; Paris, 1665). Muffat could have heard either.

the movement's cautious musical language, especially compared with its model. After the opening change from D minor to G minor, Lully modulates to C major by bar 5. By bar 5 of Muffat's piece, the music has returned to the tonic and remains in the tonic or dominant for the rest of the strain.

This lack of adventure may have been the result of youthful inexperience. But it is not out of place in *Florilegium secundum* where Muffat's main priority seems to have been in providing music that 'avoided excesses'.[14] The first strain of '35. Les Ramonneurs' from fifth suite provides a further example of the avoidance of excess: the music starts in G minor and modulates to B flat major by bar 4. But it then moves straight to the dominant and stays there for the remainder of the eight-bar strain. It is not inconceivable that Lully, in a similar situation, would have inserted a further modulation before arriving at the dominant.

If there is nothing in the two volumes of *Florilegium* that quite matches the best movements of *Armonico tributo*, it is not surprising that Muffat returned to the latter as a basis for the music of his 1701 *Auserlesene Instrumental-musik*. Muffat's claim on the title page that these 'douzes rares Concerts' are set in 'un style nouveau' is misleading: movements are taken from all five sonatas of *Armonico tributo*, albeit in an expanded and revised form. Admittedly, as in *Florilegium secundum*, there is an index giving the date of composition of each 'concert' and Muffat makes it clear that the collection is largely retrospective, but *Armonico tributo* fails to receive any specific mention. It is the dance movements of *Armonico tributo* that provide the bulk of the material for reuse. There are many changes of detail, and a much greater emphasis is placed on the division between the trio and *tutti* passages. However, Muffat's revisions do not necessarily involve expansion; for example, the Gavotta in 'Sonata I' of *Armonico tributo* loses its petite reprise in its later version, and the second *Grave* from the same sonata of the earlier collection is considerably shortened in the revision. The earlier version is one of Muffat's most original and striking pieces; it is hard to understand why he should have truncated it so ruthlessly. Most important of all is Muffat's treatment of the inner and bass parts of the dance music. Example 8.8 compares the first *tutti* of the rondeau from the third sonata with the revision of the same material in 'Concerto II, Cor Vigilans' from *Auserlesene Instrumental-musik*. The preceding trio music is largely the same in both versions but, in the *tutti* quoted in the example, only the first violin line remains unaltered.

The change of lower parts is not strictly necessary; Muffat could easily have reused his original material with little alteration. But the fact that Muffat worked in this way shows how the tradition of providing new inner parts for previously written dance music still seems to have been astonishingly potent at the start of the eighteenth century. It seems that Muffat did not tire of writing dance music: the preface to *Auserlesene Instrumental-musik* mentions a probable third volume of

---

[14] Wilson, *Georg Muffat*, p. 29.

192   The Courtly Consort Suite in German-Speaking Europe, 1650–1706

Ex. 8.8.   'Rondeau' in G. Muffat, Armonico Tributo, Sonata III; *Auserlesene Instrumentalmusik* (Passau, 1701), Concerto II

Florilegium suites.[15] Unfortunately, Muffat died in three years later in 1704 and it never appeared.

Unlike Mayr's and Muffat's suite collections, which are all in dated printed editions, the main body of Johann Christoph Pez's output is preserved in undated manuscript sources. As a result, it is very difficult to establish a chronology of his work. Only a comparatively small amount was printed, which includes two sets of trios by Roger in Amsterdam. The first set, *Sonata da camera à Tre ... Opera seconda*, was advertised in 1706 as 'Neuf suittes de Mr Pez à 2 flûtes ou violons & Basse Continue qui sont son Opera seconda' and a further set, *Sonata da camera à Tre ... Opera terza* followed in about 1716. A larger-scale collection, *IX Overtures a quatro, 2 Violini, Hautbois, Alto & Basso* is listed in the 1759 catalogue of Nicolas Selhof's library, but no longer exists.[16] Pez's trios seem to have had extraordinarily wide manuscript dissemination; perhaps as a result, there is considerable disagreement between sources.

Fortunately, the details of Pez's musical career are preserved, and they do provide some assistance with the dating of his music. After a period of study in Italy, Pez arrived in 1694 at the court of Joseph Clemens, Archbishop-Elector of Cologne. Joseph Clemens' court had suffered more than most from war; at the time of his accession in 1688, and during the ensuing period of military conflict, it was in miserable circumstances. The electoral palace was damaged so badly during the French occupation of Bonn in 1689 that the court had to move to Lüttich.[17] But in the comparative tranquillity of the later 1690s, there was a remarkable recovery; by the end of the century, the Bonn *Residenz* had been restored and the court had become synonymous with extravagant entertainment, high taxation and profligate spending. Pez was appointed *Kapellmeister* in 1696, but probably as a result of the turmoil caused by the War of the Spanish Succession, left Joseph Clemens' service in 1701 and moved to Maximilian II Emanuel's court in Munich where he must have met Mayr. Like Mayr, he was obliged to leave in 1706. Pez's last post was at the Württemberg *Hofkapelle* in Stuttgart. The wide dissemination of his music suggests that it was highly regarded by his contemporaries: performances probably continued for some years after the composer's death in 1716.

Pez's knowledge of French music must surely have come from Joseph Clemens' court, which was amongst the most pro-French in Germany. This, combined with the study in Italy, meant that he was in an ideal position to write in both Italian and French styles. An early influence may also have been Joseph Clemens' 'Vice-Maistre de Musique', Charles Rosiers. The latter's *Pieces choisies, a la maniere Italienne* (Amsterdam, 1691), a collection of trios for two recorders and bass, may well inhabit a tradition of trios for these instruments reflecting the court's

---

[15] Ibid., p. 78.

[16] N. Selhof, *Catalogue d'une trés belle bibliotheque de livres* (The Hague, 1759; facsm. A. Hyatt King (ed.), Amsterdam, 1973), p. 217, entry 2335.

[17] See: B.A. Wallner (ed.), *J.C. Pez, Ausgewählte Werke*, DTB vol. 35 (Augsburg, 1928), preface, p. xxxiv.

straightened circumstances of the late 1680s.[18] Despite the collection's title, not all the music is in the Italian style. In the *entrée*-like opening to 'Sonata XII', Rosiers has French elements existing alongside the Italian.

The 1706 date of Pez's *Sonata da camera à Tre ... Opera seconda* means that he must have been composing trios before his move to Stuttgart, and it is reasonable to suppose that many were composed at Joseph Clemens' court. It seems that Pez was continuing the tradition of trios for two recorders and bass established by Rosier. Certainly, both Roger's editions specify 'Due Flauti e Basso' and one manuscript source for many of these trios, *B-Br* MS III 1077 Mus, gives 'la flûte' for the upper instrument. The range of this part suggests a recorder. Only the top part of MS III 1077 Mus survives, but the title of the manuscript, 'Pieces en trio faites exprés pour la flûte par Mr Pezt' clearly implies a pair of like treble instruments. Given the number of manuscript sources that also specify 'flute', it seems that two recorders and bass was Pez's preferred instrumentation for many of these trios. However, there are also a large number of trio suites by Pez that exist in transposed versions: clearly, instruments other than recorders were involved.

Perhaps the important difference between the two Roger editions and the manuscript sources is in the length of suites. The suites in both the Roger editions are mostly shorter than many of their manuscript counterparts: the number of movements in each suite is never less than three or more than seven. This is in contrast to the manuscript versions where there can be as many as thirteen movements. The considerable disparity between printed and manuscript sources can be seen in by comparing the fifth suite from MS III 1077 Mus with its printed counterpart. The movements in the manuscript are:

Ouverture/Aria/Bourée/Gavotte/Menuet/Trio/Gavotte[II]/Sarabande/Air,/
Menuet[II]/Menuet[III]/Gigue

The concordant 'suitte 1' in Roger's Op. 3 omits all three menuets, the second gavotte, the sarabande and the air. The trio is retitled as a minuet. Roger inserts an additional air from an otherwise unknown source. This, and the many similar variants in Roger, point to a more simplified form of suite. Perhaps this was a reflection of the limitations of the amateur player; it may also indicate a change of taste away from the thirteen- and fourteen-movement German-Lullian suite of the 1680s and 1690s. It is also possible that Roger drew on whatever material was available, and rearranged order and content to suit the purposes of his edition. Around 1707, the English publisher Walsh reissued six of the suites from Roger's op. 2 in London, and three further suites from the same source were incorporated into an undated collection published by Walsh, Hare and Randall.

---

[18] The title page specifies the instrumentation as 'Propres à joüer sur la Flute, le Violon & autres Instruments', but the part books themselves are headed 'Flauto Primo', 'Flauto Secondo' and 'Basone' for all seven suites of the collection.

If we turn now to the manuscript sources, MS III 1077 Mus. is not alone in surviving incomplete. Of the four principal manuscript sources of Pez's trio suites, only two (*F-Pn* 4°Vm 848 (1–3) and *D-W* Cod. Guelf. 268 Mus. Hdschr.), have complete sets of parts. There is considerable disagreement in these sources over contents and order of movements although Cod. Guelf. 268 Mus. Hdschr. is nearest to the Roger editions than any of the other manuscripts. Bourées and gavottes seem to suffer particularly in this respect and there is frequent confusion over the identity of these two dances. Gavottes are often labelled as bourées and bourées as gavottes. In many cases, changes in movement order seem to have been made on the whim of a particular scribe, but some of the alterations seem little more than gratuitous. Perhaps Pez himself was responsible for some of the variants, although none of the four manuscript sources listed above can be shown to have definite links with the composer himself.

The fourth suite in Cod. Guelf. 268 Mus. Hdschr. contains movements that are also found in manuscript *D-HRD* MS Fü 3629. Seemingly on the basis of a 1728 catalogue of the collection now in D-HRD, these movements are tentatively ascribed to Telemann in the modern catalogue of Telemann's works.[19] But given that the three manuscript sources and Roger's printed edition all ascribe this music to Pez, Telemann's authorship seems unlikely.[20] On the other hand, a menuet from Steffani's 1693 opera, *La libertà contenta*, found its way into the thirteenth suite of MS III 1077.

The suites in manuscript *D-SÜN* Schloß MS 59 also pose a number of problems. Unfortunately, the manuscript itself disappeared in the mid-1990s, and its present whereabouts are unknown. It appears from RISM A/II that the manuscript contains two part books, one in the French violin clef, and one in the soprano clef.[21] No other parts survive, although some of the material also exists in trio sources.[22] The watermark apparently dates the paper as being no earlier than 1693, and it is

---

[19] 'Des Herren General Major Freÿ Herrn Von SonsFeldt Musicalisches Cathallogium' is reproduced in facsimile in J. Kindermann (comp.), *Die Musikalien der Bibliotheca Fürstenbergiana zu Herdringen*, Deutsches Musikgeschichtliches Archiv Kassel, Katalog der Filmsammlung 20/21, (Kassel, 1987–1988), pp. 142–76. See also M. Ruhnke, *Georg Philipp Telemann Thematisch-Systematisches Verzeichnis seiner Werke*, (3 vols, Kassel, 1984–1999), vol. 2, Anh. 42: C1.

[20] RISM A/II also suggests that Telemann is the composer of this suite and lists a further Pez source in *D-W* with the shelfmark Cod. Guelf. 268a Mus. Hdschr. (Records 451.508.544 and 451.544.547 generated online at http://biblioline.nisc.com) Neither I, nor the department of manuscripts in *D-W*, can confirm the existence of such a manuscript or shelf mark. I am grateful to Renate Giermann, *Handschriftenabteilung D-W*, for her help in this matter.

[21] RISM A/II, record 450.027.724.

[22] The only microfilm of the collection gives nothing but the first treble line.

probable that Schloß MS 59 dates from the early years of the eighteenth century.[23] The manuscript contains four suites ascribed to Pez, and five anonymous suites where Pez's authorship can be confirmed by concordances with other sources.

Schloß MS 59 also poses questions of instrumentation: there are frequent 'sollo' and 'tuti' markings and the part divides into two at various points. This division sometimes lasts for entire movements. With so much missing, any assumption about Schloß MS 59 is unwise, but if it is a trio manuscript, then the part divisions and solo markings seem to indicate the need for more than one player to a part. But it is also possible that these are larger-scale consort pieces, and that Schloß MS 59 contained more than three instrumental parts. In addition, two suites in the manuscript also exist in Dresden versions for oboes, bassoon and four-part string ensemble although it is difficult to know which version came first.

The second rondeau from 'Intrade à. Mr. pez' in Schloß MS 59 is also included in '12me. Suitte, M.r. Pez', a suite in the 'dessus' and 'basse' part books compiled by Charles Babel (manuscript M. 1092).[24] M. 1092 also includes two further suites 'de M.r. Pez' and, from concordant sources there is no doubt that some of the music is indeed by him. But, as we have seen, suites copied by Babel usually contain music from a wide variety of different sources. And Babel himself does not always seem to be certain of their authorship. (See page 195.) There can be no guarantee that any of the movements in these suites without a concordance are genuinely by Pez.

Many of Pez's trio suites combine French and Italian elements; indeed, there are few that are exclusively in either the Lullian or Italian manner. And, as in Mayr's *Pythagorische Schmids-Fűncklein*, Pez often combines different stylistic elements within the same movement. Example 8.9 shows the opening of 'Ouverture XI' from MS III 1077 Mus. Despite the absence of all but the upper part, we can see that Pez uses the slow-fast structure of the French *ouverture*, but fills it with music that appears to be written in the Italian manner.

All Pez's trio suites have an abstract introductory movement: on this evidence, it seems that Pez saw such movements as an essential part of the suite. They are variously labelled as 'Intrada', 'Ouverture' 'Simphonia' or 'Sonata' although not all these titles reflect their contents with any degree of accuracy. Pez often favoured the bourée as the first dance to follow the opening abstract movement. But in 'Intrada Vll' of MS III 1077 Mus., this concept is taken one stage further by specifically including the *bourrée* as part of the opening sequence:

    Intrada/bourée/adagio/intrada da capo

---

[23] W. Churchill, *Watermarks in paper in Holland, England, France, etc., in the XVII and XVIII centuries and their interconnection* (Amsterdam, 1935), watermark 29.

[24] These part books, in the private collection of Christopher Hogwood, are discussed more fully in the previous chapter.

'Cette nouvelle harmonie' 197

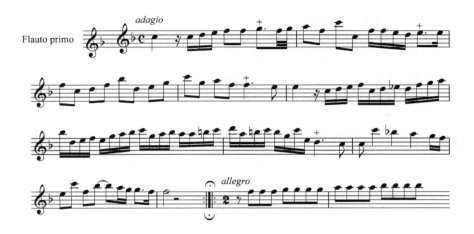

Ex. 8.9.   J.C. Pez, 'Ouverture XI' (*B-Br* MS III 1077 Mus)

Muffat had inserted a 'Balletto' into the opening sequence of the fourth sonata of *Armonico tributo* and Pez may have been following his example, although German sonatas often included dance-related music, especially gigues. But the insertion of a bourée into an opening sequence in this manner is extremely rare. Pez's sequence is particularly effective, and it is strange that he does not seem to have repeated the experiment.

Most of Pez's suites for larger ensembles are now preserved in *D-ROu*, and these are catalogued in *DTB*.[25] Most, if not all, of them appear to have been written for the Württemberg *Hofkapelle* after Pez moved to Stuttgart in 1706. But a consort suite by Pez appears in the so-called Möller manuscript (*D-B* Mus. MS 40 644). (See Chapter 7.) Pez's suite is the second in the group of consort pieces written in score at the start of the manuscript. Unfortunately, the final pages of this suite have not survived, and the chaconne is incomplete. It is an important work: even if the chronology of music in the manuscript still remains uncertain, it is clear that this is one of Pez's earliest-known consort suites. The score is unlabelled but, in the trio movement, 'Tacet l'Taille' appears over the third line. If work on the manuscript was started in 1703, this suite probably pre-dates Pez's move to the Württemberg *Hofkapelle* at Stuttgart in 1706. The movements are:

Intrada/Rondeaux/Gigue[I]/Aria/Gique[II]/Ciaconne

The opening *intrada* is, in many ways, the most interesting movement: it has two sections; a triple-metre adagio is followed by a common-time presto. Example 8.10 gives the opening of the first section.

---

[25]   Wallner, *Pez, Ausgewählte Werke*.

Ex. 8.10. J.C. Pez, 'Intrada. à 2 Violin. I Viol. è Cont:' (*D-B* Mus. MS 40 644), 'Intrada'

In structure, this movement with its slow introduction and imitative, quick, second section is reminiscent of the French *ouverture*. But, as we can see in Example 8.10, the triple-time opening is nothing like the usual opening of an *ouverture*. Once again, we can see Pez, like Mayr, using a structure from one musical style in combination with the musical language from another. Any overall judgement of the musical quality of Pez's suites is hindered by sources that have only survived in an incomplete state, and the lack of agreement between the sources. In such a large corpus of work, it would be surprising if Pez had maintained an even quality throughout, and there are many instances where Pez seems to rely too much on sequential repetition of phrases. However, there are works where Pez is clearly more inspired, and these make fine additions to the consort-suite repertoire.

In discussing the work of Mayr, Muffat and Pez, it is clear that there was a move at the turn of the seventeenth century towards the combination of different musical styles, typically the French and Italian. Muffat appears to have been the earliest exponent of this with his *Armonico tributo* collection, but Mayr was probably the first, with his *Pythagorische Schmids-Füncklein*, to write complete suites in this manner. And, as I have argued above, it is possible that Muffat may have been influenced by Mayr. Pez worked with Mayr at Munich, but it is likely that many of his trios had been written by then and that his own attitude towards the mixing of styles had been established while he was in the service of Joseph Clemens. In Pez's case, we may well be considering a case of parallel development rather than direct influence.

Chapter 9
Einer teutschen Führung
Vienna, the Imperial Court

The Viennese imperial court suite presents considerable differences to the suite in the rest of Europe, and merits consideration as a separate genre. It is possible that the suite in Vienna was influenced more by courtly fashion, and particularly by dynastic politics, than anywhere else in Europe. The influence of politics on the Viennese suite will provide a particular focus for this chapter.

The balance of political power changed in Europe during the second half of the seventeenth century. As Jeroen Duindam has put it 'halfway through Louis XIV's reign, the Spanish crown indeed ceased to be the preponderant courtly example and counterpoint for the French'.[1] The increasing weakness of the Spanish branch of the house of Habsburg created a power vacuum that led to intense rivalry between France and the Austrian branch of the Habsburgs. Even if the position of Holy Roman Emperor 'was more important for its ceremonial dignity than for any real power it offered', the only ruler with the power to oppose Louis XIV was the head of the Austrian Habsburgs, Emperor Leopold I.[2] And while 'from the late 1680s onwards, Vienna and Versailles indubitably were the two prime foci of European court life', there were occasional attempts to reduce tension between Paris and Vienna.[3] A secret treaty between Louis XIV and Leopold was drawn up in 1668: had it been signed, the result would have been to carve up the Spanish Habsburg inheritance between the two major powers. In the end, it was never signed, but details leaked out, and relations between Vienna and Spain were soured for some years.[4] So it is hardly surprising that there was intense pressure on Leopold, at least in the early part of his reign, to disassociate himself from anything to do with France. In what has been called a 'battle of images' between Paris and Vienna, the results sometimes bordered on the ridiculous:[5] in 1666, the efforts of Grémonville, the French ambassador in Vienna, to present a French ballet at court in the presence of the Emperor nearly resulted in a major diplomatic incident.[6] In similar vein,

---

[1] J. Duindam, *Vienna and Versailles; the courts of Europe's dynastic rivals, 1550–1780* (Cambridge, 2003), p. 16.

[2] J. Spielman, *Leopold I of Austria* (London, 1977), p. 20.

[3] Duindam, *Vienna and Versailles*, pp. 16–17.

[4] Spielman, *Leopold I*, p. 56.

[5] Duindam, *Vienna and Versailles*, p. 290.

[6] The entire incident is described in M. Vaillancourt, 'Instrumental Ensemble Music at the Court of Leopold I (1658–1705)', (Ph.D. diss., University of Illinois at Urbana-

Eucharius Gottlieb Rinck, the first biographer of Leopold I, wrote the following description of the dancing of the Empress and the *Hofdamen* (high-ranking female members of the Viennese court):

> Dieses war doch niemals auf frantzö[s]ische manier/sondern vielmehr eine art von teutschen führungen, welche der gravität dieses höchsten oberhauptes gemäß [war].⁷ (But this was never in the French manner; but on the contrary, a style of German leading that, in its gravity, was appropriate for high royalty.)

What Rinck meant by 'teutschen führungen' is not exactly clear, but his biography had seized every opportunity to belittle the French and it seems that, once again, he was doing everything possible to avoid the suggestion of French influence. But political rivalry, or even hostility, does not seem to have prevented cultural cross-fertilization. The Turks presented a constant and real threat to the region throughout much of Leopold's reign. That did not stop a 'sumptuous Cavalcade' processing along the streets of Vienna 'nobly apparelled after the Turkish fashion'.⁸

As Emperor, Leopold was required to travel to other areas of Europe, and he was clearly influenced by his visit to Munich in 1658. Kerll's opera *L'Oronte* was performed along with a tournament opera performed on horseback, *Applausi festivi*.⁹ A similar event, *Il Mondo Festeggiante* had also been given in Florence during the previous year. Therefore, it was hardly surprising when the imperial court organized a tournament opera and equestrian ballet to celebrate Leopold's wedding to the Spanish Princess, the *Infanta* Margarita, in December 1666. The publicity surrounding this event was far-reaching and highly successful. Schmelzer's music for the equestrian ballet was printed in two editions, one by Matteo Cosmerovio (*RISM* S 1660) and the other as part of the *Diarii Europæ* (*RISM* S 1661).¹⁰

Champaign, 1991), pp. 241–2 and Nettl, 'Die Wiener Tanzkomposition', p. 53. However, in both cases, much of the information is taken from E.G. Rinck, *Leopolds des Grossen Röm. Käysers wunderwürdiges Leben und Thaten aus geheimen nachrichten eröffnet* (4 vols, Leipzig, 1709).

⁷ Rincke, *Leopolds des Grossen*, vol. 1, p. 94. Julio Bernhardt von Rohr's *Einleitung zur Ceremoniel-Wissenschaft* (Berlin, 1729), Chapter V, ¶8, and largely a rewrite of Rincke, transfers this epithet of 'German leading' to Leopold himself (Etwas besonders war es, daß der Römische Kayser Leopoldus niemahls Frantzösisch tantzte, sondern vielmehr eine Art von einer Teutschen Führung beobachtete).

⁸ J. Burbury, *A relation of a journey of the Right Honourable my Lord Henry Howard, From London to Vienna and thence to Constantinople* (London, 1671), p. 44.

⁹ See H. Watanabe-O'Kelly, *Triumphall Shews, Tournaments at German-speaking Courts in their European Context 1560-1730* (Berlin, 1992), pp. 88–9.

¹⁰ Both editions are set in moveable type full score, but the layout suggests that the printer of *Diarii Europæ* was copying S 1660.

Even if a dynastic marriage was a political event of great importance, it is curious that the equestrian ballet for Margarita's birthday in 1667 is seldom mentioned. A two-stave reduction exists in the second volume of *A-Wn* Mus. Hs. 16 583. The title is:

> Arien des Ross Balletts zu dem Geburts dag Ihro Maÿl: der Regierenden Kaÿserin Margarita. 12. Julÿ. 1667. (Arias from the equestrian ballet for the birthday of her majesty, the reigning Empress Margarita. 12 July 1667.)

A further manuscript source (*CZ-KRa* A 4682) is unfortunately incomplete, but it includes music for two trumpets.[11]

The generic term 'Arien' is not the usual one for a Viennese suite. *Balletto* was used with far greater frequency, and in the most important surviving source of J.H. Schmelzer's dance music, the two volumes of *A-Wn* Mus. Hs. 16 583 (hereafter, 16 583[I] and [II]), *balletto* or 'ballet' is used as the generic term for a single suite in all but ten of the ninety-four suites. In these ten, 'aria' is the chosen generic term, as in the 'Arien des Ross Balletts' quoted above. Somewhat confusingly, the plural, *balletti*, does not always imply a collection of suites: it can still refer to a single suite. For clarity, and for the purposes of identification, I shall use *balletto* as a generic title for the Viennese suite. *Balletti* will be used in the same way to denote the plural.

Given the strong links between Vienna and Italy, dating back well into the previous century, it is hardly surprising that Italian musicians traditionally held the higher-ranking posts in the *Hofkapelle*. Antonio Bertali had succeeded Giovanni Valentini as *Kapellmeister* in 1649, and Felice Sances followed Pietro Verdina in the same year as *Vice-Kapellmeister*.[12] Leopold maintained the tradition; Sances became *Kapellmeister* and he was succeeded by Antonio Draghi. In fact, the only non-Italian musician in a high-ranking post during Leopold's reign was Johann Heinrich Schmelzer who became *Vice-Kapellmeister* in 1671 and *Kapellmeister* in 1679.[13] Leopold himself was a musician, although the suggestion that 'il possede en perfection la Musique' (he understood music perfectly) is surely an exaggeration.[14] In fact, it seems that he may have had tuition in music from Wolfgang Ebner and Bertali.[15]

---

[11] *AMA*, vol. 5/1, p. 505.

[12] L. von Köchel, *Die kaiserliche Hof-Musikkapelle in Wien von 1543 bis 1867* (Vienna, 1869), p. 58.

[13] Ibid., pp. 62–5.

[14] C. Freschot, *Memoires de la cour de Vienne, contenant remarques d'un voyager curieux sur l'état present de cette cour, & sur les intérêts* (2nd edn., Cologne, 1705), pp. 110–111.

[15] G. Brosche, 'Die musikalischen Werke Kaiser Leopolds I. Ein systematisch-thematisches Verzeichnis der erhaltenen Komposition' in G. Brosche (ed.), *Franz Grasberger zum 60. Geburtstag* (Tutzing, 1975), p. 28.

If Lully's dance music was an integral part of his operas and opera-ballets, the Viennese *balletto* was usually inserted into the Italian operas given at the imperial court, almost as an afterthought. In any case, it appears that the composition of the *balletti* was left to musicians, including Leopold himself, who had a particular specialisation as composers of dance music. Thus, the Viennese *balletto* has a direct link not just with the stage, but also with staged dance. Many *balletti* can be associated with particular dramatic works and there are very few instances where suites do not appear to have originated as dance music or as instrumental music related to the stage.[16]

While there is often no introductory movement at the start of a Viennese *balletto*, an *intrada* was often used to herald the entrance of a particular character in a similar manner to the French *entrée*, but this was by no means a hard and fast rule. As we can see in Table 9.1, there was a wide variety of opening movements.

Table 9.1: Opening movements of the *balletti* by Johann Heinrich Schmelzer in *A-Wn* Mus. Hs. 16 583[I]

Balletto title	Opening movement
Monstri Ballett ist gedanzt worden den 16. Febr. 1665.	Balletto.
Paueran Ballett. ist gedanzt worden den 20. Aprile 1665.	[untitled]
Der Ninfen Ballett	Allemande
Der Monstri Ballett	[untitled]
Balletto der Capritiosi ist gedanzt worden den 4 Marzti 1666	Courente
Der Amanti Ballett	[untitled]
Der Bacchi Ballett	Allemande
Ballett zu dem geburtsdag (sic) ihro Maÿ. der Keyserlichen Braudt ist gedanzt worden den 12. Juli 1666	Courente

---

[16] See: E. Wellesz, *Die Ballet-Suiten von Johann Heinrich und Anton Andreas Schmelzer. Ein Beitrag zur Geschichte der Musik an österreichischen Hofe im 17. Jahrhundert, Sitzungsberichte der Kais. Akademie der Wissenschaften in Wien, vol. 176/5* (Vienna, 1914), and F. Hadamowsky, 'Barocktheater am Wiener Kaiserhof. Mit einem Spielplan (1625–1740)' in *Jahrbuch der Gesellschaft für Wiener Theaterforschung, 1951-2* (Vienna, 1955), pp. 71–98.

Balletto title	Opening movement
Ross Ballett	Courente
Balletto beider Kaÿl: princessinen ist gedanzt worden dem 18. 9bris 1666	Courente
Balletto der Cavalieri ist gedanzt worden den 22. 7bris 1666.	Buorea
Die anderte Intrada	Balletto
Balletto der Dame ist gedanzt worden im Febr 1667	Intrada
Balletto, genandt das Narrenspitall ist gedanzt worden den 21. Febr 1667	Intrada der pulicinelli
Gran Ballo der wider zur Vernunft gekommen.	Buorea.
Balletto der Amoretti und Trittonni. ist gedanzt worden im Febris 1667	Balletto
Das Köch Ballett	[untitled]
Das Windt Ballett	[untitled]
Der Ciclopi oder schmidt Ballett ist gedanzt worden im Febr. 1667	[untitled]
Das Affen Ballet	[untitled]
Folgt das Lamentierliche auß leuthen uber den unseligen Todt St. Fasching,... den 22. Febr. 1667	Campanella

On the other hand, the *retirada* was commonly used as the closing movement. Unlike the gigues or sarabandes that were used as a closing movement in many German suites, the *retirada* was often deeply serious. There could be several shifts of key within the movement, and chromaticism allied to sharp dissonance was also quite common. Although less chromatic or dissonant than some, the *retirada* in *A-Wn* Mus. Hs. 19 265 is particularly fine, and the start is quoted in Example 9.1. Unfortunately, the composer is unknown.

Ex. 9.1.   *A-Wn* Mus. Hs. 19 265, 'Retirada'

Titles indicate that many Viennese *balletti* in 16 583 were meant as character dances. However, without knowledge of the dance itself, and the nature of the stage productions, it is not always easy to see what Schmelzer was trying to describe. But it is clear that he could produce programmatic music of great character, and also of great humour. The so-called 'Fechtschule balletto' is a good example of this. Here, there are vivid descriptions of combat, and the painful results of combat. The surviving source for this piece, in *CZ-KRa*, appears to have been lost not long after Karl Nettl edited it for *DTÖ*.[17] The *balletti* by Hoffer in the same volume show that Nettl's editing was not always completely reliable (see page 206), so it is unfortunate that it has only been preserved in his edition.

I have argued earlier that the allemande was not danced at the German courts after about 1630. In Vienna, the opposite appears to be true: the allemande appears in *balletti* that have their origins as stage works. There can be no doubt that these movements were danced: the title of J.H. Schmelzer's 'Paueran Ballett' of April 1665 specifically refers to dancing ('ist gedanzt worden') and an allemande opens the second part, 'Der Ninfen Ballet'. The first strain of this allemande is given in

---

[17]   P. Nettl (ed.), *Wiener Tanzmusik in der zweiten Hälfte des siebzehnten Jahrhunderts*, DTÖ, vol. 56 (Vienna, 1921).

Example 9.2, and the individual character of the music seems to suggest a character movement, almost certainly with its own specially created choreography.

Ex. 9.2.   J.H. Schmelzer, '*Der Ninfen Ballet*' (16 583[I]), 'Allemande'

It is likely that the other allemandes in 16 583 are character movements and were treated in the same way.

Example 9.2 above shows how the allemande from 'Der Ninfen Ballet' is written in a two-stave format. Both volumes of 16 583 use the same two-stave format throughout. These two stave versions are usually known as *particelle*. They contain nothing more than the outer parts of the original score with the occasional addition of a figured bass. 16 583 is not unique in this; other Viennese *balletti* are preserved in the same way. These outer parts were usually straightforward copies of the original first violin and bass parts, but a degree of arrangement was needed in those pieces with more complex instrumentation. Details of the instrumentation are sometimes supplied in the title, sometimes in the score itself.

It has been suggested that these *particelle* may be keyboard arrangements.[18] But this is doubtful. Example 9.3 compares the first strain of 'Ballete De S. Mayeste Imperiale' in *D-OB* MO 1037 with the first strain of 'Allemande: 30ª.' in *A-Wn* Mus. Hs. 18 710.[19]

Both are almost certainly by Leopold I and both probably originated as consort pieces. MO 1037 is a collection of keyboard pieces and arrangements compiled in 1695 by the Ottobeuren organist, Pater Honorat Reich, and Mus. Hs. 18 710 is a *particella* score. The difference between the two is clear. *Arpeggiando* figuration and occasional inner parts, both typical of seventeenth-century keyboard writing, are all to be found in the MO 1037 keyboard arrangement; *arpeggiando* figuration

---

[18] D. Smithers, *The Music and History of the Baroque Trumpet before 1721* (Carbondale & Edwardsville, 1973, repr. 1988), p. 175.

[19] Facsimile ed., R. Hill (ed.), *Ottobeuren, Benediktiner-Abtei, Bibliothek und Musik-Archiv MO 1037*, 17th Century Keyboard Music, vol. 23 (New York, 1988), p. 125.

Ex. 9.3.   D-OB MO 1037, 'Ballete De S. Mayeste Imperiale'; A-Wn Mus. Hs. 18 710, 'Allemande: 30[a]'

and inner parts are conspicuously absent from the simple treble and bass parts of Mus. Hs. 18 710.

However, the two volumes of 16 583, along with a further *particella* of music by Johann Heinrich Schmelzer's son, Andreas Anton, do allow us to identify an evolutionary process and suggest a purpose for the existence of these collections. Egon Wellesz catalogued these volumes early in the twentieth century, but his work was not consistent.[20] Despite his recognition that 16 583 is in two volumes, Wellesz's numbering system runs consecutively from the first *balletto* of volume one to the last *balletto* of volume two. Ninety-two *balletti* are listed from both volumes, but, in fact, there should be ninety-four. Despite clear titling, Wellesz grouped together, without explanation, and in a way that he did not do elsewhere, the three ballets of 'Arien zu der Opera des 13. Februari 1668'.[21] The title of 16 583[I]) is:

> Arien zu den Balletten, welche an der Röm: Kaÿl: Maÿl: Leopoldi des Ersten &c. hoff, in dero Residenz-Statt Wienn, Von dem 16. Febr 1665 bis den 23. Febr des 1667isten Jahres gehalten worden. Erstes Buch Componiert Von Johann Heinrich Schmelzer Keÿl: Camer Musico.

16 583[II] has no surviving title page, but a pencilled note is written on the reverse of the front cover giving 'Schmelzer; Jo. Heinr.' as the composer. It is dated 1667–1672, and '2do Buch' is added at the end. The collection of *balletti* by Andreas Anton Schmelzer (*A-Wn* Mus. Hs. 16 588, hereafter 16 588) has the title:

> Arien zu den Balletten, welche an der Keyserl. Kögl. Meÿl. Leopoldi des I^{tn}. Hoff. vom 15^{tn} 9ber Año 1680. bis auf den Fasching 1685 gehalten worden. Componirt von Andreas Antonius Schmelzer. Erstes Buch.

The closing date of 'Fasching 1685' has been added in pencil within a space obviously left vacant for it. During the copying of the two volumes of 16 583, the titles describing the *balletti* and the circumstances of their performances underwent a change of style. In the first volume, these titles have obviously been added later: they were squeezed into any available space. At the start of the second volume, the titles are similar but, in the later parts of the manuscript, space is regularly provided to record copious details of the occasion, the date and the participating dancers. Clearly, these later titles were written at the same time as the music. Such detail would seem to suggest that, in addition to the preservation of the music, these manuscripts evolved to be a musical diary of important court occasions. Music and titles were again written at the same time in 16 588, but the information

---

[20] Wellesz, *Die Ballet-Suiten*, pp. 30–43.

[21] Neither Wellesz, ibid., p. 34, nor Hadamowsky, *Barocktheater*, p. 74, have been able to trace the origins of this opera.

given in each title is even more comprehensive. However, there is one important change in 16 588. The vacant space left in the opening page for the insertion of a closing date suggests that each *balletto* was added as soon as it became available for copying and not retrospectively, as was probably the case with much of 16 583. This may explain the extra detail given in the titles: it would have been fresh in the mind of the copyists.[22] Not surprisingly, music by Leopold I himself is also preserved in this way. It seems that *A-Wn* Mus. Hs. 18 710 originally contained eight suites by the Emperor, each labelled 'Aria'.[23] Again, the elaborate decoration of the first letters of some of the titles suggests that *particelle* scores had become synonymous with the high-quality preservation of courtly dance and evolved to become highly stylized records of court music making.

Most of the material discussed so far in this chapter was probably part of Leopold's own court library. However, it is not the only major source for the music of the imperial court. The Liechenstein collection in Kroměříž is particularly important as it contains a great deal of Viennese music that is not found elsewhere. It contains complete sets of instrumental parts for works by J.H. Schmelzer that would otherwise only be known through the *particelle* reductions. The history of the collection in Kroměříž has been well documented, especially in its most recent catalogue, and the collection itself has become far more accessible in recent years.[24] Karl Liechenstein-Castelcorno was the Bishop of Olomouc during the period following the Thirty Years War until his death in 1695. At his behest, music was gathered together in order to service the needs, both sacred and secular, of his court at Kroměříž. Vienna clearly exerted a strong influence on what was included in the collection: the Kroměříž *Kapellmeister*, Pavel Vejvanovský, had studied in Vienna, and the Bishop maintained personal contact with both Johann Heinrich Schmelzer and one of the imperial court organists, Alessandro Poglietti.

It seems that a regular stream of correspondence and compositions of all types was sent from Vienna to Kroměříž.[25] In the case of Poglietti's music, this was often autograph material, but it appears that a team of local copyists headed by Vejvanovský was responsible for most of the copying.[26] It seems that Vejvanovský also copied music for a personal collection.[27] But where parallel Viennese sources also exist, it is clear that substantial changes were sometimes made, especially in the order of movements. This may have resulted from piecemeal dispatching of

---

[22] There is an interesting parallel between the Schmelzer *particelle* scores and the manuscripts of French dance music copied retrospectively by Philidor in the 1690s (see also Chapter 2)

[23] The subsequent movements have no such groupings and are in other hands.

[24] The preface to *AMA*, vol. 5/I has provided the information for the remainder of this paragraph.

[25] P. Nettl, *Die Wiener Tanzkomposition in der zweiten Hälfte des siebzehnten Jahrhunderts*, Studien zur Musikwissenchaft, vol. 8 (Vienna, 1921), pp. 166–75.

[26] *AMA*, vol. 5/I, preface, p. 32.

[27] Ibid., p. 33.

scores from Vienna; it may also reflect personal interventions by the Kroměříž copyists. These changes, especially to music by Johann Heinrich Schmelzer, will be discussed later in the chapter.

The surviving sets of parts in Kroměříž use both a four-part and five-part string body; it is, of course, possible that some of the *à 4* music was originally *à 5*. With few exceptions, two violins, two violas and bass seem to have been used to create a five-part texture, although Poglietti seems to have preferred a viola da gamba to the second viola. Four-part works were scored either for two violins, one viola and bass or for a single violin, with two violas and bass. Given the changes that seem to have occurred when Viennese music was transferred to Kroměříž, we must be wary of accepting Kroměříž sources as being a wholly accurate reflection of practices at Leopold's court. A set of *balletti* by the violinist and imperial court composer, Joseph Hoffer, is unusually preserved in part books rather than reduced score (*A-Wn* Suppl. mus. 1809). It confirms the use of the single violin, two violas and bass ensemble.[28] We have no fully scored sources of Leopold's own work directly from imperial sources, but it appears that he too preferred the combination of violin, two violas and bass for his own *balletti* compositions.[29]

It has also been suggested that the Viennese *Hofkapelle* provided 'the period's best orchestra', though it is difficult to see how such a qualitative claim could be substantiated.[30] It does seem, however, that more was spent on the musical establishment in Vienna than any other aspect of court life. Leopold's first biographer, Eucharius Gottlieb Rinck, lists the court expenditure for the year 1705. Rinck's evidence is not always reliable, but the overall picture is clear: the court musicians (*Hof-musici*) were paid a total of '43,702fl.', the largest amount for any individual category.[31] Wind players in the form of bassoonists, trombonists, trumpeters and cornettists all seem to have been available during Leopold's reign, and this is confirmed by the scoring of works celebrating such events as royal birthdays. The Kroměříž source of Schmelzer's 'Balletto di Centauri Ninfe et Saluatici ... per la festa À Schönbrun, 1674' (*CZ-KRa* A 764) is particularly lavish with its three choirs of instruments: '5 Viole Radopiati', '3 Piffari et un fagotto', '2 Cornetti Mutti et 3 Tromboni'. Likewise, Poglietti's 'Fastnacht Baletten' (*CZ-KRa* A 877) is scored for four trumpets, and a five-part string group with two figured harpsichord parts.

---

[28] In P. Nettl (ed.) *Wiener Tanzmusik in der 2. Hälfte der 17. Jahrhunderts,* DTÖ, vol. 56, (Graz, 1921), the scoring of Hoffer's second *balletto* is, without comment, changed to two violins, one viola and bass. There are also a number of seemingly gratuitous alterations to the musical text.

[29] Fully scored *balletti* by Leopold are preserved in manuscript *S-Uu* IMhs 053:006 and various *CZ-KRa* sources.

[30] *AMA*, vol. 5/I, p. 31. It is possible that the origins of this claim, though not cited as such, come from Rinck, *Leopolds des Grossen*, vol 1, p. 85. Rinck describes the *Hofkapelle* as 'unvergleichlichen' (unparalleled).

[31] Rinck, *Leopolds des Grossen*, vol. 1, p. 149.

Not all music for celebration was treated to such richness of scoring: many of the surviving fully scored works for royal occasions were for strings alone or smaller combinations of wind and strings. Although we do not know the circumstances surrounding its composition, manuscript *A-Wn* Mus. Hs. 18 968 contains three works 'l'Autore Ferdinando Tobia Richter' that are typical of the Viennese court repertoire for smaller mixed combinations of instruments. The first of them, a 'Sonata à 7' is dated 1685 and is clearly independent from the two following *balletti*, both of which have their own opening sonatas.[32] But all three works appear to have been copied at the same time, and were probably written shortly after the commencement of Richter's employment in 1683 as one of the imperial court organists.[33] Both *balletti* are written out in score, but no sets of parts survive. It is difficult to see how the first of these could, as Nettl suggests, be for trumpets and strings.[34] The two parts in question lie completely outside the range of natural trumpets and demand too much agility to be written for slide trumpets, even if such instrumentation was likely. However, Nettl is right in one respect: the nature of these two parts seems far more appropriate to wind instruments, and they are clearly meant to form a contrast of sonority with the main body of strings. Almost certainly, they are not oboe parts: as we shall see, oboes do not appear to have arrived in Vienna until at least the late 1690s. The most likely possibility is that they are *cornetto* parts. At least one *cornetto* player was engaged in the imperial *Hofkapelle* between 1680 and 1708 and it is probable that some of the trumpeters were also cornettists. We have seen that *cornetti* were specified in the 'Balletto di Centauri Ninfe et Saluatici', but they also appear to have been used for more intimate occasions. Poglietti scored his 'Sonata à 3' (*CZ-KRa* A 615) for 'Cornetto: Flautto Fagotto con Organo', and there is no reason to suppose that this was an isolated example.[35] The contrast between the top parts of Richter's G minor *balletto* and the genuine trumpet music in the third *balletto* of Mus. Hs. 18 968 ('Balletti à Cinque 2 Trombe i Violino i Violetta i Viola con Violone') is marked. Here, the trumpet parts are totally idiomatic and unlike the two upper parts of the previous *balletto*. They do not play in every movement and are silent in the sarabande and aria. In the allemande, the first trumpet doubles the first violin, but the second trumpet has an independent part. Music with trumpets was clearly important at the imperial court: the 'Distinta Specificatione' inventory of music written for the Viennese court has a separate entry for 'Sonate con Trombe Sollenni'. It is unfortunate that more of it does not survive.

---

[32] Nettl's account of the manuscript is incorrect: he gives the wrong shelfmark and states that the first *balletto* is signed 'Ferd. Tobias Richter, 1685'. Neither *balletto* in this manuscript is signed in this way. See: Nettl, *Die Wiener Tanzkomposition*, p. 156.

[33] Köchel, *Die kaiserliche Hof-Musikkapelle*, p. 358.

[34] Nettl, *Die Wiener Tanzkomposition*, p. 156.

[35] *AMA*, vol. 5/I, entry 388. See also: M. Collver and B. Dickey, *A Catalog of Music for the Cornett* (Bloomington and Indianapolis, 1996), p. 64.

While the *balletti* written by Johann Heinrich Schmelzer's son, Andreas Anton, are only preserved in manuscript 16 588 in *particella* format, some of the titles give instrumental indications. Thus, the second of A.A. Schmelzer's three *balletti* danced on 15 November 1680 is described as 'mit sallmaÿ, geige und einen fagott'. The third *balletto* of this set mentions a 'Jägerhorn' in its title; elsewhere in 16 588, Schmelzer asks for a choir of strings with 'trumel und flote' and, somewhat exotically, a choir of strings with four harps. Presumably, the *sallmaÿ* belonged to the same family of instruments as the *Piffari* used by Schmelzer in the 'Balletto di Centauri Ninfe et Saluatici' and elsewhere. According to Bruce Haynes, these instruments were 'probably Renaissance shawms'.[36] Oboes themselves seem to have come to the imperial court rather later than many of the German courts. Franz and Roman Glätzl were *Hofkapelle* oboists from 1701 although it seems that the instrument was in use by 1698.[37] As in other parts of Europe, oboes were added to existing string music. In the fourth of Hoffer's 1694 *balletti* (*A-Wn* Suppl. mus. 1809), 'hautbois' has been added to the first violin part by a later hand. However, if manuscript *A-Wn* Suppl. mus. 1077 is typical, then oboes and bassoons were sometimes used with great caution. Suppl. mus. 1077 is an anonymous six-movement *balletto*, but only the second movement, 'Ciaccona', uses wind instruments. Even then, the three oboes and bassoon are only used for the main sections of the 'Ciaccona'; the variation sections are for strings alone.

It has been suggested that the oboe's delayed introduction to the imperial *Hofkapelle* was a result of a personal 'aversion to French music' on the part of the Emperor himself.[38] It is therefore important to examine the nature of this personal aversion, if it existed at all, and gauge the extent of any French musical influence at the imperial court. Given the political intrigues that I discussed at the start of the chapter, it is unlikely that large-scale operas and ballets by French composers were ever given at the imperial court during Leopold's reign. Paul Nettl is probably right when he suggests that 'under these circumstances, the French ballet in Vienna virtually became a black market commodity. It was confined to the house of the French Ambassador, and occasionally to surreptitious [performances] in the houses of the nobility'.[39]

Leopold's personal tastes may well have been entirely different. Indeed, contemporary reports from sources outside the realms of political intrigue present rather a different picture. Casimir Freschot, writing in 1705, offered this assessment of Leopold's own command of the French language:

---

[36] B. Haynes, *The eloquent Oboe* (Oxford, 2001), p. 156.

[37] Köchel, *Die kaiserliche Hof-Musikkapelle*, p. 362; Haynes, *The eloquent Oboe*, p. 156.

[38] Haynes, *The eloquent Oboe*, p. 156.

[39] Nettl, *Die Wiener Tanzkomposition*, p. 53.

> L'Empereur parle fort bien les Langues Latine, Italienne, Espagnole & Françoise
> ... Il repond en toutes ces Langues avec beaucoup de facilité & d'élégance.[40]

A similar picture emerges of the Viennese themselves:

> The Inhabitants [of Vienna], generally speaking, are courteous and affable, and as well bred as any in *Germany*, by reason of the Court, and the concourse of French and Italians, whose behaviour and fashion they happily emulate: And many, besides their own Tongue, and the Latine (which they speak very fluently) speak Italian and French.[41]

This apparent cultural diversity is also present in some Viennese dance music. The 'Ariæ Ad ingressum Suæ Maiestatis et egressum' (*A-Wn* Mus. Hs. 19 265) contains an extended bransle suite; nothing could be more intrinsically French, and it is by no means an isolated example. Bransle sequences or individual bransle movements feature in the suites of Poglietti, even though his duties as one the imperial court organists may not have brought him into regular contact with the dance music of the *Hofkapelle* (see Table 9.2).

Table 9.2: Suites by Poglietti in *CZ-KRa* that contain bransles or bransle-derived movements

Shelf-mark	Manuscript title	Instrumentation	Movements
A 768	Ballets a 5. d. Al: de Pogl.	[Unlabelled first violin part]/ Viol: 2do./ Violetta/ Gamba/ Basso di viola/ Cembalo	Entree/Gavotte/Branle/ Amener/Courente/ Branle [II]/Menuette/ Allemande/ Sarabande/Passamezo/ Bouree/Retiree
A 770*	Ballett à 5. d. Al: de. Pogl.	Violino 1°/Violino 2do/ Alto di viola/Gamba/ Basso di viola/Cembalo	Entree/Branle/ Menuette/ Allemande/Courente/ Sarabande/Gigue/ Turtillione/Bouree/ Retiree

---

[40] Freschot, *Memoires*, p. 109.
[41] J. Burbury, *A relation of a journey*, p. 44.

Shelf-mark	Manuscript title	Instrumentation	Movements
A 772	Baletti Francesi a 5: dal Sigre: Alexandro de Poglietti:	Violino 1mo/Violino 2do/ Viola 1ma/Viola 2^{a}/ Cembalo o Violone	Intrada/Allemanda/ Menuette/Bouree/ Bransle gay/Canarie/ Retirade
A 773	Baletti Francesi Dal Sigr: Alexandro de Poglietti	Violino 1mo/Violino 2do/ Alto; Tenore; Cembalo ô viol: da Basso	Sonat[a]/Allemande/ Amener/Gavotte
A 877*	Ballett à. 5. *(sic)* d. A: de. Pogl.	Tromba 1^{a} (x2)/Tromba 2da/ Tromba 3^{a}/Tenor Tromba/ Violino ò flagolletto/ violetta/Alto/Gamba/ Basso di viola/Cembalo (x2)	Toccatina di Trombe/ Intrada/Branle/ Branle gaÿ/ Amener/Gavotte/ Sonatina a 4.Trombe/ Sonatina di viol:/ Sonata de 2: Tromb. 2. violin/ Gavotte/Sonata a 11.

*Note*s:

Shelfmarks with an asterisk denote autograph material.The order of the last two movements in A 770 has been reversed in AMA Vol. 5/1. The second copy of Tromba 1^{a} in A 877 does not have the opening 'Toccatina di Trombe' copied into it. In the same 'Ballet à 5', *AMA* Vol. 5/1 wrongly gives the Basso di viola as a 'T[enor] Vla'.

However, Poglietti's bransles are not always idiomatic in content or sequence of movements. For example, the 'Branle gay' in A 772 has all the characteristic cross rhythms and rhythmic ambiguity of the traditional *branle gay*, but uses a single quaver upbeat rather than the characteristic quaver and crotchet of the traditional French version. But the fact remains that this is basically French music; perhaps some of these bransles were specifically written for dancing in the French style, either on stage or in the ballroom. It is tempting to associate such works with private performances given in the houses of Viennese nobility.

Private performances of French-inspired repertoire may also have been responsible for *Concors discordia* (Nuremberg, 1695), a collection of suites by the Austrian composer Benedikt Anton Aufschnaiter. At the time of the collection's publication, Aufschnaiter seems to have been working in Vienna in the service of Count Ferdinand Ernst von Trautmannsdorf, a Viennese nobleman. Although the edition was dedicated to the 'Augusti et serenissimi Romanorum Regis

Joseph I' (later Emperor Joseph I), Aufschnaiter appears to have had little or no connection with Leopold's *Hofkapelle*. Certainly, the collection is in the German-Lullian tradition and stands outside the suite writing of the imperial court. As well as the printed edition, a number of manuscript copies also exist: *S-Uu* IMhs 134:013, *S-Uu* IMhs 012:016 and *S-VX* Mus. MS 6; the latter compiled by the Swedish amateur musician Nils Tiliander. The existence of a printed edition and three manuscript copies suggests that the collection was widely circulated. It is not difficult to see why. The music is attractive and well crafted, but undemanding on players and listeners. It is reasonable to suppose that even the least skilled court musicians could make something of the suites in this collection. Example 9.4 shows the opening of the fantasia from the third suite in the collection: despite the quick tempo, there is nothing that is especially technically demanding.

Ex. 9.4.   B.A. Aufschnaiter, *Concors discordia* (Nuremberg, 1695), Suite III, 'Fantasia'

The part books give the title 'Serenada.1' above the first suite, but only numbers thereafter. Presumably, each of the remaining suites was also intended to be a serenade. Niedt's 1706 *Handleitung zur Variation* gives the following definition of a serenade:

> [*Serenata*] means evening music or a *Ständgen* [i.e. Ständchen] and comes from *Sereno*, cheerful, light, bright, because such evening music is usually presented in cheerful, light, and clear weather. However, a *Serenata* is by no means a regular little piece, such as a Gavotte or Allemande, but rather a *Concert* consisting of many pieces, voices, and instruments.[42]

He goes on to say that, strictly speaking, a serenade should be a vocal piece, but allows that there are also 'purely instrumental' examples.[43] Perhaps Niedt had Aufschnaiter's pieces in mind: they clearly fit his definition and the implied cheerful and bright nature of the music itself. It may be no coincidence that Fux's 1701 *Concentus Musico-Instrumentalis*, likewise dedicated to Joseph I, also contains a serenade as its first suite. (See Chapter 10.) Perhaps this was a popular entertainment at Joseph's court.

There is some variation in the instrumentation of *Concors discordia*. The two opening suites are scored for one violin, two violas and bass: a second violin is added for the four remaining suites. In the second violin part book, these two *à 4* opening suites are marked 'tacet'. This is curious in a French-influenced printed collection: as we have seen, the second violin would normally duplicate the first. It has been suggested that this 'may have been simply a matter of convenience and, perhaps, also of economy'.[44] This seems unlikely: the edition itself shows no other signs of parsimony. In any case, printing a further set of pages from the same typesetting can hardly have been expensive or inconvenient. The lack of a doubled violin part in these first two suites may be the result of nothing more than the absence of a specific instruction to a printer ignorant of the French tradition. The other suites of the collection use part doubling in the traditional French manner though the scoring is *à 4* instead of *à 5*. As in the music of the German *Lullists*, the first and second violin parts diverge in the trio sections to play independent lines.

A problem of the trio instrumentation arises in one of the manuscripts copies, *S-VX* Mus. MS 6. Although incomplete, enough of Mus. MS 6 survives to suggest that the instrumentation of this source differed from the printed edition. 'Viol: 1$^{mo.}$'

---

[42] F. E. Niedt, *Handleitung zur Variation* (Hamburg, 1706, repr. 1721; trans. by P. Poulin and I. Taylor as *Friederich Erhardt Niedt /The Musical Guide*, Oxford, 1989), p. 145.

[43] Ibid., p.145.

[44] P. Whitehead, 'Austro-German Printed Sources of Instrumental Music, 1630 to 1700', (Ph.D. diss., University of Pennsylvania, 1996), p. 370.

and 'Viol: 2$^{do.}$' are written out on facing pages. Curiously, 'Viol: 1$^{mo.}$' corresponds to the original 'Violino Primo' part of the printed edition, but 'Viol: 2$^{do.}$' is a copy of the soprano clef 'Viola Prima' part. This presents a problem in the suites in the printed edition with the 'Violino Secondo' part. Although we cannot be sure that a further, now lost, manuscript violin part was available, the transfer of the original first viola part to the second violin appears to represent a scoring reduction, making some of the trio sections unplayable. This may reflect an earlier source than the publication copy, or it may be a scribal error.

Only four of the suites start with an *ouverture*: the first starts with a *ciaconna* and the fifth with an *entrée*. There is also a clear distinction between chaconne and passacaglia. The two examples of the former are little more than sequences of repeated phrases. But the passacaglia, which also uses simple phrase repetition, is loosely based on the rondeau format with an opening *grand couplet* that appears at various times during the movement. None of these movements uses a repeated bass line formula. There are no character movements and, along with the 'purely instrumental' nature of the serenade, it seems that the collection was always intended as being purely instrumental.

It is possible that the anonymous composer of manuscript suite *S-Uu* IMhs 064:013 may have been Austrian. And, like Aufschnaiter, he may also have been experimenting with the Lullian style. The Austrian origins are suggested by the closing 'Final', a Viennese *retirada* in all but name. This short and sometimes chromatic movement is shown in Example 9.5. The *taille* part has not survived complete, and I have provided a reconstruction.

As we can see in the example, the instrumentation is typically French, especially with its two copies of the treble part. There are, however, a number of differences between IMhs 064:013 and the normal German-Lullian suite. The *ouverture* starts in the normal way, but after the duple-time middle section, the final part has a '3' time signature. This is quite different from the normal final section of a Lullian *ouverture*: there is no return to the dotted rhythms of the opening. Instead, the music moves mostly in quavers and crotchets. It does not seem that this was ignorance: the opening of this *ouverture* has all the characteristics of the Lullian manner. It seems that the differences are the result of experiment. The allemande also has the same air of experimentation. The structure falls into three parts: the first and last are largely similar, but there is a triple-time central section. The remaining movements are unexceptional apart from the 'Final'.

We cannot be sure if composers like Aufschnaiter gained their knowledge of French music from other German and Austrian composers or if they had experience of Lully's works. But evidence that Lully's music was known in the region comes from Lullian sources found in the Liechenstein collection. It has already been established that manuscript A 852 in the Liechenstein collection is not, as the title page states, 'Del S: Ebner A° 1667 Die: 30: Maÿ scriptum Viennæ'.[45] Six of the

---

[45] C.B. Schmidt, 'Manuscript Sources for the Music of Jean-Baptiste Lully' in *Notes*, 44/1 (September 1987), pp. 7–32 at p. 15. *AMA*, vol. 5/I, entry 186, still lists the work as

Ex. 9.5.   *S-Uu* IMhs 064:013, 'Final'

eight movements are extracts from Lully's *L'Hercule amoureux* (LWV 17/1–4, 17/7 and 17/11). The date on A 852 may well be correct as *L'Hercule amoureux* was written in 1662. And, as I have pointed out in Chapter 2, two further Kroměříž manuscripts, A 4826 and A 873 probably originate in a single-line source of Lully's music. Vejvanovský was probably responsible for both manuscripts, which would mean that they cannot be later than 1693, the year of his death. We can therefore say with some certainty that music by Lully himself was being circulated at the

being by Ebner.

Kroměříž court by the early 1690s. It is reasonable to assume that it was also in circulation in Vienna at around the same time, if not earlier. Moreover, music in an unmistakably Lullian style was occasionally dedicated to Leopold, again calling into question his supposed resistance to anything French. Likewise, the dedication by Melchiore D'Ardespin of his French-inspired ballet music from *L'Eraclio* to Leopold (see Chapter 6) is significant. The manuscript starts with a sinfonia that is a Lullian *ouverture* in all but name, and the dance movements of each suite are very much in the Lullian manner. This association was hardly likely to be lost on the musically literate Emperor, and it is unlikely that D'Ardespin would have dedicated music to the Emperor that was likely to cause offence. Ten years later, Leopold was also the dedicatee of Cousser's *La cicala della cetra d'Eunomio*, a collection that, despite its Italian title, was firmly rooted in the Lullian style (see Chapter 6). It is possible that Cousser was looking for a new appointment at this time and, again, he would hardly have dedicated offensive music to the Emperor. It is equally unlikely that a composer so renowned for his association with the Lullian style would have considered a post at a virulently anti-French establishment. From all this, it is clear that, despite political situation described earlier in this chapter, Leopold did not have an 'aversion to French music'. If French music did not have the hold that it had elsewhere, it was certainly known and accepted at the imperial court even if the influence of Lullianism was delayed until the mid-1680s at the earliest. The delay was not a result of Leopold's personal tastes; the imperial traditions of opera and ballet were simply too strong and too conservative.

As we have seen, suites emanating from other part of the German lands usually contained a sequence of movements tied to a single key centre. But Viennese composers adopted a different approach and often used a variety of keys within their *balletti*. Even in two-movement *balletti*, the movements were often in different keys. Four of the five *balletti* by Joseph Hoffer in manuscript *A-Wn* Suppl. mus. 1809 are examples of this approach. Table 9.3 details the movements and keys of each *balletto* in the manuscript.

Table 9.3: J. Hoffer, 'Parti à.4. Sampt getantz worden von den kaÿs: Hofftanzern am Fest Leoboldi beÿ hoff 1694 Del Hoffer', (*A-Wn* S.m. 1809)

Balletto	Movement titles	Movement keys
Primo	Aria/Gavotta/Minuett	D minor /B flat major /F major
[Secondo]	Aria/Giquè/Gavotta/Aria	C major /F major /G minor /C major

Balletto	Movement titles	Movement keys
3[tio]	Entre/Aria/Minuett/ Retirada	G major /E minor /C minor /F major
[quarto]	Marsch/Aria/Minuett/Rigidon/ Minuett[II]/Minuett[III]	C major /F major /F major /F major /G minor /F major
[quinto]	Aria/Minuett/Sarabanda/ Bergamasco	F major /B flat major /G major /C major

*Note*s: Balletto numberings in brackets were added to the manuscript at a later date.

The second *balletto* of this collection, however, adopts a different approach with the last movement returning to the key of the first. Hoffer's chosen sequence of keys is not particularly elegant, but it does demonstrate the concept of a circular sequence beginning and ending in the same key. Hoffer was not alone in using this device, and similar examples can be found in the suites of Richter, Fux and the Emperor himself. However, it was not as widespread as has been suggested; only J.H. Schmelzer, appears to have used the technique with any degree of consistency.[46] An example of his usage can be seen in the seven-movement 'Balletto der Dame ist gedanzt worden im Febr 1667' (16 583[I]). Table 9.4 gives details.

Table 9.4: Keys and movements in J.H. Schmelzer, 'beder Kaÿl: Princessinen Ballet ist gehalten worden den 14 Februarÿ 1668' (*A-Wn* Mus. Hs. 16 583[II])

Movement	Key
Aria. 45[a]	D major
Gavotte. 46[a]	G major
Gagliarda. 47[a]	G major
Gavotte. 48[a]	D major
Sarabande. 49[a]	G major
Canario. 50[a]	E minor
Retirada. 51[a]	B minor - D major

---

[46] R. Hudson, *The Allemande, the Balletto and the Tanz,* 2 vols. (2 vols, Cambridge, 1986), vol. 1, p. 185.

Such key sequences are not only applied to larger-scale *balletti*. 'Balletto 2do. di Puffoni', the second of two ballets written for the Empress' birthday on 18 November 1668 (16 583[II]) only has three movements, but they are organized into a clearly defined key scheme whereby the first aria is a microcosm of the sequence as a whole. The first movement starts in F major and finishes in D minor. The second movement is in F major, and the third in D minor. As part of the technique, movements themselves sometimes start in one key and finish in another. One of the earliest examples of this in a *balletto* by J.H. Schmelzer, is in the opening *balletto* of the 'Monstri Ballett' of 16 February 1665 (16 583[I]). Here, the *retirada* starts in F sharp minor and finishes in A major. It is telling that Schmelzer was experimenting with modulation within a single dance movement at a comparatively early point in his career.

Where did Schmelzer get the idea of writing *balletti* in circular key sequences? The answer may come from his sonatas. Works such as the 'Sonata II a otto' in Schmelzer's *Sacro-profanus concentus musicus* collection of sonatas may not use circular key progressions, but the frequent use of modulation within sections suggests a parallel between sonata and *balletto*.[47] (Table 9.5 lists the key sequence of this sonata in its various sections.)

Table 9.5: Keys and sections in J.H. Schmelzer, *Sacro-profanus concentus musicus*, 'Sonata II a otto' (Nuremberg, 1662)

Bar numbers	Time signature	Keys
1-27	C	D minor
28-40	C	D minor-A major
41-71	3/2	A minor-D major
72-98	C	A minor-A major
99-120	C	A minor-D major

It is difficult to know if Schmelzer's use of circular key sequences first occurred in his *balletti* or in his sonatas. Given the association of such devices with the sonata, it seems more likely that he brought the technique from the sonata, and applied it to the suite.

---

[47] All details of this collection are taken from the modern edition: E. Schenk (ed.) *DTÖ*, vols. 111–12 (Graz, 1965).

I have already pointed to the significant differences between Viennese and Kroměříž sources. This particularly applies to J.H. Schmelzer's music. *Balletti* originally linked by their relationship to a particular opera or entertainment were often separated or copied in a different order, and we must assume that the scores were sent out from Vienna in a piecemeal fashion. For example, the February 1669 'masked serenade' in 16 583[II] has three movements: two arias and a *ciaconna*. In the Kroměříž source of the same music (A 937), the *ciaconna* is replaced by a different passacaglia, and a further three movements are added. These four additional movements are not known in any other Schmelzer source, and so we cannot be completely certain of their authorship.

There is also evidence that Schmelzer himself changed and reused material. Assuming the given dates are correct, some of the movements from the 1671 *balletto* for the birthday of the Queen of Spain (16 583[II]) were used again for the well-known 'Sonata Con Ariæ à 5 Viol: et 4 Trombe Col Timpani per libito' from the following year (*CZ-KRa* A 465). There is no Vienna version of the latter, but the Kroměříž version contains a note on the wrapper that appears to come from Schmelzer himself.

It is possible that Schmelzer may also have been responsible for the expansion of the two movement *balletto* that comes at the end of 16 583[I] into the Kroměříž seven-movement version, 'Serenata: a.5. Vom Smeltzer' (*CZ-KRa* A 760).[48] It is unlikely that a copyist would have taken such trouble. In the Vienna source, the first movement, the well-known *campanella*, is written on two staves: most unusually, inner harmonies are also included. The other movement, 'Aria Lamentevole' is written in the normal way, with just bass and treble lines. In the complete set of parts that make up A 760, these two movements become part of a larger seven-movement structure including regular repeats of the *campanelæ*. The sequence of *campanelæ* and laments in this *balletto* is complex, but the correct order is clearly indicated by the insertion of the instruction 'Campanelæ ut Supra' after each *lamento*. The full sequence of movements and repeats in A 760 is as follows:

Seranata/Ciaccona/Campanelæ/Lamento [I]/Campanelæ ut Supra/[Lamento II]/Campanelæ ut Supra e finisce.[49]

The 'Seranata' is scored for five-part strings in all its sections, the following movements for four-part strings. Although there are examples throughout the German repertoire of five-part abstract opening movements being followed by four-part dances, it seems more likely that, as in A 465, Schmelzer combined material here from at least two different sources. This appears to be confirmed by the separate existence of the 'Seranata' movement in manuscript *CZ-KRa* A

---

[48] The editorial commentary in the modern edition of this work makes no reference to the *A-Wn* source. See: B. Clark (ed.), *J.H. Schmelzer, Serenata con altre Ariae* (St Ives, 2004).

[49] *AMA*, vol. 5/I omits the first repeat of the *campanella*. (Record 585.)

746. A duplicate set of parts for the complete *balletto* exists as *CZ-KRa* A 905. It is possible that these parts are merely an additional set made for a performance with more players than usual. Although in a different hand, they are identical in all respects to A 760.

There are other sources of *balletti* by J.H. Schmelzer that exist outside Vienna and Kroměříž. A manuscript of three suites appears to have originated in Vienna, but is now in Uppsala (*S-Uu* IMhs 011:016:1–3). One of these contains music by Schmelzer. The manuscript is dated 'Vienna, 26 May 1671', and has the name 'Assieg' on the wrapper. No information has come to light regarding the identity of Assieg, but his name is found on a number of different manuscript sources, all of which seem to originate in Vienna. Despite its shelf mark, IMhs 011:016:1–3 is a single manuscript in the form of four part books, each containing three suites. The conclusion of each suite is shown by the marking 'NB. X'. The wrapper title, 'Sonata Aria Gique Retirada Couranta Sarabanda à Violino 2. Violetto e Basso Contin. Assieg. Wien. d. 26. Maÿ. 1671' appears to be a collective one applying to all three suites. In the second suite, the two viola parts are marked 'NB. Violetta' and 'NB. Viola di Braccio', but it is not clear if this instruction is also meant to apply to the third suite. No composer is mentioned. The first suite has some of the features of a Viennese *balletto*: it ends with a *retirada*, and two of its four movements are in the key of B flat major and two in D major. The contents of the second suite do not suggest similar origins, and much of the work, especially the opening sonata, is technically awkward and not particularly imaginative.

The last of these three *balletti* is more interesting. It contains music from J.H. Schmelzer's 'Balletto, genandt das Narrenspitall ist gedanzt worden den 21. Febr 1667'. In 16 583[I], this *balletto* starts with the widely copied 'Intrada der pulicinelli', and this is clearly the source for the title 'Delli Policinelli', which is placed at the head of IMhs 011:016:1–3.[50] In fact, only the first four movements of 'Delli Policinelli' are taken from Schmelzer's original ballet; the remainder appear to be from an unknown source, and may not be by Schmelzer at all. There is little agreement between the two sources over order of movements, and it seems likely that the copyist of the *S-Uu* source was only concerned to extract four movements in the same key from the original *balletto*, presumably for instrumental performance. Another *S-Uu* manuscript, IMhs 008:015, is headed '12. Sonata, Allemand, Courant, Gavott, Sarab:, Gique, Sonatina. à 4 Viol: ê Bass: Giovanni Henrico Schmelzer'. It also bears Assieg's name. The manuscript does not appear to be complete: there are parts for two violas but, despite the title, only one violin. The quality of the music in this manuscript is poor: we should treat the attribution to Schmelzer with the greatest suspicion.

J.H. Schmelzer died in 1680 after contracting the plague. His son Andreas Anton took over his duties as a composer of the ballet music for the various court entertainments. It has been suggested that the music of Andreas Anton Schmelzer

---

[50] This *intrada* is also found in a hitherto-unrecognised manuscript source in *S-N* Finspong 9098.

does 'not evince the great variety and musical interest of his father's'.[51] This claim requires examination. Example 9.6 shows the first strain of 'Intrada 193' from 16 588.

Ex, 9.6.   A.A. Schmelzer, 'Balletto von gartnerinne' (16 588) 'Intrada N° 193'

It is typical of many such movements in this manuscript: the strains are organized clearly and the material is inventive. We have also seen that Andreas Anton's instrumentation was colourful and often highly original. From the titles given in 16 588, it is clear that there were changes in the circumstances governing the performances of the ballets themselves. Visiting dignitaries appear to have taken an increasing part in the dancing. In addition, a greater number of character dances were inserted, perhaps reflecting the presence of professional or more experienced dancers. The music obviously had to reflect these changes and the dances for the visitors are often short and simple, no doubt making the task of the dancing masters much easier when it came to teaching the choreography. Many of Andreas Anton's *balletti* contain no more than two or three dances, but this is a reflection of the choreography, not the music. All this suggests that Andreas Anton was working within narrow confines, and that the comparisons of his music with his father's may be unnecessarily harsh. Unfortunately, it seems that the only sources of his *balletti* are the two-stave reductions given in 16 588. A reassessment

---

[51]   R. Schnitzler & T. D. Walker, 'Schmelzer, Andreas Anton' in *New Grove* 2, vol. 22, p. 526.

of Andreas Anton Schmelzer's work cannot really begin until further material is recovered.

Most of the music that I have discussed in this chapter has had direct links with the stage. Music originating in the ballroom appears to be rare, as do suites intended for purely instrumental performance. As we have seen, the music in IMhs 011:016:1–3 may have been intended for the latter purpose, and there are a number of works in *CZ-KRa* that do not appear to fall into the category of dance music originally intended for the stage. The suite in manuscript A 758 seems to stand apart from most of J.H. Schmelzer's other dance music. It is written for violin, two violas, and a figured 'Organo ò Basso di Viola'. A sonata prefaces the dance movements, and the entire suite remains in the key of G minor. The sarabande has an unusual structure: there are three strains; one each of eight, twelve and four bars. Only the first and third strains are repeated. This is a far more complex structure than that of any sarabande in Schmelzer's stage-related *balletti*, although it is possible that special choreography could have been created for it. However, the presence of the sonata does seem to confirm that this suite was meant for instrumental performance. *CZ-KRa* A 899 presents rather more of a problem. Entitled 'Arie Con la Mattacina à4. Dal Smelzer', it includes an introductory sonata. The *mattacina* itself is not written in the triple-metre traditionally assigned to this dance, although the tempo marking 'presto' suggests something of its usual character, which is meant to be wild, even demonic. Again, the presence of a sonata, combined with a dance of unusual characteristics, seems to suggest an instrumental work, and not one with its origins in music for the stage.

The question of how the Viennese *balletto* differs from the suite in the rest of Austria and the surrounding areas falls outside the scope of this book. However, it is clear that the *balletti* discussed in this chapter mostly represent an entirely different tradition from the suite in the rest of the German lands. Even though they were often subservient to the needs of the operas with which they shared the stage, their quality is often extremely high. In particular, it must be considered a matter of great regret that so much of J.H. Schmelzer's work only exists in the two-stave collections of 16 583.

Chapter 10
Eine frische Frantzösische Ouverture ihnen allen zu præferiren
Conclusion and Case Studies

Despite a general decline in music printing in Germany and Austria,[1] the revitalization of the court suite by the German Lullists carried the genre well into the eighteenth century. 'Auf jetziger Zeit wol-bekannte Frantzösische Art' (in the well-known French style of the present day) is how Jacob Scheiffelhut described his 1707 collection of suites in the German-Lullian style, *Musicalisches Klee-Blatt*.[2] Despite the War of the Spanish Succession and military conflict with France at the start of the eighteenth century, there can be little doubt that the influence of Lully was still strong amongst musicians in Germany at this time. But German musical taste was still apparently preoccupied with the differences between French and Italian music. Johann Mattheson spends a good deal of time dealing with the matter in the first chapter of the third part of his treatise, *Das Neu-Eröffnete Orchestre* (Hamburg 1713). His view of the suite also appears to have changed little from those of the German Lullists of the previous century:

> Ob sich auch gleich die Italiäner die gröste Mühe von der Welt mit ihren Symphonien und Concerten geben/welche auch gerwitz überaus schön sind/so ist doch wol eine frische Frantzösische Ouverture ihnen allen zu præferiren. Denn/nechst der Composition einer solchen Pieçe mit ihrer Suite à la Francoise, ist die Excecution in ihrem Genere, welche die Frantzosen derselbigen geben/so admirable, so unie (sic) und so ferme, daß nichts darüber seyn kan.[3] (Even if one also says that Italians take the greatest pains of anybody with their simphonies and concertos which are, as we know, also extremely fine, it is still a vigorous French *ouverture* that is to be preferred above all. Then next to the composition of such a piece with its suite in the French manner, is the execution of the genre, which the French give to the same: so admirable, so unified and so contained; nobody can surpass it.)

---

[1] H. Lenneberg, *On the Publishing and Dissemination of Music 1500–1850* (Hillsdale, New York, 2003), pp. 60–1.

[2] L. Gerheuser, *Jacob Scheiffelhut und seine Instrumentalmusik* (Augsburg, 1931), p. 44.

[3] J. Mattheson, *Das neu-eröffnete Orchestre* (Hamburg, 1713; facsm. D. Bartel (ed.), Laaber, 2004), p. 226.

Tellingly, Mattheson continues to link the French manner and 'die Excecution', in other words, performance practice. Even the traditional German description of French music as lively resurfaces in the use of 'frische' in conjunction with the *ouverture*. To illustrate this further, I am presenting three case studies that demonstrate the continuing influence of Lully's music not just on the music of the courts, but also on the music of the towns. Accordingly, Johann Christian Schieferdecker's *XII. musicalische Concerte* will show the influence of the French manner on an eighteenth-century town musician. Johann Joseph Fux's *Concentus musico-instrumentalis* will show how French influence was consolidating in Vienna at the turn of the century. And a little-known manuscript suite by 'Johan Fischer' will show how the same influence was reaching the areas outside Vienna.

Johann Christian Schieferdecker seems doomed to be principally remembered as the man who married Anna Margreta, daughter of Dietrich Buxtehude. Marriage to Anna Margreta was a condition of being appointed successor to Buxtehude as organist and *Werkmeister* of the *Marienkirche* in Lübeck and, famously, she and the post were turned down by both Mattheson and Handel.[4] Schieferdecker had worked with Buxtehude for a year as his assistant and appears to have married Anna Margreta just before her father's death in 1707. Accordingly, he became the Lübeck organist. The marriage itself was short-lived; Anna Margreta died in 1709. Unfortunately, much of Schieferdecker's work has been lost, and *XII. musicalische Concerte, bestehend aus etlichen Ouverturen und Suiten,* (Hamburg,1713) is his only known instrumental composition. The collection is detailed in Table 10.1.

Table 10.1: Contents of: J.C. Shieferdecker, *XII. musicalische Concerte, bestehend aus etlichen Ouverturen und Suiten* (Hamburg, 1713)

Title	Contents	Instrumentation	Key
1.Concert	Ouvertur/Passepied/Entrée/ Chaconne/ Giquée	Hautbois I-III/ basson/violino I-II/ violin III & viola/ bassus continuo	A minor
2.Concert	Ouvertur/Bourée/ Gavotte/ March/ Saraband/Menuet alternativement/ Trio/Menuet da capo	Hautbois I-III/ basson/violino I-II/ violin III & viola/ bassus continuo	B flat major

---

[4] C. Snyder, *Dieterich Buxtehude, organist in Lübeck* (New York, 1987; revised edn.; Rochester, 2007), pp. 103–104.

Eine frische Frantzösische Ouverture ihnen allen zu præferiren   229

Title	Contents	Instrumentation	Key
3.Concert	Ouvertur/Gavotte/Rondeau/ Rigadon/ Sarabanda/Menuet alternativement/ Concert/Menuet da capo	Hautbois I-III/ basson/violino I-II/ violin III & viola/ bassus continuo	C minor
4.Concert	Prelude/Aria/March/Menuet alternativement/Trio/Menuet da capo/ Bourée/Sarabanda/Giquée	Hautbois I-III/ basson/violino I-II/ violin III & viola/ bassus continuo	C major
5.Concert	Ouverture/Rondeau/Bourée/ Menuet/ Aria/Rigadon/Trio/ Rigadon da capo/ Giquée	Hautbois I-III/ basson/violino I-II/ violin III & viola/ bassus continuo	D minor
6.Concert	Simphonie/Aria/Gavotte/ Rondeau/ Menuet/Aria hautbois solo/Giquée	Hautbois I-III/ basson/violino I-II/ violin III & viola/ bassus continuo	D major
7.Concert	Ouvertur/Gavott/Sarabanda Menuet/ Chaconne/Giquée	Hautbois I-III/ basson/violino I-II/ violin III & viola/ bassus continuo	F minor
8.Concert	Ouvertur/Concert/Sarabanda/ Gavott en Rondeau/Menuet/Trio/ Menuet da capo/Giquée	Hautbois I-III/ basson/violino I-II/ violin III & viola/ bassus continuo	F major
9.Concert	Ouvertur/Courante/Sarabanda/ Aria/ Menuet/Bourée alternativement/ Bourée da capo	Hautbois I-III/ basson/violino I-II/ violin III & viola/ bassus continuo	G minor
10.Concert	Ouvertur/Gavott/Aria/Menuet alternativement/Trio/Menuet da Capo/ Chaconne	Hautbois I-III/ basson/violino I-II/ violin III & viola/ bassus continuo	G major
11.Intrada *à 4*	Intrada/March/ Rigadon/Menuet/ Deuett. alternativement/Menuet da capo/Sarabanda/Giquée	Hautbois I-II/basson I-II	F major

Title	Contents	Instrumentation	Key
12.Prelude *à 4*	Prelude/Ouvertur/Sarabanda/ Menuet alternativement/Duetto/ Menuet da capo/Chaconne	Hautbois I-II/basson I-II	C major
[13.]Concert	Ouverture/Gavott/Bourée/Menuet alternativement avec l'trio/Trio/ Menuet da capo/Chaconne	Hautbois I-III/ basson/violino I-II/ violin III & viola/ bassus continuo	C minor

Note: The 'bassus continuo' part is not figured anywhere in the collection.

Schieferdecker had been educated at the Leipzig *Thomaskirche* at a time when Johann Schelle was *cantor* and Kuhnau was organist. He also studied at the university. With this background, Schieferdecker must certainly have come into contact with consort suites written by town musicians. But by the end of the century, the separate tradition of tradition of carefully organized consort-suite writing discussed in Chapter 3 had all but died out. Only in the keyboard repertoire did it extend into the following century. For example, Johann Kuhnau's *Neüer Clavier Übung Andrer Theil* (Leipzig, 1692) was reprinted no less than four times, the last being 1726.

So where did Schieferdecker gain his knowledge of the French music that clearly had such an influence on *XII. musicalische Concerte*? It seems that Lully's music was starting to circulate in the towns at the end of the seventeenth century.[5] And Scheiffelhut's reference to the 'well-known' French manner is especially significant as he was not a court musician, but a town musician in Augsburg. However, the progress of this influence was much slower in the towns than it was in the courts, and it is unlikely that Schieferdecker came across French music in any significant amounts before he left Leipzig. He had encountered opera while at Leipzig University, but this was Italian. So it seems almost certain that prolonged contact with the French style came at the Hamburg opera where Schieferdecker worked between 1702 and 1706 and where Johann Georg Conradi and Cousser had introduced French elements during the 1690s. It is even possible that he may have known Cousser's highly influential *Composition de musique*. The opening of the *ouvertures* to the first suites of both *Composition de musique* and *XII. musicalische Concerte* contain intriguing similarities in the treble lines and harmonic progressions. Schieferdecker's harmonic scheme may be less expansive than Cousser's, but it is still essentially the same. And, as we have seen, Cousser's six suites are arranged in a rising sequence of keys from A minor to G major (see page 124). With additional major and minor pairings, Schieferdecker's ordering

---

[5] For instance, it appears that French music is mentioned in the Lübeck book auctions of 1695. I am grateful to Stephen Rose for passing this information onto me.

of the keys in suites I–X is, again, essentially the same. The breaking of the sequence for the eleventh and twelfth suites (see Table 10.1 above) was probably dictated by the need to write in a comfortable key for the wind band instruments Schieferdecker uses at this point.

XII. musicalische Concerte was issued as eight part books:

> Hautbois Primo /Hautbois Secundo /Hautb. Tertio /Basson /Violino Primo / Violino Secundo /3. Violin and Viola /Bassus Continuo

It is likely that the viola was intended as an alternative, and not a supplement, to the third violin.[6] According to the preface, the collection is 'vollstimmig gesetzt worden' (set for a full ensemble), and *vollstimmig* may well refer to Schieferdecker's practice of having, in all *tutti* passages, each oboe doubling the corresponding violin line. One of the most striking features of the instrumentation of the collection is the frequent use of concerto-like solo writing. The Italian solo concerto was certainly known in early eighteenth-century Germany; Albinoni's concertos, for example, were apparently widely circulated at this time.[7] And 'Roger built up his list by actively seeking out saleable Italian instrumental music'.[8] However, solo writing in suites at this time was hardly new; Muffat had combined elements of the suite and *concerto grosso* into his *Armonico Tributo* collection, and the trio for two oboes and bassoon was an important factor in the writing of Lully and his German imitators.

A further influence may have been Johann Christian Schickhardt who arrived in Hamburg just before the publication of his Op. 13 *VI. Concerts à Deux Violons, Deux Haubois ou Violons Basse & Basse Continue* by Roger around 1712. He also became the Hamburg agent for Roger and might have met Schieferdecker in this capacity. *VI. Concerts* are mostly concertos; Richard Maunder has suggested that they 'appear to be the earliest printed concertos ... to include parts for oboes.[9] But while the final *allegro* of Schickhardt's first 'concert' is clearly inspired by the concerto genre, there are also strong suite elements with an *ouverture* followed by an *entreé* and a menuet. Schieferdecker's mixture of concerto and suite elements may have been influenced by Schickhardt. And, of course, the term 'concert' is common to both collections.

---

[6] While the range of the second violin in many of the movements might suggest a viola rather than a violin, the presence of g" and a" at various moments would take the part above the normal range of the former.

[7] R. Maunder, *The Scoring of Baroque concertos* (Woodbridge, 2004), pp. 23 and 44. See also S. McVeigh & J. Hirshberg, *The Italian solo concerto, 1700–1760* (Woodbridge, 2004), pp. 44–5

[8] McVeigh & Hirshberg, *Italian solo concerto*, p. 47.

[9] Maunder, *Scoring of Baroque concertos*, p. 94.

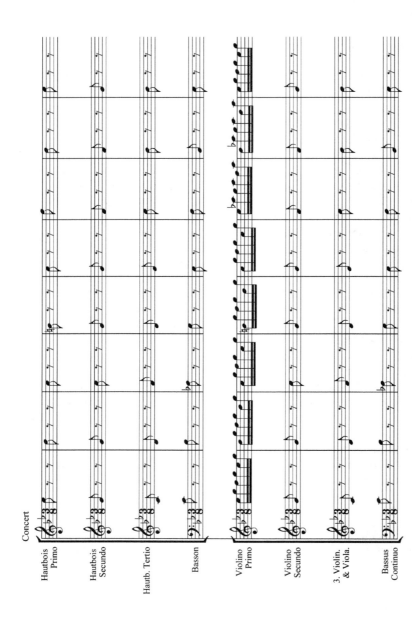

Ex. 10.1. J.C. Schieferdecker, *XII. musicalische Concerte, bestehend aus etlichen Ouverturen und Suiten* (Hamburg, 1713), Suite III, 'Concert'

It is not surprising, therefore, to see the influence of the concerto in the 'concert' movement that forms part of a menuet sequence at the close of Schieferdecker's third suite (see Example 10.1).

But it is not just the violin that is treated as a soloist; every member of the ensemble is given an opportunity for solo playing: in the splendidly exuberant prelude to the fourth suite, even the *continuo* is marked 'solo' at the start. However, it is the first oboe that is the collection's most frequently used soloist, and it is surely no coincidence that the title page and preface appears in the first oboe part book and not in the first violin. The first oboe music suggests that Schieferdecker must have had a fine and expressive player available to him in Lübeck. We should also note that many of the trio sections are for the three oboes alone, rather than the usual combination of two oboes and bassoon.

If the sixth suite is dominated by solo writing for the first oboe, there is little uniformity elsewhere in the way that solo instruments are brought together. The combinations of soloists tend to vary from movement to movement. Schieferdecker was some way from writing the later type of combined concerto and suite, labelled by Johann Adolph Scheibe as a 'Concertouverture', where the same solo instrument or combination of instruments tended to be used throughout.[10] But Schieferdecker's contribution to the early stages of this genre is significant and largely unrecognized by modern scholars.[11] Most important of all, it seems that Schieferdecker was the first town musician to have written suites in this way. Before we leave issues of instrumentation, we should note that not one of the string passages marked 'solo' in *XII. musicalische Concerte* has alternative music for any remaining *ripieno* players. The implication is clear: these suites were intended for one-to-a-part performance.

The title page of the collection lists twelve suites, but there are actually thirteen. It seems that the thirteenth suite was not originally intended as part of the collection; 'fine' appears in all part books at the end of the twelfth suite. The music is similar to the rest of the collection, albeit with oboe writing that is far less demanding than it is in the other suites. For the only time in the collection, a trio of violins is employed. Perhaps it was written for other circumstances and just tacked onto the end of *XII. musicalische Concerte*; superstition may possibly have played a part and prevented the number 13 from being used either on the title pages or in the part books.

The use of 'concert' to describe a suite was not new; Muffat had used it in *Ausserlesene Instrumental-Music* and, of course, Schickhardt has used it as well. Schieferdecker may have been thinking of no more than indicating an ensemble of mixed instruments. But if it was his intention to emphasize the French credentials

---

[10] S. Zohn, 'Bach and the *Concert en ouverture*' in G. Butler (ed.), *J.S. Bach's concerted ensemble music, the Ouverture*, Bach Perspectives, vol. 6 (Urbana & Chicago, 2007), pp. 137–56 at pp. 137–8.

[11] For example he is not mentioned in Zohn, 'Bach', or Maunder, *Scoring of Baroque concertos*.

of *XII. musicalische Concerte*, it is strange that he used 'concert' again for two individual movements where the Italian influence is at its strongest. French influence is clearly proclaimed in the preface: 'welche durchaus nach der in den Ouverturen so beliebten Frantzösischen Art' (the *ouvertures* are entirely in the popular French manner), although it is not clear if he is referring to complete suites or opening movements. And by calling his pieces 'Ouverturen und Suiten', Schieferdecker appears to be making deliberate reference to the German-Lullist collections of 'Ouvertures de theatre accompagnées de plusiers airs'. How accurate is Schieferdecker's claim that he is following the French manner?

All the suites in *XII. musicalische Concerte* start with an introductory movement followed by a sequence of dances; in nine of them, this introductory movement is a French *ouverture*. A similar *ouverture* is also present in the second of the wind band suites where it follows a prelude. The opening of the first *ouverture* of the collection has been quoted above, and it is clear that Schieferdecker was largely familiar with the Lullian idiom. But there are differences in Schieferdecker's approach that are at odds with his claim to be writing in an entirely French manner. Example 10.2 shows the start of the second section of the *ouverture* to the eighth suite.

Ex. 10.2.   Schieferdecker, *XII. musicalische Concerte*, Suite VIII, 'Ouverture'

The repeated notes and the rising phrase from the dominant to the tonic in each entry seem to look back to the type of subject that was popular in the keyboard fugues of the previous century. The material is unlike anything used by Lully or his German imitators. Perhaps Schieferdecker was thinking of Buxtehude at this point. However, it has to be said that this is one of the musically weaker moments of the collection; Schieferdecker was no Buxtehude when it came to handling this type of material.

Ouvertures are not the only movement types to open suites in this collection. The *simphonie* that opens the sixth suite was clearly intended for an ensemble of some expertise, and the first-oboe writing often makes considerable demands on the player. The structure of this movement is tri-partite; there is an opening section, a fast central section that starts with imitative entries, and a closing section that revisits the material of the opening. All this would normally indicate an *ouverture* in the French manner, and there can be little doubt that Schieferdecker had this structure in mind; it is surely no accident that the fast middle section is marked 'vistement'. However, the musical language at the start has little to do with Lully or his imitators. This use of non-French musical language inside the structure of a French *ouverture* was not new; as we have seen, both Mayr and Pez had experimented in this way.

Schieferdecker's selection of dance types is mostly French, and typical of the German *Lullists*. But there are no dances that give the impression of having originated as music for characters or groups of characters in a stage ballet. There are collections by the German *Lullists* that do not have any such movements. But the trend in suite collections at the turn of the seventeenth century was to include character movements in ever-greater numbers. The absence of them in *XII. musicalische Concerte* may reflect a lack of opportunity to write music for the stage; Schieferdecker appears not to have written any operas or ballets after leaving Hamburg.

Muffat, Cousser or any of the German *Lullists* would surely have raised a critical eyebrow at Schieferdecker's treatment of the some of the dance melodies themselves. In the menuet from the second suite, the crotchet rests in the treble part are most unusual (see Example 10.3). Given the tradition of single-line transmission of dance music during the seventeenth century, it was common practice for the melody to be written without a break. Perhaps Schieferdecker was unaware of the tradition, or chose simply to ignore it so that he could highlight the imitation of the treble by the bass. The latter is perhaps more likely and seems to confirm that, at this point and probably elsewhere, Schieferdecker was thinking in terms of instrumental performance and not practical dance music. On the other hand, he certainly does follow late seventeenth- and early eighteenth-century tradition in his use of the chaconne. This movement, with its links to royalty, was often the most impressive in terms of size and scope, and Schieferdecker's examples are no different. The two chaconnes in the collection broadly follow the same pattern; a simple beginning is followed by passages of increasing rhythmic intensity and diminution of note values. Frequent use is made of a repeated bass line formula.

236 The Courtly Consort Suite in German-Speaking Europe, 1650–1706

Ex. 10.3. Schieferdecker, *XII. musicalische Concerte*, Suite II, 'Menuet'

Finally, we come to the two wind band suites placed at the end of the main part of the collection. They are entitled '11. Concert à 4. 2. Hautbois & 2. Basson' and '12. Concert à 4. 2. Hautbois & 2. Basson'. This ensemble of pairs of oboes and bassoons is slightly different from the combination of three oboes and bassoon favoured in seventeenth-century France. Three oboes and a bassoon were certainly the norm in Germany at the start of the eighteenth century. Again, Schieferdecker seems to have ignored the French manner in this respect. But even if *the intrada* of his eleventh suite does seem to look back to Leipzig tower music of the previous century, most of the movements in these wind band suites contain a good deal that falls within the German *Lullist* tradition.

Taken as a whole, *XII. musicalische Concerte* represents a wide variety of influences. Some of the music appears to have been influenced by the music of Schieferdecker's youth in Leipzig, but there is no doubt that most of it is much nearer to the music written by court composers in imitation of Lully and the French manner. If the demise of the town music consort suite left a vacuum at the start of the eighteenth century, Schieferdecker's music makes it clear that music in imitation of Lully and the influence of the concerto was starting to fill this vacuum. The importance of this collection does not lie in its imitation of the Lullist art, which was, as we have seen, imperfect. Its importance lies in the fact that such music was written by a town musician.

Johann Joseph Fux entered the service of the Viennese imperial court in 1698, though it seems that his connections with it may date from several years earlier.[12] *Concentus musico-instrumentalis* was published in 1701, and dedicated not to the Emperor Leopold, but to his son Joseph. By this time, late in Leopold's reign, a faction of younger courtiers had formed around the heir to the imperial throne, and it is possible that Fux, through this dedication, was attempting to secure his position for the future.[13] As I pointed out in Chapter 9, Aufschnaiter's 1695 *Concors discordia* was also dedicated to Joseph, and it may not be a coincidence that both Fux and Aufschnaiter use the term 'serenade' in their collections. It is possible that Joseph particularly cultivated this form of entertainment. While Fux's serenade is quite different in content from the examples in *Concors discordia*, both collections were greatly influenced by the Lullian style. Although we have seen that French influence was reaching the imperial court by the 1690s, it is likely that other musical establishments in Vienna were able to accept Lullianism rather more quickly and fully than Leopold's own *Hofkapelle*. Perhaps Fux came across Lully's music principally at Joseph's court. It would certainly explain the dedication.

But Fux was, above all, an imperial court composer, and a closer examination of the collection also reveals it to be firmly rooted in the Viennese imperial tradition of the previous decades. The title page of *Concentus musico-instrumentalis* tells us that the collection is divided into seven 'Partitas'. A 'Catalogo' at the start of the 'Violino Primo' part book lists contents and instrumentation. Table 10.2 gives details.

Table 10.2: Contents of: J.J. Fux, *Concentus musico-instrumentalis* (Nuremberg, 1701), as given in the 'catalogo' of the first violin part-book

Partita	Contents	Instrumentation
N. I.	Serenada à 8.	'2. Trombe. 2. Hautbois e Fagotto. 2. Violini. 1 Viola. e Basso'
N. II.	Ouverture à 6.	'2. Hautbois. 2. Violini. 1. Viola e Basso'
N. III.	Ouverture à 4.	'2. Violini. 1. Viola e Basso'

---

[12] H. White, 'Fux' in *New Grove* 2, vol, 9, pp. 365–75.
[13] J. Duindam, 'Courts of the Austrian Habsburgs c.1500–1750' in J. Adamson (ed.), *The Princely Courts of Europe 1500–1750* (London, 1999, repr. 2000), p. 182.

Partita	Contents	Instrumentation
N. IV.	Ouverture à 6.	'2. Hautbois. 2. Violini. 1. Viola e Basso'
N. V.	Ouverture à 4.	'2. Violini. 1. Viola e Basso'
N. VI.	Ouverture à 4.	'2. Violini. 1. Viola e Basso'
N. VII.	Sinfonia à 2.	'1. Hautbois. 1. Flauto e Basso'

The serenade that makes up the first *partita* is quite different from any of those in *Concors discordia*: a central *ouverture* suite in the Lullian manner is placed within a further sequence of movements mostly distinguished by their use of one or more trumpets. The return of the second trumpet for the 'final', which gives virtually the same instrumentation of the opening and closing movements, seems to indicate that the serenade was intended to be played complete, and not as individual sections. Despite this, the movements do fall into three groups, and these are given in Table 10.3.

Table 10.3: Contents and groupings in Fux, *Concentus musico-instrumentalis*, 'N.I. Seranada à 8.'

Movement	Key	Instrumentation
Marche	C major	Clarino I-II/Hautbois I-II/Fagotto/Violino I-II/Viola/Basso
Guique	C major	Hautbois I-II/Fagotto/Violino I-II/Viola/Basso
Menuet	C major	
Aria	C major	Clarino I-II/Hautbois I-II/Fagotto/Violino I-II/Viola/Basso

Eine frische Frantzösische Ouverture ihnen allen zu præferiren 239

Ouverture	A minor	Hautbois I-II/Fagotto/Violino I-II/Viola/Basso
Menuet	A minor	
Trio	C major	Hautbois I-II /Fagotto
Menuet da capo	A minor	Hautbois I-II/Fagotto/Violino I-II/Viola/Basso
Guique	A minor	
Aria	A minor	Hautbois I-II (in unison)/Violino I & II (in unison)/ Viola/ Fagotto/Basso
Aria[II]	A minor	Hautbois I-II/Fagotto/Violino I-II/Viola/Basso
Bourée première	F major	
Bourée 2de.	D minor	
Bourée première *da capo*.	F major	

Intrada	C major	Clarino I/Hautbois I-II/Fagotto/Violino I-II/Viola/ Basso
Rigadon	G major	Hautbois I-II/Fagotto/Violino I-II/Viola/Basso
Ciacona	C major	Clarino I/Hautbois I-II/Fagotto/Violino I-II/Viola/ Basso
Guique	F major	Hautbois I-II/Fagotto/Violino I-II/Viola/Basso
Menuet	C major	Clarino I/Hautbois I-II/Fagotto/Violino I-II/Viola/ Basso
Final	C major	Clarino I/Hautbois I-II/Fagotto/Violino I-II/Viola/ Basso

As we can see from the table, the second group of movements has a key sequence that is quite unlike anything used by the German Lullists, but is typical of the Viennese *balletto* tradition that was discussed in the previous chapter. The *intrada* that starts the third group of movements in the table is unusual. Fanfare-like trumpet solos occur twice in this movement. There do not appear to be any parallel examples in other *intradas* by Viennese court composers, but it is possible that these fanfares in *Concentus musico-instrumentalis* reflect improvised trumpet fanfares used at the imperial court. The *ciaconna* in the third group of movements in the serenade follows the example of many of the shorter chaconnes in the German-Lullian tradition: it is little more than an extended sequence of repeated four- bar phrases. However, the varied instrumentation and the quality of Fux's invention overcome any limitations of the genre.

The remaining *partitas* of *Concentus musico-instrumentalis* are far simpler in construction. The second has a sequence of dances and character movements in the French manner preceded by a multi-sectioned sinfonia. The three suites that make up *partitas* III, V and VI are scored for strings without oboes or bassoon. Perhaps this music without wind parts comes from earlier in the 1690s. It is mainly in the Lullian style but, as we have seen, Lully's music was known in Vienna at this time. However, the influence of the *balletto* is still present: not one of these three suites remains in a single key.

There is explicit reference to the French manner in the final *partita,* which is a trio for *flauto*, oboe and bass. The range of the *flauto* part makes it likely that Fux intended a recorder. There are four movements:

Sinfonia/La joye des fidels sujests/Aire francoise-Aria Italiana/Les e'nemis Confus.

There is an almost programmatic element running through this trio: a comparison of the French and Italian styles. 'La joye des fidels sujets' is a rondeau in the French manner; the Italian manner is evident in the tri-partite opening sinfonia. But the two national styles are brought together in a remarkable way in the dual-titled 'Aire francoise-Aria Italiana'. Each of the treble instruments plays in a different style: not surprisingly, the French music is given to the oboe, an instrument closely associated with France. Perhaps it is strange that Fux did not choose the violin as the other treble instrument in the suite; this would have provided the greatest contrast between the French oboe and the Italian violin. The 'Aria Italiana' *flauto* part is written and played in a 6/8 time signature, but the oboe and bass 'French' music is written and played at the same time in ¢. (See Example 10.4.)

The notation as it stands would make any attempt at rhythmic coordination between the instrumental parts very difficult, but if the French rhythmic convention of *notes inégales* is employed in the 'Aire francoise' part, the rhythms of all three parts coincide.[14] But even here, there is a third influence in addition to the French

---

[14] I am grateful to Peter Holman for suggesting this to me.

and the Italian: Fux again follows the imperial *balletto* tradition in his use of more than one key for the movements of the suite. The principal key is F major, but the second part of the sinfonia and the 'Aire francoise-Aria Italiana' are both in D minor.

The final case study in this chapter deals with two manuscript seventeenth-century consort suites that are clearly of German origin. (They are part of a group of manuscripts with the shelf mark *GB-Lbl* MS Mus. 1585.) The first is entitled 'Partei a. 4: ... La franceise' and is dated 'Anno 1690 Der 4 Augusti', the second suite, 'Partei a. 4 ... Author Jeann Fischer' is dated 'Anno 1691 Der 19 October'.[15] The 1690 suite is attributed to 'Johan Fischer' and the 1691 suite to 'Jeann Fischer'. Both suites are preserved as sets of parts: there is no score. The violin part of the 1691 suite has the title of 'Violino Primo', but there is nothing in the writing to suggest that a second violin part originally existed. Unfortunately, the watermarks in both suites are unclear, but it is possible that the manuscripts originate in southern Germany.

Ex.10.4.   J.J. Fux, *Concentus musico-instrumentalis* (Nuremberg, 1701), 'Aire francoise, Aire Italiana'

The parts of the 1690 suite are all written in the same hand, and the same copyist appears to be responsible for at least part of the 1691 suite. In addition, it is clear that the 1691 title page is written in a way that closely resembles that of the earlier suite. (See Figure 10.1.)

---

[15]   Modern edn.: M. Robertson (ed.), *Two seventeenth-century suites for string consort by Johann Fischer of Vratislavia* (Hebden Bridge, 2005).

Fig. 10.1. Manuscripts *GB-Lbl* Mus. 1585/90 and 91, outer wrappers

Both manuscripts have seemingly been part of the same library collection: the archive numbers written on each title page are in the same hand, and the same monogram also appears at the head of each manuscript. It appears that neither suite exists in any other copies. Table 10.4 gives the instrumentation and movements of each suite.

Table 10.4: Selected contents of: *GB-Lbl* MS Mus. 1585

Abbreviated title	Movements	Instrumentation	Key
Partej a 4 | 1. Violin: | 2 Violis | Et | Basso Continuo. |La franceise |Mis En Musique |Author: Johan Fischer ... Anno 1690 | Der 4 Augusti.	Rondeaux/Ballet/ Gÿque/Gavott/ Menuet/Menuet [II]	Violino (in *scordatura* tuning)/Viola 1/Viola 2/Basso Continuo/ Basso Organo	B minor
Partej a 4 | 1 Violin | 2 Violis | Et | Basso Continuo | Author | Jeann Fischer ... Anno 1691 | Der 19 October	Sonatina/ Allemand/ Menuet/Ballet	Violino Primo/ Viola Prima/ Viola 2da/ Bassus/ Basso Continuo	B minor

For ease of identification, I shall now refer to these suites as Mus. 1585/90 and Mus. 1585/91. Given the strong links between the two manuscripts, it is reasonable to assume the 'Johan' and 'Jeann' Fischer of the title pages is the same person. Mus. 1585/90, with its heading 'La franceise' is the one that is of greatest interest in the context of this chapter but, in order to establish the identity of the composer, I shall discuss both suites.

Given that the name 'Johann Fischer' was common in the German lands at the end of the seventeenth century, the identity of this composer is not easy to establish. But there are similarities between the two Fischer suites here and six further suites by a Johann Fischer in the Liechtenstein collection in Kroměříž (*CZ-KRa*). Table 10.5 details all six.

Table 10.5: Suites by Johann Fischer in the Liechtenstein collection in Kroměříž (*CZ-KRa*)

Title	Shelf-mark	Instrumentation	Movements
Ballettæ a 4 | Violino | 2 Violæ | e | Viola	A 776	Violino (in *scordatura* tuning)/ Viola 1ª/Viola 2da/ Basso	Allamanda / Menuett /Lemasme /Boure /Menuett

Title	Shelf-mark	Instrumentation	Movements
Balletti a 4 | Violino | 2: Violæ | e | Viola | Aut: Joanne Fischer	A 777	Violino (in *scordatura* tuning) /Viola 1ma / Viola 2da/Violone	Allamanda/Gavotte/ Menuett/Boure/Menuett
Ballettæ a 4:	A 778	Violino (in *scordatura* tuning) / Viola 1ma / Viola 2^{a} / Violone	Sonatina/Balletto/Minuet/ Gavotte/Boure/Minuet/ Minuet
Balettæ a 4. | Compositæ in Melancholia Authoris ... Johann Fischer.	A 780	Violino Piculo (in *scordatura* tuning) / Viola 1ma / Viola Secunda / Cimbalo	Sonatina/Allemanda/ Menuett/Menuett/Boure/ Sarabande
Balletti ad duos Choros: | Authore D: Joanne Fischer	A 781	*Choro 1mo*: Violino 1mo / Viola 1ma/ Viola 2da / Violon *Chori 2^{di}*: Violino 1mo / Viola 1ma/ Viola 2da / Violone/Bassus Continuus	Intrada/Balletto/Guige/ Sarab/Balletto/Minuett
Balletæ à 4. | 2 Viol: / Viola di Brazzio, | Con Basso Violone. | Authore Sigre | Fischer	A 782	Violino Primo (in *scordatura* tuning)/ Violino Secundo (in *scordatura* tuning)/ Viola di Brazzio/ Violone	Allemanda/Couranda /Ballet/Minuet/Ballet/ Sarabanda/Bour/Gigue

*Note*s: A 776 & 778 do not contain Fischer's name on their title pages, but Fischer is given as the author in the 1695 inventory.

A 776 and 778 do not have an author's name on their title pages, but Fischer is given as their composer in the 1695 inventory of the collection.[16] Mus. 1585/91 is very close in style and content to these six suites. Like the opening movement of A 780, the sonatina of Mus. 1585/91 is a bipartite structure with an opening common-time section followed by an imitative triple-time section. It is not as highly-wrought or as chromatic as the sonatina in A 780, but this latter movement has a clear programmatic element, the description of Fischer's state of melancholy.

[16] A facsimile of the inventory is given in *AMA*, vol. 5/1, pp. 71–2.

The allemandes from the same two suites also contain clear parallels, as we can see in Example 10.5. Likewise, the semiquaver figuration in the violin part of the vigorous second *ballet* movement that concludes Mus. 1585/91 is very similar to the violin figuration in the suite 'ad duos Choros' (A 781).

Mus. 1585/90 uses a *scordatura* violin, and the same instrumental combination of single *scordatura* violin, two violas and bass is used in four of the six Fischer suites in *CZ-KRa*. One further *CZ-KRa* suite (A 782) also uses a *scordatura* violin, but in combination with a second *scordatura* violin, a single viola and bass. *Scordatura* writing in German consort suites was usually limited to trios of two violins and bass, and it seems that this use of *scordatura* violin tuning in a four-part instrumental combination may well be a distinguishing feature of the work of the Kroměříž Fischer. So it is significant that the same instrumental combination is used in Mus. 1585/90. The *scordatura* tuning of the latter has the top three strings tuned to F sharp, C sharp and F sharp. The bottom string is not used. But there are some differences. Compared with the Kroměříž suites listed above, which contain large amounts of double-stopping in the violin part, Mus. 1585/90 seems technically rather unadventurous. In addition, the six Kroměříž suites are often characterized by a gap between the tessitura of the violin part and the rest of the ensemble. This generates a quality of sound that is absent from Mus. 1585/90. But despite this, there are enough similarities to suggest that the Johann Fischer of the six Kroměříž suites in Table 10.5 is the same Johann Fischer of Mus. 1585/90. If we also take into account the similarities between Mus. 1585/91 and the same six suites, the case for a common authorship for all of them becomes particularly persuasive.

Who then was the Kroměříž Fischer? There are three possible candidates. As I pointed out in Chapter 7, there were at least three composers with the name Fischer were working in the German lands during the 1690s: Johann Fischer of Vratislavia, Johann Caspar Ferdinand Fischer and the Augsburg-born Johann Fischer. Jiří Sehnal and Jitřenka Pešková identify the first of these as a musician 'probably based in Wroclaw' (Vratislavia), and Robert Eitner lists the last as 'Johann Fischer III'.[17] For ease of identification, I shall use 'Fischer III' to distinguish him from the Vratislavia Fischer who will now be identified as 'Fisher IV'. It seems that Eitner was not aware of the latter, and most modern scholars have tended to assume that the Kroměříž suites are the work of Fischer III.[18] But I have already argued that the

---

[17] AMA, vol. 5/1, p.33; R. Eitner, *Biographisch-Bibliographisches Quellen-Lexikon der Muskier und Musikgelehrten der Christlichen Zeitrechnung bis zur Mitte des neunzehnten Jahrhunderts* (11 vols. Leipzig, 1900–1904; repr. Graz, 1959), vol. 3, pp. 464–5. The first two Fischers in Eitner's list did not work in the seventeenth century.

[18] Dagmar Glüxam has suggested 'parallels' between Fischer III's music and the six Fischer suites in CZ-KRa; see D. Glüxam, *Die Violinskordatur und ihre Rolle in der Geschichte des Violinspieles*, Wiener Veröffentlichungen zur Musikwissenschaft vol. 37 (Tutzing, 1999), p. 225. Meyer's list of music by Fischer III includes suites from *CZ-KRa*, but only three. See E. H. Meyer, *Die mehrstimmige Spielmusik des 17. Jahrhunderts in Nord-*

link between Fischer and *scordatura* violin writing has been overstated, and the question of the Kroměříž Fischer's identity appears to be resolved by a note that at the foot of the title page of A 780 reads:

> Compositæ in Melancholia Authoris, apud N: Solatium | quærentis, ex Vratislavia ad Neöburgiam Epum | Vratislaviensem pergentis. (On the way from Vratislavia to Neoburg with the bishop of Vratislavia, [this suite was] composed at N's house by the author in a state of melancholy and searching for solace.)

It is not clear if 'N' is an initial or an indication that Vejvanovský, the copyist of the manuscript, did not know the identity of the householder. But the note is significant; despite Fischer III's constant travelling, there is no record of him ever having visited Vratislavia. In addition, Fischer III was in Mitau for most of the 1690s and did not start his travelling until the 1700s; the *CZ-KRa* suites by Johann Fischer are all included in the 1695 inventory of the collection, and cannot be later than that date. Fischer III can therefore be ruled out as the composer of the Kroměříž suites. Likewise, there is no evidence that J.C.F. Fischer visited the area at this time, or had any connection with Vratislavia. We may assume that the Kroměříž suites must be by Fischer IV, and this assumption is strengthened by the apparently strong link between Vratislavia and the Liechtenstein court.[19]

As we have seen, Lully's music was known at the Kroměříž court by the early 1690s at the very latest, and there is no reason to think that this influence did not extend to the surrounding regions. The French influence on Mus. 1585/90 was obviously intended as a feature of the suite: the title page (shown on page 242 as part of Illustration 10.1) calls it 'La franceise'. But even when they contain little that is obviously French, many suites in the 1695 inventory of the Liechtenstein collection are termed 'Balletti Francesi'. However the musical evidence to support the title of Mus. 1585/90 is clear: the rondeaux and *gÿque* are deliberate attempts to write in the Lullian style. In the rondeaux, this is particularly apparent: each phrase starts on the second beat of a triple-time bar, exactly in the manner of a chaconne. The structure of the movement is as follows:

> Grand couplet (eight bars), *tutti*/Secondary couplet (four bars), trio/Grand couplet *tutti*/Secondary couplet (six bars), *tutti*/Grand couplet *tutti*. [Example 10.6 shows the trio *couplet.*]

---

und Mitteleuropa, Heidelberger Studien zur Musikwissenschaft, vol. 2 (Kassel, 1934), pp. 203–204. Perhaps as a result, the recent auction catalogue dealing with MS Mus. 1585 lists them both as the work of Fischer III. See: Sotheby's, *Music including the autograph manuscript of Rachmaninov's second symphony* (London, 2004), p. 42. See also RISM A/II (generated online at http://biblioline.nisc.com), records 550.264.147–550.264.152.

[19] *AMA*, vol. 5/1, p. 33.

Ex. 10.5. Allemandes in J. Fischer, 'Balettæ a 4. Compositæ in Melancholia Authoris' (*CZ-KRa* A 780) and 'Partei a. 4' (*GB-Lbl* MS Mus. 1585)

Fischer IV's writing in these rondeaux is of very high quality; it can stand comparison with the work of any of the German *Lullists*.

There is one feature of Mus. 1585/90 that is not derived from Lully's music. All the movements of this suite are linked by the use of head motifs and the same rising bass line is found at the start of every movement except the gavotte. In addition, the descending sequence in the first viola part is common to the start of every movement. Although it was mostly confined to the suites written by town musicians, the technique was known and used by court musicians in Vienna. Fischer IV himself used the technique in the allemande and courante of his suite in manuscript A 782 and again in the *intrada* and *balletto* of his suite for two string choirs in A 781. However, the restriction of linking material to the viola and bass parts of Mus. 1585/90 is unusual: it was far more common to use it as part of the melody line where the links would be obvious to the listener. If movement linking was seemingly unknown in Lully's music, and rare in the work of the German Lullists, it may be that Fischer IV was aware of this and chose to make its application less obvious. Taken as a whole, Mus. 1585/90 shows how the influence of Lully was spreading to this part of Europe. It represents a most interesting and successful foray into the world of the German-Lullian suite, albeit with some compositional techniques from other traditions. We may not know a great deal at the moment about Fischer IV, and this is clearly an area for further research; but judging from all his suites that I have discussed in this case study, he is a most interesting composer who was not afraid to experiment, and whose work deserves to be far better known.

In conclusion, all three case studies in this chapter show us how German musicians were experimenting with various styles at the start of the eighteenth century. On the other hand, practices associated with French performance in the seventeenth century continued to be used until well into the eighteenth; for example, J. S. Bach's so-called 'orchestral' suite in C major (BWV 1066) has both oboes doubling the first violin in the *tuttis* of the dances and the *ouverture*. The traditional French emphasis on the treble line is thus retained. But there was a genuine move amongst many of them towards a stylistic synthesis, even if, as we have seen, understanding of national style was often flawed. And, despite its clear association with courtly French music, the consort suite was as much a part of this movement as any other musical genre. Georg Muffat wrote more on the German-Lullian tradition than anyone else at the time. It is fitting that we should let him have the last word. The following extract from the preface to *Florilegium secundum* may not have represented the views of all German musicians, but it certainly represented the views of many German ruling families:

> This is how to play the Ballets on violins in the manner of the most famous Jean-Baptiste de Lully (which we here will understand in all its purity, and which is admired and praised by the most accomplished musicians in the world), a

manner so sensible that one might scarcely think of anything more graceful or beautiful.[20]

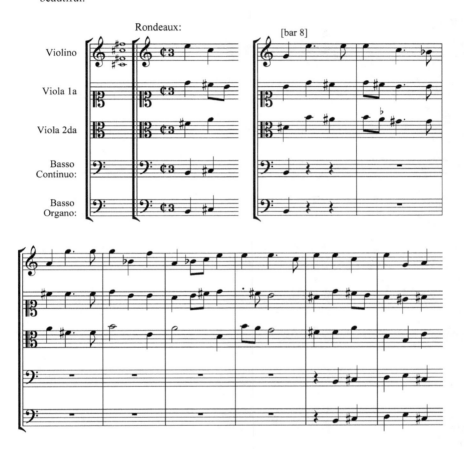

Ex. 10.6.   J. Fischer, 'Partei a. 4: ... La franceise'(*GB-Lbl* MS Mus. 1585), 'Rondeaux'

---

[20]   D. Wilson, (ed. and trans.), *Georg Muffat on Performance Practice* (Bloomington and Indianapolis, 2001), p. 31.

Bibliography

Books and Articles before 1800, including facsimile and modern reprintings

Arbeau, T., *Orchesographie en traicte en forme de dialogve* (Langres, 1589; trans. M.S. Evans, New York, 1948, repr. 1967).

Blainville, [?] de, *Travels through Holland, Germany, Switzerland and Other Parts of Europe ... by the late Monsieur de Blainville*, trans. Turnbull, G. W. Guthrie, G. (3 vols, London, 1757).

Brossard, S. de, *Dictionaire de Musique, contenant une explication des termes Grecs, Latins, Italiens, & François les plus usitez dans la Musique* (Paris, 1703; facsm. F. Knuf (ed.), Hilversum, 1965).

Burbery. J. (trans.), *The History of the Sacred and Royal Majesty of Christina Alessandra Queen of Swedland With the Reasons of her late Conversion to the Roman Catholique Religion* (London, 1658).

Burbury, J., *A relation of a journey of the Right Honourable my Lord Henry Howard, From London to Vienna and thence to Constantinople* (London, 1671).

Chappuzeau, S., *L'Europe vivante, ou relation nouvelle, historique & politique de tous ses estats* (Paris, 1667).

Dumanoir, G., *Le mariage de la musique avec la dance; contenant la reponce au livre des treize pretendus Academistes, touchant ces deux arts* (Paris, 1664; repr. Paris, 1870).

Freschot, C., *Memoires de la cour de Vienne, contenant remarques d'un voyager curieux sur l'état present de cette cour, & sur les intérêts* (2nd edn., Cologne, 1705).

Lauze F. de, *Apologie de la danse et la parfaicte methode de l'enseigner tant aux Caualiers quáux dames* (n.p., 1623; trans. J. Wildeblood, London, 1952).

Manoir, G. du, *Le mariage de la musique avec la dance; contenant la reponce au livre des treize pretendus academistes, touchant ces deux arts* (Paris, 1664; repr. Paris, 1870).

Mattheson, J., *Der vollkommene Kapellmeister* (Hamburg, 1739; facsm. Kassel, 1954).

Mattheson, J., *Das neu-eröffnete Orchestre* (Hamburg, 1713; facsm. D. Bartel (ed.), Laaber, 2004).

Menestrier. C., *Des representations en musique anciennes et modernes* (Paris, 1681).

Merian, M., *Theatri Europœi Fuenffter Theil*, vol. 6 (Frankfurt am Main, 1663; online facsm. www.bibliothek.uni-augsburg.de/dda/dr/hist/we_00001-00021).

Mersenne, M., *Harmonie Universelle contenant la theorie et la pratique de la musique* (Paris, 1636; facsm. Paris, 1963).

Niedt, F.E., *Handleitung zur Variation* (Hamburg, 1706, repr. 1721; trans. by Poulin, P. and Taylor, I. as *Friederich Erhardt Niedt/The Musical Guide*, Oxford, 1989).

P[atin], C., *Relations historiques et curieuses de voyages en Allemagne, Angleterre, Hollande, Boheme, Suisse, & c. Par C.P.D.M. de la Faculté de Paris* (Rouen, 1676).

Quantz, J.J., *Essai d'une methode pour apprendre à jouer de la flute taversiere avec plusieurs remarques pour servir au bon gout dans la musique* (Berlin, 1752), Reilly, E.R. (trans.), *On Playing the Flute; the classic of Baroque music instruction*, (Boston, 2001).

Rinck, E.G., *Leopolds des Grossen Röm. Käysers wunderwürdiges Leben und Thaten aus geheimen nachrichten eröffnet* (4 vols, Leipzig, 1709).

Rohr, J.B. von, *Einleitung zur Ceremoniel-Wissenschaft* (Berlin, 1729).

Rousseau, J., *Traité de la Viole* (Paris, 1687).

Selhof, N., *Catalogue d'une trés belle bibliothe`que de livres ... auquel suit le catalogue d'une partie tres considerable de livres de musique* (The Hague, 1759; facsm. Hyatt King, A. (ed.), Amsterdam, 1973).

Taubert, G., *Rechtschaffener Tanzmeister oder gründlicher Erklärung der Frantzösischen Tantz-Kunst bestehend in drey Büchern* (Leipzig, 1717; facsm. K. Petermann (ed.), Munich, 1976).

Walther, J., *Musicalisches Lexicon Oder Musicalische Bibliothec* (Leipzig, 1732; facsm. Kassel, 1953).

Books and Articles after 1800

Albertyn, E., 'The Hanover orchestral repertory, 1672–1714: significant source discoveries', *Early Music*, 33/3 (2005), pp. 449–71.

Anthony, J.R., *French Baroque Music from Beaujoyeulx to Rameau* (3rd edn., Portland, Oregon, 1997).

Babel, R., 'The Duchy of Bavaria. The Courts of the Wittelsbachs c.1500–1750' in Adamson, J. (ed.), *The Princely Courts of Europe 1500–1750* (London, 1999; repr. 2000),.

Baselt, B., 'Philipp Heinrich Erlebach und seine VI Ouvertures, begleitet mit ihren darzu schicklichen Airs, nach französischer Art und Manier (Nürnberg, 1693)' in Fleischhauer, G, Ruf, W, Siegmund, B, Zschoch, F. (eds.), *Michaelsteiner Konferenzberichte*, vol. 49 (Michaelstein, 1996), pp. 9–30.

Beckmann, G., *Das Violinspiel in Deutschland vor 1700* (Leipzig, 1920).

Béhar, P. and Watanabe-O'Kelly, H. (eds.), *Spectaculum Europæum* (Wiesbaden, 1999).

Benoit, M. (ed.), *Musiques de cour; chapelle, chambre, écurie, 1661–1733* (Paris, 1971).

Bepler, J., 'Cultural life at the Wolfenbüttel court, 1635–1666' in H. Schmidt-Glintzer (ed.), *A Treasure House of Books: the library of Duke August of Brunswick-Wolfenbüttel* (Wolfenbüttel, 1998), pp. 131–146.
Berend, F., *Nicolaus Adam Strungk (1640–1700), sein Leben und seine Werke* (Freiburg, c.1913).
Bettenhäuser, E. (ed.), *Familienbriefe der Landgräfin Amalie Elisabeth von Hessen-Kassel und ihrer Kinder*, Veröffentlichungen der Historischen Kommission für Hessen, vol. 56 (Marburg, 1994).
Bourdelot, P. and Bonnet, P., *Histoire de la musique et des ses effets depuis son origine jusqu'a présent* (Paris, 1715; repr. 4 vols, Amsterdam, 1725).
Bowles, E. A., *Musical Ensembles in Festival Books, 1500–1800* (Ann Arbor, 1989).
Braun, W., 'The "Hautboist;" an Outline of Evolving Careers and Functions' in W. Salmen (ed.), *The Social Status of the Professional Musician from the Middle Ages to the 19th Century* (New York, 1983), pp. 125–58.
Brosche, G., 'Die musikalischen Werke Kaiser Leopolds I. Ein systematisch-thematisches Verzeichnis der erhaltenen Komposition' in Brosche, G., (ed.) *Franz Grasberger zum 60. Geburtstag* (Tutzing, 1975).
Buch, D., *Dance music from the Ballets de cour, 1575–1651: historical commentary, source study, and transcriptions from the Philidor manuscripts* (Stuyvesant, New York, c.1993).
Buch, D., 'The Influence of the *Ballet de cour* in the Genesis of the French Baroque Suite' *Acta Musicologica*, vol. 57 (1985), pp. 94–109.
Burgess, G., 'The Chaconne and the Representation of Sovereign Power in Lully's *Amadis* (1684) and Charpentier's *Medée* (1693)' in McCleave, S. (ed.), *Dance & music in French baroque theatre: sources & interpretations* (London, 1998), pp. 81–104.
Chafe, E.T., *The Church Music of Heinrich Biber*, Studies in Musicology, vol. 95 (Ann Arbor, 1987).
Chan, M. and Kassler, J.C. (eds.), *Roger North's The Musical Grammarian 1728* (Cambridge, 1990).
Churchill, W., *Watermarks in paper in Holland, England, France, etc., in the XVII and XVIII centuries and their interconnection* (Amsterdam, 1935; repr. 1967).
Collver, M., & Dickey, B., *A Catalog of Music for the Cornett* (Bloomington and Indianapolis, 1996).
Davidsson, A., *Catalogue Critique et Descriptif des Imprimés de Musique des XVIe et XVIIe Siècles Conservés a la Bibliothèque de l'Université Royale d'Upsala Tome II* (Uppsala, 1951).
Dreyfus, L., *Bach's continuo group* (Cambridge, Mass., 1987).
Duindam, J., 'The Courts of the Austrian Habsburgs c.1500–1750' in Adamson, J., (ed.) *The Princely Courts of Europe 1500–1750* (London, 1999; repr. 2000) p. 165–87.
Duindam, J., *Vienna and Versailles; the courts of Europe's dynastic rivals, 1550–1780* (Cambridge, 2003).

Eitner, R. *Biographisch-Bibliographisches Quellen-Lexikon der Muskier und Musikgelehrten der Christlichen Zeitrechnung bis zur Mitte des neunzehnten Jahrhunderts* (11 vols, Leipzig, 1900–1904; repr. Graz, 1959).
Engelbrecht, C., *Die Kasseler Hofkapelle im 17. Jahrhundert und ihre anonymen Musikhand-schriften aus der Kasseler Landesbibliothek* (Kassel, 1958).
Engelbrecht, C., Brennecke, W., Uhlendorff, F, Schaefer. H. J., *Theater in Kassel aus der Geschichte des Staatstheaters Kassel von den Anfängen bis zur Gegenwart* (Kassel, 1959).
Erdmann, H., *Schwerin als Stadt der Musik* (Lübeck, 1967).
Finscher, L., (ed.), *Die Musik in Geschichte und Gegenwart* (20 vols, Kassel & Stuttgart, 1999–2008).
Frandsen, M. E., *Crossing confessional boundaries: the patronage of Italian sacred music in seventeenth-century Dresden* (Oxford, 2006).
Fürstenau, M., *Zur Geschichte der Musik und des Theatres am Hofe zu Dresden* (2 vols, Dresden, 1861–2).
Gerheuser, L., *Jacob Scheiffelhut und seine Instrumentalmusik* (Augsburg, 1931).
Glüxam, D., *Die Violonskordatur und ihre Rolle in der Geschischte des Violinspieles*, Wiener Veröffentlichungen zur Musikwissenschaft, vol. 37 (Tutzing, 1999).
Göhler, A. (comp.), *Verzeichnis der in den Frankfurter und Leipziger Messkatalogen der Jahre 1564 bis 1759 angezeigten Musikalien* (3 vols, Leipzig, 1902).
Gottwald. C., (ed.) *Die Handschriften der Gesamthochschul-Bibliothek Kassel, Landesbibliothek und Murhardsche Bibliothek der Stadt Kassel*, vol. 6 (Wiesbaden, 1997).
Gustavson, B., (ed.), *Lüneburg, Ratsbücherei, Mus. ant. pract. 1198*, 17th Century Keyboard Music, vol. 22 (New York and London, 1987).
Gustavson, B., 'Babel, Charles' in L. Finscher (ed.), *Die Musik in Geschichte und Gegenwart*, Personenteil 1(Kassel, 1995), pp. 1250-1251.
Gustavson, B., 'France' in Silbiger, A. (ed.), *Keyboard music before 1700* (New York, 1995, repr. 2004), pp. 90–146.
Gustavson, B., with Leshinskie, M., *A thematic locator for the works of Jean-Baptiste Lully* (New York, 1989).
Hadamowsky, F., 'Barocktheater am Wiener Kaiserhof. Mit einem Spielplan (1625–1740)' in *Jahrbuch der Gesellschaft für Wiener Theaterforschung, 1951–2* (Vienna, 1955) pp. 71–98.
Harding, R., A thematic catalogue of the works of Matthew Locke with a calendar of the main events of his life (Oxford, 1971).
Harris-Warrick, R. and Cecomte, N., 'Branle' in M. Benoit (ed.), *Dictionnaire de la musique en France aux XVIIe et XVIIIe siècles* (Paris, 1992).
Haynes, B., *The Eloquent Oboe* (Oxford, 2001).
Haynes, B., *Music for Oboe, 1650–1800* (2nd. edn., Berkeley, 1992).
Henshall, N., *The myth of absolutism: change and continuity in Early Modern European monarchy* (London and New York, 1992).
Herissone, R., 'The Magdalen College Part Books, origins and contents' in *Chronicle* 29 (1996).

Hilton, W., *Dance and Music of Court and Theater, Selected Writings of Wendy Hilton*, Dance and Music, vol. 10 (Stuyvesant, New York, 1997).
Hofmann, H-G., 'Singballett' in Finscher, L. (ed.), *Die Musik in Geschichte und Gegenwart*, Sachteil 8 (Kassel, 1998), pp. 1409–1411.
Hogwood, C., *Music at court* (London, 1977).
Holman, P., *Four and Twenty Fiddlers: the Violin at the English Court* (Oxford, 1993, repr. 1995).
Holman, P., 'From Violin Band to Orchestra' in J. Wainwright, P. Holman (eds.), *From Renaissance to Baroque: change in instruments and instrumental music in the seventeenth century* (Aldershot, 2005).
Houle, G., *Meter in Music, 1600–1800* (Bloomington & Indianapolis, 1987).
Hudson, R., *The Allemande, the Balletto and the Tanz* (2 vols, Cambridge, 1986).
Hudson, R., *The Folia, the Saraband, the Passacaglia, and the Chaconne: the historical evolution of four forms that originated in music for the five-course Spanish guitar* (4 vols, Neuhausen-Stuttgart, 1982).
Israël, C., *Uebersichtlicher Katalog der Musikalien der Ständischen Landesbibliothek zu Cassel* (Kassel, 1881).
Jurgens, M. (ed.), *Documents du Minutier central concernant l'histoire de la musique (1600–1650)* (Paris, 1974).
Kindermann, J. (comp.), *Die Musikalien der Bibliotheca Fürstenbergiana zu Herdringen*, Deutsches Musikgeschichtliches Archiv Kassel, Katalog der Filmsammlung 20/21, Kassel, 1987–1988).
Klingensmith, S., *The utility of splendour: ceremony, social life, and architecture at the court of Bavaria, 1600–1800*, Otto, C. F. and Ashton, M. (eds.), (Chicago, 1993).
Köchel, L. von, *Die kaiserliche Hof-Musikkapelle in Wien von 1543 bis 1867* (Vienna, 1869).
Koletschka, K., 'Esias Reußner der Jüngere und seine Bedeutung für die deutsche Lautenmusik des XVII. Jahrhunderts' in Adler, G. (ed.), *Studien zur Musik*, vol. 15 (Vienna, 1928), pp. 7–45.
Latham, R.C. and Matthews, W., (eds.) *The Diary of Samuel Pepys,* (11 vols, London, 1970–83, repr. 1995).
Le Cocq, J., 'The Early *Air de Cour*, the Theorbo, and the Continuo Principle in France' in Wainwright, J. and Holman, P. (eds.), *From Renaissance to Baroque; change in instruments and instrumental music in the seventeenth century* (Aldershot, 2005),.
Lenneberg, H., *On the Publishing and Dissemination of Music 1500–1850* (Hillsdale, New York, 2003).
Lesure, F., *Bibliographie dés éditions musicales publiées par Estienne Roger et Michel-Charles le Cène, Amsterdam, 1696–1743* (Paris 1969).
Macclintock, C. (ed.), *Readings in the history of music in performance* (Bloomington & Indianapolis, 1979, repr. 1982).
Malortie, K. von, *Der Hannoversche Hof unter dem Kurfürsten Ernst August und der Kurfürstin Sophie* (Hanover, 1847).

Massip, C., *La Vie des musiciens de Paris au temps de Mazarin (1643–1661)*, La Vie musicale en France sous les roi Bourbons, vol. 24 (Paris, 1976).
Maunder. R., *The scoring of Baroque concertos* (Woodbridge, 2004).
McGowan, M., *L'Art du ballet de cour en France 1581–1643* (Paris, 1978).
Mcveigh, S. and Hirshberg, J., *The Italian solo concerto, 1700–1760* (Woodbridge, 2004).
Meyer, E.H., *Die mehrstimmige Spielmusik des 17. Jahrhunderts in Nord- und Mitteleuropa,* Heidelberger Studien zur Musikwissenschaft, vol. 2 (Kassel, 1934).
Möller, E., 'Die Weimarer Noteninventare von 1662 und ihre Bedeutung als Schütz-Quellen' in Breig, W. (ed.), *Schütz-Jahrbuch 1988* (Kassel, 1988), pp. 62–85.
Morton, C. (ed.), *A journal of the Swedish Embassy in the years 1653 and 1654. Impartially written by the Ambassador Bulstrode Whitelocke. First published from the original manuscript by Dr. Charles Morton* (2 vols, London, 1771, repr. 1885).
Nef, K., *Geschichte der Sinfonie und Suite* (Leipzig, 1921).
Nettl, P., *Die Wiener Tanzkomposition in der zweiten Hälfte des siebzehnten Jahrhunderts*, Studien zur Musikwissenchaft, vol. 8 (Vienna, 1921).
Noack, E., *Musikgeschichte Darmstadts vom Mittelalter bis zur Goethezeit*, Beiträge zur Mittelrheinischen Musikgeschichte, vol. 8 (Mainz, 1967).
Noack, E., *Wolfgang Carl Briegel. Ein Barockkomponist in seiner Zeit* (Berlin, 1963).
Norlind, T., 'Zur Geschichte der Suite' in *Sammelbände der Internationalen Musikgesellschaft*, vol. 7 (Leipzig, 1905–1906), pp. 172–203.
Nussbaum, F. L., *The Triumph of Science and Reason 1660–1685* (New York, 1953, repr. 1962).
Owens, S.K., 'The Württemberg *Hofkapelle* c.1680–1721', (Ph.D. diss., Victoria University of Wellington, 1995).
Owens, S.K., 'Upgrading from Consorts to Orchestra' in Wainwright, J. and Holman, P. (eds.), *From Renaissance to Baroque: change in instruments and instrumental music in the seventeenth century* (Aldershot, 2005), pp. 227–236.
Owens, S.K., 'Ducal musicians in the clouds: the role of seventeenth-century German Singballet' in *Context: Journal of music research*, vol. 24 (2002), pp. 63–67.
Patalas, A., *Catalogue of Early Music Prints from the Collections of the Former Preußische Staatsbibliothek in Berlin, kept at the Jagiellonian Library in Cracow* (Kraków, 1999).
RISM A/II records are generated at: http://biblioline.nisc.com
Robertson, M.N., 'The consort suite in the German-speaking lands, 1660–1705' (Ph.D. diss., University of Leeds, 2004).

Rosow, L., 'Power and display: music in court theatre' in Carter, T. and Butt, J. (eds.), *The Cambridge history of seventeenth-century music* (Cambridge, 2005), pp. 197–240.
Ruhnke, M., *Georg Philipp Telemann Thematisch-Systematisches Verzeichnis seiner Werke*, (3 vols, Kassel, 1984–1999).
Sachs, C., 'Die Ansbacher Hofkapelle unter Markgraf Johann Friedrich (1672–1686)' in M. Seiffert (ed.), *Sammelbände der Internationalen Musikgesellschaft*, vol. 9 (Leipzig, 1909–1910), pp. 105–137.
Sadie, S. and Tyrrell, J. (eds.), *The New Grove Dictionary of Music and Musicians* (29 vols, 2nd edn., London, 2001).
Sandman, S.G., 'The wind band at Louis XIV's court' in *EM* 5 (1977/1), pp. 27–37.
Scheibert, B., *Jean-Henry D'Anglebert and the Seventeenth-century Clavecin School* (Bloomington, 1986).
Schmidt, C.B., 'The Amsterdam editions of Lully's music: a bibliographical scrutiny with commentary' in Heyer, J. (ed.), *Lully studies* (Cambridge, 2000), pp. 100–165.
Schmidt, C.B., 'The geographical spread of Lully's operas during the late seventeenth and early eighteenth centuries: new evidence from the livrets' in Heyer, J. (ed.), *Jean-Baptiste Lully and the music of the French baroque* (Cambridge, 1989), pp. 183–211.
Schmidt, C.B., 'Newly Indentified Manuscript Sources for the Music of Jean-Baptiste Lully', *Notes*, 44/1 (September 1987), pp. 7–32.
Schneider, H., *Chronologisch-thematisches Verzeichnis sämtlicher Werke von Jean-Baptiste Lully* (Tutzing, 1981).
Schneider, H., 'J. C. F. Fischers Orchestersuiten, ihre Quellen und stilistische Einordnung' in Fischer, L. (ed.), *J.C.F. Fischer in seiner Zeit: Tagungsbericht Rastatt 1988* (Frankfurt am Main, 1994), pp. 83–4.
Scholz, H., *Johann Sigismund Kusser (Cousser) Sein Leben und seine Werke* (Leipzig, 1911).
Schwab, H.W., 'The Social Status of the Town Musician' in Salmen, W. (ed.), trans. H. Kaufman & B. Reisner, *The Social Status of the Professional Musician from the Middle Ages to the 19th. Century*, Sociology of Music, vol. 1 (New York, 1983), pp. 33–59.
Sehnal, J. & Pešková, J., *Caroli de Liechtenstein Castelcorno episcopi Olumucensis operum artis musicae collectio Cremsirii reservata*, Artis Musicæ Antiquioris Catalogorum, vol. 5 (2 vols, Prague, 1998).
Shepherd, W. R., *Shepherd's Historical Atlas* (ninth edition, New York, 1964).
Sievers, H., *Hannoversche Musikgeschichte* (Tutzing, 1979).
Smithers, D., *The music and history of the baroque trumpet before 1721* (Carbondale & Edwardsville, 1973; repr. 1988).
Snyder, K. J., *Dieterich Buxtehude, organist in Lübeck* (New York, 1987; revised edn.; Rochester, 2007).

Sotheby's, *Music including the autograph manuscript of Rachmaninov's second symphony* (London, 2004).
Spagnoli, G. (ed.), *Letters and documents of Heinrich Schütz, 1656–1672; an annotated translation* (Ann Arbor, 1990).
Spielman, J., *Leopold I of Austria* (London, 1977).
Spitta, P., *Johann Sebastian Bach* (2 vols, Leipzig, 1873).
Spitzer, J. and Zaslaw, N., *The birth of the orchestra: history of an institution, 1650–1815* (Oxford, 2004).
Stampfl, I., *Georg Muffat Orchesterkompositionen. Ein musikhistorischer Vergleich der Orchestermusik 1670–1710* (Passau, 1984).
Strunk, O., (ed.) *Source Readings in Music History*, (New York, 1950; rev. edn.), Treitler, L. (ed.), (New York and London, 1998).
Thormahlen, W., 'Georg Muffat – a document for the French manner?', *EM* vol. 31/1 (2003), pp. 110–115.
Timms, C., *Polymath of the baroque: Agostino Steffani and his music* (Oxford, 2003).
Ulrich, B., 'Die Pythagorischen Schmids-Füncklein', Sammelbände der Internationalen Musikgesellschaft, vol. 9/1 (1907), pp. 75–82.
Vaillancourt, M.G., 'Instrumental ensemble music at the court of Leopold I (1658–1705)', (Ph.D. diss., University of Illinois at Urbana-Champaign, 1991).
Vierhaus, R., trans. J. Knudsen, *Germany in the Age of Absolutism* (Cambridge, 1988; repr. 1991).
Wade, M.R., *Triumphus nuptialis danicus: German court culture and Denmark* (Wiesbaden, 1996).
Ward, J.M., 'Newly Devis'd Measures for Jacobean Masques' *Acta musicologica* vol. 60/2 (May–August, 1988), pp. 111–142.
Watanabe-O'Kelly, H., *Triumphall Shews, Tournaments at German-speaking Courts in their European Context 1560–1730* (Berlin, 1992).
Watanabe-O'Kelly, H., *Court culture in Dresden from Renaissance to Baroque* (Basingstoke, 2002).
Watanabe-O'Kelly, H. and Simon A., *Festivals and ceremonies: a bibliography of works relating to court, civic and religious festivals in Europe, 1500–1800* (London, 2000).
Webber, G., *North German Church Music in the age of Buxtehude* (Oxford, 1996).
Wellesz, E., *Die Ballet-Suiten von Johann Heinrich und Anton Andreas Schmelzer. Ein Beitrag zur Geschichte der Musik an österreichischen Hofe im 17. Jahrhundert, Sitzungsberichte der Kais. Akademie der Wissenschaften in Wien, vol. 176/5* (Vienna, 1914).
Whitehead, P., 'Austro-German Printed Sources of Instrumental Music, 1630 to 1700', (Ph.D. diss., University of Pennsylvania, 1996).
Wilson, D. (ed. and trans.), *Georg Muffat on Performance Practice* (Bloomington and Indianapolis, 2001).

Wollny, P., 'Zur Thüringer Rezeption des französischen Stils im späten 17. und frühen 18. Jahrhundert' in Seidel, W. and Wollny, P. (eds.), *Ständige Konferenz Mitteldeutsche Baroquemusic in Sachsen, Sachsen-Anhalt und Thüringen e. V.*, Jahrbuch 2001 (Schneverdingen, 2002), pp. 140–52.

Zobeley, F. (comp.), *Die Musikalien der Graffen von Schönborn-Wiesentheid* (Tutzing, 1967).

Zohn, S., 'Bach and the *Concert en ouverture*' in Butler, G. (ed.), *J.S. Bach's concerted ensemble music, the Ouverture*, Bach Perspectives, vol. 6 (Urbana & Chicago, 2007), pp. 137–56.

Music, including facsimile editions, selected online editions and selected modern editions

Abel, C-H., *Erstlinge Musicalischer Blumen Bestehend in Sonatinen, Allemanden, Corranten, Sarabanden und Giquen... Pars Prima* (Frankfurt am Mayn, 1674).

Abel, C-H., *Erstlinge Musicalischer Blumen Bestehend in Sonatinen, Allemanden, Corranten, Sarabanden und Giquen... Pars Secunda* (Frankfurt am Mayn, 1676).

Abel, C-H., *Dritter Theil Musicalischer Blumen Bestehend in Allemanden, Correnten, Sarabanden, und Giquen* (Frankfurt am Main, 1677).

Aufschnaiter, B.A., *Concors discordia, amor et timori augusti et serenissimi Romanorum regis Josephi* (Nuremberg, 1695; ed. K. Ruhland, Altötting, 1988).

Ballard, R. (ed.), *Pièces pour le violin a quatre parties* (Paris, 1665; M. Roche (ed.), Paris, 1971).

Bleyer, G., *Lüst-Müsic Nach ietziger Frantzösicher Manier gesetzet bestehend von unterschiedlichen Airn, Bourreen, Gavotten, Gagliarden, Giqven, Chansons, Allemanden, Sarrabanden, Couranden &c* (Leipzig, 1670).

Bononcini, G., *Arie, Correnti, Sarabande, Gighe, & Allemande ... Opera Quarta* (Bologna, 1671)

Briegel, W.C., *Erster Theil. Darinnen begriffen X Paduanen, X Galliarden, X Balleten, und X Couranten. Mit 3. oder 4. Stimmen* (Erfurt, 1652).

Briegel, W.C., *Allemanden/Couranten/Sarabanden/Balleten und Chiquen/Mit 2. oder 3. Stimmen sambt dem General-Bass* (Jena, 1664).

Cazzati, M., *Correnti balletti galiarde a 3 è 4* (Venice, 1659).

Cousser [Kusser], J.S., *Composition de musique Suivant la Methode Francoise* (Stuttgart, 1682; R. Bayreuther (ed.), *Suiten für Orchester*, Musikalische Denkmäler, vol. 11, Mainz, 1994).

Clark, B. (ed.), *J.H. Schmelzer, Serenata con altre Ariae* (St Ives, 2004).

Cousser [Kusser], J.S., *Apollon Enjoüé contenant six Ouvertures de Theatre accompagnees de plusiers airs* (Stuttgart, 1700); R. Bayreuther (ed.), *Suiten für Orchester*, Musikalische Denkmäler, vol. 11, Mainz, 1994).

Cousser [Kusser], J.S., *Festin des Muses contenant six Ouvertures de Theatre accompagnees de plusiers airs* (Stuttgart, 1700).
Cousser [Kusser], J.S., *La Cicala della Cetra d'Eunomio* (Stuttgart, 1700).
D'Anlebert, J-H, *Pieces de Clavecin* (Paris, 1689).
Drese, A., *Erster Theil Etlicher Allemanden, Couranten, Sarabanden, Balletten, Intraden und andern Arien* (Jena, 1672).
Druckenmüller, G.W., *Musicalisches Tafel-Confect; Bestehend in VII. Partyen Balleten, Allemanden, Couranten, Sarabanden &c.* (Schwäbisch Hall, 1668; Traub, A. and Bergmann, H. (eds.), Denkmäler der Musik in Baden-Württemberg, vol. 4, München, 1996).
Écorcheville, J., *Vingt suites d'orchestre du XVIIe siècle français, publiées d'après un manuscrit de la Bibliothèque de Cassel* (2 vols, Paris, 1906; repr. 1970).
Erlebach, J.P., *VI Ouvertures Begleitet mit ihren darzu schicklichen airs, nach Französischer Art und Manier* (Nuremberg, 1693).
Erlebach, J.P., *VI Sonate à Violino e Viola da Gamba col suo Basso Continuo, che si possono prattricar anche a due Violini, essendovi à tal fine aggiunta la Parte del Violino secondo* (Nuremberg, 1694).
Fischer, J., *Neu-Verfertiges Musicalisches Divertissement* (Augsburg, 1700).
Fischer, J., *Tafel-Musik Bestehend In Verschiedenen Ouverturen, Chaconnen, lustigen Suiten, auch einem Anhang von Pollnischen Däntzen à 4 & 3 Instrumentis* (Hamburg, 1702).
Fischer, J., *Musicalische Fürsten - Lust, Bestehend anfänglich In unterschiedenen schönen Ouverturen, Chaconnen, lustigen Suiten und einen curieusen Anhang Polnischer Täntze* (Lübeck, 1706).
Fischer, J.C.F., *Le Journal du Printems, Consistant en Airs, & Balets à 5. Parties, & les Trompettes à plaisir* (Augsburg, 1695; H. J. Moser (ed.), DDT, vol. 10, Graz, 1958).
Furchheim, J. W., *Musicalische Taffel-Bedienung Mit 5.instrumenten, als 2.Violinen, 2.Violen 1.Violon Benebenst dem General-Bass* (Dresden, 1674).
Fux, J.J. *Concentus musico-instrumentalis in septem partitas* (Nuremberg, 1701; Rietsch, J. (ed.), DTÖ, vol. 47, Graz, 1919).
Gester, J-L. (ed.), *Johann Ernst Rieck Neue Allemanden, Giques, Balletten*, Convivium Musicum vol. 2 (Stuttgart, 1994).
Hill, R. (ed.), *Keyboard music from the Andreas Bach Book and the Möller Manuscript*, Harvard Publications in Music, vol. 16 (Harvard, 1991).
Hill, R., (ed.), *Ottobeuren, Benediktiner-Abtei, Bibliothek und Musik-Archiv MO 1037*, 17th Century Keyboard Music, vol. 23 (New York, 1988).
Horn, J.C., *Parergon musicum oder Musicalisches Neben-Werck Bestehend in allerhand anmuthigen Allemanden, Couranten, Ballo und Sarabanden ... Ersten Theil* (Erfurt, 1663).
Horn, J.C., *Parergon musicum oder Musicalisches Neben-Werck Bestehend in fünff angenehmen Grossen-Balletten... Andern Theil* (Erfurt, 1663).
Knöp, L., *Ander Theil Newer Paduanen, Galliarden, Arien, Allemanden, Balletten, Couranten, und Sarabanden* (Bremen, 1660).

Krieger, J.P., *Die Lustige Feldmusik* (Nuremberg, 1704; mod. editions: suite 1, suites 1 & 2, R. Eitner (ed.), *Monatshefte für Musik-Geschichte*, vol. 29/10, Leipzig, 1895; suite 3, M. Seiffert (ed.), Organum vol. 3/9, Leipzig, 1925).

Kuhnau, J., *Neüer Clavier Übung Andrer Theil* (Leipzig, 1696; repr. Monumenta Musicæ Revocata 20; Firenze, 1996).

Löwe von Eisenach, J-J., *Synfonien, Intraden, Gagliarden, Arien, Balletten, Couranten, Sarabanden. Mit 3. oder 5. Instrumenten* (Bremen, 1657-8).

Lully, J-B., *Proserpine* (Paris, 1680; online facsm. http://www.library.unt.edu/music/special-collections/lully/browse/proserpine-1st-edition-1680).

Lully, J-B., *Le Temple de la paix* (Paris, 1685: online facsm. http://www.library.unt.edu/music/special-collections/lully/browse/ballet-du-temple-de-la-paix-1st-edition-1679).

Lully, J-B., *Le Temple de la paix. Ballet. Dansé devant sa Majesté à Fontainebleau* (Amsterdam, n.d.).

Lully, J-B., *Ouve[r]ture du Triomphe de l'amour avec tous les airs de violon* (Amsterdam, n.d.).

Lully, J-B., *Les trios des opera de Monsieur de Lully*, 2 vols. (Amsterdam, 1690-91).

Lully, J-B., *Ouverture avec tous les airs de violons de l'opera de Persée* (Amsterdam, 1682).

Lully, J-B., *Ouverture avec tous les airs de Violons de Lopera(sic) d'Amadis fait à paris par Mons. Baptist de Lully. Imprimee à Amsterdam par Iean Philip Heus 1684* (Amsterdam, 1684).

Lully, J-B. and Collasse. P., *Achilles et Polixene* (Paris, 1687).

Mayr, R.I., *Pythagorische Schmids-Füncklein* (Augsburg, 1692).

Mayr, R.I., *Arion Sacer, à 4. Strom[enti] e Basso Continuo* (Regensburg, 1678).

Mráček, J.S. (ed.), *Seventeenth-Century Instrumental Dance Music in Uppsala University Library, Instr. mus. hs 409*, Musica Svecica Saeculi XVII:5, Monumenta Musicae Svecicae, vol. 8 (Stockholm, 1976).

Muffat, G., *Armonico tributo cioé sonate di camera commodissime a pocchi, ò a molti stromenti* (Salzburg, 1682; E. Schenk (ed.), DTÖ, vol. 89, Vienna, 1953).

Muffat, G., *Suavioris harmoniæ instrumentalis hyporchematicæ, Florilegium primum* (Augsburg, 1695); H. Rietsch (ed.), DTÖ, vol. 2, Vienna, 1894).

Muffat, G., *Suavioris harmoniæ instrumentalis hyporchematicæ, Florilegium secundum* (Passau, 1698; H. Rietsch (ed.), DTÖ, vol. 4, Vienna, 1895).

Muffat, G., *Exquisitioris harmoniæ instrumentalis gravi-jucundæ selectus primus, duodecim rarioribus* [commonly known as 'Ausserlesene Instrumental-musik'] (Passau,1701; ed. H. Rietsch, DTÖ, vol. 23, Vienna, 1904; ed. E. Schenk, DTÖ, vol. 89, Graz, 1953).

N[?], B. N. (comp.), *Exercitium musicum Bestehend in auszerlesenen Sonaten, Galliarden,Allemanden, Balletten, Intraden, Arien, Chiquen, Couranten, Sarabanden, und Branlen* (Frankfurt am Main, 1660).

Nettl, P. (ed.) *Wiener Tanzmusik in der zweiten Hälfte des siebzehnten Jahrhunderts* DTÖ, vol. 56 (Vienna, 1921).
Pachelbel, J., *Partie a 4 in F sharp minor*, Gwilt, R. (ed.), (Hungerford, 1998).
Pez, J.C., *Sonate da camera a tre, due flauti et basso del signore Christophoro Pez, opera seconda* (Amsterdam, n.d.).
Pez, J.C., *Sonate da camera a tre, due flauti et basso del signore Christophoro Pez, opera terza* (Amsterdam, n.d.).
Prætorius, M., *Terpsichore* (Wolfenbüttel, 1612; Oberst, G. (ed.), *Gesamtausgabe der musikalischen Werke von Michael Praetorius,* vol. 15, Wolfenbüttel, 1929).
Rasch, R.A. (ed.), '*T Uitnement Kabinet* (10 vols, Amsterdam, 1973–78).
Reincken, J.A., *Hortus musicus recentibus aliquot flosculis sonaten, allemanden, couranten, sarbanden et giquen* (n.p., n.d.; J.C.M. van Riemsdijk (ed.), Amsterdam, 1888).
Reusner, E., *Musicalische Gesellschaffts ergetzung bestehend in Sonaten, Allemanden, Couranten, Sarabanden, Gavotten, und Giguen* (Brieg, 1670).
Reusner, E., arr. Stanley, J.G., *Musicalische Taffel-erlustigung bestehend in allerhand Paduanen, Allemanden, Couranten, Sarabanden, Gavotten, Balletten und Giguen von Esias Reusnern* (Brieg, 1668).
Robertson, M., (ed.), *Two seventeenth-century suites for string consort by Johann Fischer of Vratislavia* (Hebden Bridge, 2005).
Roche, M. (ed.), *Pièces pour le Violon a Quatre Parties de Differents Autheurs Ballard, 1665* (Paris, 1971).
Rollin, M. & Vaccaro, J-M. (eds.), *Œuvres de Pinel* (Paris, 1982).
Rosiers, C., *Pieces choisies, a la maniere Italienne de Monsieur Charles Rosiers* (Amsterdam, 1691).
Rossi, L., *L'Orfeo,* (C. Bartlett (ed.), Huntingdon, c.1997).
Rothe, W.E., *Erstmahlig Musicalische Freuden - Gedichte Unterschiedliche Paduanen, Alemande, Balletten, Couranten und Sarabanden* (Dresden, 1660).
S[?], J. A., *Zodiaci musici, in XII. Partitas Balleticas, veluti sua Signa divisi. Pars 1.* (Augsburg, 1698; ed. H. J. Moser, DDT vol. 10, Graz, 1958).
Schein, J.H., *Banchetto musicale Newer anmutiger Padouanen, Gagliarden, Courenten und Allemanden* (Leipzig, 1617; D. Krickeberg (ed.), Newe Ausgabe sämtlicher Werke, vol.9, Kassel, 1967).
Schieferdecker, J.C., *XII. Musicalische Concerte, bestehend aus etlichen Ouverturen und Suiten* (Hamburg, 1713).
Schmelzer, J.H., *Sacro-profanus concentus musicus* (Nuremberg, 1662; E. Schenk (ed.) DTÖ, vols. 111–12 (Graz, 1965).
Seyfrid, J.C., *Erster Theil neuer Balletten, Allemanten, Arien, Couranten und Sarabanden* (Erfurt, 1656).
Seyfrid, J.C., *Ander Theil neuer Paduanen, Baleten, Arien, Couranten und Sarabanden* (Jena, 1659).

Speth, J., *Ars magna consoni et dissoni* (Augsburg, 1693; Fedtke, T. (ed.), Kassel, 1973).
Vitali, G.B., *Balletti, correnti, gighe, allemande, e sarabande à violino, e violone, ò spinetta con il secondo violino a beneplacito* (Bologna, 1673).
Wallner, B.A. (ed.), *J.C. Pez, Ausgewählte Werke*, DTB vol. 35 (Augsburg, 1928).
Werra, Ernst von (ed.), *Orchestermusik*, DDT vol. 10 (Leipzig, 1902, repr. Graz, 1958).

Index

Abel, Clamor Heinrich 95, 114–6, 173
   Drey Opera Musica 115
   Erstlinge Musicalischer Blumen 95, 114–6
Actes royaux 74
ad placitum 98, 100–102
Albinoni, Tomaso 231
Albertyn, Erik 116
allemande 20, 38, 45, 48–50, 54, 73, 75–7, 79, 87, 93, 99, 105, 107, 109, 112, 114, 143, 159, 169, 171, 176, 178, 206–7, 212, 217–8, 245, 248
Amsterdam 40, 43, 62–3, 117–8, 130, 143, 193
Ansbach 26, 117, 122–3, 133, 149–50
Anthony, James R. 129
Appartement, see court entertainments and ceremonies
Arbeau, Thoinot 50–51
   Orchesographie 50
aria (air) 8, 12, 25, 39, 97, 100, 164, 179, 186, 189, 194, 197, 203, 210, 212, 222–4, 240–41
Arnold, Georg 18
Arnstadt 17
Artus, *see* Leborgne, Jean Artus
Assieg 224
Aufschnaiter, Benedikt Anton 129, 215–8
   Concors discordia 166, 237
Augsburg 5, 141, 143, 145–6, 149, 175, 230, 245
August, Duke of Braunschweig-Lüneburg 12
'Auß meines Hertzens Grunde' 154
Aux-Cousteaux, Artus 74

Babel, Charles 40, 47, 58, 165–7, 169–72, 196
Babel William 170
Bach, Johann Sebastian 248

Baden-Durlach 75
ball, *see* court entertainments and ceremonies
Ballard, Christophe, publishing house of, 42, 117–8
   Pièces pour le violin a quatre parties 49, 88
ballet 2–4, 7–12, 15, 17, 19, 23–5, 43, 59, 66, 79, 81–2, 93, 119, 147–8, 172, 183, 185, 189, 201, 203, 209, 213, 220, 222, 224–5, 235; *see also* court entertainments and ceremonies, *grand ballet*
ballett (*ballet*) 2, 25, 35, 47, 93, 96–7, 99–100, 104, 245, 248
balletto 2, 35, 47, 197, 203–4, 206–7, 209–13, 220–26, 240–41
ballo 2, 35, 37, 47, 50, 105, 107, 111
Barre (Barrey) 47, 167
Baselt, Bernd 137, 140
basse contrainte 128, 132, 147, 152
bassoon 20–21, 129–30, 151, 155, 159–60, 162, 184, 196, 213, 231, 233, 236, 240; *see also* instrumentation
bataglia 50
Bautzen 115
Beck, Pleickard Carolus
   1. Theil neuer Allemanden, Balletten, Arien 97
Becker, Dieterich 89
Behr, Samuel 11–12
   L'Art de bien danser 11
Belleville, Jacques de 57, 67, 84
Bepler, Jill 9
Berlin 3, 8, 160
Bernabei, Giuseppe Antonio 147
Bertali, Antonio 203
Biber, Heinrich 24
Blainville, de 5, 16

Bleyer, Georg 21, 30, 100, 109–10, 111, 115–6, 119–21, 133, 144, 185
   Lüst-Müsic 21, 109–10, 115–6, 120–21
Bodecker, Johann Friedrich 3
Bonn 193
Bononcini, Giovanni Maria
   Arie, Correnti, Sarabande, Gighe, & Allemande 32
Bontempi, Giovanni Andrea 18, 29
   Il Paride im musica 29
bourée 26, 88, 161, 169, 178, 195–7
bransle (brawl) 11, 13, 15, 25, 39, 51, 53, 66, 87–8, 109, 121, 214–5
   bransle suite 46, 50–53, 57, 64, 82, 87–8, 96–8, 109, 114, 121, 125, 129, 133, 142, 214
      amener (à mener) 51–2, 87
      bransle de Piotou (Poictou) 51–2
      bransle double 51, 52, 87–8
      bransle gay 51–2, 87
      bransle simple 51–2, 82, 87, 109
      montirande 51–2, 87–8
bransle de village 130, 133
Braunschweig 115
Brieg 105, 108
Briegel, Wolfgang Carl 54, 98–101, 104
   Erster Theil. Darinnen begriffen X. Paduanen 98–9
   Allemanden/Couranten/Sarabanden/ Balleten und Chiquen 99
Bremen 49, 115
Breüil, Louis de 8
Brossard, Sébastien de 32, 35, 58, 60, 64, 128
   Dictionaire 47, 58
Bruslard (Brülar, Brullard) 67, 88
Buch, David J. 45
Buisson, de 63
Burckart, J. V. 163, 164
Burgess, Geoffrey 4
Buxtehude, Anna Margreta 228
Buxtehude, Dietrich 228, 235

canarie 37–8, 147, 161; *see also* gigue
Capricornus, Samuel 7
Caroubel, Pierre Francisque 18

Cazzati, Maurizio 30, 32
   Correnti balletti galiarde 30
Celle 18–9, 66, 114, 160, 164, 169
chaconne 50, 60, 62, 90, 127–8, 130, 132–3, 144, 147, 152, 185–7, 197, 218, 235, 240, 246; *see also ciaconna*
Chafe, Eric 24
Chappuzeau, Samuel 6, 65
   Suite de L'Europe vivant 19
character movements 129, 132–3, 157, 186, 189, 206–7, 218, 235, 240
Charles I, King of England 84
Charles II, King of England 13
Charpentier, Marc-Antoine
   Medée 128
Christian Ernst, Margrave of Brandenburg-Bayreuth 29, 93
Christina, Queen of Sweden 13, 40, 81, 84, 175
ciaconna 187, 218, 223, 240; *see also* chaconne
Clemens, Joseph 5, 193–4, 199
Coberg, Johann 173
Coleman, Charles 97
Collasse, Pascal 42
concert 4, 16, 172, 191, 217, 231, 233–4
concerto 184, 227, 231, 233, 236
'Concertouverture', *see* suite
Conradi, Johann Georg 122, 230
Constantin, Louis 4, 65–7, 73, 84, 87
Coques, Gonzales 13
Corelli, Arcangelo 172, 180–81
corrente (courente) 2, 30, 32, 47, 54; *see also* courante
Cosmerovio, Matteo 202
Cotta, Johann 26
coucher, *see* court entertainments and ceremonies
courante 2, 11, 13, 15, 25–6, 30, 32, 35, 45–6, 50, 52–4, 66, 77, 79, 81, 85, 87, 93, 98–101, 104–9, 114, 121, 127, 129, 170, 177–8, 189, 248; *see also corrente*
court ballets 8–9, 11
   'Ballet Royal du Dereglement des Passions', *see* manuscript *F-Pn Rés. F. 499*

Ballet von Zusammenkunft u. Wirkung derer VII Planeten, see manuscript *D-Dl* Mus. 2/F/31
naissance de la paix, La 81
réjouissance des dieux, La 3
Triumphirende Liebe, Die 7, 9, 12
court entertainments and ceremonies; *see also* ballet
   appartement 5
   ball 13, 15–16, 84
      concluding a wedding banquet 13
      opening with a bransle 15, 87
      placing of musicians 13
   ballet de cour 3, 9–11, 15
   carnival season 4–5, 7
   carousel 6, 16
   coucher 4–5
   divertissement 17, 19, 128
   equestrian ballet 75, 202–3
   lever, 4–5
   opera 4, 8 16, 29, 59–60, 79, 93, 119, 132–3, 147–8, 177, 195, 202. 204, 213, 220, 223, 226, 230, 235
   payments 3, 66
   Singballet 8
   Wirtschaft 7
Cousser (Cusser, Kusser), Jean Sigismund 20–21, 26, 28, 117, 119, 122–3, 125, 127–30, 132–3, 137, 142, 149, 151 178 184–5, 189, 220, 230, 235
   Adonis 133
   Apollon enjoüé 129–30, 132–3
   La cicala della cetra d'Eunomio 129 132–3, 220
   Composition de musique 20, 28, 40, 53, 119, 121–3, 125, 127–9, 132–3, 137, 142-3, 152, 166, 182, 186, 230
   Festin des muses 129–30, 132–3
   Julia 132
Crestot, Claude 73
Crestot, Jean (La Haye, La Haÿe) 73–4, 84–5
Croix, Adrien de la 67, 84

dancing master 3, 8–9, 27, 40, 42, 49, 67, 74, 111, 225
D'Anglebert, Jean-Henry 28
   Pieces de Clavecin 27

D'Ardespin, Melchiore 147, 220
   L'Eraclio, see manuscript *A-Wn* Mus. Hs. 19 171
Darmstadt 26, 117, 160
D'Artus, Louis 74
de suite, see suite
Denner, Johann Christoph 160
Depure, Michel 9–10
Descartes, René 81
Diarii Europæ 202
Diesener, Christoph 66
Diesener (Diesineer), Gerhard 66–7, 75, 79, 82, 86, 117
'Distinta Specificatione' 212
Draghi, Antonio 203
Dresden 12–13, 17–18, 21, 29, 102, 104–5, 196
Drese, Adam 20, 27, 47, 59, 65, 75. 79, 86, 110–11
   Allem. Cour. Baett. 114
   Erster Theil Etlicher Allemanden 27, 46, 59, 110, 175
Druckenmüller, Georg Wolfgang 48
   Musicalisches Tafel-Confect 48
Düben, Andreas 86
Düben collection 84
Düben collection database 86
Düben, Gustav 84, 86
Düben Peter, 86
Duindam, Jeroen 201
Dumanoir (Du Manoir), Guillaume 57, 67, 74, 84, 98
Düsseldorf 16

Ebner, Wolfgang, 203, 218
Écorcheville, Jules 67, 73–7, 82
   Vingt suites 67, 75, 83
'Eins-Drey und Drey Eins oder habile Violiste, das', *see* manuscript *S-Uu* IMhs 015:012
Eitner, Robert 149, 245
Elisabeth Dorothea, Landgravine of Hessen-Darmstadt 26
Emeraud, Anthoine 39
en suite, see suite
entrée 3, 9, 11–12, 15, 50, 63, 82, 143, 152, 162, 173, 186, 189, 194, 204, 218, 231

equestrian ballet, *see* court entertainments and ceremonies
Erlebach, Philipp Heinrich 23, 32, 116, 133, 136–7, 139–41, 178, 185, 189
   VI. Ouvertures 32, 133. 136–7, 141
   VI. Sonate 23, 32, 136–7
Essex, John
   The Dancing Master 53
Exercitium musicum, *see* Wust, Balthasar Christoph

Fabricius, Werner
   Deliciae harmonicae oder Musicalische Ergötzung 116
Farinel (Farinelli), Jean-Baptiste 164, 167, 172
Ferdinand Maria, Elector of Bavaria 5
Finspong collection 65, 88
Fischer (III), Johann 133, 149–50, 152, 155, 157, 159–60, 245–6
   Himmlischen Seelenlust 150
   Musicalisch Divertissement 149
   Musicalische Fürsten-Lust 150, 156
   Neuverfertigtes musicalisches Divertissement 150–52, 154–5, 157
   Tafel-Musik 25, 47, 150, 155–7, 159
Fischer (IV, of Vratislavia), Johann 149, 160, 228, 241, 243–6, 248
Fischer, Johann Caspar Ferdinand 141–3, 145, 149, 189, 245–6
   Le journal du printems 50, 141–3, 145
'Folia, la' 63
Frankfurt am Main 57, 93, 143
Freising 175
French violin bands in Germany and Sweden, *see* Hofkapelle
Freschot, Casimir 213
Friedrich Carl, Duke of Württemberg and Teck 122
fugue 119, 179, 235
Furchheim, Johann Wilhelm 104–5
   Musicalische Taffel-Bedienung 105, 114
Fux, Johann Joseph, 221, 237, 240–41
   Concentus Musico-Instrumentalis 217, 228, 237–8, 240

galliard 25, 96, 99

Gallot, Jaques 63
gavotte (*gavott*, *gavotta*) 37, 50–53, 87, 107–10, 114, 121, 130, 161–2, 164, 172–3, 178–9, 189, 191, 194–5, 217, 224, 248
gigue (*gigha*) 21, 26, 37–8, 45, 99, 105–8, 114, 127, 147, 161–2, 164, 168–70, 176, 178–9, 181, 186, 189, 194, 197, 205; *see also canarie*
gigue angloise 37
Göbel, Gottlieb 145
Göhler, Albert 105, 114, 145
Gotha 17, 98, 162
Gottwald, Clytus 73
grand ballet 9, 11–12; *see also* ballet
Gumprecht, Johann 93
Gustafson, Bruce 37

Hague, The 13, 165
Hake, Hans
   Ander Theil Newer Pavanen 25
Hamburg 55, 117, 122, 129, 160, 230–31, 235
Handel, George Frideric 228
Hanover 18–19, 37, 47, 58, 114, 116, 160, 164–7, 169–70, 172–3
Haye (Haÿe), La, *see* Crestot, Jean
Haynes, Bruce 155, 160, 213
Henriette Adelaide, Electoral Princess of Savoy 5, 16
Herissone, Rebecca 167
Herwig, Christian 75, 82
Heus, Amsterdam publishing house of 62–3, 117, 130
Hilton, Wendy 3, 128
Hire, Philippe de la 73
Hoffer, Joseph 206, 211, 213, 220–21
Hof-Journal, Dresden 13
Hofkapelle 16–18, 20, 26, 37, 47, 57–8, 64, 66, 75, 82, 86, 104, 116, 122–3, 133, 164, 167, 169, 193. 197, 203, 211–14, 216, 237
   foreign musicians in 18, 29, 67, 150, 164; *see also* Mazzuchelli, Paolo
   French violin bands 18–20, 40, 66, 84, 175
   oboe bands 115, 156, 160–62, 164
   reorganisation of 18

salary arrears 18
size of 16–18
Hogwood, Christopher 165
Holman, Peter 1, 81
Horn, Johann Caspar 23, 32, 99
　Parergon musicum 23, 25, 32, 54, 99, 101, 136
Hudson, Richard 32, 35

instrumentation 119, 128, 144–5, 151, 155, 159, 167–9, 217, 231, 233, 240, 245; *see also scordatura*
　different ensembles within the same suite 21–2, 76–7
　doubling of outer parts 20–22, 77, 123, 130, 145, 151, 162, 217, 248
　reduction of ensemble size 40, 218
　wind parts 21, 130, 141–2, 155; 194, 196; 233, 236, 240 *see also* bassoon, oboe, *Hofkapelle* oboe bands
intrada 88, 196–7, 204, 236, 240, 248
Isabella Angelika von Montmorency, Princess of Mecklenburg-Schwerin 18

J.A.S. 143, 145–6; *see also* Schmierer, J.A.
　Zodiaci musici in XII partitas balleticas 143, 145–6
Janssens, Hieronymous 13
Jena 27, 59, 110
Johann Georg II, Elector of Saxony 12
Joseph I, Holy Roman Emperor 215–7, 237
Joseph Clemens, Archbishop-Elector of Cologne 5, 193–4, 199

Kassel 3, 16, 20, 22, 29, 49, 53, 65–6, 73–6, 79–82, 84–6, 88, 98
Keiser, Reinhard 61
　Hercules und Hebe 60
Kerll, Johann Caspar
　L'Oronte 29, 202
Kircher, Athanasius 24, 30
　Musurgia universalis 24
Knöp, Lüder 20, 25, 49–50
　Ander Theil Newer Paduanen 20, 25, 49
Krieger, Johann Philipp, 161–2, 164

Die Lustige Feldmusik 161–2
Kroměříž 42, 105, 119, 210–11, 219–20, 223–4, 245–6
Liechenstein collection 42, 160, 210, 243
Kroninger, Lorenz 145
Krünner, Christian 8
Kuhnau, Johann 230
　Biblischer Historien 176
　Neüer Clavier Übung Andrer Theil 230
Kusser, *see* Cousser

Lauze, F. de 46, 51
　Apologie de la Danse 46, 51
Lavoizière, Nicolas, 73
Lawes, William 97
Lazarin 67, 84
Leborgne, Jean Artus 74–5
Liechenstein-Castelcorno, Karl, Bishop of Olomouc 210
Leipzig 11, 23, 54, 99, 109, 115–6, 145, 230, 236
Leopold I, Holy Roman Emperor 1, 147, 201–4, 207, 209–11, 213, 216, 220, 237
lever, *see* court entertainments and ceremonies
'Livre pour la flute Seul', *see* manuscript D-HVl MS IV 417
Locke, Matthew 97
Louis XIV, King of France 1, 4, 6, 57, 73, 121, 160, 201
loure 161
Löwe von Eisenach, Johann-Jacob 54, 101
　Synfonien, Intraden, Gagliarden 101
Lübeck 84, 97, 228, 233
Lully, Jean-Baptiste 7, 24, 28–9, 37, 40, 42, 57, 59–60, 62–3, 73, 88, 116–9, 120–21, 123, 127–8, 130, 132, 142–3, 149, 164, 180, 190–91, 204, 218–9, 227–8, 230–31, 235–7, 240, 246, 248
　Achilles et Polixene (LWV 74) 42
　Acis et Galathée (LWV 73) 63
　Amadis (LWV 63) 62
　Atys (LWV 53) 59
　Ballet des Saisons (LWV 15) 128
　Ballet royal de Flore (LWV 40) 128

Bellerophon (LWV 57) 63
'Entractes d'Oedipe' (LWV 23) 190
L'Hercule amoureux (LWV 17) 219
Monsieur de Pourceaugnac (LWV 41) 127
Ouverture avec tous les airs de violons de L'opera de Persée 130
Proserpine (LWV 58) 132
Psyché (LWV 56) 127
temple de la paix, Le (LWV 69) 42, 118
Thésée (LWV 51) 59
Tous Les Airs de Violon de l'Opera D'Amadis 61, 63, 130
trio des opera de Monsieur de Lully, Les 63
triomphe de l'amour, Le (LWV 59) 119
lute 1, 13, 38, 93, 96, 105, 107
Lüttich 193

Magdalen College part books, *see* manuscript *GB-Cmc* F-4-35, 1–5
manuscripts
    A-Wn Mus. Hs. 16 583: 43, 203, 206–7, 209–10, 221–4
    A-Wn Mus. Hs. 16 588: 43, 209–10, 213, 225–6
    A-Wn Mus. Hs. 18 710: 207, 209–10
    A-Wn Mus. Hs. 18 968: 212
    A-Wn Mus. Hs. 19 171: 147
    A-Wn Mus. Hs. 19 265: 205, 214
    A-Wn Suppl. mus. 1077: 213
    A-Wn Suppl. mus. 1809: 211, 213, 220
    A-Wn Suppl. mus. 1813: 63
    A-Wn Suppl. mus. 23982: 161
    B-Br MS III 1077 Mus: 194–6
    CZ-KRa A 465: 223
    CZ-KRa A 4682: 203
    CZ-KRa A 4826: 42, 219
    CZ-KRa A 615: 212
    CZ-KRa A 746: 224
    CZ-KRa A 758: 226
    CZ-KRa A 760: 223–4
    CZ-KRa A 764: 211
    CZ-KRa A 772: 215
    CZ-KRa A 776: 160, 244
    CZ-KRa A 777: 160
    CZ-KRa A 778: 160, 244
    CZ-KRa A 780: 160, 244, 246
    CZ-KRa A 781: 160, 245, 248
    CZ-KRa A 782: 160, 245, 248
    CZ-KRa A 801: 30, 119–21, 185
    CZ-KRa A 847: 119–20, 144
    CZ-KRa A 852: 218–9
    CZ-KRa A 873: 42, 219
    CZ-KRa A 877: 211
    CZ-KRa A 899: 226
    CZ-KRa A 905: 224
    CZ-KRa A 937: 223
    D-B Mus. MS 16481/2: 38
    D-B Mus. MS 30274: 37, 170
    D-B Mus. MS 40 644 (Möller manuscript): 173, 197
    D-Dl Mus. 2/F/31: 12
    D-Dl Mus. 2026 - N - 1-8: 21
    D-DS Mus. MS 1221: 47, 164–5, 167, 169–70
    D-DS Mus. MS 1227: 47, 165, 167, 169–71
    D-HRD MS Fü 3629: 195
    D-HVl MS IV 417: 165, 170–71
    D-Kl 2° MS mus. 60b³: 162
    D-Kl 2° MS mus. 61: 57, 66–7, 73–7, 79, 81–4, 86, 98
    MS mus. 61a: 88
    MS mus. 61b¹: 57, 73, 77
    MS mus. 61b¹ᵃ: 53, 73
    MS mus. 61b²: 32, 75, 105
    MS mus. 61d²: 76–7
    MS mus. 61d³: 73, 77
    MS mus. 61d⁴: 75, 79
    MS mus. 61d⁵: 76, 81
    MS mus. 61d⁶: 74
    MS mus. 61d⁷: 22, 74–6, 85, 88
    MS mus. 61d⁸: 49
    MS mus. 61e: 67, 75, 79
    MS mus. 61f: 66, 73, 77, 79, 81
    MS mus. 61g: 57, 81
    MS mus. 61h: 79, 82
    MS mus. 61i: 75
    MS mus. 61k¹: 73, 77
    MS mus. 61k⁴: 81, 85
    MS mus. 61m: 76–7
    D-Kl 4° MS mus.148: 66–7, 82
    MS mus.148a: 82
    MS mus.148c¹: 82

MS mus.148c^2: 82
MS mus.148c^3: 82
MS mus.148e: 82
D-OB MO 1037: 207
D-SÜN Schloß MS 59: 195–6
D-W Cod. Guelf. 268 Mus. Hdschr.: 195
D-W Cod. Guelf. 270 Mus. Hdschr.: 61
D-W Cod. Guelf. 295 Mus. Hdschr.: 132
F-Pn Rés. F. 494: 40, 75, 79
F-Pn Rés. F. 496: 15
F-Pn Rés. F. 497: 15
F-Pn Rés. F. 498: 79
F-Pn Rés. F. 499: 10, 79
F-Pn Rés. F. 529: 142
F-Pn Rés. F. 533: 32, 75
F-Pn 4°Vm 848 (1–3): 195
F-V MS Mus. 1163: 161
GB-Cmc F-4-35, 1-5 (Magdalen College part books): 165–6, 169–70, 172
GB-Lbl Add. MS 31438: 97
GB-Lbl Add. MS 39569: 170
GB-Lbl MS Mus. 1585: 241, 243–6, 248
M. 1092: 165–6, 169–70, 196
S-N 9094: 88
S-N 9096:5: 88
S-N 9096:10: 88
S-N 9096:15: 88
S-N 9098: 88
S-Uu Ihre 281-2/3: 35, 89-90
S-Uu IMhs 008:015: 224
S-Uu IMhs 011:016:1-3: 224, 226
S-Uu IMhs 012:016: 216
S-Uu IMhs 013:020: 163–4
S-Uu IMhs 013:021: 163–4
S-Uu IMhs 015:010: 159
S-Uu IMhs 015:011: 159
S-Uu IMhs 015:012: 150
S-Uu IMhs 064:007: 63–4
S-Uu IMhs 064:011: 162, 164
S-Uu IMhs 064:013: 218
S-Uu IMhs 064:014: 59
S-Uu IMhs 134:013: 216

S-Uu IMhs 409: 40, 73–4, 83–7, 89, 98, 104, 109
S-VX Mus. MS 6: 59–61, 216–7; see also Tiliander, Nils
Marais, Marin
    Pièces en trio 130
Marie Thérèse, Queen of France 73
mattacina 226
Mattheson, Johann 122, 227–8
    Das Neu-Eröffnete Orchestre 227
Maunder, Richard 231
Maximillian Gandolf, Archbishop of Salzburg 180–81
Maximillian II Emanuel, Elector of Bavaria 5, 175–7, 193
Mayer, Johann Andrea 122
Mayr, Rupert Ignaz 133, 175–9, 193, 198–9, 235
    Arion Sacer 175, 185
    Pythagorische Schmids-Fincklein 143, 175–7, 179, 186, 196, 199
Mazuel, Michel 67, 84
Mazzella, Salvatore
    Balli, correnti, gighe, sarabande 47
Mazzuchelli, Paolo 29, 67; see also *Hofkapelle*, foreign musicians in
menuet 26, 50, 53, 127–9, 147, 156–7, 159, 161–2, 164, 168, 172–3, 178, 189, 194–5, 231, 233, 235
Mercure, Jean 93
Mersenne, Marin 15, 30, 48, 51–2
    Harmonie universelle 23, 51
Meyer, Ernst Hermann 160, 163–4
Mitau 149, 246
Möller manuscript, see manuscript *D-B* Mus. MS 40 644
montirande 51–2, 87–8
Mráček, Jaroslav 73, 84, 86–7
Muffat, Georg 8, 21, 24–30, 37–9, 48, 117, 129, 136, 141–2, 160, 175–7, 179–91, 193, 197, 199, 231, 235, 248
    Armonico Tributo 30, 39, 181, 191, 197, 199, 231
    Auserlesene Instrumental-musik 25, 180, 182, 184, 191, 233
    Florilegium collections 175, 177, 182–4, 193

Florilegium primum 24, 37–8, 179, 181–2, 184, 186–9
Florilegium secundum 21, 25, 28–9, 48, 133, 184, 188–91, 248
  on bowing 26
  on ornamentation 28–9
Munich 5, 7, 16–17, 29, 147, 160, 164, 175, 193, 199, 202
Musicien Maistre de Dance, Le 43

Nassau-Weilburg 160
Nau, Stephen 81, 84
Niedt, Friederich Erhardt 217
  Handleitung zur Variation 217
Nettl, Karl 206, 212–3
Norlind, Tobias 45
Norrköping, *see* Finspong collection
North, Roger 9, 40
notes inégales 240

oboe (*hautbois*) 20–21, 129–30, 132, 155, 159, 160–61, 163, 167, 169, 184, 193, 196, 212, 231, 233, 235–6, 240
  arrival of in Vienna 212–3
oboe band, see *Hofkapelle*
Osnabruck 164, 169
ouverture 2, 11, 37, 42, 46, 50, 52, 63, 79, 118–20, 123, 125, 127, 130, 133, 136–7, 139–43, 145, 147, 151–2, 157, 159, 161–4, 168, 170, 172–3, 179, 185–6, 189, 194, 196, 198, 218, 220, 227–8, 230–31, 234–5, 238, 248
  harmonic structure at opening of 119, 141, 147
  in the *ballet de cour* 9
ouverture suite, *see* suite
Owens, Samantha 7, 11, 133

Pachelbel, Johann 38–9
Paduan (*Paduana, Padouana,* 'Pavin') 1, 84, 99–100, 107
Paris 4–5, 7, 10, 49, 57, 65–7, 73–4, 84, 88, 116, 118, 127, 142–3, 161, 201
  foreign visitors to 4, 66, 142, 175

German musicians visiting 26, 28–9, 57, 66–7, 79, 117, 119, 121–2, 129, 133, 149, 175, 180, 189
particella 207, 209, 210, 213
Partie, see suite
Pasquini, Ercole 180
passacaglia (passacaille) 50, 90, 128, 162, 179, 182, 189, 218, 223
Passau 8, 48, 181, 189
passepied 130, 161, 172
Patin, Charles 16–7
Pepys, Samuel 15
petite Escurie, la 74
Pez, Johann Christoph 21, 172–3, 175, 179, 181, 193–9, 235
  IX Overtures a quatro 193
  Sonata da camera ... (Neuf suittes) Op. 2 47–8, 193–4
  Sonata da camera ... Op. 3 193–4
Pezel, Johann 115
Philidor manuscripts, *see* manuscripts *F-Pn*
Philidor, André Danican 10–11, 79–81
Picart, Nicholas 84
Pinel, Germain 96
Poglietti, Alessandro 210–12, 214
Pohle, David 57, 75, 82, 85
Pointel, Amsterdam publishing house of 62–3, 117–8, 130
Praetorius, Michael 18, 39–40 51
  Terpsichore 18, 39–40, 51
prelude ('Præludium') 63, 105, 114, 169–70, 172, 233–4

Quantz, Johann Joachim 24

Rameau, Pierre
  Maître à danser, la 53
Rechnungen aus dem Kammerverlag 66; *see also* court entertainments and ceremonies, payments
Regensburg 117
Reich, Pater Honorat 207
Reincken, Johann Adam 55
  Hortus musicus 55
Residenz 6, 16, 193, 209
retirada 205, 218, 222, 224
Reusner, Esaias 104–11, 114–5
  Delitiae testudnis 105, 107

Musicalische Gesellschaffts 108–9, 115
   arr. Stanley, Johann Georg
   Musicalische Taffel-erlustigung 35,
      105–8, 111
Richter, Ferdinand Tobias 212, 221
Rieck, Johann Ernst 93, 96
   Neue Allemanden, Giques, Balletten
      93, 96
Rinck, Eucharius Gottlieb 202, 211
RISM A/II 2, 63, 89, 195
ritournelle 128, 130, 132
Roger, Amsterdam publishing house of 43,
   47–8, 143, 193–5, 231
Rogers, Benjamin 84
Rome 180–81
rondeau 50, 123, 127–8, 130, 132, 144,
   147, 159, 169, 172, 182, 191, 196,
   218, 240, 246, 248
Rosenmüller, Johann 54, 99
   Paduanen, Alemanden, Couranten,
      Balletten, Sarabanden 54
   Sonata da Camera cioe Sinfonie 48, 99
Rosiers, Charles 193–4
   Pieces choisies, a la maniere Italienne
      193
Rossi, Luigi 79
   L'Orfeo 4, 59, 73, 79
Rothe, Wolf Ernst 100, 104–5, 110–11, 115
   Erstmahlig musicalische Freuden-
      Gedichte 25, 35, 102–4
Rousseau, Jean 27–8
Rudolf August, Duke of Braunschweig-
   Lüneburg 17
Rudolstadt 23, 100, 104, 109, 115–6, 133,
   136
   court inventory 116, 141

Salzburg 24, 180–81, 187
Sances, Felice 203
sarabande (*saraband, sarabanda*) 25, 32,
   35, 45, 47, 50, 52–3, 55, 66, 75, 77,
   80–81, 87, 93, 99–100, 104–7, 109,
   114, 121, 152, 161, 172, 177–9,
   186, 189, 194, 205, 212, 226
   differences between type 32, 35, 101
Scheibe, Johann Adolph 233
Scheiffelhut, Jacob 230
   Musicalisches Klee-Blatt 227

Schein, Johann Hermann 53–4
   Banchetto musicale 53–4
Schelle, Johann 230
Schickhardt, Johann Christian 231, 233
   VI Concerts à Deux Violons Op. 13 231
Schieferdecker, Johann Christian 230–31,
   233–6
   XII. musicalische Concerte 228,
      230–31, 233–6
Schlackenwerth 141
Schmelzer, Andreas Anton 43, 187, 209,
   213, 224–6
Schmelzer, Johann Heinrich 43, 82, 88,
   187, 203, 206, 209–11, 213, 221–4,
   226
   Arie per il balletto à cavallo
      (equestrian ballet) 75, 202
   'Fechtschule balletto' 206
   Sacro-profanus concentus musicus 222
Schmidt, Carl 117–8
Schmierer, J.A. 146, 147; *see also* J.A.S.
Schneider, Herbert 142–3
Schwartzkopff, Theodor 129
Schwerin 18, 66, 149–50, 159–60
scordatura 96–7, 150, 245–6; *see also*
   instrumentation
Selhof, Nicolas 110, 193
Sénecé, Antoine Bauderon de 73
serenade 217–8, 223, 237–8, 240
Seyfferts, Wolffgang 102
Seyfrid, Johann Christoph 99, 116
   Ander Theil neuer Paduanen 100
   Erster Theil neuer Balletten,
      Allemanten 99
sinfonia (*simphonie*, 'Simphonia',
   'Synfonia') 101, 147–8, 173, 176,
   179, 186, 196, 220, 227, 235,
   240–41
Singballet, see court entertainments and
   ceremonies
sonata 30, 39, 45, 55, 82, 96, 105, 108,
   114, 181, 191, 196–7, 212, 222,
   224, 226
sonata da camera, *see* suite
sonatina 96, 114, 224, 243
song, strophic 12
Sophie Elisabeth, Duchess of
   Mecklenburg-Güstrow 21

Speth, Johann 145–6
    Ars magna consoni et dissoni 146
Spitzer, John 16, 20, 28
Stampfl, Inka 141
Stanley, Johann Georg 105, 107, 110 *see also* Reusner, Esaias
Steffani, Agostino 164–5, 175
    La libertà contenta 195
Steneken, Konrad
    Hortulus musicus 116
Stockholm 13, 40, 49, 65, 81, 84–6, 175
Störl, Johann Georg Christian 129
Strasbourg 93, 96
Strattner, Georg Christoph 75
Strobel, Valentine 93, 96
Strungk, Nicolaus Adam 61
Stuttgart 6, 121–2, 129, 149, 160, 194, 197
    Württemberg *Hofkapelle* at 7, 193, 197
suite; *see also* bransle suite
    generic terms for 35, 46–48, 50, 184, 203; see also *balletto*
    as functional dance music 48–9, 147–8, 188–9, 204
    'classical' order 45, 50, 64, 87
    circular key sequences in 220, 221–2, 240
    common key centre in 53–4, 58–9, 81, 86, 162, 220, 240
    'Concertouverture' 233
    dramatic excerpts 59–64, 79–81, 132–3, 148, 152, 176, 189, 226 *see also* character movements
    en suite (*de suite*) 35, 46, 105, 109
    equated with entourage 46
    equated with *sonata da camera*
    organisation of 49–50, 54–5, 86–7, 93, 96–7, 99, 104–12, 114–6, 123, 127, 130, 137, 143, 151–2, 157, 159, 176, 178, 181, 184–6, 189, 194, 224, 230–31, 233–5
    Partie (*Parthyen*) 143, 161, 241
    pastiche suite 57–8, 73
    performance 25, 28, 116, 147, 233; *see also* instrumentation
    sonata da camera 47–8, 58, 99
    variation techniques (movement linking) in 54, 57, 105, 139, 248
Sweden 65, 74, 81, 84

Taubert, Gottfried 49
    Rechtschaffener Tanzmeister 49
Telemann, Georg Philipp 195
Theatri Europæi 4, 15
Thirty Years War 6–7, 17, 29, 54, 65–6, 93, 100, 160, 210
Thomas, Christoph 66
Thormahlen, Wiebke 27, 29
Thun, Johann Ernst von, Archbishop of Salzburg 180
Tiliander, Nils 216; *see also* manuscript S-VX Mus. MS 6
traquenard 50
Trautmannsdorf, Count Ferdinand Ernst von 215
Treu, Paul 123, 129

Uppsala 89, 105, 224
'T Uitnement Kabinet 42

Valentini, Giovanni 93, 203
Valois (Valoÿ), Stephan 37, 167, 169–70, 172
variation techniques, *see* suite
Vejvanovsky, Pavel Josef 42, 210, 219, 246
Venice 48
Venturini, Francesco 171
Verdier, Pierre 84, 87
Verdina, Pietro 203
Versailles 201
Vienna 1, 17, 43, 47, 49, 58, 101, 119, 147–8, 201–3, 206, 210–15, 218 220, 223–4, 228, 237, 240, 248
Vigne, Philipp la 18
Vingt-quatre Violons du Roy 28, 74
Voye-Mignot, de la 73
    Traité de musique 73
Voÿs, la 73, 84
Vratislavia 1, 149, 160, 245–6

Walsh, London publishing house of 194
Walsh Hare and Randall, London publishing house of 194
Walther, Johann Gottfried 119–21, 179
    Musicalisches Lexicon 121
War of the Spanish Succession 175, 193, 227

Webber, Geoffrey 29
Weimar 27, 65, 75, 85–6, 110
Weißenfels 161
Wellesz, Egon 209
Werra, Ernst von 145–6
Whitehead, Paul 89, 129
Whitelock, Sir Bulstrode 13, 84
Wilhelm V, Landgrave of Hessen-Kassel 17
Wilhelm VI, Landgrave of Hessen-Kassel 4, 66, 79, 85
Wilhelm VII, Landgrave of Hessen-Kassel, 66

Wilson, David 182
Wirtschaft, see court entertainments
Witt, Christian Friederich 162, 164
Wolfenbüttel 17–18, 101, 117, 133
Wollny, Peter 85–6
Wust, Balthasar Christoph 93, 96–7, 143
   Exercitium musicum 57, 74, 89, 93, 96–8, 100, 116

Zaslaw, Neal 16, 20, 28
Zuber, Gregor 89
   Paduanen, Galliarden, Arien 97

CPSIA information can be obtained
at www.ICGtesting.com
Printed in the USA
BVHW081959100619
550635BV00010B/144/P